MW01200016

2000 YEARS AGO

the day missed their h⟨...⟩
ble prophecy. Today, t⟨...⟩
the same mistake. Once again, the LORD has raised up voices in
the wilderness to speak the truth. This is their account!

Benjamin Baruch

"Reading *The Day of the LORD is at Hand* helped me understand
how close the hour of Christ's return really is. I am disturbed by
the weakness of leadership and so little warning and help coming
from the pulpit. I hope there is enough time to become ready. Benjamin, thank you for your faithfulness."

Sylvia S.

"I have viewed your video "The Day of the LORD is at Hand" seven
times and read your book three times. I want to say thank you for
being obedient to the LORD. Your video and book have encouraged me with answers to many questions I had about the Day of
the LORD."

Sandee B.

"I worked for a Christian book store for three years and have about
500 books in my personal library. Now, I can throw 99% of them
away. Through the years I have read many books, watched other
Christians, listened to many pastors of every denomination, via
churches, TV, Internet. As I studied my Bible, I knew something
was very wrong in the Church's interpretation of God's word, and
the lives Christians were choosing to lead. I thought it was me, my
self-will trying to bend others' understanding of the Word to my
own. This book has completely redirected my prayer life, waking
life, how I look at others and how much more I love them. Actually, this book has changed me for what life remains; already preparing for the future, but very much at peace and I have joy."

Jan A.

"For years I have studied Scripture, read all the end time books
available to help me know what to do as a Christian. I have had
many dreams that I knew were from the Lord concerning terrible
times coming upon us. After reading your book, what Jesus
warned and my own sense of coming trouble makes sense. It's in
the Scripture, and The Day of the LORD is at Hand has settled all
doubts, we must be ready."

Ruth G.

The Day of the LORD is at Hand

Isaiah 13:6

Second Edition

By
Benjamin Baruch

"Howl ye; for the day of the LORD *is* at hand; it shall come as a destruction from the Almighty" (Isaiah 13:6).

"Behold, he cometh with clouds; and every eye shall see him, and they *also* which pierced him: and all kindreds of the earth shall wail because of him. Even so, Amen" (Revelation 1:7).

The Day of the Lord is at Hand *Isaiah 13:6*
By Benjamin Baruch

First Edition:	September, 1998
Second Edition:	March, 2004
Second Printing:	April, 2005

You may order a copy of the book or other teaching materials by Benjamin Baruch including the two hour DVD of the Day of the LORD message through our web site.

| Author's website: | www.benjaminbaruch.com |
| Book website: | www.thedayofthelordisathand.com |

ISBN: 0-976457-49-0
Published by:
Get Ready Publishing, Inc.
PO Box 58
Westcliffe, CO 81252
www.getreadypublishing.com

DEDICATION

This book is dedicated to my **LORD AND SAVIOR, JESUS CHRIST,** who alone is Holy and Righteous and worthy of all praise, glory, and honor. He is the KING of Kings and the LORD of Lords, the only-begotten Son of the Father, Who in His great love and mercy has saved us from the wrath that is to come. And by His faithfulness, He causes His chosen ones to stand in robes of righteousness. By His grace we are appointed to walk in good works, which He has prepared before the foundation of the world, and having so blessed us with His love and mercy, He bestows upon us the greatest of honors, He calls us His friends.

"Unto me, who am less than the least of all saints, is this grace given, that I should preach among the Gentiles the unsearchable riches of Christ; And to make all men see what is the fellowship of the mystery, which from the beginning of the world hath been hid in God, who created all things by Jesus Christ" (Ephesians 3:8-9).

"For thus hath the Lord said unto me, Go, set a watchman, let him declare what he seeth.... and he hearkened diligently with much heed: And he cried, A lion: My lord, I stand continually upon the watchtower in the daytime, and I am set in my ward whole nights: And, behold, here cometh a chariot of men, with a couple of horsemen. And He answered and said, Babylon is fallen, is fallen; and all the graven images of her gods he hath broken unto the ground" (Isaiah 21:6-9).

"But I certify you, brethren, that the gospel which was preached of me is not after man. For I neither received it of man, neither was I taught it, but by the revelation of Jesus Christ" (Galatians 1:11-12).

"Therefore take heed, so that the thing spoken of in the Prophets may not come upon you: 'BEHOLD, YOU SCOFFERS, AND MARVEL, AND PERISH; FOR I AM ACCOMPLISHING A WORK IN YOUR DAYS, A WORK WHICH YOU WILL NEVER BELIEVE, THOUGH SOMEONE SHOULD DESCRIBE IT TO YOU.'" (Acts 13:40-42 NAS)

PREFACE

First, I wish to thank my dear friend Shannon; without your help, the current edition of this book would never have been possible. Your help and encouragement were instrumental in allowing me the opportunity to share the prophetic words I have received from the Lord Jesus Christ with many of the elect in this last hour.

I also wish to thank the many men of wisdom who have been raised up in this last hour to speak the truth to America, including Kato Mivule, David Wilkerson, Dumitru Duduman, Henry Gruver and countless others who have had the courage to speak the truth to the American people. They shall stand in white among the saints of the ages, who have been faithful in proclaiming the true word of God. I have been blessed to meet each of these men, save brother Duduman, who went to be with the Lord in early 1996. His suffering at the hands of our enemies is an inspiration to us all.

The contents of this book are a summary of the revelation that the servants of Jesus Christ are speaking to America and her church in this final hour. The word of the Lord is always hard for the natural man to bear. It exposes our sin and demands we change.

The word of God is always the truth. Even if no man receives it, it remains true. In addition, if a word is from God, then the day shall declare it.

This is such a word. I pray, dear reader, you will take the time to read the words of this book and to prayerfully test them in the Spirit and in the word of God.

May the Lord Jesus Christ bless you all.

Benjamin Baruch

The Day of the LORD is at Hand

Benjamin Baruch

TABLE OF CONTENTS

FOREWORD

For years, the body of Christ has been misled with false interpretations of the prophecies surrounding the Second Coming of Jesus Christ. All over the earth, millions of Christians embrace these false teachings. These false teachings have deceived a backslidden people that Jesus Christ will rescue born-again Christians to safety before any trouble comes. These false doctrines also teach that Christians can live a life of ease, allowing the passions of the flesh to rule over them, while their hearts are full of the love of the world allowing them to continue in deliberate sin, while believing they have eternal security.

Few Christian authors have dug as deeply into the word of God and correctly applied the end of the age prophecies to current events as Benjamin Baruch. He has uncovered the true message of the sealed prophecies surrounding the last days.

Spring of 2000 I came across *The Day of the LORD is at Hand*, a work full of insight and warning; I could not put the book down until the end. I had started writing *Revelation Six Get Ready* in 1998 and needed a clearer understanding of Bible prophecy. I knew exactly what Christ said about the end times, and understood that Christians would have to endure the Great Tribulation. However, the books of Daniel, Isaiah, Jeremiah, other prophecies in Scripture, as well as the Revelation of John, held keys to help us understand the *"more specifics"* of how the end of the age will unfold.

This volume did what I hoped it would: bring to light detailed instructions and specific world events found in Scripture, helping the reader understand the birthing of the coming kingdom of God! As Christ put it—

"So when you see the desolating sacrilege spoken of by the prophet Daniel, standing in the holy place (let the reader understand), then let those who are in Judea flee to the mountains; let him who is on the housetop not go down to take what is in his

8

house; and let him who is in the field not turn back to take his mantle. And alas for those who are with child and for those who give suck in those days! Pray that your flight may not be in winter or on a sabbath. For then there will be great tribulation, such as has not been from the beginning of the world until now, no, and never will be. And if those days had not been shortened, no human being would be saved; but for the sake of the elect those days will be shortened" (Mathew 24:15-22 RSV).

Jesus admonished us to pay attention and learn the lesson from the fig tree. *"Immediately after the tribulation of those days the sun will be darkened, and the moon will not give its light, and the stars will fall from heaven, and the powers of the heavens will be shaken; then will appear the sign of the Son of man in heaven, and then all the tribes of the earth will mourn, and they will see the Son of man coming on the clouds of heaven with power and great glory; and he will send out his angels with a loud trumpet call, and they will gather his elect from the four winds, from one end of heaven to the other. 'From the fig tree learn its lesson: as soon as its branch becomes tender and puts forth its leaves, you know that summer is near. So also, when you see all these things, you know that he is near, at the very gates'"* (Matthew 24:29-33 RSV).

Indeed, we must discern the season of the end of the age as it starts to come forth, like the tender leaves of the fig tree in spring. If you do not understand these warnings and are unprepared, you, your family and your Christian brethren run a great risk of suffering more than necessary or even dying prematurely. Worst, you could be among the foolish Christians who are left-behind, barred from joining the marriage feast of the Lamb.

Therefore, as Christians we must be ready, for Christ said, *"You also must be ready; for the Son of man is coming at an unexpected hour"* (Luke 12:40). Even though most believers anticipate Christ's soon return; many will be caught off-guard. Jesus Christ warned His church that the end of the age would be a time of great deception, and a time of many false prophets. In the midst of this great deception, many will not hear the voice of the Holy Spirit leading God's people to safety during the coming hour of testing. *The Day of the Lord is at Hand* will challenge you to wake up, seek Christ, embrace the cross, learn to store your treasures in heaven, learn to be led by the true Holy Spirit and live with eager anticipation of Christ's soon return.

May Christ open your eyes to the truth as you read this important and timely message by Benjamin Baruch.

Pastor Charles Pretlow
Executive Director, Get Ready Publishing
and–author of *Revelation Six Get Ready*

INTRODUCTION

My name is Benjamin. I am neither an author nor a prophet. My educational background is in Business and Finance. I have spent over 20 years preparing for a career as a professional money manager, first acquiring a license as a Certified Public Accountant and then as a Chartered Financial Analyst. In 1995, I was promoted to Director of Investments and was informed that I would be responsible for managing several institutional investment accounts. Suddenly, I was responsible for directing investment policy for millions of dollars in America's stock market. I was honored, elated and I was scared.

Wall Street is a dangerous place, full of deception, where mistakes can be costly, very costly. I walked back to my office wondering, "What do I do now?" "Where do I start?" I had all of the advanced training, thousands of hours of exhaustive research, and years upon years of work experience with an intensity you cannot even imagine. What I did next began to change my career and my entire life. I knelt down in my office and prayed.

The Lord honored my prayers, and He blessed the work of my hands; my first year's results were outstanding, yet by early 1996 I knew the market was at risk, and that one day large, spectacular losses would occur. Therefore, in early 1996 I began to pray in earnest. I usually arrived at the office around 5 a.m., and the first thing I did every day was to pray and ask the Lord? "show me the end of this matter." Almost a year passed and I had not received an answer; then one day, shortly after my 40th birthday, I heard from the Lord.

This book is a summary of the word the Lord revealed unto me. It is also a warning to the Church and to our nation. I stand as one small voice among the many men of wisdom the Lord has raised up in this last hour declaring what the Spirit is saying to the churches:

"THE LORD GOD ALMIGHTY IS STANDING NOW READY TO JUDGE THE ENTIRE EARTH!"

CHAPTER 1

"TAKE HEED THAT NO MAN DECEIVE YOU"
Matthew 24:4

Jesus Christ began to answer the question His disciples posed regarding the signs of His Second Coming and the end of the age in Matthew 24. The Lord's first response was a warning for the last days would be a time of greatest deception the world has ever seen, with false christs, false teachers and false doctrines abounding such that even the elect would find themselves deceived if they did not take heed. Jesus continued His answer saying, *"For many shall come in my name, saying, I am Christ; and shall deceive many."*[1]

There would be many who come in the name of Jesus Christ proclaiming the truth that Jesus of Nazareth is the Messiah of Israel, yet they would be false teachers and false prophets, who would teach and deceive many. The word for "deceive" is *planao*[2] (plan-ah'-o), which means to go astray from the truth, to err, seduce, wander, and be out of the way. *"But evil men and seducers shall wax worse and worse, deceiving, and being deceived."*[3]

The word used of "seducers" is *goes*[4] (go'-ace), which means a wizard (as muttering spells), an imposter, and a seducer! These false teachers are actually speaking spells and evil enchantments with the words of their false doctrines. This is the terrible time Jesus warned us would come at the end of the age *"Little children, let no man deceive you: he that doeth righteousness is righteous, even as he is righteous. He that committeth sin is of the devil; for the devil sinneth from the beginning."*[5]

THE PARABLE OF THE FIG TREE

In the twentieth century, the world has witnessed the budding of the fig tree, which is the restoration of the nation of Israel back to their land. This is the sign spoken of by the prophets signaling we are in the last days and that the Lord is coming back soon. Jesus spoke of this sign in a parable. The Lord taught many parables, but this is the only one He instructed us to learn the meaning of, for this is the sign that He is standing at the door.

> *"Now learn a parable of the fig tree; When his branch is yet tender, and putteth forth leaves, ye know that summer is nigh: So likewise ye, when ye shall see all these things, know that it is near, even at the doors"* (Matthew 24:32-33).

Israel is the fig tree, and her leaves came forth in the early part of this century. We are living in the last days spoken of by the prophets of Israel, and the Lord is now standing at the door. We are presently entering into the midnight hour, and the darkest part of the night lies just ahead. The purpose of this book is to reveal the mystery of the Revelation of Jesus Christ, hidden by God from those who are wise in their own eyes, and revealed unto babes. I shall give insight and understanding to the writings of the prophets, and reveal the true order of the events that will precede the Second Coming of our Lord.

Two thousand years ago, the religious leaders of Israel were looking for the coming of the Messiah, yet having misunderstood the true meaning of Bible prophecy, they missed their hour of visitation. Today, the religious leaders of the Christian Church are making the same mistake, having misunderstood Bible prophecy regarding the Second Coming of the Lord. Their hour of visitation is at hand, and the Lord is coming as a thief in the night, in ways of which they are unaware. Once again, the Lord has raised up men of wisdom in the wilderness to speak the truth, and to warn the Church of the impending judgment, which must begin in the house of God.

JUDGMENT BEGINS IN THE HOUSE OF GOD

> *"For the time is come that judgment must begin at the house of God: and if it first begin at us, what shall the end be of them that obey not*

the gospel of God? And if the righteous scarcely be saved, where shall the ungodly and the sinner appear" (1 Peter 4:17-18)?

The Judgment of God always begins within His house. God revealed His forthcoming judgments concerning ancient Israel to the prophet Ezekiel. *"The LORD said to him, 'Go through the midst of the city, even through the midst of Jerusalem, and put a mark on the foreheads of the men who sigh and groan over all the abominations which are being committed in its midst" But to the others He said in my hearing, "Go through the city after him and strike; do not let your eye have pity, and do not spare. "Utterly slay old men, young men, maidens, little children, and women, but do not touch any man on whom is the mark; and you shall start from My sanctuary." So they started with the elders who were before the temple."*[6] Before addressing the issues of what is about to come, I shall first attempt to summarize the consensus view of end time prophecy held widely today within the Church in America, and by the power of God's spirit, also correct the errors contained therein.

THE CHURCH IN AMERICA HAS BEEN DECEIVED

The Church in America is looking for the Second Coming of Jesus with the following assumptions and expectations:

1. The signs of Matthew 24:6-8 represent the signs that we are in the last days.
2. A union of ten nations will rise to global power representing a revived Roman Empire.
3. The Antichrist will sign a seven-year peace treaty marking the beginning of the Great Tribulation, a 7 year time-period.
4. America is strangely absent from the prophetic writings.
5. The Church will be raptured out of the earth before the beginning of the seven-year tribulation.
6. The Church is looking forward to a great end-time revival before the hour of judgment begins.

Each of these commonly held views are wrong and are based upon vain thinking with no Scriptural basis whatsoever. Through the course of this text, I will address and correct these errors. Some will dismiss this message, refusing to believe the leadership of the Church could be deceived. Yet the Lord warned us specifically to "take heed that no man deceive you" and the Lord does not give idle warnings, for the warnings and admonitions of the Lord are themselves prophecy of what will come. The Lord is actually saying: *"In the last days, the majority will be deceived, take heed that it doesn't happen to you!"* Not only is deception of the Church possible, it was prophesied to happen!

> *"For the time will come when they will not endure sound doctrine; but after their own lusts shall they heap to themselves teachers, having itching ears; And they shall turn away their ears from the truth, and shall be turned unto fables."*[7]

I have not written this book seeking to enter into a debate with theologians nor to introduce controversy or dissension, but the word of God will always divide. My mission is to publish the word of truth for the remnant which my God shall call and to provide a true witness to the word of prophecy. I shall do both through the grace of my Lord. I will show the Biblical basis for this message, while revealing the true meaning of the prophecies including the order and the detail of events, which will shortly come to pass.

THE EARLY BIRTH PAINS OF THE KINGDOM

What then is the sign of the end of the age and the Second Coming of the Lord? Prophecy teachers point to the statements made by Jesus in Matthew 24 as the answer:

> *"And ye shall hear of wars and rumors of wars: see that ye be not troubled: for all these things must come to pass, but the end is not yet. For nation shall rise against nation, and kingdom against kingdom: and there shall be famines, and pestilences, and earthquakes, in divers places. All these are the beginning of sorrows"* (Matthew 24:6-8).

These *signs* Christ spoke of can be cited as the evidence that we are in the *last days*. Jesus said these signs are only the beginning of sorrows that the earth must endure before the Great Tribulation, but they are not the sign of the end of the age. Scripture warns us, *"Knowing this first, that there shall come in the last days scoffers, walking after their own lusts, And saying, Where is the promise of his coming? for since the fathers fell asleep, all things continue as they were from the beginning of the creation."*[8] The time of the end would witness scoffers who would deride the message of truth regarding the return of the Lord. The word used for scoffers is *empaiktes*[9] (emp-aheek-tace'), which means a de- rider, and a false teacher, a mocker or a scoffer. At the time of the end, these scoffers will be found as false teachers within the Church itself.

THE PERSECUTION OF THE TRUE BELIEVERS

Present day prophecy teachers completely miss the next point the Lord makes in His discourse regarding the events of the end of the age:

> *"Then shall they deliver you up to be afflicted, and shall kill you: and ye shall be hated of all nations for my name's sake. And then shall many be offended, and shall betray one another, and shall hate one another. And many false prophets shall rise, and shall de- ceive many. And because iniquity shall abound, the love of many shall wax cold. But he that shall endure unto the end, the same shall be saved. And this gospel of the kingdom shall be preached in all the world for a witness unto all nations; and then shall the end come"* (Matthew 24:9-14).

Following the signs which are the *"beginning of sorrows,"* the Lord tells us *"then"* the true believers will be delivered up to be afflicted *"and they shall kill you and you shall be hated of all na- tions."* An intense persecution will precede the Great Tribulation, and will come suddenly upon many as a snare! One day soon, the majority of the people in the Church will awaken and realize that their leaders, who did not warn them of the coming persecution, deceived them and lied. The *"many"* who consider themselves Christian will then be *"offended"* and *"betray"* one another. American believers are neither emotionally nor spiritually pre- pared for the sudden and intense persecution which is about to fall upon them, and when it comes, and it will surely come, the major- ity will be utterly devastated.

The word for "many" in the original Greek is *polus* (pol-oos'); which means most, plenteous or the majority. Jesus is warning us, in the midst of intense worldwide persecution, the majority of pro- fessing Christians will become offended, and betray one another. Only a faithful few will continue to hold the true profession of the faith—that Jesus Christ is Lord and He is the only Way, the only Truth and the only Life.

"If the world hates you, you know that it has hated Me before it hated you. If you were of the world, the world would love its own; but because you are not of the world, but I chose you out of the world, therefore the world hates you. Remember the word that I said to you, 'A slave is not greater than his master.' If they persecuted Me, they will also persecute you; if they kept My word, they will keep yours also. But all these things they will do to you for My name's sake, because they do not know the One who sent Me."[10]

The word in Greek for "offended" is *skandalizo* (skan-dal-id'-zo), which means to entrap, and to trip up (figuratively, to stumble or entice to sin, apostasy). Nominal professing Christians will stumble and fall under the persecution, and will deny the faith. These apostate believers will then turn on and betray the true brethren of the Lord. The word for "betray" in the Greek is *paradidomi* (par-ad-id'-o-mee), which means to surrender, to yield up, or to deliver. The Greek for "hate" is *miseo* (mis-eh'-o), meaning to detest and to persecute. Jesus has warned us that a worldwide persecution is coming before the tribulation. This persecution will be so intense that the majority of those claiming to be Christian will become offended and stumble into apostasy, and they shall then deliver up the chosen ones to persecution unto death! Only those who endure unto the end will be saved. The Greek word for "endure" is *hupomeno*[11] (hoop-om-en'-o), which means to remain, to bear trials, to persevere. Only those who remain faithful to the Lord, enduring patiently the trials of this persecution, will be saved.

Jesus warned of a worldwide persecution of the true believers. *All nations* will hate the chosen ones of the Lord. Dear reader, this includes the United States of America where, up to the hour of this writing, believers have enjoyed unprecedented freedom. Yet in the Lord's own words, we know this will change and a time of violent persecution will come very soon in America.

The flash points of judgment are all at hand; the spirit of greed, the spilling of innocent blood, perversion and pride cover our land.

A generation of American Christians has been watching the early birth pains convinced by their teachers that the next event would be the rapture of the Church, yet what must follow next is persecution—intense persecution. The twentieth century has witnessed more martyrs for the name of Jesus Christ than any other. Today in many nations, thousands of believers are dying every day. America too will witness such sorrows before the *sign of the end.*

THE SIGN OF THE END OF THE AGE

Jesus tells us after the worldwide persecution of the Church, then we will see the sign which marks the beginning of the end of the age: the abomination of desolation, spoken of by Daniel the prophet, standing in the holy place!

> *"When ye therefore shall see the abomination of desolation, spoken of by Daniel the prophet, stand in the holy place, (whoso readeth, let him understand:) Then let them which be in Judaea flee into the mountains: Let him which is on the housetop not come down to take any thing out of his house: Neither let him which is in the field return back to take his clothes. And woe unto them that are with child, and to them that give suck in those days! But pray ye that your flight be not in the winter, neither on the Sabbath day: For then shall be great tribulation, such as was not since the beginning of the world to this time, no, nor ever shall be"* (Matthew 24:15-21).

The sign which marks the end of the age, and the beginning of the Great Tribulation, is the stopping of the daily altar sacrifice on the Temple Mount and the setting up of the abomination of desolation in the holy place. The Lord tells those in Judea to flee immediately, for this event marks the beginning of the Great Tribulation! Jesus also warns us to pray that our flight will not come in winter or on a Sabbath day. This warning is also prophetic. The Lord is actually telling us the Great Tribulation will begin during winter and on a Sabbath day. The warning is to His remnant. They are to pray that their flight would not come during this time for the remnant are to be in position early, before the world is snared on that day! We are also warned that those with child, still needing milk, will experience woe on that day. This is also a spiritual prophecy, for those who are babes in the faith and still needing the milk of the Word will have great trouble standing on that day.

What exactly does Daniel the prophet tell us about the abomination of desolation? In chapter 12, we learn that from the stopping of the daily sacrifice, which is the morning and evening oblation offering of the temple worship, to the setting up of the abomination that brings desolation, there shall be 1,290 days. *"And from the time that the daily sacrifice shall be taken away, and the abomination that maketh desolate set up, there shall be a thousand two hundred and ninety days."*[12]

Daniel prophesies about the abomination in chapter 11, writing that the Antichrist *"shall pollute the sanctuary"* and *"shall take away the daily sacrifice."*[13] He shall then set up the abomination of desolation upon the holy place. Scripture warns that the Antichrist is a *"vile person to whom they shall not give the honor of the kingdom."*[14] This man will be considered vile, and will have been passed over for the title of king. He is a prince who will be rejected and considered unworthy to rule. Daniel continues telling us *"but he shall come in peaceably, and obtain the kingdom by flatteries."*[15] The false messiah will come in under the disguise of peace, and will conquer the earth with flattering words. We are also told *"And after the league made with him he shall work deceitfully: for he shall come up, and shall become strong with a small people."*[16] The false messiah will work deceitfully following a league or an alliance of a small group of people who have seized the kingdom by deception. Daniel continues, *"he shall do that which his fathers have not done, nor his father's fathers."*[17] He shall accomplish the goal, of which his ancestors were incapable, uniting a worldwide empire under a single crown once again.

> *"And in his estate shall stand up a vile person, to whom they shall not give the honour of the kingdom: but he shall come in peaceably, and obtain the kingdom by flatteries.... And after the league made with him he shall work deceitfully: for he shall come up, and shall become strong with a small people. He shall enter peaceably even upon the fattest places of the province; and he shall do that which his fathers have not done, nor his fathers' fathers"* (Daniel 11:21-24).

After he seizes power, the false messiah will exalt himself above every god, speak blasphemy against the God of heaven, and prosper until the time of the indignation is accomplished. *"For that that is determined shall be done."*[18] The events of the Great Tribulation and the coming false messiah have been determined, or predestined to occur; and they shall be accomplished. The Scripture refers to this time as "the indignation." In Hebrew, this word is *za` am*[19] (zah'-am), which means fury, especially of God's displeasure with sin. The proper translation is anger, indignation, or rage. The last days upon planet earth will be a time of the outpouring of God's wrath and judgment for the sins of mankind. This outpouring will continue until the indignation of the Lord is complete!

> *"And arms shall stand on his part, and they shall pollute the sanctuary of strength, and shall take away the daily sacrifice, and they shall place the abomination that maketh desolate. And such as do wickedly against the covenant shall he corrupt by flatteries: but the people that do know their God shall be strong, and do exploits. And they that understand among the people shall instruct many:... And the king shall do according to his will; and he shall exalt himself, and magnify himself above every god, and shall speak...against the God of gods, and shall prosper till the indignation be accomplished: for that that is determined shall be done"* (Daniel 11:31-36).

Some scholars teach that Antiochus Epiphanes fulfilled these prophecies when he desecrated the temple and stopped the daily sacrifice around 164 B.C. This is incorrect. Antiochus Epiphanes only foreshadowed these events. Chapter 11:27 instructs that this king will do mischief and speak lies, but he shall not prosper *"for yet the end shall be at the time appointed."*[20] He will not succeed—for God has appointed the end to occur within the days of his rule. This tells us these events occur at the time of the end. In Daniel 12:1 we are also told *"and at that time"* which refers to the preceding events of chapter 11, *"there shall be a time of trouble, such as never was."* This is the time of the end, *"the time of Jacob's trouble,"*[21] which was prophesied by Jeremiah. This is the Great Tribulation at the end of the age, and Israel shall be delivered out of it! God will yet preserve and deliver a chosen remnant in the midst of the most terrible time the world has ever known.

This is the time of the end when *"... they that be wise shall shine as the brightness of the firmament; and they that turn many to righteousness as the stars for ever and ever. But thou, O Daniel, shut up the words, and seal the book, even to the time of the end: many shall run to and fro, and knowledge shall be increased."*[22] The prophecy tells us *"knowledge shall be increased"* at the time of the end. In the secular world, the knowledge of mankind will greatly increase in the last days. In the spiritual world, the knowledge of prophetic truth will also be increased at the time of the end. Read this entire book, Dear Reader, and witness the amazing knowledge the Lord is now revealing to His people.

> *"And at that time shall Michael stand up, the great prince which standeth for the children of thy people: and there shall be a time of trouble, such as never was since there was a nation even to that same time: and at that time thy people shall be delivered, every one that shall be found written in the book.... And they that be wise shall shine as the brightness of the firmament; and they that turn many to righteousness as the stars for ever and ever. But thou, O Daniel, shut up the words, and seal the book, even to the time of the end"* (Daniel 12:1-4).

THE IMAGE OF THE BEAST

The *"abomination that maketh desolate"* is the *"image of the beast,"* which will be set upon the Temple Mount in Jerusalem. The apostle John was also given insight into these days in the book of Revelation. In John's vision of chapter 13, he saw a beast with seven heads and ten horns rising up from the sea. One of the heads was wounded unto death, and then healed, and the whole world wondered after the beast.

The horn, which was wounded, is the Antichrist. He will be given a mouth to utter blasphemy, and power to continue 42 months, which is 3½ years. John saw another beast coming out of the earth, with two horns as a lamb, appearing to be innocent and harmless, but possessing the mouth of the dragon. This beast will speak for the great dragon. This is the false prophet, who will stand before the Antichrist, and cause all the people of the earth to worship the beast, and to make an image of the beast. This is the abomination of desolation, which will be set upon the Temple mount. The setting up of the image of the beast is the abomination, for it profanes the holy place in Jerusalem. It also violates the law of the Lord our God, where men are commanded to worship only the Lord, and are prohibited from making and worshipping graven images. The false prophet leads mankind to worship the image of the beast, and the dragon, which gave his power to the beast.

"And he opened his mouth in blasphemy against God.... And it was given unto him to make war with the saints, and to overcome them.... And I beheld another beast coming up out of the earth; and he had two horns like a lamb, and he spake as a dragon,... and causeth the earth and them which dwell therein to worship the first beast, whose deadly wound was healed. And... that they should make an image to the beast.... And he causeth all... to receive a mark in their right hand, or in their foreheads: And that no man might buy or sell, save he that had the mark,... Here is wisdom. Let him that hath understanding count the number of the beast: for it is the number of a man; and his number is Six hundred threescore and six" (Revelation 13:6-18).

Satan has attempted from the beginning to counterfeit the work of the true Messiah. In his efforts to deceive mankind, the Antichrist will appear to the nations as having received a *"deadly wound"* which is healed, presenting a counterfeit resurrection. He will then require that no one may buy or sell without his mark, which is the number of his name, 666. I will discuss the number of the beast in chapter 7, *"Here is the mind which has wisdom."*

DANIEL'S SEVENTY WEEKS PROPHECY

The stopping of the sacrifices is also mentioned in Daniel's prophecy of the seventy weeks. This prophecy is the single most important prophecy in the entire Scripture, for in it, we are given insight into the timing of the coming of the Messiah.

"Seventy weeks are determined upon thy people and upon thy holy city, to finish the transgression, and to make an end of sins, and to make reconciliation for iniquity, and to bring in everlasting righteousness, and to seal up the vision and prophecy, and to anoint the most Holy. Know therefore and understand, that from the going forth of the commandment to restore and to build Jerusalem unto the Messiah the Prince shall be seven weeks, and threescore and two weeks: the street shall be built again, and the wall, even in troublous times. And after threescore and two weeks shall Messiah be cut off, but not for himself: and the people of the prince that shall come shall destroy the city and the sanctuary; and the end thereof

shall be with a flood, and unto the end of the war desolations are determined. And he shall confirm the covenant with many for one week: and in the midst of the week he shall cause the sacrifice and the oblation to cease, and for the overspreading of abominations he shall make it desolate, even until the consummation, and that determined shall be poured upon the desolate" (Daniel 9:24-27).

Daniel's seventy weeks prophecy has fascinated scholars over the centuries. The seventy weeks represent weeks of years, which have been determined, predestined to occur upon both the nation of Israel and the holy city of Jerusalem. Daniel writes that *"from the going forth of the commandment to restore and to build Jerusalem unto Messiah the Prince shall be seven weeks and sixty two weeks... and after sixty two weeks shall Messiah be cut off, but not for himself."*[23]

Daniel has revealed the timing of the coming of the Messiah. He first refers to Him as Messiah the Prince, speaking of His Second Coming as ruler of the earth. He then refers to Him as the Messiah who would be *"cut off, but not for himself."* This refers the First Coming, when the Messiah would come not as a Prince, but as a servant who would die for the nation. In perfect literal fulfillment of Daniel's prophecy, Jesus Christ was born *sixty-two weeks* from the first decree to rebuild Jerusalem, after which He shed His precious blood on the Feast of Passover as the Holy Lamb of God. Jesus fulfilled the prophecy of His First Coming exactly as Daniel prophesied almost 500 years earlier!

WHO HAS BELIEVED OUR REPORT

Isaiah spoke of the suffering of the Messiah of Israel, declaring that He would be cut off, not for His own sins, but for the sins of the people. *"But he was wounded for our transgressions, he was bruised for our iniquities...and with His stripes we are healed."*[24]

This is Yeshua, Who is the Son of the Most High God. He was beaten and bruised for our sins, and wounded for our transgressions. Moreover, by the stripes, which were cut into His back, we are healed. He was taken on the feast day of Pesach, which the Gentiles call Passover, and was brought as a lamb to the slaughter. On that day, they massacred my Lord. And it was for me that He died. Yes, for all of us who are the little flock of the Father, whom

Isaiah calls *"a remnant."*[25] He did not even open His mouth in protest, and without a word of complaint, He laid His life down and was *"cut off"* from the land of the living. *"For God so loved the world, that he gave his only begotten Son, that whosoever believeth in him should not perish, but have everlasting life."*[26] It pleased our Father in Heaven, to bruise His Son that we His children might not perish but obtain life everlasting. Therefore, Jesus made His soul *"an offering for sin"* and the Father God declares, *"My righteous servant shall justify many!"*

"Who hath believed our report? And to whom is the arm of the LORD revealed? For he shall grow up before him as a tender plant, and as a root out of a dry ground: he hath no form nor comeliness; and when we shall see him, there is no beauty that we should desire him. He is despised and rejected of men; a man of sorrows, and acquainted with grief: and we hid as it were our faces from him; he was despised, and we esteemed him not. Surely he hath borne our griefs, and carried our sorrows: yet we did esteem him stricken, smitten of God, and afflicted. But he was wounded for our transgressions, he was bruised for our iniquities: the chastisement of our peace was upon him; and with his stripes we are healed. All we like sheep have gone astray; we have turned every one to his own way; and the LORD hath laid on him the iniquity of us all. He was oppressed, and he was afflicted, yet he opened not his mouth: he is brought as a lamb to the slaughter, and as a sheep before her shearers is dumb, so he openeth not his mouth.... for he was cut off out of the land of the living: for the transgression of my people was he stricken. And he made his grave with the wicked, and with the rich in his death; because he had done no violence, neither was any deceit in his mouth. Yet it pleased the LORD to bruise him;... He shall see of the travail of his soul, and shall be satisfied: by his knowledge shall my righteous servant justify many; for he shall bear their iniquities" (Isaiah 53:1-11).

THEY SHALL SMITE THE JUDGE OF ISRAEL WITH A ROD

The prophet Micah declares *"they shall smite the judge of Israel with a rod upon the cheek."*[27] This is Jesus, for He is both King and Judge of Israel. Throughout the Scripture, the prophets testify that the Lord Himself would come to save His people. And He did come, just as Daniel prophesied He would, and He was then *"cut off, but not for himself."* *"For unto us a child is born, unto us a son is given: and the government shall be upon his shoulder: and his name shall be called Wonderful, Counselor, The mighty God, The everlasting Father, The Prince of Peace. Of the increase of his government and peace there shall be no end, upon the throne of David, and upon his kingdom, to order it, and to establish it with judgment and with justice from henceforth even forever. The zeal of the LORD of hosts will perform this."*[28]

THE LORD SHALL PROVIDE HIMSELF A LAMB

Many of the prophets of Israel have spoken of the Lord coming Himself, to save His people, and to die in their place. Abraham's heart was torn when the Lord commanded him to offer up Isaac as a sacrifice and a burnt offering. In Genesis we read how the great patriarch of the faith obeyed, and prepared to kill his only son. This commandment by the Lord foreshadowed the Lord sending His son to die for the people. Abraham and Isaac departed alone, leaving with only the fire and the wood. Isaac questioned his father, *"My father.... Behold the fire and the wood: but where is the lamb for a burnt offering? And Abraham said, My son, God will provide himself a lamb for a burnt offering."*[29] Abraham's answer was prophetic, for the Lord had determined to provide Himself, as the Lamb of God, to be the burnt offering for the sins of the world. His words in the Hebrew read *"Elohiym yir'eh low haseh la` olaah baniy."* Truly the Scripture declares, *"God will provide Himself a lamb."*

THEY HAVE PIERCED MY HANDS AND FEET

David prophesied of the crucifixion of the Lord in Psalm 22. This prophecy includes the words spoken by the Lord as He hung upon the cross. *"My God, my God, why hast thou forsaken me?"*[30] cried the Lord. The bulls of Bashan are the evil spirits, which attacked the Lord while on the cross. *"... strong bulls of Bashan have beset me.... They gaped upon me with their mouths, as a ravening and a roaring lion.... my heart is like wax, it is melted.... and my toungue cleaves to my jaws."*[31] The prophecy even describes the mocking of the crowd: *"All they that see me laugh at me.... He trusted in the LORD... let him deliver him."*[32] These very words of scorn were spoken against our Lord on that day. *"... and thou hast brought me into the dust of death. For dogs have compassed me...they pierced my hands and my feet"*[33] cries the Messiah of Israel. Who has believed our report? To whom is the arm of the Lord revealed? Who hears from God? Let him reveal it! The Lord has spoken! Hear Him!

> *"My God, my God, why hast thou forsaken me? why art thou so far from helping me, and from the words of my roaring?... Our fathers trusted in thee: they trusted, and thou didst deliver them. They cried unto thee, and were delivered: they trusted in thee, and were not confounded. But I am a worm, and no man; a reproach of men, and despised of the people. All they that see me laugh me to scorn: they shoot out the lip, they shake the head, saying, He trusted on the LORD that he would deliver him: let him deliver him, seeing he delighted in him.... Be not far from me; for trouble is near; for there is none to help. Many bulls have compassed me: strong bulls of Bashan have beset me round. They gaped upon me with their mouths, as a ravening and a roaring lion. I am poured out like water, and all my bones are out of joint: my heart is like wax; it is melted in the midst of my bowels. My strength is dried up like a potsherd; and my tongue cleaveth to my jaws; and thou hast brought me into the dust of death. For dogs have compassed me: the assembly of the wicked have enclosed me: they pierced my hands and my feet.... They part my garments among them, and cast lots upon my vesture.... Save me from the lion's mouth: for thou hast heard me from the horns of the unicorns. I will declare thy name unto my brethren: in the midst of the congregation will I praise thee.... For the kingdom is the LORD's: and he is the governor among the nations.... They shall come, and shall declare his righteousness unto a people that shall be born, that he hath done this"* (Psalm 22:1-31).

HEAR O ISRAEL, THE LORD OUR GOD, THE LORD IS ONE!

Yeshua is the Messiah of Israel. He is the Good Shepherd who laid down His life for His sheep, and having loved His own who were in the world, He loved them until the end. Even while the Lord hung on the cross, He continued to think about each one of His chosen ones. He endured all of this suffering so we could escape the wrath, which is soon to come. This is His agape love. This is the death to self, which His gospel demands. He is the Way, the Truth and the Life, and no one comes to the Father by any other name. Yeshua is the Lord, and let all the earth be silent before Him! Every one of the prophets of Israel testified of Him! Hear O Israel, The Lord our God, The Lord is One. Blessed be His glorious Name whose Kingdom is forever and ever!

HIS NAME IS WRITTEN KING OF KINGS AND LORD OF LORDS

In exact fulfillment of the prophecies, Jesus Christ rose on the third day, as the first fruits of the resurrection from the dead. Jesus is about to return to this earth, and now He will be called *"Faithful and True"* for He will now judge the entire earth. Each of us will stand before Him very soon. His eyes are as flames of fire, and His clothes have been dipped in blood. He is the lamb who was slain, and having endured the suffering of the cross and its shame, He now comes to smite the nations! He will tread them in the winepress of His fierce wrath! Jesus spoke of this judgment of the earth when He said, *"I am come to send fire on the earth; and what will I, if it be already kindled? But I have a baptism to be baptized with; and how am I straitened till it be accomplished! Suppose ye that I am come to give peace on earth? I tell you, Nay; but rather division."*[34] Yeshua was straitened until His baptism on the cross was accomplished. His words, *"I am come to send fire on the earth"* will now be fulfilled. *"Alas! for that day is great, so that none is like it: it is even the time of Jacob's trouble; but he shall be saved out of it."*[35]

> *"And I saw heaven opened, and behold a white horse; and he that sat upon him was called Faithful and True, and in righteousness he doth judge and make war. His eyes were as a flame of fire, and on his head were many crowns; and he had a name written, that no man knew, but he himself. And he was clothed with a vesture dipped in blood: and his name is called The Word of God. And the armies which were in heaven followed him upon white horses, clothed in fine linen, white and clean. And out of his mouth goeth a sharp sword, that with it he should smite the nations: and he shall rule them with a rod of iron: and he treadeth the winepress of the fierceness and wrath of Almighty God. And he hath on his vesture and on*

his thigh a name written, KING OF KINGS, AND LORD OF LORDS" (Revelation 19:11-16).

THE SIXTY-TWO WEEKS AND THE FIRST COMING

The birth and death of the Messiah were prophesied exactly in Daniel's seventy weeks. Present day theologians assume the seven weeks must be added to the sixty-two weeks, and that sixty-nine weeks occurred between the first decree to rebuild Jerusalem, issued by Artaxerxes in the time of Nehemiah, until the First Coming of Jesus Christ. They also assume the sixty-nine weeks was fulfilled at the time of the crucifixion. Both of these assumptions are incorrect, and inconsistent with the words of Daniel's prophecy and the true historical record. Sir Isaac Newton, one of the greatest minds the world has ever known, was a devoted student of the book of Daniel. He wrote *Observations upon the prophecies of Daniel and the Apocalypse of St. John*, which was published six years after his death in 1733. Newton was an expert in both ancient history and ancient languages. He also studied the prophecies of Daniel in depth throughout his lifetime.

Newton reasoned that the weeks of years represent Sabbath years, which occur every seven years on the Jewish calendar. Therefore, Daniel's prophecy of the seventy weeks must be understood from the Jewish calendar, which is lunar-based, and not based on the solar calendar of the pagan world. Newton confirmed the sixty-two weeks were fulfilled at the birth of Christ. *"Now Nehemiah came to Jerusalem in the 20th year of Artaxerxes, while Ezra continued there.... and finished the wall the 25th day of the month of Elul,* [36] *in the 28th year of the king, that is in September in the year of the Julian Period 4278. Count now from this year three score and two weeks of years, that is 434 years, and the reckoning will end in September in the year of the Julian period 4712, which is the year in which Christ was born, according to Clemens Alexandrinus.... and other ancients, and this was the general opinion, till Dionysious Exiguus invented the vulgar account, in which Christ's birth is placed two years later.... How after these weeks Christ was cut off, and the city and sanctuary destroyed by the Romans, is well known."*[37]

Newton also understood the seven weeks must represent the time near the end of the age between a second restoration of the nation of Israel and the second command to rebuild Jerusalem. The Second Coming of the Messiah, this time as a Prince, would then follow after seven Sabbath years, or a total of forty-nine Jewish years, from the issuing of the second decree. Newton wrote, *"This part of the prophecy, being therefore not yet fulfilled, I shall not attempt a particular interpretation of it, but content myself with observing, that as the seventy and sixty two weeks were Jewish weeks, ending with sabbatical years, so the seven weeks are the compass of a Jubilee, and begin and end with actions proper for a Jubilee, and of the highest nature for which a Jubilee can be kept: and that since the commandment to return and to build Jerusalem, precedes the Messiah the Prince 49 years; it may perhaps come forth not from the Jews themselves, but from some other....The manner I know not. Let time be the interpreter."*[38] Forty-nine years is the cycle of time between the years of Jubilee. The Jubilee of the Lord is the year of redemption, and is also known as the favorable year of the Lord. The law of the Jubilee is contained in Leviticus, and the trumpet to announce the Jubilee is blown after the Day of Atonement, on Yom Kippur.

THE YEAR OF JUBILEE—SEVEN WEEKS OF YEARS

Newton wrote: *"This prophecy of the Messiah... relates to both comings, and assigns the times thereof.... We avoid also the doing violence to the language of Daniel, by taking the seven weeks and sixty two weeks for one number. Had that been Daniel's meaning, he would have said sixty nine weeks, and not seven weeks and sixty two weeks, a way of numbering used by no nation. In our way the years are Jewish weeks ending with sabbatical years, which is very remarkable.... Others either count by Lunar years, or by weeks not Judaic: and, which is worst, they ground their interpretations on erroneous chronology...."*[39] The seven weeks, then, represent a Jubilee period of 49 years, seven sabbatical weeks of seven years each, followed in the fiftieth year by the year of Jubilee.

The year of Jubilee is holy throughout all the land. It is the year of redemption of all property, freedom for slaves, and a year of rest and restoration for both the land and the people of Israel. Daniel's prophecy of the seven weeks which precedes the Second Coming of the Lord, uses the exact same words in the Hebrew as the law of Jubilee contained in Leviticus.

> *"And thou shalt number seven sabbaths of years unto thee, seven times seven years; and the space of the seven sabbaths of years shall be unto thee forty and nine years. Then shalt thou cause the trumpet of the jubilee to sound on the tenth day of the seventh month, in the day of atonement shall ye make the trumpet sound throughout all your land. And ye shall hallow the fiftieth year, and proclaim liberty throughout all the land unto all the inhabitants thereof: it shall be a jubilee unto you; and ye shall return every man unto his possession, and ye shall return every man unto his family. A jubilee shall that fiftieth year be unto you: ye shall not sow, neither reap that which groweth of itself in it, nor gather the grapes in it of thy vine undressed. For it is the jubilee; it shall be holy unto you: ye shall eat the increase thereof out of the field. In the year of this jubilee ye shall return every man unto his possession"* (Leviticus 25:8-13).

The trumpet to announce the Jubilee is a war trumpet, and it is blown on Yom Kippur. John heard the same war trumpet when he was caught up in the spirit to witness the Revelation of the Day of the Lord. It began with the blowing of the war trumpet to announce the final Jubilee of Israel. *"I was in the Spirit on the Lord's day, and heard behind me a great voice, as of a trumpet."*[40] John is speaking of more than just a Sabbath day, for the Revelation is the Day of the Lord. The prophets declare in several places the Day of the Lord begins during a Jubilee. The Messiah proclaims, *"For the day of vengeance is in mine heart, and the year of my redeemed is come."*[41] The Jubilee is the favorable year of the Lord, and the year of redemption by God. In Isaiah 61, which declares the ministry of the Messiah, the Spirit prophesies of the Second Coming of the Messiah, this time in judgment: *"To proclaim the acceptable* (Jubilee) *year of the LORD, and the day of vengeance of our God."*[42] The year of Jubilee is the key to understanding the fulfillment of the redemptive plan of God and will be discussed further in chapter 12 entitled *"Return, Oh LORD, how long."*

The Second Coming of the Messiah as Prince will be preceded by the final seven weeks of years and then the final Jubilee. The Second Coming begins in a way few understand, for the mystery of the revelation of Jesus Christ has been hidden from the beginning of time, only revealed to a few until this final hour. The Messiah of Israel is both a conquering King and a humble servant. In His First Coming, Jesus Christ came as the suffering servant, and as the Passover lamb, to die for the sins of His people. In the Second Coming, our Lord will come forth as the Lion from the tribe of Judah and as the Mighty Deliverer. His First Coming was through a supernatural birth in the natural. His Second Coming will also begin with a supernatural birth, only this time in the spirit. A company of men will become born again totally, and filled with the Spirit without measure. These are the 144,000, who are pictured as standing with the Lamb in the book of Revelation. These men are the vanguard of the Lord, and they will fulfill in their lives the second half of the seven-year ministry of the Jesus Christ, which occurs during the Great Tribulation. This is the mystery of the Revelation of the Word of God fulfilled literally, which is Christ in us, the hope of glory. Though it is hard to comprehend, dear reader, hold your objections for a moment and open your heart and mind and consider that the Second Coming is in fact preceded by the revelation of Jesus Christ in His people during the Great Tribulation. This is what is revealed in Luke 17:30 when Luke wrote, "... *in the day when the Son of man is revealed.*" The context of this verse is the beginning of the Great Tribulation, but we are told in Luke's account that on this day the Son of man will be revealed! This is at the same time that the abomination of desolation is seen on the Temple mount, as declared by Matthew. On the same day, the Son of man is revealed within a remnant of His people, as declared by Luke. Then the Lord will begin the second half of His seven-year ministry upon the earth.

Newton understood this, and reasoned that sometime during the twentieth century, Israel would be restored during a Jubilee year, and would then issue a decree to rebuild Jerusalem. After forty-nine years, the final Jubilee of Israel would begin, after which the Messiah the Prince would come. The final Jubilee was announced by the blowing of the war trumpet on Yom Kippur on October 11, 1997. The Jubilee year is based on the sacred calendar of Israel, which actually begins in the month of Nissan or March. The trumpet on Yom Kippur announces the coming Jubilee and instructs

Israel to forgo planting following the fall harvest. The 70th Jubilee of Israel began on March 28th, 1998 and concluded on March 18, 1999. We are now in the midst of the eighth week which ends in March of 2006. Based upon Daniel's prophecy, the "man-child" of the book of Revelation who will fulfill the second half of the Messiah's seven year ministry in the earth must therefore be born into the world on or before March of 2006. This would fulfill literally the prophecy that Messiah the Prince would come after seven weeks and before the end of the eighth week. This birth of the man-child does require that the tribulation must also begin at that time. As in the case of the first coming, the birth of the Messiah preceded his ministry by 30 years. Similarly, the birth of the man-child may precede the beginning of their ministry during the Great Tribulation. Consider this: if the religious leaders at the time of the First Coming had been told the Messiah had come as prophesied by Daniel, they would protested in unbelief. Yet, he had come, only as a small child, and his ministry would begin in 30 years. So too now, the birth of the man-child of Revelation may also precede the ministry of this company for a period of time.

The Messiah's first coming was preceded by 62 sabbatical weeks, or 434 years based on the Jewish calendar, which Newton confirms perfectly from the decree issued by Artaxerxes till the birth of Christ. [43] The prophecy foretold His coming into the world at the time of his birth exactly. Note Daniel tells us *"and after [sixty-two weeks] shall Messiah be cut off."*[44] The Messiah is not cut off at sixty-two weeks but *"after."* He came exactly at the sixty-two weeks, and then later was cut off. Daniel also writes *"he* (the prince) *shall confirm the covenant with many for one week."*[45]

Scholars all agree this is the 70th week of the prophecy, and in the midst of the 70th week, the prince shall cause the sacrifice and the oblation to stop. This refers to the stopping of the sacrifices of the Temple mount.

THE SEVENTIETH WEEK OF DANIEL

"Seventy weeks are determined upon thy people and upon thy holy city, to finish the transgression, and to make an end of sins, and to make reconciliation for iniquity, and to bring in everlasting right-

eousness, and to seal up the vision and prophecy, and to anoint the most Holy" (Daniel 9:24).

Jesus began his ministry walking out of the wilderness of Jordan, and was first baptized by John, and then filled with the Holy Spirit. He then walked among His people as the Good Shepherd, the humble servant of God, who sought His lost sheep for 3½ years. Jesus then died for their salvation as the Holy Lamb of God. Modern scholars have made many errors regarding Bible prophecy. Jesus has a seven-year ministry upon the earth. This seven-year ministry is the 70th week of Daniel, and it is already half over. He is Messiah the Prince, Who will confirm His covenant with His people for one week, which is seven years. He has already confirmed the covenant by Grace and Truth. In His first 3½-year ministry as a humble servant sent to be the Holy Lamb of God, He walked in perfect obedience to the Law of the Lord. Jesus is about to begin the second half of His ministry on the earth. During this second 3½ years, which is known as the *"time of Jacob's trouble"*[46] Jesus will again confirm His covenant with His people, only this time He will be born again within His remnant as the Messiah Prince who is both Lord of lords and King of kings. In the second half of His seven year ministry on the earth, He will not come among us as a lamb anymore.

No, this time, He will be revealed within the remnant of His people as THE LION FROM THE TRIBE OF JUDAH! *"Behold, the people shall rise up as a great lion, and lift up himself as a young lion: he shall not lie down until he eat of the prey, and drink the blood of the slain."*[47]

AND TO ANOINT THE MOST HOLY

The Lord will accomplish the complete fulfillment of all prophecy during the 70th week. *"Seventy weeks are determined... to finish the transgression, and to make an end of sins, and to make reconciliation for iniquity, and to bring in everlasting righteousness, and to seal up the vision and prophecy, and to anoint the most Holy."*[48] Within the seventy weeks, transgression will be finished and sin will end. The Lord shall also *"make reconciliation for iniquity."* The word for "reconciliation" is *kaphar*[49] (kaw-far'), which means to cover, to be merciful, and to forgive. The Lord will bring a complete cancellation of the charges against His elect during the seventy weeks. The vision of the prophets is also to be sealed up by the end of the seventieth week. The word "to seal up" is *chatham*[50] (khaw-tham'), which means to close up and to seal. The word for "vision" is *chazown*[51] (khaw-zone'), which means a dream, or a revelation and the word for "prophecy" is *nabiy'*[52] (naw-bee'), which speaks literally of a prophet or an inspired man. The verse literally means, during the seventieth week, the Lord will give final pardon for sins, and seal up the revelation of the prophets of God. Prophecy and revelation continue unto the last days, and are only sealed up at the end of the seventieth week.

The final act of the seventy weeks is *"to anoint the most Holy."* The word "to anoint" is *mashach* [53] (maw-shakh'), which means to cover with oil, to anoint and to consecrate. *Mashach* is also the title of the Messiah, which means the Anointed One. After the sixty-two weeks, Jesus was anointed with the Holy Spirit in fulfillment of this prophecy. The word for "most" in the Hebrew is *kodesh*[54] (ko'-desh), which means a sacred or consecrated place, or that which is most holy. The Hebrew word for "holy" in this text is *kaadaashiym*. The reference for this word is to the same *kodesh*, but the text actually reads *kodesh kaadaashiym*, which means the holiest of the holy places. Scholars assume this speaks only of the anointing of Jesus Christ in His first 3½-year ministry. This prophecy is dual, and will be fulfilled twice for the holiest place will be anointed once again, during the second half of the seventieth week which is the time period of the great tribulation.

The Scripture defines that which is considered most holy by the Lord. *"Anything which a man sets apart to the LORD out of all that he hath... is most holy to the Lord."*[55] That which is the Lord's portion, and which has been set apart unto Him, is the most holy of the Lord. *"And thou shall put the mercy seat upon the ark of the testimony in the most holy place."*[56] That which has been set apart unto the Lord, shall have the mercy seat of God placed there in the spiritual. Remember that the New Covenant fulfills in the spirit, all of the substance of the Old Covenant, which was given to Israel in the natural. Jesus was born in the natural, under the law of the Old Covenant, and was anointed as the most holy place. Not a temple made with hands, but by the Lord. In the Second Coming, the Lord is preparing another temple to dwell in. This temple is also the *"most holy"* for it, too, has been consecrated, and set apart for God. *"And they shall call them, The holy people, the redeemed of the LORD: and thou shalt be called, Sought out, A city not forsaken."*[57] The redeemed of the Lord are the most holy, and they shall endure until the end of the tribulation, and they will see the sign of the Son of Man in the heavens!

This holy remnant is also called the holy seed in Scripture. *"Then said I, Lord, how long? And he answered, Until the cities be wasted without inhabitant, and the houses without man, and the land be utterly desolate, And the Lord have removed men far away, and there be a great forsaking in the midst of the land. But yet in it shall be a tenth, and it shall return, and shall be eaten: as a teil tree, and as an oak, whose substance is in them, when they cast their leaves: so the holy seed shall be the substance thereof."*[58] This seed is the portion set apart unto the Lord. They are His special treasure, and in the last half of the seventieth week of Daniel, which is the Great Tribulation, the holy seed, which is the most holy, shall again be anointed. *"And that which is left... it is a thing most holy of the offerings of the LORD made by fire."*[59] In the harvest of the earth, which is coming, the most holy shall endure the fire, and remain. *"The most holy gifts, reserved from the fire, every offering of theirs... which they shall render to Me, shall be most holy."*[60]

The most holy are reserved from the fire, they are the Lord's portion. The fire, which is coming, will purify the people of God, but the most holy remnant are already pure. They are the first fruits of the Lord and need not be burned. *"And it shall come to pass, that in all the land, saith the LORD, two parts therein shall be cut off and die; but the third shall be left therein. And I will bring the third part through the fire, and will refine them as silver is refined, and will try them as gold is tried: they shall call on my name, and I will hear them: I will say, It is my people: and they shall say, The LORD is my God."*[61] The most holy place is the temple of the Lord in the heart of the sanctified believer. The Song of Solomon presents a picture of the remnant, hidden in the wilderness, and coming forth leaning on Him. *"Who is this that cometh up from the wilderness, leaning upon her beloved?"*[62] The Lord is their beloved, and they lean upon Him. They have no strength of their own, for their strength is in the Lord. The prophecy for the tribe of Benjamin is also a picture of the remnant: *"And of Benjamin he said, The beloved of the LORD shall dwell in safety by Him; and the Lord shall cover him all the day long, and he shall dwell between his shoulders."*[63]

> *"And, behold, the glory of the God of Israel came from the way of the east: and his voice was like a noise of many waters: and the earth shined with his glory.... and I fell upon my face... the spirit took me up, and brought me into the inner court; and, behold, the glory of the LORD filled the house. And I heard him speaking unto me out of the house; and the man stood by me. And he said unto me, Son of man, the place of my throne, and the place of the soles of my feet, where I will dwell in the midst of the children of Israel for ever, and my holy name, shall the house of Israel no more defile.... by their abominations that they have committed: wherefore I have consumed them in mine anger.... Thou son of man, show the house to the house of Israel, that they may be ashamed of their iniquities: and let them measure the pattern. And if they be ashamed of all that they have done, show them the form of the house,... and all the ordinances thereof,... and all the laws thereof: and write it in their sight, that they may keep the whole form thereof, and all the ordinances thereof, and do them. This is the law of the house; Upon the top of the mountain the whole limit thereof round about shall be most holy"* (Ezekiel 43:2-12).

The Lord admonishes all believers to *"Watch ye therefore, and pray always, that ye may be accounted worthy to escape all these things that shall come to pass, and to stand before the Son of man."*[64] Those who are accounted worthy to stand and endure the hour of testing are the most holy of the Lord. They have sanctified their lives to the Lord, and they stand separated unto God.

AND HE SHALL CAUSE THE SACRIFICE TO CEASE

Jesus, as the servant Messiah, confirmed His Father's covenant by keeping the law perfectly, and then dying as the Passover lamb for the sins of the world. Jesus came forth from the Father to confirm His covenant for one week. *"[H]e shall confirm the covenant with many for one week: and in the midst of the week he shall cause the sacrifice and the oblation to cease.*"[65] In the midst of the week, at the end of His first 3½ years of ministry, the Lord Jesus Christ gave His own life as the perfect sacrifice, and thereby did away with the need for the sacrificial system of the Old Covenant. *"Sacrifice and offering and burnt offerings and offering for sin thou wouldest not, neither hadst pleasure therein; which are offered by the law; Then said he, Lo, I come to do thy will, O God. He taketh away the first, that he may establish the second. By the which will we are sanctified through the offering of the body of Jesus Christ once for all."*[66]

The prophecy also says because of *"the overspreading of abominations, he shall make it desolate, even until the consummation."*[67] At the coming of Jesus Christ, the land was filled or *"overspread"* with abominations, and therefore it was made desolate until the *"consummation."* The *"consummation"* means until the time of the end. After the death of Jesus Christ upon the cross, in literal fulfillment, the Romans came and stopped the Temple sacrifice, destroying the Temple and the nation, leaving the land desolate. The Romans enacted a property tax shortly after the death of our Lord based on the number of trees on a piece of property. The Jews, being shrewd tax planners, promptly cut down most of the trees, and thus the land became a desolate wilderness. Again, the prophecy was fulfilled literally. The phrase *"until the consummation"* means that the sacrifice will stop, and the land will remain desolate until the time of the end. Only after the return to the land, which began in the late 19th century, did the Jews began to replant the trees and restore the land. Soon Israel will begin to rebuild the physical Temple of the Lord, and their first step will be to restart the daily sacrifice. While Israel is rebuilding the Temple, the Lord will rebuild His Temple made without hands in the Spirit, the temple in the hearts of His people. Today in Israel, the Orthodox Jews are preparing to rebuild the Temple. The altar has already been prepared, and the priesthood trained in the Levitical laws of sacrifice. All that remains is for the Jews to be given access to the Temple Mount. Following the next Arab-Israeli war, they will be given permission to start the altar as the first step in rebuilding the Temple. Once the sacrifice is started again, it will again be stopped and then the second half of the 70th week of Daniel will begin. The stopping of the sacrifice on the Temple

Mount and the subsequent setting up of the abomination of desolation will mark the beginning of the Great Tribulation! I will discuss the ministry of the Lord Jesus Christ during the second half of the 70th week in detail in the chapter entitled *"The LORD shall be the hope of His people."*

THE OTHER PRINCE WHO IS COMING

In addition to revealing the timing of the first and Second Coming of Messiah, Daniel also reveals another prince shall come. He is mentioned when we are told *"and the people of the prince that shall come, shall destroy the city and the sanctuary"*[68] speaking of the Roman destruction of Jerusalem in 70 AD. This is the Antichrist, to whom I shall refer as the little prince. He comes in his own name, rising out of the empire which was once ancient Rome, and he makes his appearance to the world, taking his seat of authority as a "prince." It is of this prince Jesus spoke saying, *"I am come in my Father's name, and ye receive me not: if another shall come in his own name, him ye will receive."*[69] Jesus Christ had come in His Father's name, and the nation had rejected Him as Messiah. The Lord prophesied another messiah would come one day in his own name, and him the nation would receive.

CONFIRMATION OF THE OTHER COVENANT

The little prince will also confirm a covenant with the many for a period of one week. In the midst of this confirmation, he, too, will stop the daily sacrifice on the temple mount and cause the oblation to cease. What is this covenant with the many? This covenant was made by Israel without the Lord. It was made in the flesh. In Scripture it is called the *"covenant with death,"*[70] because it was made with the sons of darkness, and will be confirmed by the Antichrist. This other covenant was made with the *"many."* After Israel enters into a covenant of its own making, a peace treaty with the many, then the little prince, who is to come, will confirm it for a period of seven years. The Hebrew word for "confirm" is *"gabar"* (gaw-bar'), which means to strengthen, or make stronger. Satan is still attempting to counterfeit all the works of the true Messiah, thus he creates his own covenant with Israel, and his false messiah will confirm this covenant for seven years.

Therefore, we know that the little prince shall confirm a peace treaty, which Israel will sign with her enemies. Some of the new Bible versions mistranslate this verse implying the little prince will make the covenant. This is not the true interpretation. He only confirms it. He makes it stronger, giving his seal of approval to it and his strength in supporting and enforcing it.

Thus, the perfect counterfeit is in place. Jesus Christ confirms the true covenant between Israel and God His father, while the little prince confirms the covenant created by his father, the Devil. This confirmation sets the stage for the last half of the 70th week, which begins when the little prince stops the sacrifice, and then the Great Tribulation comes as a snare upon all mankind. Both princes will then fulfill their covenants with Israel; the true Messiah, Jesus Christ, comes as the LION OF JUDAH to deliver His *"remnant"* and to judge the entire earth, while the little prince comes as the *"son of perdition"* [71] to cast the final deception upon the nations.

THE COVENANT WITH RABIN

On September 13, 1993, on the eve of Rosh HaShanah which begins the civil New Year of Israel, exactly 3,000 witnesses gathered on the White House lawn to watch Yitzack Rabin and Yasser Arafat sign what would be called the Peace and Security Agreement. The Western news media would announce to the world, *"Today, on the White House lawn, 3,000 witnesses gathered to observe the signing of the most historic peace treaty in the history of mankind, for today, after nearly 4,000 years of conflict, the descendents of Isaac and Ishmael have made peace."* [72] Notice the name of the man who signed the treaty. Rabin. The word for "many" in the Hebrew is *"la rabim."* Rabin's name is inferred within the prophecy! The number 3,000 is also the covenant number of God. When Moses received the law and came down from the mountain, and saw the children of Israel had made the golden calf, three thousand died in the ensuing judgment. *"And the children of Levi did according to the word of Moses: and there fell of the people that day about three thousand men."* [73] When the Holy Spirit fell on Pentecost, three thousand were saved, a sign that the Lord had accepted the New Covenant. *"Then they that gladly re-*

ceived his word were baptized: and the same day there were added unto them about three thousand souls."[74]

The Lord uses the same covenant number of 3,000 to alert us that this is the final covenant spoken of by the Prophet Daniel. This covenant with the many, the covenant Israel initiates with hell itself, it is the covenant with Rabin. The Lord also has given us other signs to witness we are at the door. The year 1997 was the 3,000th anniversary of Jerusalem. Three thousand years ago, David built an altar, and made Jerusalem the capital of Israel. Today, the descendents of David are preparing another altar, which they will start to build immediately after Israel takes back the Temple Mount. Isaiah speaks of this covenant and the apostate leaders who would rule Israel in the last days: *"Wherefore hear the word of the LORD, ye scornful men, that rule this people in Jerusalem. Because ye have said, We have made a covenant with death, and with hell are we at agreement; when the overflowing scourge shall pass through, it shall not come unto us: for we have made lies our refuge, and under falsehood have we hid ourselves."*[75]

Isaiah calls the leaders of modern apostate Israel *"scornful men"* for they reject the word of God, and the promise God made to Abraham, through whom the Jewish people inherited the right to possess the land of Israel. God never gave actual ownership of the land to Israel, they are merely allowed to live there and they have no legal right to surrender the land of Israel to their enemies. *"The land shall not be sold forever: for the land is mine."*[76]

The Lord has never authorized signing a peace treaty with His enemies or surrendering any part of the land. Isaiah calls the leaders of this apostate people who enter into such a treaty "scoffers", for they mock the word of the Lord promising the land of Israel to Abraham and his descendants forever.

Rabbi Charlop wrote, *"It is clear and simple that the Jewish People must never, Heaven forbid, cede any part of the Land. Any concession of a piece of land, whether large or small, that is blessed with the holiness of Eretz Yisrael, is considered a form of 'denying a connection to the Land.' Anyone upon whom rests the name of Israel is forbidden to deny his Judaism or his connection to the Land of Israel.... We learn from our forefathers, that for as long as Abraham thought to share the Land with Lot, God did not speak with him. We see clearly that it is forbidden to agree to cede even part of the Land... and God is angered by this as if the entire Land was given over. I would like to point out that the ruling handed down by the Rabbis of Israel during the previous government—that there is a clear prohibition to withdraw from any part of Eretz Yisrael—is still true and valid today. In fact, this government is obligated even more to preserve the Land of Israel, and is forbidden to sign any document that means the handing over of parts of the Land. Furthermore, if such a document is signed, it has no validity. May Hashem preserve us and our Holy Land in our control."* [77]

Isaiah called the leaders of apostate Israel who entered into this agreement, scoffers. Prime Minister of Israel Yitzach Rabin mocked the promises of God and was quoted as saying the Bible is not a grant deed for the land of Israel. These apostate leaders of Israel who signed the covenant claimed they did not believe in *"greater Israel,"* and God's promise to Abraham for the land in Genesis 12:7. *"And the LORD appeared unto Abram, and said, Unto thy seed will I give this land: and there builded he an altar unto the LORD, who appeared unto him."* On the day of Rabin's assassination, the Torah teaching for the Sabbath, which began that evening, was the Abrahamic Covenant and this passage of Scripture. This promise to Abraham and his seed is the foundation of the faith of the elect and the Lord does not tolerate those who mock His Holy word. This same promise is repeated in the law of the Lord, which was given to Israel before they entered into the land. We do well to heed this command!

"You shall utterly destroy all the places where the nations whom you shall dispossess serve their gods, on the high mountains and on the hills and under every green tree. And you shall tear down their altars and smash their sacred pillars and burn their Asherim with fire, and you shall cut down the engraved images of their gods, and you shall obliterate their name from that place. You shall not act like this toward the LORD your God. But you shall seek the LORD at the place which the LORD your God shall choose from all your tribes, to establish His name there for His dwelling, and there you shall come. And there you shall bring your burnt offerings, your

sacrifices, your tithes, the contribution of your hand.... and rejoice in all your undertakings in which the LORD your God has blessed you. You shall not do at all, what we are doing here today, every man doing whatever is right in his own eyes; for you have not as yet come to the resting place and the inheritance which the LORD your God is giving you.... And you shall rejoice before the LORD your God, you and your sons, and daughters.... Be careful that you do not offer your burnt offerings in every cultic place you see, but in the place which the LORD chooses in one of your tribes, there you shall offer your burnt offerings, and there you shall do all that I command you."[78]

The Lord does not tolerate mixing paganism with the worship of the true God of Israel, and we shall see in this text that the modern Christian church has embraced many pagan rituals in the worship of God. The Lord does not change. Paganism remains an abomination before our God, and the tribulation, which is immediately ahead, will cleanse the land of this wickedness! Both the idolater and their idols shall be consumed in the fire that is coming!

THE COVENANT WITH DEATH

Shimon Peres, in his book *"The New Middle East,"* states the reason Israel entered into the Peace and Security Agreement is they are tired of war. He continues his discussion saying we have signed this agreement "so that the overflowing scourge of war will pass us by."[79]

His statements are almost an exact quote of the prophecy in Isaiah 28. After the treaty was signed, and the terrorist bombs began to explode in Jerusalem, Shimon Peres went to the scene of the bombing of bus number 18, which was targeted twice. The crowds greeted him by shouting, *"You have signed a covenant with death,"* again quoting literally the very words the prophet Isaiah spoke concerning this peace covenant. The name *"Peres"* was first written in the Bible 2,500 years earlier, in the judgment pronounced against the King of Babylon.[80] *Peres* is translated *"Thy kingdom is divided."* Shimon Peres was the architect of the peace plan through which Israel agreed to surrender her land for peace, thus dividing its kingdom. The name of the man responsible for this plan is Peres. The verdict: your kingdom is divided!

THE COVENANT WITH DEATH
SHALL BE DISANNULLED

Isaiah 28 continues saying, *"this covenant with death will be disannulled, and your agreement with hell shall not stand."* Isaiah reveals this treaty, signed with the forces of hell in the spiritual world, shall not stand. No, this covenant will not bring peace at all, for the other side of this covenant is war. A great war is coming! It will be called World War III before it is over! This is the battle of Ezekiel 38. Isaiah goes on to say that the critics of this agreement would complain, *"The bed is too short on which to stretch out, And the blanket is too small to wrap oneself in."* [81] The treaty would be deemed inadequate; it would not solve the conflict or bring peace, for it was signed with the father of lies.

After Rabin was assassinated in 1995, the leaders of the world gathered in Jerusalem at his funeral service. *"Each speaker called for the confirming of the Middle East peace accord so that the life of Rabin would not be in vain. They called for an agreement with his grave to continue the peace process. We watched as the world leaders came and confirmed the Middle East peace process. Standing in the front row of Rabin's funeral were the world leaders and a prince of the Roman empire."* [82] Jerusalem and the Middle East peace process had now been moved onto the center stage of world politics. The death of Rabin gave new meaning to the prophecy regarding the covenant with death. The covenant with the many, the covenant with Rabin, now truly had become the covenant with the grave. The Lord gives a final warning admonishing you: do not mock this prophecy, unless you want the bands that bind you to be made stronger! The prophet also tells us the timing for it refers to events at the end of the age, for at that time the Lord will bring His judgment upon the entire earth!

> *"Your covenant with death shall be disannulled, and your agreement with hell shall not stand.... For the LORD shall rise up as in mount Perazim, he shall be wroth as in the valley of Gibeon, that he may do his work, his strange work; and bring to pass his act, his strange act. Now therefore be ye not mockers, lest your bands be made strong: for I have heard from the LORD God of hosts a consumption, even determined upon the whole earth."* [83]

The Lord describes His judgment as *"consumption."* The word used is *kalah*[84] (kaw-law'), which means a complete destruction, to be utterly consumed—a determined full and utter end! The Lord has determined that "consumption" shall come in the whole land! And will you not fear Him? Indeed, in the days ahead all flesh shall learn the fear of the Lord! *"For though thy people Israel be as the sand of the sea, yet a remnant of them shall return: the consumption decreed shall overflow with righteousness. For the Lord GOD of hosts shall make a consumption, even determined, in the midst of all the land."*[85]

THE WAR OF EZEKIEL 38

The covenant with death will be cancelled by war! The prophet Ezekiel describes this war; in chapter 37, the prophet is shown a valley full of dry bones. This is a picture of the whole house of Israel having been destroyed as a nation; they lay scattered among the gentile nations as dry bones. *"Then he said unto me, Son of man, these bones are the whole house of Israel: behold, they say, Our bones are dried, and our hope is lost.... Thus saith the Lord GOD; Behold, O my people, I will open your graves, and cause you to come up out of your graves, and bring you into the land of Israel.... And shall put my spirit in you, and ye shall live, and I shall place you in your own land: then shall ye know that I the LORD have spoken it, and performed it."*[86] In the midst of this judgment, Israel declares, *"Our hope is lost."* Most Americans cannot comprehend what it means to have lost all hope. Israelis have known this all too well. God begins speaking to these bones for they are His people, and though the Lord judged His nation Israel for rejecting His truth, He has never forsaken His people. In the last days, God promises to restore His chosen people to their own land a second time. As Newton declared, *"Let time be the interpreter."*

"Thus saith the Lord GOD; Behold, I will take the children of Israel from among the heathen, whither they be gone, and will gather them on every side, and bring them into their own land: And I will make them one nation in the land upon the mountains of Israel.... I will save them out of all their dwellingplaces, wherein they have sinned, and will cleanse them: so shall they be my people, and I will be their God.... they shall also walk in my judgments, and observe

> *my statutes, and do them... I will make a covenant of peace with them; it shall be an everlasting covenant with them: and I will.... set my sanctuary in the midst of them for evermore. My tabernacle also shall be with them: yea, I will be their God, and they shall be my people. And the heathen shall know that I the LORD do sanctify Israel"* (Ezekiel 37:21-28).

Ezekiel continues prophesying that after Israel is restored to the land, and then the Lord will call forth from the north a great nation from the land of Magog with many allies. This prophecy speaks to the ancient tribes who lived in the land that is now Russia. This is the land of Magog, they shall come, along with Persia, Ethiopia, and Lybia, in a great alliance formed against Israel. The Lord says they will come against the mountains of Israel, *"which have always been waste."* This speaks of the desolation lasting almost 2,000 years until the land was restored. The prophet speaks of this attack against the land of Israel saying, *"thou shalt come into the land that is brought back from the sword."* The land of Israel fell under the sword of the Romans. This great army, which will attack Israel, is described as a *"storm"* and it *"shall be like a cloud to cover the land."* In the next war, Israel will be overrun, and her enemies will cover the land like a cloud.

> *"And the word of the LORD came unto me, saying, Son of man, set thy face against Gog, the land of Magog... and prophesy against him.... Thus saith the Lord God; Behold, I am against thee, O Gog.... And I will turn thee back, and put hooks into thy jaws, and I will bring thee forth, and all thine army, horses and horsemen, all of them clothed with all sorts of armour.... Persia, Ethiopia, and Libya with them.... and many people with thee.... in the latter years thou shalt come into the land that is brought back from the sword, and is gathered out of many people, against the mountains of Israel, which have been always waste: but it is brought forth out of the nations, and they shall dwell safely all of them. Thou shalt ascend and come like a storm, thou shalt be like a cloud to cover the land, thou, and all thy bands, and many people with thee"* (Ezekiel 38:1-9).

Do not fear, Israel, though these great armies shall come against you, the Lord himself shall defend Israel! God says at that time, *"My fury shall come up in my face!"* and *"in my jealousy and in the fire of my wrath,"* God will respond and fight Israel's enemies

Himself! Then there shall be a great shaking in the land of Israel! God is going to literally shake the entire nation when He strikes His enemies with the rod of His wrath. The Lord describes the sword that He will call forth against the enemies of Israel. This sword will rain upon them with an overflowing rain of fire and brimstone! In addition, great hailstones shall fall to the earth and the ground itself shall shake for the wrath of the Lord, which is poured out. This prophecy describes the thermonuclear weapons, which Israel will use as its last line of defense. This is a literal prophecy. The *"great hailstones"* which shall fall are the byproduct of an atmospheric detonation. The intense heat of a nuclear weapon causes huge hailstones to form, and then fall from the sky. The ground will shake as well, when the enemies of Israel fall upon the mountains, under the fire of the wrath of God!

"And it shall come to pass at the same time when Gog shall come against the land of Israel, saith the Lord GOD, that my fury shall come up in my face. For in my jealousy and in the fire of my wrath have I spoken, Surely in that day there shall be a great shaking in the land of Israel.... And I will call for a sword against him throughout all my mountains, saith the Lord GOD: every man's sword shall be against his brother. And I will plead against him with pestilence and with blood; and I will rain upon him, and upon his bands, and upon the many people that are with him, an overflowing rain, and great hailstones, fire, and brimstone. Thus will I magnify myself, and sanctify myself; and I will be known in the eyes of many nations, and they shall know that I am the LORD" (Ezekiel 38:18-23).

THE NEXT AND FINAL ARAB-ISRAELI WAR

Warnings of a renewed Arab-Israeli war in the Middle-East have been with us for years. In the late 1990's, the news was filled with stories of imminent war in the Middle East. *"The next and final Arab-Israeli war could come as early as the second half of 1998... The feeling in the (Arab) war camp is that most of the major concessions have been gained (through the peace process)."*[87] Finally, the Russian Arab war camp could not attack Israel without first finding a way to neutralize America and the best way *"would be by using nuclear armed terrorist to blackmail the US into inaction, but we have assumed that is unlikely... Until now that is..."*[88]

As early as April of 1998, US intelligence services began to report that the United States may find itself attacked as part of this conflict. One such example is The Terrorism and Security Monitor, which reported *"THE US PREPARES FOR BIOCHEM ATTACK. US Defense Secretary William Cohen announced the creation of 10 new emergency teams to help domestic agencies respond quickly to attacks with chemical or biological weapons... the Pentagon is involved in a federal government effort to train first-response teams to deal with chemical, biological, or other (nuclear) emergencies in 120 of the largest US cities. Cohen stated 'This is not something that is a scare tactic. It is a reality, so we have to be prepared.' Acting Army Secretary Robert Walker 'The experts tell us it's not 'if' but 'when' a weapon of mass destruction will be used in this country."*[89] For the first time, in the late 1990's the US public was beginning to be told the coming war would be fought in part, on the US homeland.

Following the events of September 11th, 2001, the next world war began almost invisibly as the President of the United States formally declared war on an ideology he called "terrorism". Shortly thereafter the US invaded Afghanistan and then Iraq. Both of these military occupations continue and now the press is filled with rumors of war with Iran which is moving to arm itself with nuclear weapons. These wars now being waged by the United States in the Middle-East and Asia are the beginning of what will become World War III. By the Spirit we know these are the "beast wars" for the forces of Antichrist are manipulating American policy from behind the scenes and setting the stage for battle of Ezekiel 38 in which Israel and the United States will be attacked by an alliance of nations. Amazingly the American public, and much of the American church, actually supports this madness. Under the guise of promoting democracy in these countries, the actions of the United States are hardening the resolve of our enemies and depleting the military resources of the country in advance of the attack upon our nation. Many of the troops on the ground in Iraq are actually National Guard units. This fact establishes how thinly stretched US military forces are, yet the American people scarcely seem to notice, and for the most part could not care less.

In late 2004, an expert on American foreign policy from one of the Ivy League think tanks spoke to a large group of seemingly intelligent Americans. He spoke at great length how the US policy of creating a democratic government in Iraq was doomed to failure, concluding that the leadership that promoted such madness must be either mentally impaired or insane. The majority of the listening audience concurred and offered their opinion of how foolish and ignorant the present administration must be to pursue such an obviously doomed agenda. No one in the room even stopped to consider that the true agenda has been carefully hidden from the public eye, veiled within lies and deceptions, while the wars in Iraq and Afghanistan are actually pursuing another agenda. This agenda was designed in hell, and is built upon lies and deceit, for the purpose of bringing the world to brink of destruction, and ordering the events of history in order to allow the coming judgment upon America and to open the door for the Antichrist to rise to power and to seize the throne of world government.

The daily news continues to reveal evidence of the gathering storm, which as dark clouds now cover the horizon. Only those with an ear to hear, can discern the thunder of God's prophetic word, which warns His remnant, prepare for summer.

> *"And he said, Amos, what seest thou? And I said, A basket of summer fruit. Then said the Lord unto me, the end is come upon my people of Israel; I will not again pass by them any more."*[90] *"Now learn a parable of the fig tree; When her branch is yet tender, and putteth forth leaves, ye know that summer is near."*[91] *"Then was the iron, the clay, the brass, the silver, and the gold, broken to pieces together, and became like the chaff of the summer threshingfloors; and the wind carried them away."*[92]

After this Great War, the Lord will no longer hide His face from Israel. From that point forward, God says they shall know that He is the Lord.

JERUSALEM, THE STUMBLING BLOCK OF THE NATIONS

The Peace and Security Agreement is silent on the subject of the city of Jerusalem. The architects did not even attempt to negotiate the holy city. They knew they would never get an agreement on

Jerusalem; their strategy was to leave Jerusalem out of the peace process in hope that the parties would be so committed, that Jerusalem could be negotiated at the end. This strategy is doomed to fail. The Lord tells us after the covenant with death is cancelled by the war, He will then rise up as in mount Perazim and He will be *"wroth."*[93]

"For the LORD shall rise up as in mount Perazim, he shall be wroth as in the valley of Gibeon, that he may do his work, his strange work; and bring to pass his act, his strange act."[94] The Lord will then begin to *"do his work,"* which He calls *"His strange work,"* and *"to bring to pass His act, His strange act."* The strange work of the Lord is the judgment of God, which begins with the next war. God refers to His judgment as *"His strange act"* for the Lord takes no joy in the judgment of the wicked. It also appears as *"a strange act"* to the people of God, who in spite of the many warnings, will be taken completely off-guard, and surprised when the judgment falls.

The prophet Zechariah speaks of the city of Jerusalem, which in the last days will become a "stumbling block" to all the nations. Jerusalem is to become a burden for all peoples, and all who attempt to come against Jerusalem shall be destroyed. This prophecy is already being fulfilled, as the nations of the world are all focused on the question of Jerusalem. The UN itself has spent the majority of its energies attempting to deal with the problem of Jerusalem. Over a third of the UN Security Council actions deal with Israel. The Lord proclaims, *"though all the people of the earth be gathered together against Jerusalem"*[95] in that day the Lord Himself will fight for His people. He will then open the eyes of Judah, while smiting all of Israel's enemies with blindness.

"Behold, I will make Jerusalem a cup of trembling.... And in that day will I make Jerusalem a burdensome stone for all people: all that burden themselves with it shall be cut in pieces, though all the people of the earth be gathered together against it. In that day, saith the LORD, I will smite every horse with astonishment, and his rider with madness: and I will open mine eyes upon the house of Judah, and will smite every horse of the people with blindness" (Zechariah 12:2-4).

The Lord declares in that day, He will defend Jerusalem Himself. And those that are feeble among His people shall be as valiant as David, and the house of David shall be as God, and as the angel of the Lord before them. The Lord himself will destroy these nations, which have gathered to come against Israel and to capture Jerusalem.

"In that day shall the LORD defend the inhabitants of Jerusalem; and he that is feeble among them at that day shall be as David; and the house of David shall be as God, as the angel of the LORD before them. And it shall come to pass in that day, that I will seek to destroy all the nations that come against Jerusalem" (Zechariah 12:8-9).

The Lord then will pour out His spirit upon my brethren in Yisrael, and they shall see the light of the Lord. Their eyes will be opened and they will recognize Yeshua is Messiah, and they will know it was Him Whom they pierced. And everyone will mourn for their sin, and for the Lord Whom they rejected. But the Lord, who is so rich in His great mercy, will pour out His spirit of healing. A fountain of the Holy Spirit will open for my brethren in Yisrael, and they will weep, and cast themselves down on their faces before the Lord. And He will have compassion on them, as a Father Who has found His lost son whom He feared was dead. Oh, there shall be such mourning, followed by such great rejoicing, when the remnant of Yisrael is turned again unto the Lord!

"And I will pour upon the house of David, and upon the inhabitants of Jerusalem, the spirit of grace and of supplications: and they shall look upon me whom they have pierced, and they shall mourn for him, as one mourneth for his only son, and shall be in bitterness for him, as one that is in bitterness for his firstborn."[96] *"In that day there shall be a fountain opened to the house of David and to the inhabitants of Jerusalem for sin and for uncleanness.... And one shall say unto him, What are these wounds in thine hands? Then he shall answer, Those with which I was wounded in the house of my friends."*[97]

Following the next war, Israel will then take back the Temple Mount, and the Orthodox Jews will set up an altar and begin again the daily sacrifice. Thus, the stage will be set for the Great Tribulation to begin. The true Messiah, the Lord Jesus Christ, whom Daniel calls "Messiah the Prince", Who is the King of Kings and Lord of Lords, will then begin to fulfill the second half of His seven-year ministry on this earth. He will once again confirm the covenant, which His Father made with Israel, only now He will come as the LION OF JUDAH and as THE JUDGE OF THE EN-TIRE EARTH. To those whose robes are white, and who walk before Him in holiness and truth, and are washed in His blood, which He shed as the Lamb of God, He comes now as the **MIGHTY DELIVERER!**

To those who have rejected His truth and despised His grace, He comes with the full fury of the wrath of God and to the backsliders within the corrupt church of Laodicéa, He comes with a fire to purify and to cleanse, for the wedding feast is about to begin, and each of the guests must put on a robe of white. If we refuse to repent, and to cleanse our hearts by the washing of His word, if we are truly His, then He will do this work by FIRE! And the little prince, he is just a small bit player, who is only reading his lines, and he has only a small part in the story of the Revelation of Jesus Christ, THE SON OF THE MOST HIGH GOD, and THE HOLY ONE OF ISRAEL. BARUCH HASHEM! AMEN!

"Fear God, and give glory to him; for the hour of his judgment is come: and worship him that made heaven, and earth, and the sea, and the fountains of waters" (Revelation 14:7).

CHAPTER
2

"THEY THAT UNDERSTAND AMONG THE PEOPLE SHALL INSTRUCT MANY"
Daniel 11:33

The book of Daniel contains many prophecies in the form of visions and dreams revealing the events of the end of the age, and the kingdoms, which would come to power preceding the coming of the Lord. Much of the book is in symbolic form and requires interpretation. Daniel himself inquired of the angel what would be the fulfillment of the visions that he saw. *"I heard, but I understood not: then said I, O my Lord, what shall be the end of these things? And he said go thy way, Daniel: for the words are closed up and sealed till the time of the end."*[1]

THE BOOK IS SEALED UNTIL THE TIME OF THE END

The angel responds to Daniel, telling him the prophecies contained in his visions are to be sealed until the time of the end, and that no further explanation would be given. It is little wonder that men of God who labored to read this sealed book over the many centuries of the church age failed to discern the true meaning. The book of Daniel is sealed, and its true meaning has been kept secret until the time of the end. Only then, will the Lord open the book, and its true meaning be revealed. The prophet Isaiah speaks of the Lord sealing up prophecy saying: *"And the vision of all is become unto you as the words of a book that is sealed, which men deliver to one that is learned, saying, Read this, I pray thee: and he saith, I cannot; for it is sealed: And the book is delivered to him that is not learned, saying, Read this, I pray thee: and he saith, I am not learned. Wherefore the Lord said, For as much as this people draw near me with their mouth, and with their lips do honour me, but have removed their heart far from me, and their fear toward me is taught by the precept of men: Therefore, behold, I will proceed to do a marvellous work among this people, even a marvellous work and a wonder: for the wisdom of their wise men shall perish, and the understanding of their prudent men shall be hid.*"[2] The Lord declares in the word that He turns His face away from His people because of their sins.

> *"The vision is become as a book that is sealed.... Forasmuch as this people draw near me with their mouth... but have removed their heart far from me, and their fear toward me is taught by the precept of men"* (Isaiah 29:11-13).

Such was also the case in the time of Samuel the prophet. *"And the child Samuel ministered unto the LORD before Eli. And the word of the LORD was precious in those days; there was no open vision."*[3] The Lord had sealed up vision, and closed the meaning of the prophetic writings because of the great sin of the people. Today, our nation and people are under the same curse, for the land is full of wickedness, and there is no open vision. *"We do not see our signs; There is no longer any prophet, nor is there any among us who knows how long."*[4] Yet God always preserves a remnant, and this handful of remnant saints can still hear and receive the word of the Lord! How awesome is our God!

MEN OF WISDOM SHALL COME

This is the hour which has been appointed for the books to be unsealed, and for the men of wisdom to raise their voices in the wilderness declaring to the whole world: *Make straight the way of the Lord, for the Day of the LORD is at hand!*

When the prophecy teachers speak about the end times, they all miss one sign—those with insight will come and give understanding to the many. God himself has prepared these chosen ones. Until now, they have been hidden away, like David and his mighty men in the cave at Adullum. *"And he hath made my mouth like a sharp sword; in the shadow of his hand hath he hid me."*[5] These messengers have been prepared like Joseph, waiting in prison until the day of his showing unto Israel. The life of Joseph was filled with suffering and sorrow until the appointed time for his rising among the people. Joseph first had to be purged with fire before the Lord would use him. Rejection and repudiation, hatred and jealousy, false accusation and abandonment were all used by the Lord to purify Joseph for the hour of his ministry to the people.

The men of wisdom, whom the Lord is now raising up, have walked the same path. This must be, for whenever God chooses to use a man, He first must empty him. The fires endured by these broken ones have been intense. The Lord has prepared them *"by the spirit of judgment, and by the spirit of burning."*[6] Out of these flames, the Lord has forged for Himself a people with a faith made of steel. In their mouths, He has placed a sharpened swift sword. They shall teach the people the truth, and shall cast down all the altars of Baal!

"And they that understand among the people shall instruct many: yet they shall fall by the sword, and by flame, by captivity, and by spoil, many days. Now when they shall fall, they shall be [helped] with a little help: but many shall cleave to them with flatteries. And some of them of understanding shall fall, to try them, and to purge, and to make them white, even to the time of the end: because it is yet for a time appointed" (Daniel 11:33-35).

Why haven't the prophecy teachers told us to look for the men of wisdom? And where would you expect them to be found? These anointed messengers of the Lord will be found in the wilderness, even as John the Baptist came before the First Coming of the Lord. Isaiah speaks of these messengers and where they will be found:

THE VOICES IN THE WILDERNESS CRY OUT

"The voice of him that crieth in the wilderness, prepare ye the way of the LORD, make straight in the desert a highway for our God. Every valley shall be exalted, and every mountain and hill shall be made low: and the crooked shall be made straight, and the rough places plain: And the glory of the LORD shall be revealed, and all flesh shall see it together: for the mouth of the LORD hath spoken it" (Isaiah 40:3-5).

On the eve of the First Coming of the Messiah, His messenger was found in the wilderness before His showing to the common people. His father, Zacharias prophesied of John:

> *"And thou, child, shall be called the prophet of the Highest: for thou shall go before the face of the Lord to prepare His ways; To give knowledge of salvation unto His people by the remission of their sins, Through the tender mercy of our God; whereby the dayspring from on high has visited us, To give light to them that sit in darkness and in the shadow of death, to guide our feet into the way of peace. And the child grew, and waxed strong in spirit, and was in the deserts till the day of his shewing unto Israel"* (Luke 1:76-80).

John was not sent to speak to the religious leaders who ruled the people in their own wisdom, having rejected the truth of God. John was sent instead to the poor, the sinners and the outcasts. Jesus speaks of John and tells us that John fulfilled another prophecy in addition to Isaiah 40: *"Jesus began to say unto the multitudes concerning John, What went ye out into the wilderness to see? A reed shaken with the wind? But what went ye out for to see?... A prophet? yea, I say unto you, and more than a prophet. For this is he, of whom it is written, Behold, I send my messenger before thy face, which shall prepare thy way before thee. Verily I say unto you, Among them that are born of women there hath not risen a greater than John the Baptist:... For all the prophets and the law prophesied until John. And if ye will receive it, this is Elias, which was to come."*[7]

THIS IS ELIJAH WHO IS TO COME

The Lord reveals a mystery, for John the Baptist fulfilled the prophecy of the coming of Elijah in the Spirit. Elijah was the greatest prophet in the history of Israel, and he appeared suddenly, in one of the nation's darkest hours. Israel had fallen into terrible apostasy, and a great evil had assumed the throne. King Ahab ruled under the dominance of the wicked Queen Jezebel and their iniquity covered the land like a cloud. False prophets proclaimed the doctrines of the baals and the people had forgotten the Lord Jehovah ruled Israel. It was in this, the darkest hour in the history of the nation, that the great Elijah suddenly appeared out of the wilderness. In Malachi, the Lord promises to send Elijah again before His return on the great Day of the Lord.

"For, behold, the day cometh, that shall burn as an oven; and all the proud, yea, and all that do wickedly, shall be stubble: and the day that cometh shall burn them up, saith the LORD of hosts, that it shall leave them neither root nor branch. But unto you that fear my name shall the Sun of righteousness arise with healing in his wings; and ye shall go forth, and grow up as calves of the stall. And ye shall tread down the wicked; for they shall be ashes under the soles of your feet in the day that I shall do this, saith the LORD of hosts. Remember ye the law of Moses my servant, which I commanded unto him in Horeb for all Israel, with the statutes and judgments. Behold, I will send you Elijah the prophet before the coming of the great and dreadful day of the LORD: And he shall turn the heart of the fathers to the children, and the heart of the children to their fathers, lest I come and smite the earth with a curse" (Malachi 4:1-6).

ELIJAH MUST COME AGAIN

This prophecy in Malachi will be fulfilled again, at the Second Coming of the Lord, when He comes to judge the earth with fire! We are instructed in this prophecy to *"remember the law of Moses."* Why does the Lord remind the people to remember the law? Because in the last days, a great apostasy will come, and the people will have forsaken the law, turning the grace of God given to them through Jesus, into a license for sin. God promises that He will send Elijah the prophet again, before the coming of the great and dreadful day of the Lord. Jesus referred to this prophecy, and told us that John fulfilled it in his First Coming. Yet, this prophecy also speaks of the Second Coming—the great and dreadful day of the Lord.

Dear Reader, know and understand, the events of the First Coming parallel the Second Coming. Elijah, or one, who comes in his office and anointing, shall also appear before the Second Coming. The land will again be found covered in deep darkness, and the people will have turned from the truth. The false prophets of Baal will again spin their web of deception, and the throne will be ruled by a weak king like Ahab under the dominance of a wicked woman like Jezebel. Such is the present hour, and Elijah is about to come forth suddenly, as if out of the wilderness. He will burst forth from outside of the organized religious institutions of our day, for many of them have fallen under the influence of Baal. We are told of only one interaction that John had with the religious leaders, when they came out to see him. His response was direct and to the point:

> *"But when he saw many of the Pharisees and Sadducees come to his baptism, he said unto them, O generation of vipers, who hath warned you to flee from the wrath to come? Bring forth therefore fruits meet for repentance: And think not to say within yourselves, We have Abraham to our father: for I say unto you, that God is able of these stones to raise up children unto Abraham. And now also the axe is laid unto the root of the trees: therefore every tree, which bringeth not forth good fruit, is hewn down, and cast into the fire"* (Matthew 3:7-10).

The messengers of the Second Coming, the men of wisdom who will give understanding to the many, will also be found in the wilderness. They will be rejected by the religious leaders and sent instead to the poor and the outcasts, who will hear the true words of God. It will not be just one voice this time. No, before the Second Coming, many men and women will come forth and raise their voices proclaiming, *"The Day of the LORD is at hand!"*

These men of understanding among the people *"shall instruct many."* They will share the revelation knowledge they have received from the Lord with many others. It will be their passion, for the word of God will burn within these men. Yet we are also told that these men of understanding would be tested, and that they would fall and when they fall, they will be helped with a little help, and many would join them with flatteries or hypocrisy.

HERE IS THE MIND WHICH HAS WISDOM

What signs do we have that we can use to identify the men of wisdom, who have the true understanding of the Scripture? How will we discern their voice and message from all the other voices, which will be speaking at the time of the end?

It has been the practice of kings to test their wise men with riddles, for this was the proof that they were indeed men of wisdom. Our Lord uses the same test, providing riddles in Scripture as prophetic mysteries, by which we may know and discern that those who can answer the riddle truthfully have the mind of wisdom. This wisdom is not of human knowledge, or higher learning, though the men of understanding whom God calls may possess both. The mind of wisdom spoken of in the Scripture is one to whom the secret mysteries of God have been revealed by the Spirit. These mysteries are not discovered, nor are they reasoned with the mind of man, but God reveals them to whomever he chooses to reveal them. As Daniel exclaims, *"Blessed be the name of God for ever and ever; for wisdom and might are his: and he changeth the times and the seasons: he removeth kings, and seteth up kings; he giveth wisdom to the wise.... he revealeth the deep and secret things, he knoweth what is in the darkness."*[8]

Scripture gives us three spsecific tests we can use to identify the men of understanding who have the mind of wisdom. First, everything they speak and teach must confirm and be consistent with both the whole counsel of God, which is His Torah, and the testimony of the prophets. *"To the law and to the testimony: if they speak not according to this word, it is because there is no light in them."*[9]

Second, they are able to count the number of the beast, and identify the Antichrist before he is revealed to the world. *"And I stood upon the sand of the sea, and saw a beast rise up out of the sea.... the beast which I saw was like unto a leopard, and his feet were as the feet of a bear, and his mouth as the mouth of a lion: and the dragon gave him his power, and his seat, and great authority.... Here is wisdom. Let him that hath understanding count the number of the beast: for it is the number of a man; and his number is Six hundred threescore and six."*[10]

Third, the men of wisdom are also able to solve the riddle of the woman, Mystery Babylon, and the beast on which she rides as spoken in Revelation 17. *"I saw a woman sit upon a scarlet coloured beast, full of names of blasphemy, having seven heads and ten horns. And the woman was arrayed in purple and scarlet colour, and decked with gold and precious stones and pearls, having a golden cup in her hand full of abominations and filthiness of her fornication: And upon her forehead was a name written,* **MYSTERY, BABYLON THE GREAT, THE MOTHER OF**

HARLOTS AND ABOMINATIONS OF THE EARTH.... here is the mind which hath wisdom."[11]

Each of the above tests will be answered in chapter 7 entitled *"Here is the mind which has wisdom"* to prove to you, dear reader, that this message is indeed from men of God.

THE DREAM OF THE KING OF BABYLON

First, I wish to discuss some of the key prophecies contained in the writings of Daniel. They are a glimpse into the events of the end of the age. The first of these prophecies are revealed to King Nebuchadnezzar in a dream, which greatly troubles him. He then asks the wise men of his kingdom to tell him both the dream and its interpretation. None of the magicians could answer the king in this matter so the king became enraged, and ordered all the wise men of the kingdom to be killed. Daniel, whose life was now at risk, sought the Lord for the revelation of the king's dream and God answered him in a night vision. In thanksgiving, Daniel declares the sovereignty of the Lord. The Lord alone changes times and seasons, the Lord alone removes and establishes kings. The Lord alone gives wisdom unto the wise, and He alone reveals the deep and secret things.

> *"Then was the secret revealed unto Daniel in a night vision. Then Daniel blessed the God of heaven. Daniel answered and said, Blessed be the name of God for ever and ever: for wisdom and might are his: And he changeth the times and the seasons: he removeth kings, and setteth up kings: he giveth wisdom unto the wise, and knowledge to them that know understanding: He revealeth the deep and secret things: he knoweth what is in the darkness, and the light dwelleth with him"* (Daniel 2:19-22).

Daniel then answers the king, giving the glory in this matter to the Lord, and declaring that the God in heaven revealed this secret. The king's dream reveals that which will come in the latter days. Daniel was not given the meaning and the interpretation of the dream for any wisdom that was in him, for it was the Lord who revealed the matter. Even as the Lord showed Daniel the king's dream, it is the Lord who unseals the prophetic writings in this last hour.

"Daniel answered in the presence of the king, and said, The secret which the king hath demanded cannot the wise men, the astrologers, the magicians, the soothsayers, shew unto the king; But there is a God in heaven that revealeth secrets, and maketh known to the king Nebuchadnezzar what shall be in the latter days.... But as for me, this secret is not revealed to me for any wisdom that I have more than any living, but for their sakes that shall make known the interpretation to the king, and that thou mightest know the thoughts of thy heart" (Daniel 2:27-30).

"Thou, O king, sawest, and behold a great image. This great image, whose brightness was excellent, stood before thee; and the form thereof was terrible. This image's head was of fine gold, his breast and his arms of silver, his belly and his thighs of brass, His legs of iron, his feet part of iron and part of clay. Thou sawest till that a stone was cut out without hands, which smote the image upon his feet that were of iron and clay, and brake them to pieces. Then was the iron, the clay, the brass, the silver, and the gold, broken to pieces together, and became like the chaff of the summer threshing floors; and the wind carried them away, that no place was found for them: and the stone that smote the image became a great mountain, and filled the whole earth" (Daniel 2:31-35).

After making known the king's dream, Daniel then gives the interpretation:

"This is the dream; and we will tell the interpretation thereof before the king. Thou, O king, art a king of kings.... Thou art this head of gold. And after thee shall arise another kingdom inferior to thee, and another third kingdom of brass, which shall bear rule over all the earth. And the fourth kingdom shall be strong as iron: forasmuch as iron breaketh in pieces and subdueth all things: and as iron that breaketh all these, shall it break in pieces and bruise. And whereas thou sawest the feet and toes, part of potter's clay, and part of iron, the kingdom shall be divided; but there shall be in it of the strength of the iron, forasmuch as thou sawest the iron mixed with miry clay. And... so the kingdom shall be partly strong, and partly broken. And whereas thou sawest iron mixed with miry clay, they shall mingle themselves with the seed of men: but they shall not cleave one to another, even as iron is not mixed with clay. And in the days of these kings shall the God of heaven set up a kingdom,

which shall never be destroyed.... Then king Nebuchadnezzar fell upon his face.... The king answered unto Daniel, and said, Of a truth it is, that your God is a God of gods, and a Lord of kings, and a revealer of secrets, seeing thou couldest reveal this secret" (Daniel 2:36-47).

THE IMAGE OF MYSTERY BABYLON THE GREAT

The image of the king's dream represents the ruling kingdoms of the earth from that time until the First Coming of the Messiah. Nebuchadnezzar, the king of Babylon, is the head of gold and ancient Babylon is the first kingdom. Next, Media-Persia would come to power, represented by the silver arms. Third, Greece under Alexander the Great would conquer and rule the earth, represented by the thighs of brass. Finally, Rome would come, pictured by the legs of Iron. These four empires precede the First Coming of the Lord. Lastly, we are shown that Rome, after its collapse, would be divided into ten kingdoms, portrayed by the ten toes mixed with iron and clay. Thus, the vision of this great statue is our first clue to the prophetic revelation of the end of the age, and the identification of Mystery Babylon. When we look at a statue, we tell who it is by the face. We do not think to ask, *"Whose toes are those?"* Once you identify a statue by its face, you know the name for the whole body. This is the image of Mystery Babylon the Great, the ruling kingdom of the earth. Each of the successive kingdoms, which would come and rule after Babylon is also part of the Mystery Babylon. The image of the king's dream represents the kingdom of Satan, which would rule over the earth in various times and places.

This is why the identity of Mystery Babylon has confused so many while her name and place of authority change throughout time; her identity has been hidden. Only through the revelation of the Spirit can those with the mind of wisdom see and discern her. I will speak much more on the dimensions of Mystery Babylon in subsequent chapters, but for the moment let me summarize by stating Babylon was both a kingdom, or a political power, and a religion in its first manifestation. Nebuchadnezzar was both king and god to the citizens of ancient Babylon. In its future forms, we will see that Mystery Babylon divides itself into a separation of church and state, depicted by the two legs of iron. The false religion of Babylon has continued from that time until the present with its identity hidden from the people, for the great deceiver comes as an angel of light.

One of the principles of Bible prophecy is dualism, where prophecy repeats itself in similar, almost identical fashion. This principle was first revealed by Joseph interpreting the Pharaoh's dream, *"The dream was doubled unto Pharaoh twice; it is because the thing is established by God, and God will shortly bring it to pass."*[12] That which is established by the Lord is always doubled in prophetic revelation. The coming of the Messiah is one such example. The ancient Israelites looked for the Lord to come as deliverer from the rule of Rome not realizing He would first come as the Lamb of God.

The prophecies of His coming will be fulfilled twice. The fact that the modern church is making the same mistakes as the nation of Israel 2,000 years ago is another such dualism. The Lord sending His messengers speaking in the wilderness to the poor is a third. The fact that only a remnant recognized His First Coming is also being repeated. Joseph, Mary, Simeon, Anna and a few others recognized the time of the First Coming of the Lord.

> *"There was a man in Jerusalem whose name was Simeon.... and it was revealed unto him by the Holy Ghost, that he should not see death, before he had seen the Lord's Christ.... There was one Anna, a prophetess.... but served God with fastings and prayers night and day. And she coming in that instant gave thanks likewise unto the Lord, and spake of him to all them"* (Luke 2:25-39).

Today, on the eve of the Second Coming, a small remnant has also been shown the Day of the LORD is at hand. In Daniel's prophecies, we find further examples of this dualism.

THE FOUR KINGDOMS, WHICH PROCEED THE RETURN OF THE LORD

Daniel receives a second vision of four kingdoms, which would rise to power on the earth before the Second Coming of the Lord. These parallel the first four revealed in King Nebuchadnezzar's dream in amazing ways.

"Daniel spake and said, I saw in my vision by night, and, behold, the four winds of the heaven strove upon the great sea. And four great beasts came up from the sea, diverse one from another. The first was like a lion, and had eagle's wings: I beheld till the wings thereof were plucked, and it was lifted up from the earth, and made stand upon the feet as a man, and a man's heart was given to it. And behold another beast, a second, like to a bear, and it raised up itself on one side, and it had three ribs in the mouth of it between the teeth of it: and they said thus unto it, Arise, devour much flesh. After this I beheld, and lo another, like a leopard, which had upon the back of it four wings of a fowl; the beast had also four heads; and dominion was given to it. After this I saw in the night visions, and behold a fourth beast, dreadful and terrible, and strong exceedingly; and it had great iron teeth: it devoured and brake in pieces, and stamped the residue with the feet of it: and it was diverse from all the beasts that were before it; and it had ten horns. I considered the horns, and, behold, there came up among them another little horn, before whom there were three of the first horns plucked up by the roots: and, behold, in this horn were eyes like the eyes of man, and a mouth speaking great things" (Daniel 7:2-8).

THE LION WITH WINGS OF AN EAGLE
BRITAIN AND AMERICA

A lion with eagle's wings represents the first kingdom. This is England and her colonies in America. England is the Lion. The house of Windsor, the Royal family of England, has as its symbol the heraldic beast, which has the head of a lion. America, symbolized by the eagle's wings, comes out of England. Thus, in the prophetic parallel, England and America represent Babylon—the head of gold. Both England and ancient Babylon were known for the splendor and majesty of their royalty. Both empires also had kings who went insane while in power. Historians recorded the insanity of members of the British monarchy including the well-known madness of King George III.[13] The story of the madness of Nebuchadnezzar is contained in Daniel.

"The same hour was the thing fulfilled upon Nebuchadnezzar: and he was driven from men, and did eat grass as oxen, and his body was wet with the dew of heaven, till his hairs were grown like eagles' feathers, and his nails like birds' claws. And at the end of the

days I Nebuchadnezzar lifted up mine eyes unto heaven, and mine understanding returned unto me, and I blessed the most High, and I praised and honoured him that liveth for ever, whose dominion is an everlasting dominion, and his kingdom is from generation to generation: And all the inhabitants of the earth are reputed as nothing: and he doeth according to his will in the army of heaven, and among the inhabitants of the earth: and none can stay his hand, or say unto him, What doest thou" (Daniel 4:33-35)?

THE BEAR DEVOURING MUCH FLESH
COMMUNIST RUSSIA

The second kingdom is likened unto a bear and represents Russia with its counterpart Media-Persia. This beast is told to arise and devour much flesh, and so the Communist empire has been the bloodiest in terms of murder. It is interesting that Media-Persia came to power in an alliance of two peoples, while the Soviet revolution was led by two men—Trotsky and Lenin. Adding to the parallel is that the communists killed the royal family after the revolution. According to historians, when the Medes and Persians seized power, they executed the royal family of Belshazzar. The Media-Persia Empire endured the rule of seven kings, and then fell to Alexander's armies. Michael Gorbachev was the seventh Premier of the Soviet Union at the time of its collapse.[14]

THE LEOPARD WITH FOUR HEADS: NAZI GERMANY

Next, we see the leopard, which is Nazi Germany and its parallel of ancient Greece under Alexander the Great. Historians recount how Alexander conquered the world in record time and died at a young age. In the modern era, the Nazi Blitzkrieg or lightning war is a similar fulfillment. Another striking parallel between Alexander and Hitler is they both ruled for 12 years.[15] We are told in the prophecy that the leopard had four heads, and when the horn of Greece was broken, four heads came to power. When Greece fell, four kings came to power and divided the kingdom.

"Therefore the he goat waxed very great: and when he was strong, the great horn was broken; and from it came up four notable ones toward the four winds of heaven.... And the rough goat is the king of Grecia: and the great horn that is between his eyes is the first king. Now that being broken, whereas four stood up for it, four kingdoms

shall stand up out of the nation, but not in his power" (Daniel 8:8, 21-22).

In perfect parallel fulfillment, when Nazi Germany fell, the allies divided Germany and Berlin into four districts, ruled by four kings, American, British, French and Russian. After a time, the four kingdoms, which succeeded Greece, were absorbed into two kingdoms—one in the east and the other in the west. The kingdom in the west ultimately dominated and subdued the eastern empire in the rise to power of ancient Rome. This foreshadows the birth of the final Antichrist kingdom. In the modern era, the four-part division of Germany was also absorbed into two kingdoms—of East and West. The US-led NATO alliance rose to power in the West, while Russia and its Warsaw Pact subdued the eastern half. In exact parallel fulfillment, the eastern half collapsed with the fall of the Berlin wall in 1989. Now the fourth beast will subdue the empires of the world, which is the New World Order of the United Nations. This final empire has been given birth in, and modeled after, the United States of America.

THE FALL OF ROME
AND THE DESTRUCTION OF AMERICA

The parallels between ancient Rome and modern America are also very real. The eagle symbolized both empires and both were formed as republics with an elected body of representatives called the Senate. When Rome conquered its subject states, it allowed them to maintain regional autonomy under the dominion of Rome. The United States federal government, and its rule over the state republics, is a copy of this model of government. The United Nations, when brought to full power, will continue the same format. The nations of the world will have rights and autonomy similar to the states of America, while the central government of the United Nations will retain absolute sovereignty in whatever area it chooses.

The evolution of the Roman government from a democratic republic to a fascist state of despotic tyranny will also repeat itself as the New World Order comes to power. Rome fell from within, its demise the result of the hedonism and the immorality of its people. America, too, is crumbling from within; and the moral decline of the leaders of our nation is now the subject of the tabloid papers. Rome lost her freedoms and the Emperor became a despot in the final days. America, too, is about to lose her freedom under the weight of Executive Orders, and the tyranny of UN domination.

After her collapse, Rome divided into ten regional powers, signified by the ten toes. The emergency plans under the Federal Emergency Management Agency (FEMA) call for the division of government in time of national crisis into ten FEMA regions. The collapse of the Roman Empire resulted in the division of power described as ten toes, and in the last days, these toes will give birth literally to the ten kings of the Beast Empire. The parallel fulfillment is that, out of the destruction of America, the UN will assume full global power and bring about the rule of the Antichrist. The United Nations has already divided the earth into ten regional power blocs with North America as number one.

The United States is also a type of Israel. God created Israel under the Old Covenant to bring the Messiah into the world. America was raised up by the Lord under the New Covenant, to share the truth of the Messiah with the world. Israel was destroyed as a nation during the reign of her 42nd king.[16] President George W. Bush is the 42nd President of the United States of America.

The ten toes of the collapsed Roman Empire are described as a mixture of clay and iron. We are told *"they shall mingle themselves with the seed of men."*[17] This reference foretells the strategy of the ten kings to use intermarriage to consolidate their power. The reference to the toes as a mixture of clay and iron also speaks of the demonic nature of this group. Clay is used to describe mankind in scripture, while the iron speaks of spiritual power. Many historians recount the arranged marriages among the ruling class of Europe, where the wealthiest families of the earth have been engaging in intermarriage for hundreds of years.

The *LA Times* writes of one such family, *"The Hapsburgs are keeping up the age old family tradition of strategic marriage."* [18] These are the descendants of the rulers of the collapsed Roman Empire. They are the descendents of the ten toes, which survived the collapse of Rome. These rulers will give birth to the ten kings of the beast. These ten kings will be literally born into this group of families. This small group, who call themselves the Elite, formed an alliance, which they call The Order of the Illuminati, through which they will create the final One World Government of Lucifer.

THE SECRET ORDER OF THE ILLUMINATI

The Order of the Illuminati has remained unseen for centuries, only recently beginning to allow press about itself. *The Economist* magazine published one of the few articles ever written about the Order entitled "The Good Network Guide" in December 1992. It discussed the various secret societies of the world, ranking them in terms of power, secrecy and exclusivity. The article covered The Skull and Bones fraternity, the Communist Party, The Trilateral Commission, and Freemasonry, among others.

Each of these groups was formed by, and is controlled by, the Order of the Illuminati. The last organization discussed was the Order of the Illuminati itself, which was given the highest ranking in all categories:

"Beyond all these networks lies the mother of all networks, the Order of the Illuminati, known to some as the True Rulers of the World.... Though this secret body has hovered unseen over all history, its most public flowering was in the Enlightenment. Adam Wieshaupt, a former Jesuit... revealed its purpose and system of mutual surveillance to the world on May 1st, 1776.

Since then the order has taken a keen interest in another newborn of that year. It is significant that many American presidents have been Illuminati; some have been killed by the Illuminati; and the Illuminati symbol of the eye in the pyramid still graces the dollar bill. The conspiracy is immense and terrifying.... It is the network of those who run networks. Given its power, you should assume that anyone writing about the order must be lying or part of a conspiracy to confound you. In wondering about the Illuminati, merely remember this. You have never arrived."[19]

This order is the league made with the Antichrist. These are the Luciferians, who serve the prince of the air of the present age. The seal of the Great Pyramid on the dollar bill is their symbol, which reads *"Annui Coeptis"* and *"Novus Ordo Seclorum."* The translation from Latin means, "Announcing the Birth of the New World Order." This is the New World Order of the beast, and the government of the US is the model for this Order, a union of independent states under a supreme central government. The model has now been extended to the world with the formation of the United Nations, and after the next world crisis, engineered by the Order, the UN will be brought to full global power.

Press stories on the Illuminati are rare. One of the few stories to be published in recent years states: *"Many of the world's power brokers and power seekers will wind their way up a narrow, avalanche-prone Alpine valley in the remote eastern resort of Davos this week for six days of deal-making, deep thinking and fun. Headliners at this year's World Economic Forum, which opens Thursday, include Microsoft billionaire Bill Gates, U.S. House Speaker Newt Gingrich, top Russians and, as usual, key players from the Middle East. The group of Illuminati, including top scientists and experts in a range of fields will have their pick of a bewildering array of meetings."*[20]

"And after the league made with him he shall work deceitfully: for he shall come up, and shall become strong with a small people. He shall enter peaceably even upon the fattest places of the province; and he shall do that which his fathers have not done, nor his fathers' fathers" (Daniel 11:23-24).

The ten horns of the beast are the rulers of the Order who will consolidate the power of the UN, and give it unto the beast. I will discuss what the Order plans to do to the modern nation of Babylon as they bring their New World Order to full power in the chapter entitled *"Babylon the Great is fallen, fallen."* The motto of this group is *"Ordo Ab Chao"* which means, *"Order out of Chaos."* The beast will soon create a world crisis to compel the nations of the earth to surrender their sovereignty to the UN in order to preserve the "peace and security" of the planet. This is how the prince enters "peaceably" and takes the throne by "intrigue" and "deception." He is doing the work of his father, the father of lies, and there is no truth in him.

"And the ten horns which thou sawest are ten kings, which have received no kingdom as yet; but receive power as kings one hour with the beast. These have one mind, and shall give their power and strength unto the beast" (Revelation 17:12-13).

THE NEW WORLD ORDER OF
THE LION, THE BEAR AND THE LEOPARD

In Revelation chapter 13, the apostle John sees the same beast empire in a vision:

> *"And I stood upon the sand of the sea, and saw a beast rise up out of the sea, having seven heads and ten horns, and upon his horns ten crowns, and upon his heads the name of blasphemy. And the beast which I saw was like unto a leopard, and his feet were as the feet of a bear, and his mouth as the mouth of a lion: and the dragon gave him his power, and his seat, and great authority"* (Revelation 13:1-2).

The beast John witnesses is comprised of the lion, the leopard and the bear. It also has ten horns, but now seven heads are apparent and the eagle's wings are missing. Now it is one beast, united in power, which it receives from the dragon. This is the fourth beast witnessed by Daniel, which evolves out of the ten toes of the ruined Roman Empire and comes to power out of an alliance of the English, German and Russian nations. America is no longer in the prophetic picture, for she has been judged and destroyed immediately before the beast empire comes to power. *"The first was like a lion, and had eagle's wings: I beheld till the wings thereof were plucked, and it was lifted up from the earth, and made stand upon the feet as a man, and a man's heart was given to it."*[21]

After the wings are plucked from the lion, which is symbolic of the destruction of America, the lion is lifted up above the earth. This symbolizes the lion will be the head of the final beast empire. The dominion and seat of authority of the final Antichrist empire will reside in England. The Antichrist is pictured as a lion, for he will come out of the royal family of England. The lion also is symbolic of the false messiah who comes to conquer the earth as a counterfeit of the true Messiah, the Lion from the tribe of Judah.

The lion is then made to stand upon its feet as a man, and a man's heart is given to it. The Antichrist is the heart of a man given to the lion. He is the *"king of fierce countenance"* who *"understanding dark sentences, shall stand up."*[22] We are told *"his power shall be mighty, but not by his own power."*[23] The Antichrist will rule in the power of the dragon *"and his mouth as the mouth of a lion...*

the dragon gave him his power, and his seat, and great authority."[24] The prophecy that the lion will be mighty, but not of his own power, is also fulfilled by the lion's use of the eagle's wings. Over the centuries, when using its wings, it appeared as an eagle, and it used the power of America to be mighty. Now, endued with the power of the dragon, the lion destroys the eagle, and then is lifted up as it rises to power over the entire earth!

> *"And in the latter time of their kingdom, when the transgressors are come to the full, a king of fierce countenance, and understanding dark sentences, shall stand up. And his power shall be mighty, but not by his own power: and he shall destroy wonderfully, and shall prosper, and practice, and shall destroy the mighty and the holy people.... and by peace shall destroy many: he shall also stand up against the Prince of princes; but he shall be broken"* (Daniel 8:23-25).

AND BY PEACE HE SHALL DESTROY MANY

We are told, *"by peace shall (Antichrist) destroy many."*[25] This is the mission of the United Nations, to preserve peace and security, and it is by peace that the final beast empire comes to power and *"he shall destroy wonderfully."*[26] The destruction that he brings will be incredible, fantastic. Note also he destroys two people groups, *"and he shall destroy the mighty and the holy people."*[27] The term *"people"* refers to nations. First, he destroys the mighty nation, the one remaining world super power at the time of his ascension to the throne. Then he turns to destroy the holy people. This speaks of the final judgment on America, the mighty people, and then the persecution of the saints of the Most High. Daniel is then shown that during the reign of the last world empire, the King of Kings will come and establish His kingdom upon the earth, which shall be an everlasting kingdom.

> *"I beheld till the thrones were cast down, and the Ancient of days did sit, whose garment was white as snow, and the hair of his head like the pure wool: his throne was like the fiery flame, and his wheels as burning fire. A fiery stream issued and came forth from before him: thousand thousands ministered unto him, and ten thousand times ten thousand stood before him: the judgment was set, and the books were opened.... I saw in the night visions, and, be-*

hold, one like the Son of man came with the clouds of heaven, and came to the Ancient of days, and they brought him near before him. And there was given him dominion, and glory, and a kingdom, that all people, nations, and languages, should serve him: his dominion is an everlasting dominion, which shall not pass away, and his kingdom that which shall not be destroyed" (Daniel 7:9-15).

Daniel then is told the meaning of the vision of the fourth beast.

"These great beasts, which are four, are four kings, which shall arise out of the earth.... The fourth beast shall be the fourth kingdom upon earth, which shall be diverse from all kingdoms, and shall de-vour the whole earth, and shall tread it down, and break it in pieces. And the ten horns out of this kingdom are ten kings that shall arise: and another shall rise after them; and he shall be diverse from the first, and he shall subdue three kings. And he shall speak great words against the most High, and shall wear out the saints of the most High, and think to change times and laws: and they shall be given into his hand until a time and times and the dividing of time" (Daniel 7:17-25).

THE ONE WORLD GOVERNMENT
OF THE UNITED NATIONS

The fourth beast will be diverse, for it is different from all the others. The final world government comes to power by an alliance of nations through treaties. The United Nations is the fourth beast. The UN is unlike any other world empire, for it comes to power by deception, promising peace and security. The ten horns are ten kings who will rule this beast system in its short time upon the earth, and the Antichrist, the little horn, subdues or overthrows three of them in his rise to power. He then makes war with the saints of the Most High, and prevails against them. *"And he shall speak great words against the most High, and shall wear out the saints of the Most High."*[28] He wears them out in slave labor camps in which the believers will be persecuted. He changes times and laws, speaking of his violation of the covenant of God and the stopping of the altar sacrifice on the temple mount. We are told the saints of the Most High are given into his hand: *"they shall be given into his hand until a time and times and the dividing of time."*[29] The time and times and a dividing of time is the 3-1/2 years that the prince rules the beast empire. The apostle John also speaks of this period of rule in Revelation 13:

> *"And there was given unto him a mouth speaking great things and blasphemies; and power was given unto him to continue forty and two months. And he opened his mouth in blasphemy against God, to blaspheme his name, and his tabernacle, and them that dwell in heaven. And it was given unto him to make war with the saints, and to overcome them: and power was given him over all kindreds, and tongues, and nations. And all that dwell upon the earth shall worship him, whose names are not written in the book of life of the Lamb slain from the foundation of the world. If any man have an ear, let him hear. He that leadeth into captivity shall go into captivity: he that killeth with the sword must be killed with the sword. Here is the patience and the faith of the saints"* (Revelation 13:5-10).

THE ANTICHRIST—THE OTHER LION WHO IS COMING

The lion is given a mouth, the mouth of the man of sin, and power for 42 months, which is 3½ years. It is given to him to make war with the saints, and to overcome them. We are also told, whoever leads others into captivity, he must also go into captivity. This is the reason why saints are chosen to go into captivity under the beast. They have led others into captivity by their lifestyle of idolatry. Dear reader, if your lifestyle includes idolatry in any form, you are leading others into captivity by your example. If you do not repent of this sin now, you will go into captivity with the many.

Daniel is given a further vision of these kingdoms in chapter 8. The goat refers to Greece, and the four notable ones speak of the division of Alexander's empire into four parts. Then the vision takes us to the time of the end, when the little horn, the Antichrist comes to power. We are told that he, the prince, will magnify himself, and lift himself up after he takes away the daily sacrifice. The stopping of the daily sacrifice marks the beginning of the second half of the 70th week of Daniel's prophecy. This begins his reign of terror upon the earth for a time, times and half a time. We are then given a clue to the timing of the events during the Great Tribulation, for from the day that the sacrifice stops, which marks the beginning of the 3½ years, there shall be 2,300 days.

This is a mistranslation. The original text reads *"ereb"* (eh'-reb) and *"boqer"* (bo'-ker) which literally means 'evenings' and "mornings." Thus, from the day that the daily sacrifice is taken away, there shall be 2,300 evenings and mornings. These count the number of missed sacrifices, which were required at both evening and morning.

> *"And I saw in a vision; and it came to pass, when I saw, that I was at Shushan in the palace, which is in the province of Elam; and I saw in a vision, and I was by the river of Ulai"* (Daniel 8:2).

> *"Therefore the he goat waxed very great: and when he was strong, the great horn was broken; and from it came up four notable ones toward the four winds of heaven. And out of one of them came forth a little horn.... and it waxed great, even to the host of heaven; and it cast down some of the host and of the stars to the ground, and stamped upon them. Yea, he magnified himself even to the prince of the host, and by him the daily sacrifice was taken away.... and it cast down the truth to the ground; and it practiced, and prospered. Then I heard one saint speaking, and another saint said unto that certain saint which spake, How long shall be the vision concerning the daily sacrifice, and the transgression of desolation, to give both the sanctuary and the host to be trodden under foot? And he said unto me, Unto two thousand and three hundred days* (evenings and mornings)*; then shall the sanctuary be cleansed"* (Daniel 8:8-14).

Daniel is then given the explanation of the vision. He is told that the vision is of the time of the end of the world. The angel then explains that the ram is the kingdom of Media and Persia and that the goat is the king of Greece. At the time of the end, another king will come out of one of the four kingdoms, which rose out of the empire of Greece. This king will arise when the transgressors have come to full power. This king, the prince who shall come, will have a fierce countenance, and will understand dark sentences. These dark sentences speak of the occult nature of the prince's power and the dark words are of evil.

> *"And I heard a man's voice.... Gabriel, make this man to understand the vision.... he said unto me, Understand, O son of man: for at the time of the end shall be the vision.... Behold, I will make thee know what shall be in the last end of the indignation: for at the time ap-*

pointed the end shall be. The ram which thou sawest having two horns are the kings of Media and Persia. And the rough goat is the king of Grecia: and the great horn that is between his eyes is the first king. Now that being broken, whereas four stood up for it, four kingdoms shall stand up out of the nation, but not in his power. And in the latter time of their kingdom, when the transgressors are come to the full, a king of fierce countenance, and understanding dark sentences, shall stand up. And his power shall be mighty, but not by his own power: and he shall destroy wonderfully, and shall prosper, and practice, and shall destroy the mighty and the holy people.... and by peace shall destroy many: he shall also stand up against the Prince of princes; but he shall be broken without hand.... shut thou up the vision; for it shall be for many days.... and I was astonished at the vision, but none understood it" (Daniel 8:16-27).

At the end of the prophecy, Daniel is told to go his way, for the book shall be sealed until the time of the end. The wicked shall continue in wickedness, and none of the wicked shall be able to understand these things, but the wise shall understand. We are then told that from the timing of the abomination of desolation, which is the statue of the beast erected upon the holy place, there shall be 1,290 days and blessed are they who wait for and see the 1,335th day.

"And he said, Go thy way, Daniel: for the words are closed up and sealed till the time of the end. Many shall be purified, and made white, and tried; but the wicked shall do wickedly: and none of the wicked shall understand; but the wise shall understand. And from the time that the daily sacrifice shall be taken away, and the abomination that maketh desolate set up, there shall be a thousand two hundred and ninety days. Blessed is he that waiteth, and cometh to the thousand three hundred and five and thirty days. But go thou thy way till the end be: for thou shalt rest, and stand in thy lot at the end of the days" (Daniel 12:9-13).

THE TIMING OF THE GREAT TRIBULATION

I shall now show you how these day counts fit together. From the stopping of the sacrifice, there are 2,300 evenings and mornings, or 1,150 days. From the time the abomination is being set up there shall be 1,290 days. In Revelation we are told there is period of five months when the earth is covered in darkness.

Here is the mystery of this matter. From the day the sacrifice stops, there are 1,150 days of sunlight, then 150 days of darkness, for a total of 1,300 days. The image of the beast is erected 10 days after the sacrifice stops, which gives us the total of 1,290 days from when the abomination is erected on the holy place.

"And the fifth angel sounded, and I saw a star fall from heaven unto the earth: and to him was given the key of the bottomless pit. And he opened the bottomless pit; and there arose a smoke out of the pit, as the smoke of a great furnace; and the sun and the air were darkened by reason of the smoke of the pit. And there came out of the smoke locusts upon the earth: and unto them was given power, as the scorpions of the earth have power. And it was commanded them that they should not hurt the grass of the earth, neither any green thing, neither any tree; but only those men which have not the seal of God in their heads. And to them it was given that they should not kill them, but that they should be tormented five months: and their torment was as the torment of a scorpion, when he striketh a man" (Revelation 9:1-5).

The timing of the Great Tribulation can be presented as follows.

Total time from beginning of the sign of the sacrifice stopping:
|———————————— 1,300 days —————————————|
Stopping of the sacrifice for 2,300 evening and mornings:
|———————— 1,150 days ——————|
Days of Darkness at the end of the tribulation period:
                          |—— 5 months or 150 days ——|
Time from setting up the abomination:
        |———————————— 1,290 days ——————————|
Time between the sacrifice stopping and the abomination being set up:
|— 10 days —|

"He that hath an ear, let him hear what the Spirit saith unto the churches; He that over- cometh shall not be hurt of the second death"

(Revelation 2:11).

CHAPTER
3

"THEN THE WORD OF THE LORD CAME UNTO ME"
Jeremiah 1:4

The Lord declares in His word that He will do nothing without first revealing the matter to His servants, the prophets. God always reveals what He is about to do, through those individuals who can hear His voice. He calls them His servants, the prophets. *"Surely the Lord GOD will do nothing, <u>but he revealeth his secret unto his servants the prophets</u>. The lion hath roared, who will not fear? the Lord GOD hath spoken, who can but prophesy?"*[1]

The Lord always raises up prophets from among the people to bring the final warning before the sword of judgment falls in the land. The prophets of God were ordinary men, whom the Lord called from among the common people. The Lord does not call great men, nor does He call the wealthy, or those who are wise in their own eyes. The Lord says He looks unto the humble and those with a broken and contrite heart. The appointment of a prophet is of the Lord alone. Many men have appointed themselves leaders in the Church, but no man can appoint himself a prophet before God. The modern Church tends to revere the prophets of old, yet they were simple men whom the Lord called and gifted with an ear to hear His voice. Their ministry was to simply tell the people those things which God had said.

I AM NEITHER A PROPHET NOR A PROPHET'S SON

Amos was such a prophet; he speaks of his calling by the Lord saying *"I was no prophet, neither was I a prophet's son; but I was a herdsman, and a gatherer of sycamore fruit."*[2] Amos was a simple farm worker. Would we listen today if the Lord called a migrant farm worker as a prophet? What if the man He called was a tax collector? Many within the modern Church believe the Lord no longer calls prophets to declare His word to the people. They assume this must be true because they themselves have never heard the voice of the Lord. How foolish of these men! This is not true, and it is not what the Scriptures teach. They have created this doctrine from their experience. Truly, the Scripture declares they *"have walked after the imagination of their own heart."*[3] Paul writing to the Ephesians teaches the five-fold ministry of the Church includes *"he gave some, apostles; and some, prophets; and some, evangelists; and some, pastors and teachers."*[4] The Church does not believe the Lord has forsaken the ministry of the pastor or teachers! Why, then, would the Lord forsake the ministry of His prophets?

In many of today's churches, the pastor has been exalted to the position of authority and teacher, while the other offices are missing. This is not the Biblical model. In this last hour, the Lord is restoring the five-fold ministry to the true Church. Prophecy has not ended with the writings of the New Testament, and the Lord still speaks to His people. The modern Church has been deceived in so many ways. There are two prophets coming at the time of the end.[5] These are the two witnesses, who shall prophesy against the nations for 1,260 days, and then they will be martyred. The ministry of prophecy obviously continues to the very end of the age. Remember Daniel prophesied that men with wisdom, who understood these things, would come and give insight to the many. In order to understand these mysteries, you must hear from God.

And when the Lord speaks to you, who can but prophesy? I have been able to hear the voice of the Lord from my youth. I was surprised to learn recently that the majority of Christians have never heard His voice. From my earliest experience as a believer, hearing the voice of the Lord was a normal part of my walk of faith. I will share with you three instances, not to lift myself up, but to confirm to you, dear reader, I am a man who hears from God. These words also contain a prophetic message for you, as well.

I ONLY WANTED TO MOVE YOU

In 1977, the Lord spoke to me one morning, saying, *"I want you to go to the World Evangelism conference in San Diego. Do not seek directions, for I will lead you as you drive your car."* I obeyed the Lord and when the day came, I began to drive to San Diego. I said to the Lord *"I am on the freeway now, and all I know is to drive to San Diego and you promised to direct me. Lord please, don't let me get lost."* The Lord answered immediately, but He did not mention the directions: *"I have cancelled your hotel reservation...."* Then He paused and I said nothing. The Lord continued, *"and they have given your room away...."* Again He paused as if waiting for me to respond but I would not answer. *"And the hotel is full."* That was all. My reservation cancelled, my room gone, and the hotel full. I did not know what to say, so I looked up to heaven and thought, *"What do you want me to do, sleep in my car?"* He spoke again. *"When you get to the hotel, don't get upset, just sit in the lobby and wait for me. I will get you a room. I only wanted to move you."* When I got to the hotel, the manager and the desk clerk were very upset. I had a confirmed reservation, and they had a full hotel! I told them *"Don't worry, I am sure you will find me a room, I'll just sit in the lobby and wait."*

A MAN WHOM I HAVE BEEN CHASING FOR MANY YEARS

The events of that weekend could fill an entire book. The Lord poured out His anointing with power I had never seen before in my life, and spoke many times with an audible voice. After the conference, I began to drive home with another believer who had been my roommate. His name was Kevin, and I was taking him to a hotel in Anaheim. As we were driving up the freeway, people in other cars began to honk, and roll down their windows. They were weeping and shouting at us. I looked at Kevin and we were both puzzled by this. We did not know what was going on. I rolled down my window and they began to yell, *"Who are you? Who are you?"* At that point, we knew the anointing had come upon them. We did not answer them. The Lord then began to speak audibly to both of us. *"I want you to pray that I remove My anointing from you, for I am sending you back to My church, and they can not receive you in My presence."*

As we continued driving, the Lord began to speak again to both of us in an audible voice. *"When you get to the hotel in Anaheim, a man whom I have been chasing for many years will crash into your car in the parking lot. Get out of the car and speak to him the words that I give you. And don't worry about the car. It will just be a little ding. And besides, it's My car."* I responded *"Lord, I thought I had the pink slip on this car?"* *"Everything in the earth is mine, including your car."* I turned to Kevin and said, *"Let's try to see this accident happen. We have to watch when we get to the hotel. This will be fun."* When we arrived at the hotel, we did not see a thing. We only felt and heard a big bang! I got out of the car, pointed my finger at the man, and said, *"I don't know who you are, but the Lord told us we would meet you this way."*

"The Lord says to you, if you don't return to Him and repent of your sin, He is going to kill you. This is your last warning!" He was visibly shaken by my words. I then got into my car and drove off. I never even asked the man his name.

The next incident occurred in 1979 in the land of Israel. I had been asking the Lord for permission to go the Holy Land for years. I would pray often *"Lord, I want to go to Israel, can I go?"* It was always the same answer, *"No, not yet."* Then one day, while I was praying and asking Him again, I was surprised when He said, *"You can go Friday."*

YOU ARE IN THE WRONG PLACE, GET BACK ON THE BUS

I had the most incredible trip to the land. The Lord even provided me a personal tour guide for the entire two weeks. At the end of my trip, I was returning to Jerusalem from a kibbutz outside Tel Aviv. I had to make a bus transfer in a small city. I got out my map, and found the city next to the major freeway from Tel Aviv to Jerusalem. I thought, *"This will be easy to find."* The bus passed under the freeway and stopped in the town square and I got off.

Sabbath was about to begin, and the city square was deserted. As I stood there, I heard someone behind me: *"Binyamin, you are in the wrong place, get back on the bus."* I could not imagine who would know my name here, so I turned around to see who was speaking to me, and there was no one there! Again, I heard Him:

"Binyamin, you are in the wrong place, get back on the bus." At this point, I knew it was the Lord, but rather than getting on the bus, I got out my map. I then held up the map to the sky so the Lord could read it!

I told Him, *"Lord, I have to go to Jerusalem to get my things, remember, and I checked this map, and look, Lord."* He did not even mention the map, but now He spoke with a loud voice: *"I created this entire country! I know where you are and you are in the wrong place! Get back on the bus. It is leaving. I don't want to have to argue with you again."*

YOU ARE IN MY PERFECT WILL RIGHT NOW

At this point, the Lord was literally yelling at me. And what did I do? I thought to myself, *"I know the Lord wants me on this bus, so I better get on it. But if this is a mistake, He won't hear the end of it, until He gets me out this mess."* I still trusted my little map. Oh, how foolish I was to doubt the Lord. I got onto the bus and turned to a woman who was seated next to me, and I asked her, *"Is this Petrovia?"*

"No," she said, *"it's the next town."* I still had the map in my hand, so I showed it to her and asked, *"What's wrong with this map?"* *"Oh, that's the tourist map. They made a typo, and reversed the cities."* She knew of this error! And God had to yell at me to get me to obey Him. I began to repent, asking the Lord, *"please forgive me, I will never doubt you again, Lord."* I was very embarrassed and I began to wonder why God had said *"again."* How many times had I argued with the Lord, and not realized it! He began to speak, *"You are in my perfect will right now, and I have sent you to the woman you just spoke with to bring to her and her family My truth."*

Yaffa and I began to talk, and she invited me to spend the evening with her family and to stay the night at her home. I arrived around 10 PM. The entire family was waiting to have dinner with me. Her father began weeping as he thanked God for the honor of having an American in his home. All of us were weeping as I told him *"The honor is mine, for the God of Israel is truly the King of the Universe, and I am only His humble servant. I am the one who is honored to be here in His land and with you His people."*

At that point, Yaffa's brother came in the room. She told me he was the only survivor from his division in the Sinai tank battle of the Yom Kippur war. His tank had also been hit, and an armor-piercing round killed all of the other crewmembers, but it did not touch him. The titanium round also detonated the tank's ammunition, and the crew was completely burned in the ensuing flames, but the fire did not even kindle upon his body.

He walked out of that battle the only survivor of Israel. Now I had the honor to share with him and his family, the truth about Yeshua the Messiah. Lest you are tempted to think I am a great man of God, remember He uses foolish things to confound those wise in their own eyes.

These stories are all true. Events such as these one never forgets. I still look back with amazement at the things the Lord did in my life. These words God that spoke were also meant for you, dear reader: The Lord is about to cancel your reservations and all of the plans you have made in this land. Do not get upset. He is preparing another place for you. He just wants to move you. The Lord is going to create a huge crash in this country. He wants to speak to the people of America who have not been listening to Him.

For the apostates, this is your final warning! And it won't be a little ding this time. He is going to destroy this nation by the time He is through. To His remnant the Lord says, *"You are in the wrong place. You have been following the map you have made for your life, but your map is wrong! You must get on the bus that is coming. You must find God's plan for your life. Everything is about to change. You will not recognize this nation in the near future."*

I WISH TO SPEAK TO THIS PEOPLE

When I began praying about the stock market in early 1996 I had not heard God's voice for years. I had become back-slidden and had fallen away from the Lord. Shortly after God answered me, and showed me what was to come, I was speaking to a group of employees about our retirement plan. After I finished my presentation, the Holy Spirit began to fall upon me, and I heard the Lord say unto to me, *"I wish to speak to this people."*

I thought to myself, *"I don't know what He is going to say, but I have a feeling people are going to get mad at me."* I answered the

Lord under my breath, *"If you wish to speak Lord, go ahead and speak."* I began to share how I had been praying all year, and that God had just answered me. I told them I did not have time, and this was not the proper place to share what He said, but if they were believers, they had better pray.

I then began to cry softly. My crying turned into weeping as I remembered what I had seen in the Spirit. The weeping turned into wailing, and I fell face down on the conference room table and began to cry aloud before the great and awesome Day of the LORD. I then heard Him say, *"Stand on your feet!"* As I stood upon my feet, I noticed my right hand was raised to heaven. It seemed to me as if I was watching everything at this point, and I wondered what the Lord would do next.

The Spirit of the Lord then spoke in a loud voice: *"The Lord God Almighty is standing now ready to judge the entire earth!"* That evening at home the Lord said to me *"They are going to fire you, but do not fear, you are not being fired, you are being delivered."* Everything the Lord has ever told me has always come to pass. I no longer doubt Him. I cannot make Him speak to me, but oftentimes He answers me quickly when I call upon His name. I do not consider myself a prophet, or a great man of faith. I only write this book and testify of these things because He told me, *"Warn the people."*

I HAVE CALLED YOU FRIENDS

The Lord always reveals His secrets to those who are close to Him. The first example is when God revealed to His friend Abraham His plans to destroy Sodom. *"Shall I hide from Abraham that thing which I do?"*[6] God always warns His friends when He is ready to bring His judgment. Jesus told us: *"Henceforth I call you not servants; for the servant knoweth not what his lord doeth: but I have called you friends; for all things that I have heard of my Father I have made known unto you."*[7]

If we are His friends, then we will hear His voice. The Lord declared this: *"My sheep hear my voice, and I know them, and they follow me."*[8] There is ample precedent for the Lord revealing His plans to His chosen people in advance. With the greatest event in the history of the world about to occur, the Lord is again warning

His friends. Would you not warn your friends? I would. That is why I am writing this book. Dear reader, you are being warned. Listen to His voice!

The Lord uses the example of the lion roaring as a warning of the judgment to come. *"The lion has roared, who will not fear? The Lord GOD hath spoken, who can but prophesy?"*9 The Lord Jesus Christ also refers to the lion as a symbol of this last hour, when the lion has come out of hiding, and the plans of the prince are now being revealed to God's people. *"The lion is come up from his thicket, and the destroyer of the Gentiles is on his way; he is gone forth from his place to make thy land desolate; and thy cities shall be laid waste, without an inhabitant."*10 Who will not fear?

*"The wicked flee when no man pursueth: but the righteous are bold as a lion."*11 The people who can hear from the Lord are the true prophets. They bear the indignation of the Lord, and their ministry is to warn the people to turn from their sins, lest they be consumed in the judgment. Their voices are in the minority, and they are always found in the wilderness, rejected by the religious leaders of the day. The true messengers of the Lord are always rejected by the majority of the people, who prefer to listen to the false prophets preach a message of peace and prosperity. Thus it is today, as well.

PROPHETS STILL SPEAK

The Church is in desperate need of the true prophetic voice of God to be brought forth in this last hour. The prophets of God are the eyes in the body of Christ. They are the seers who announce to the people the warnings of the Lord. The true prophets have always had the spiritual discernment to understand their times. It was the function of the prophet to admonish, to warn, to reprove and to denounce existing sin. The prophets are also called as watchmen. They are set upon the walls of Zion to blow the trumpet and to warn of coming danger. The true prophets receive their prophetic office directly from the Lord.

The life of a prophet is of hardship and suffering, loneliness and rejection. The true word of God has always been hard to bear, and the people have always rejected the true messengers of the Lord. *"And the LORD, the God of their fathers, sent word to them again and again by His messengers, because He had compassion on His people and on His dwelling place; but they continually mocked the messengers of God, despised His words and scoffed at His prophets, until the wrath of the LORD arose against His people, until there was no remedy."*[12] The message of the true prophets will cause men to shun their company, and to speak all manner of evil against them.

They are cast out by friends and family, rejected by the nation at large, but the Lord Jesus Christ is faithful to send His warnings to the people time, and time again.

God has chosen a very hard path for the vessel to be used as His mouthpiece. The life of the messenger with the genuine prophetic call is not immune to the valleys of depression. This is all part of the package. A true prophet of the Lord lives a lonely life. The revelation of Christ can only come in the solitary place away from the crowds and noise of the vendors and their religious wares. The prophets are burdened vessels, for they see the vision and the lateness of the hour. They know the night is far spent and the day is at hand.

The prophet's character is very likely to be one of shifting moods, unpredictable at times and not likely to be found mingling with the religious. He is serious, sober and not easily persuaded to compromise. His lot is most likely found hidden away on the backside of the desert alone with God. He is the one with a heart for justice, righteousness, honor and integrity. His words may come across as harsh and cruel, but to the one with spiritual perception, his words are received to awaken to righteousness.

The higher the calling into His purposes, the hotter the fires required to purify the servant. The greater the responsibility, the greater and more intense the fires to perfect will become. This is the cost of prophetic ministry.[13]

Those who can hear the Lord's voice directly, and who have been chosen to speak to the Lord face-to-face hold the highest prophetic office. *"Hear now My words: if there is a prophet among you, I, the LORD, shall make Myself known to him in a vision; I shall speak with him in a dream. Not so, with My servant Moses, he is faithful in all My household. With him I speak mouth to mouth,*

*Even openly, and not in dark sayings, and he beholds the form of the Lord. Why then were you not afraid to speak against My servant Moses?"*14

When a man or woman of God speaks the true word of the Lord; their ministry and message will always produce hatred and scorn in the minds of their listeners. *"Blessed are ye, when men shall hate you, and when they shall separate you from their company, and shall reproach you, and cast out your name as evil, for the Son of man's sake. Rejoice ye in that day, and leap for joy: for, behold, your reward is great in heaven: for in the like manner did their fathers unto the prophets. But woe unto you that are rich! for ye have received your consolation."*15

The prophets of God are not trained in the religious schools of man, nor are they raised up from among the leadership of the organized Church. None of the prophets of Israel came from the priesthood. They were all called and prepared by God alone. The appearance of Elijah is such an example. *"And Elijah the Tishbite, who was of the inhabitants of Gilead, said unto Ahab, As the LORD God of Israel liveth, before whom I stand."*16 Elijah's only qualification was that he stood before the Lord God of Israel.

Nothing more was said of him. He was an ordinary man who knew his God. John the Baptist was of similar origins, trained on the backside of the desert wilderness. *"And the child grew, and waxed strong in spirit, and was in the deserts till the day of his showing unto Israel."*17 John had no university or seminary training. He just appeared as the forerunner of the Lord Jesus Christ. God's ways are not man's ways. He still uses the foolish things of this world to confound the wise. Many people have rebuked me for speaking the word of the Lord saying, *"By what authority do you speak these words?"* My answer: *"By the authority of the Lord Jesus Christ, the God of Israel."*

THE JUDGMENT OF ANCIENT ISRAEL

God judged ancient Israel for departing from the truth, and turning to the worship of idols and for following the gods of the pagans. The Lord in His mercy always sent His prophets to warn the people to repent and return to the Lord, or they would be judged and the nation destroyed. Jeremiah, Isaiah, Ezekiel and many others came and preached the word of the Lord, but the people always refused to listen, turning their ears to the false prophets, while rejecting, and in many cases, killing, the true prophets of the Most High God.

Each of the prophets of Israel spoke of the specific judgment that would come in their time, but they also spoke of the Day of the LORD, which is the final judgment upon the whole earth. This is another example of the principle of dualism, where the message of the prophets would be fulfilled twice. First, to the specific people to whom it is addressed and then again, at the end of the age. Jeremiah is one such prophet who spoke to the children of Israel warning of the destruction of their nation for the sins of idolatry and immorality, which had filled the land. The prophecies of Jeremiah also speak to the last day's Church in America. The Lord never judges a nation without first sending a warning to His people. Before addressing the word of God to our nation, I must first dispel a widely-held error in the modern Church. If you fail to discern this error, you will be wide open for deception.

ISRAEL AND THE CHURCH

Many within the modern Christian Church embrace a theology which holds that Israel and the Church are two separate and distinct groups of people, and that God, therefore, is dealing with them differently. This is one more of the great deceptions to descend upon the saints in the last days. *"The concept that God is dealing with Israel in one way and the 'Gentile Church' in another is a serious contradiction in Scripture. In God's eyes there is no such thing as a 'Gentile Church'.... This is a serious heretical doctrine.... This doctrine is often referred to as 'replacement theology."*

This idea was conceived about 200 years after the cross, and later birthed at the same time the Catholic Church was birthed, during the Council of Nicaea in AD 325." [18] It was during this Council that *"the Gentile Church issued a doctrinal statement that strictly forbade any Jewish Believer to observe the law."* [19] The Church has forgotten that Paul tells Gentile believers that they have been *"grafted in among the ever present Jewish remnant that believe in Christ. He also declares that they are also citizens of the nation of Israel.*"[20]

The very name of *Yisra'el*[21] (yis-raw-ale') means ruled by God; this is the name of the nation of people who are ruled by the Lord. They are His people, and He is their God. Jesus says, *"I am the good shepherd, and know my sheep, and am known of mine. As the Father knoweth me, even so know I the Father: and I lay down my life for the sheep. And other sheep I have, which are not of this fold: them also I must bring, and they shall hear my voice; and there shall be one fold, and one shepherd."*[22] The other sheep of whom Jesus is speaking are the Gentile believers who would also be gathered into the flock, which is spiritual Israel, the true nation ruled by God. The Lord has only one people, true Israel.

THE CALLED-OUT AND CHOSEN ONES

The word "church" is actually not found in the Scripture. The original manuscripts contain the word *ekklesia*[23] (ek-klay-see'-ah); which means the called-out ones, or the chosen ones, and is used to describe a religious congregation (Jewish synagogue, or Christian community of members on earth or saints in heaven or both). The scholars translate the word *ekklesia* as the word "*church,*" but God never intended to create a separate institution apart from spiritual Israel. This false doctrine of "*replacement theology*" is a part of the last day's deception of the Church. The Spirit spoke of a great falling away in the last days. The true meaning was the last two days of creation and the great falling away began shortly after the resurrection of our Lord.

Vine's Expository Dictionary of Biblical Words defines "*ekklesia*" as, "The word is from *ek*, 'out of', and *klesis*, a 'calling' (kaleo, to call)... it is used to designate the gathering of Israel, summoned for any definite purpose, or a gathering regarded as representative of the whole nation. It has two applications to the company of Christians, (a) to the whole company of the redeemed throughout the present era. The company of which Christ said, *'I will build My Church,'* and which is further described as *'the Church which is His Body,'* (b) in the singular number to a company consisting of professed believers, and in the plural, with reference to churches in a district."[24]

Jesus spoke of His own ministry, declaring, *"But he answered and said, I am not sent but unto the lost sheep of the house of Israel."*[25] The Lord was only sent to save the lost sheep of Israel, and, dear reader, if you are not grafted into that company, you have no part in Him. When Jesus was crucified, the charge they hung on His cross was that He was the King of Israel. *"He saved others; himself he cannot save. If he be the King of Israel, let him now come down from the cross, and we will believe him."*[26] Nathanael declared this when he first met Jesus. *"Rabbi, thou art the Son of God; thou art the King of Israel."*[27]

Many students of the Scripture fail to understand Paul's writings in Romans where he declares, *"Not as though the word of God hath taken none effect. For they are not all Israel, which are of Israel: Neither, because they are the seed of Abraham, are they all children: but, In Isaac shall thy seed be called."*[28]

Paul reveals the mystery of God's election of His remnant, for not everyone who is born into natural Israel is saved, but only those who are sons of the promise. He uses the choice by God of Isaac over Ishmael as an example of this. Paul continues to expound upon the mystery that only a remnant was to be saved. *"Esaias also crieth concerning Israel, Though the number of the children of Israel be as the sand of the sea, a remnant shall be saved: For he will finish the work, and cut it short in righteousness: because a short work will the Lord make upon the earth."*[29]

The nation of Israel would number in the millions in the natural bloodlines, but only a small remnant would be saved. Dear reader, the same is true of modern Christianity, where those professing faith number in the many millions, while the true elect of God are only a small remnant. Jesus speaking of His chosen ones said, *"Fear not, little flock; for it is your Father's good pleasure to give you the kingdom."*[30] The true saints of the most High are indeed a little flock.

ALL THAT ARE TRUE ISRAEL SHALL BE SAVED

Paul also addresses the issue of whether God has cast away Israel because of the rejection of Messiah by the majority. God has always had a small remnant within the nation of Israel.

"I say then, Hath God cast away his people? God forbid.... God hath not cast away his people which he foreknew. Know ye not what the scripture saith of Elias? how he maketh intercession to God against Israel, saying, Lord, they have killed thy prophets, and digged down thine altars; and I am left alone, and they seek my life.

"But what saith the answer of God unto him? I have reserved to myself seven thousand men, who have not bowed the knee to the image of Baal. Even so then at this present time also there is a remnant according to the election of grace."[31] Paul continues to declare *"blindness in part is happened to Israel, until the fullness of the Gentiles be come in. And so all Israel shall be saved: as it is written, There shall come out of Sion the Deliverer, and shall turn away ungodliness from Jacob: For this is my covenant unto them, when I shall take away their sins.... as touching the election, they are beloved for the fathers' sakes. For the gifts and calling of God are without repentance."*[32]

All of the true spiritual Israel shall be saved. None of them will be lost, nor can those among true Israel be lost.

MY SHEEP HEAR MY VOICE
AND THEY SHALL NEVER PERISH

Jesus declares that His true sheep hear His voice, and they will follow Him. He gives eternal life to them, and they shall never perish. The Father gave the sheep to Jesus as a bride, and no man can pluck them out of the Father's hand. This is true Israel, the people governed by God, and they are a *"little flock"* and a *"remnant saved according to grace."*

"My sheep hear my voice, and I know them, and they follow me: And I give unto them eternal life; and they shall never perish, neither shall any man pluck them out of my hand. My Father, which gave them me, is greater than all; and no man is able to pluck them out of my Father's hand" (John 10:27-29).

"All that the Father giveth me shall come to me; and him that cometh to me I will in no wise cast out. For I came down from heaven, not to do mine own will, but the will of him that sent me. And this is the Father's will which hath sent me, that of all which he hath given me I should lose nothing, but should raise it up again at the last day" (John 6:37-39).

THE COMMONWEALTH OF ISRAEL

Paul writing to the Ephesians explains that the remnant Gentiles, who are saved, now belong to the commonwealth of Israel, for The Holy One of ISRAEL is the King of this commonwealth. If you are not a citizen of this nation, then your portion is the lake of fire! *"Wherefore remember, that ye being in time past Gentiles in the flesh.... at that time you were without Christ, being aliens from the commonwealth of Israel, and strangers from the covenants of promise, having no hope, and without God in the world: But now in Christ Jesus ye who sometimes were far off are made nigh by the blood of Christ."*33

This is the New Covenant, which Jesus, the Messiah of Israel bought with His own blood. This New Covenant was promised to spiritual Israel, and is only made with them: *"Behold, the days come, saith the Lord, when I will make a new covenant with the house of Israel.... For this is the covenant that I will make with the house of Israel after those days, saith the Lord; I will put my laws into their mind, and write them in their hearts... and they shall be to me a people:"*34

The name "Israel" was first given to Jacob after He wrestled with the Lord and prevailed *"And he said, Thy name shall be called no more Jacob, but Israel: for as a prince hast thou power with God and with men, and hast prevailed."*35

We know that God let Jacob prevail, much as a father plays with His son, and lets him win. Jacob prevailed because of the mercy of God. When Jesus said, *"I am only sent to the lost sheep of Israel"* He was speaking of spiritual Israel, which includes the Gentiles who have been grafted into the true vine, which is Jesus. Paul speaks of true Israel saying *"as many as walk according to this rule, peace be on them, and mercy, and upon the Israel of God."*36 The Israel of God is true Israel; these are the holy remnant comprising Jews and Gentiles, who have been made one in Christ and who follow the Lord in obedience to Him.

The Church in America has been lied to. We marvel at the blindness of the Jews who cannot see that Yeshua, Whom we call Jesus, is the Messiah of Israel. Yet, the Church is also blind to the fact that the Gentiles have been grafted into the true vine, which is spiritual Israel. Does God have two peoples, or two nations? One Christian exclaimed, *"The Church is called the bride of Christ, but Israel was called the wife of God."*

I answered this man, *"Yes, that is true. If you read Hosea, the Lord shows us the picture of the divorce He sought from natural Israel for their unfaithfulness to Him, but He will marry true Israel again at the wedding feast of the lamb and she is now His bride, betrothed to God and awaiting the blessed day!"*

The Church is also deceived on the issue of the law of God. Jesus did not come to destroy the law but to fulfill it: *"Think not that I am come to destroy the law or the prophets: I am not come to destroy, but to fulfil. For verily I say unto you, Till heaven and earth pass, one jot or one tittle shall in no wise pass from the law, till all be fulfilled."*[37] The New Covenant was promised to Israel where God said He would write the Law upon their hearts. The law has not been abolished under the New Covenant.

It is still our teacher while we walk in the flesh. Paul in Galatians is speaking to believers who have died to themselves, and are now led by the Spirit. They no longer need the law as a teacher, for they follow the Spirit and obey the law from the heart. Israel and the Church are not separate peoples in the eyes of the Lord. God has chosen one people for Himself, and that is spiritual Israel. The mystery of God is that the Lord only saved a remnant according to His grace: *"Even so then at this present time also there is a remnant according to the election of grace."*[38]

Ancient Israel fell into great sin and apostasy, was judged by God, and carried off into captivity to Babylon in the natural. The modern Church has also fallen into apostasy, and has been carried off into captivity to Babylon in the spiritual. After the rejection of the Messiah, God destroyed ancient Israel. America and her Church have also rejected the truth of the Messiah, and they, too, face destruction.

I AM THE LORD, I CHANGE NOT

God declares in Malachi that He does not change for He is the same yesterday, today and forever. The Lord is a God of judgment. He will not tolerate the murder of innocent children and the promotion of sexual immorality and sodomy without bringing His judgment. God judged Israel for turning from His truth to darkness. God's people worshiped pagan gods and engaged in all forms of wickedness. They were worshipping Asherah, the God of sexual immorality.

They were also killing their babies, the unwanted fruit of their sinful passions, by burning them alive on the altars of Molech. A fire would be built under the stone hands of the large graven image, and when the hands were red hot, they would place the newborn infants upon them. Though they turned a deaf ear to the screams of their own children, the Lord heard, and He turned His ear to the suffering cries of His little ones. His heart was turned with compassion for these poor innocent babies. In His nostrils, the fire of His wrath kindled against His now wicked nation.

He did not tarry long before bringing His judgment. Today in America, our nation worships the same evil gods, and in our modern clinics, we are again murdering His little children. Though America has turned a deaf ear to their cries, the Lord still hears. His heart breaks for each and everyone of these innocent souls. Again, the Lord has become wroth with this His Christian nation. He will not tarry long this time either.

The word of the Lord came to the prophet Jeremiah to the people of Judah, of the soon and certain judgment for their sins as a nation. This word also speaks in these last days to the believers in America, who consider themselves the people of God, yet who commit the same sins as ancient Israel. The Lord chose Jeremiah in his sovereignty, and ordained him a prophet unto the nations. This is our first clue that these prophecies extend beyond ancient Israel even unto these last days.

> *"Then the word of the Lord came unto me, saying, Before I formed thee in the belly I knew thee; and before thou camest forth out of the womb I sanctified thee, and I ordained thee a prophet unto the nations"* (Jeremiah 1:4-5).

God has established Jeremiah's word over both the nations and the kingdoms. The word "kingdom" in this context means a realm, dominion, a reign, or sovereignty. The word "nations" refers to the nation states of the Gentiles. Thus we are told Jeremiah's prophecies would rule over many countries and many empires or dominions, which would come.

"See, I have this day set thee over the nations and over the kingdoms, to root out, and to pull down, and to destroy, and to throw down, to build, and to plant" (Jeremiah 1:10).

GOD'S NATION OF THE NEW COVENANT – AMERICA

The prophet Jeremiah spoke for the Lord, telling Israel that in her early years as a nation, she was holy unto the Lord, and God's blessing and protection were upon her. All that fought against her, He destroyed. Now the Lord asks the people, *"What did I do? Why has My nation gone far from Me and walked in vanity and become vain?"*

> *"Moreover the word of the LORD came to me, saying, Go and cry in the ears of Jerusalem, saying, Thus saith the LORD; I remember thee, the kindness of thy youth, the love of thine espousals, when thou wentest after me in the wilderness.... Israel was holiness unto the LORD, and the firstfruits of his increase.... Thus saith the LORD, What iniquity have your fathers found in me, that they are gone far from me, and have walked after vanity, and are become vain"* (Jeremiah 2:1-5)?

This is also true of the history of America. When America was a youth, she was holy unto the Lord. Our nation was founded on Biblical principles of justice and truth and religious freedom. Many of our founding fathers were God-fearing souls who loved the Lord. They had come from Europe to the new world in America seeking freedom from the persecution they faced in their own land. Some of them were called separatists, for they believed the disobedient church could not be saved. They separated themselves, joining together in covenant communities seeking to honor the Lord.

One of these groups was pastored John Robbins, who preached his final message before his congregation left for America. Robbins told them he believed the Lord had called them to go into the wilderness to a new land, to build a new Jerusalem, and to restore the temple of the Lord with themselves as the living stones. These early pilgrims sought and honored the Lord. These Godly men and women built our great nation. Our heritage of freedom, peace and prosperity is the fruit of the blessings our forefathers received by their faithful obedience to the God of Israel and His Son Jesus Christ.

THE JUDGMENT OF APOSTATE AMERICA

Today, America is Christian in name only. Sin, lawlessness and wickedness fill our once great land. Dear reader, I trust I need not go on about the sad state of our once great nation, where now the land itself is defiled with the blood of over 50 million murdered innocent babies. Their blood cries out to the Lord. The HOLY ONE OF ISRAEL watches as innocent babies are slaughtered. Once again, the Lord's wrath kindles before Him. As He did in ancient Israel, He will make a quick work of judging this land. They were killing babies at the time of the First Coming of Jesus Christ. They are killing babies again! This time the Lord's response will come in one hour.

> "But your iniquities have separated between you and your God, and your sins have hid his face from you, that he will not hear. For your hands are defiled with blood, and your fingers with iniquity; your lips have spoken lies, your tongue hath muttered perverseness" (Isaiah 59:2-3).

The Lord furthers His complaint against his people that they are divorcing, remarrying and committing sexual sins with many lovers, and thus the land is greatly polluted! Isn't this a picture of America? Indeed, the Church in America is full of divorce, abortion, sodomy, and sexual immorality, even as the heathen.

> "They say, If a man put away his wife, and she go from him, and become another man's, shall he return unto her again? shall not that land be greatly polluted? but thou hast played the harlot with many lovers; yet return again to me, saith the LORD" (Jeremiah 3:1).

The Lord pleads with His people until the end to repent and return unto Him *"for I am merciful says the Lord."* Dear reader, we need only acknowledge our sin, and return to our first love, and the Lord will deliver us from the judgment that is to come. The Lord also shows us a picture of His remnant, which shall be counted worthy to endure the hour of testing, saying, *"I will take one out of a city and two of a family."*

"Go and proclaim these words toward the north, and say, Return, thou backsliding Israel, saith the LORD; and I will not cause mine anger to fall upon you: for I am merciful, saith the LORD, and I will not keep anger for ever. Only acknowledge thine iniquity, that thou hast transgressed against the LORD thy God, and hast scattered thy ways to the strangers under every green tree, and ye have not obeyed my voice, saith the LORD. Turn, O backsliding children, saith the LORD; for I am married unto you: and I will take you one of a city, and two of a family, and I will bring you to Zion" (Jeremiah 3:12-14).

Do not be tempted to trust in anything but God, for He alone is our salvation! Blessed be the name of the Lord. *"Truly in vain is salvation hoped for from the hills, and from the multitude of mountains: truly in the LORD our God is the salvation of Is-rael."*[39] The hills represent the religious institutions of man. These are the mountains, which have raised themselves up against the knowledge of God. There is no hope in religion, or in the teachings of man. Our only hope is in the Lord. He is our salvation, and His chosen ones wait for Him and Him alone.

THE LORD REPROVES THE MEN AMONG HIS PEOPLE

The Lord then speaks directly to the men of Judah, directing us to put away those things that keep us from being tender, the sins that cause us to harden our hearts. Judah represents the remnant, for they were the last tribe to go into captivity. The Lord commands the remnant to break up the fallow ground, representing our hard hearts and no longer sow our seeds among the thorns. Jesus spoke in parables about the thorny ground, which represents bad soil, choked by the cares of the world, and which cannot bear fruit for the kingdom of God.

Here the Lord tells us to turn away from the things of the world, and no longer sow to them. Sowing represents investing our seed, our time and resources into fruitless activities and sinful relation-ships, which cannot bear fruit for the kingdom, for they do not represent good soil. The Lord then commands us to turn to Him with our whole heart, for then we shall find Him!

"If thou wilt return, O Israel, saith the LORD, return unto me: and if thou wilt put away thine abominations out of my sight, then shalt

thou not remove. And thou shalt swear, The LORD liveth, in truth, in judgment, and in righteousness; and the nations shall bless themselves in him, and in him shall they glory. For thus saith the LORD to the men of Judah and Jerusalem, Break up your fallow ground, and sow not among thorns" (Jerermiah 4:1-3).

THE JUDGMENT UPON THE CHURCH IN AMERICA

This word is to both the Church and to the men and women whom God has appointed as leaders in the community of the faithful. The Lord commands us to cut away the foreskin and circumcise our hearts, speaking of that which is of the flesh, and of this world. The Lord demands that we sanctify ourselves, and walk in holiness and purity. This commandment includes a promise that if we do not obey, and seek true repentance and purify our lives, the Lord will do this work Himself by fire! Here the Lord speaks of the fire of testing that will come upon the entire world to test those who dwell upon the earth. Remember that the Lord promised His judgment would begin in the house of God—His Church!

> *"Circumcise yourselves to the LORD, and take away the foreskins of your heart, ye men of Judah and inhabitants of Jerusalem: lest my fury come forth like fire, and burn that none can quench it, because of the evil of your doings"* (Jeremiah 4:4).

> *"For the time is come that judgment must begin at the house of God: and if it first begin at us, what shall the end be of them that obey not the gospel of God"* (1 Peter 4:17)?

> *"Every man's work shall be made manifest: for the day shall declare it, because it shall be revealed by fire; and the fire shall try every man's work of what sort it is. If any man's work abide which he hath built thereupon, he shall receive a reward. If any man's work shall be burned, he shall suffer loss: but he himself shall be saved; yet so as by fire. Know ye not that ye are the temple of God, and that the Spirit of God dwelleth in you? If any man defile the temple of God, him shall God destroy; for the temple of God is holy, which temple ye are"* (1 Corinthians 3:13-17).

The Scripture testifies that we should not consider it strange that we have been appointed to walk through the fiery trial, which is to test all believers; God has appointed this trial. *"Beloved, think it* not strange concerning the fiery trial which is to try you, as though some strange thing happened unto you."[40]

Jesus himself tells His faithful ones, "Because thou hast kept the word of my patience, I also will keep thee from the hour of temptation, which shall come upon all the world, to try them that dwell upon the earth. Behold, I come quickly: hold that fast which thou hast, that no man take thy crown."[41] Now, this keeping is not as some suppose, to remove us from the hour, but rather is to preserve us through the fire even as the ancient Hebrew boys were preserved through the fiery furnace of Babylon.

THE WARNING FROM THE LORD: THE DESTROYER IS COMING

The Lord commands that this word be both declared and published, to blow the trumpet in Zion, to command the people to assemble, and to go into the safe cities. Judgment is coming upon our nation, and a great destruction shall fall upon our land. The trumpet represents the word of prophecy and is a warning of an approaching enemy, to prepare the people for war. The warning also includes instructions to gather in groups, and to move to places of refuge, for our nation is about to be destroyed.

We are then told that the lion has come up out of the thicket, which represents hiding. The lion here symbolizes the Antichrist, and as the warning trumpets are blowing in the land, the lion has come out of hiding. Today, the secret plans of the Illuminati to create a One-World government under the Antichrist are visible, and the destroyer of the gentiles is now on his way. He will make your land desolate, and your cities shall be laid waste, without inhabitant. Much has been revealed of the plans to bring the New World Order into existence shortly after the year 2000. The detailed plans of the Illuminati for the judgment upon the Church and America are contained in chapter 10, "Babylon the Great is fallen, fallen." America, your hour of judgment is upon you, and you see it not.

"Declare ye in Judah, and publish in Jerusalem; and say, Blow ye the trumpet in the land: cry, gather together, and say, Assemble yourselves, and let us go into the defenced cities. Set up the standard toward Zion: retire, stay not: for I will bring evil from the north, *and a great destruction. The lion is come up from his thicket, and the destroyer of the Gentiles is on his way; he is gone forth from his place to make thy land desolate; and thy cities shall be laid waste, without an inhabitant"* (Jeremiah 4:5-7).

The prophecy states the warning of judgment will be first declared in the tribe of Judah, and then published in Jerusalem which is in the tribe of Benjamin. This is being literally fulfilled, for this word first came forth to the children of Judah, and is now being published by the sons of Benjamin. Oh, the wonders of our God, how awesome to observe!

THE LEADERS AMONG GOD'S PEOPLE SHALL BE ASTONISHED

Once the *"anger of the Lord"* is poured out on our nation, it will not turn back, and there will be no release for the people. Further, in the day that the judgment of the Lord is revealed *"the heart of the king shall perish."* The leaders of this nation will be unable to stop the judgment of God. The freedom of America will be taken from the people, and their authority will fail. Further *"the priests shall be astonished, and the prophets shall wonder."* Your religious leaders will not see this judgment coming. The priests represent the pastors and leaders, who will be utterly astonished and amazed, because they failed to discern the judgment of America. And the false prophets shall wonder why they could not see this was coming.

> *"For this gird you with sackcloth, lament and howl: for the fierce anger of the LORD is not turned back from us. And it shall come to pass at that day, saith the LORD, that the heart of the king shall perish, and the heart of the princes; and the priests shall be astonished, and the prophets shall wonder"* (Jeremiah 4:8-9).

THE FAMINE OF HEARING THE VOICE OF THE LORD

In the book of Amos, we are told that in the last days there would be a new type of famine in the land, not a famine of bread or water, but of hearing the voice of God. The end of this famine, which is in the spirit, will be death of an even greater kind. *"Where there is no vision, the people perish."*[42] In the days of Samuel the prophet, a similar famine covered the land. *"And the child Samuel ministered unto the LORD before Eli. And the word of the LORD was precious in those days; there was no open vision.*"[43] The silence from heaven was the direct result of the wickedness and sin among the people.

This is the state of the Church in America today, where so few believers can actually hear the voice of the Lord. No, the people of God no longer hear from the Lord for they have turned to the pillow prophets who preach another gospel of peace and prosperity. These prophets cannot see the impending judgment of God upon America, because they are false prophets! Do not listen to them. They are lying to you.

"Behold, the days come, saith the Lord GOD, that I will send a famine in the land, not a famine of bread, nor a thirst for water, but of hearing the words of the Lord: And they shall wander from sea to sea, and from the north even to the east, they shall run to and fro to seek the word of the Lord, and shall not find it" (Amos 8:11-12).

The people will wander from sea to sea, and run to and fro seeking to find the word of the Lord, but they shall not find the true bread of life. The masses of people who do not know the Lord, will wander among dry places, and shall find no water for their souls. *"They shall wander from sea to sea... they shall run to and fro to seek the word of the Lord, and shall not find it."*[44] In the midst of this famine, the land is full of a counterfeit word, soulish (carnal) and religious, lacking the power of the Spirit.

The true prophetic word of God has been hidden, and reserved for the remnant. In this final hour, the Lord is uttering His voice like a trumpet, but the famine continues, for many cannot bear to hear the truth.

Isaiah declares that the people have been greatly deceived, thinking they would have peace, yet the sword that was coming would reach to the very soul. *"For the leaders of this people cause them to err; and they that are led of them are destroyed."*[45] The judgment is referred to as a wind, and it is not to cleanse or to fan, but to destroy.

"Then said I, Ah, Lord GOD! surely, thou hast greatly deceived this people and Jerusalem, saying, Ye shall have peace; whereas the sword reacheth unto the soul. At that time shall it be said to this people and to Jerusalem, A dry wind of the high places in the wil-

derness toward the daughter of my people, not to fan, nor to cleanse, Even a full wind from those places shall come unto me: now also will I give sentence against them" (Jeremiah 4:10-12).

THEY HATED KNOWLEDGE
AND DID NOT CHOSE MY FEAR

The Lord declares that He called but these people refused. They neglected God's counsel, and they spurned the reproof of the Lord. So they shall eat the fruit of their own way and in the day of calamity, they will cry out but the Lord will not answer them!

"How long, O naive ones, will you love simplicity? And scoffers delight themselves in scoffing, And fools hate knowledge? Turn to my reproof, Behold, I will pour out my spirit on you; I will make my words known to you. Because I called, and you refused; I stretched out my hand, and no one paid attention; And you neglected all my counsel, And did not want my reproof; I will even laugh at your calamity; I will mock when your dread comes, When your dread comes like a storm, And your calamity comes on like a whirlwind, when distress {and} anguish come on you.

"Then they will call on me, but I will not answer; They will seek me diligently, but they shall not find me, Because they hated knowledge, and did not choose the fear of the LORD. They would not accept my counsel, They spurned all my reproof. So they shall eat of the fruit of their own way, And be satiated with their own devices. For the waywardness of the naive shall kill them, And the complacency of fools shall destroy them. But he who listens to me shall live securely, and shall be at ease from the dread of evil" (Proverbs 1:22-33 NAS).

A GRIEVOUS WHIRLWIND OF THE LORD
IS GONE FORTH IN FURY

The Lord again refers to His judgment as a whirlwind: *"Behold, a whirlwind of the LORD is gone forth in fury, even a grievous whirlwind."*[46] The word for "whirlwind" is *ca' ar*[47] (sah'-ar), which means a hurricane, a stormy tempest, and a whirlwind. The people will be caught off-guard, thinking they would have peace.

Paul tells us of the sudden judgment which shall come in an instant, but admonishes the believers that the day should not overtake them unaware: *"For yourselves know perfectly that the day of the Lord so cometh as a thief in the night. For when they shall say, Peace and safety; then sudden destruction cometh upon them, as travail upon a woman with child; and they shall not escape. But ye, brethren, are not in darkness, that that day should overtake you as a thief."*[48]

The judgment of the Lord comes in a time when the people are looking for peace and safety. Then destruction comes suddenly! The present hour fulfills this prophecy perfectly. It appears that the cold war is over and American democracy has triumphed over Communism. The Russian threat has supposedly ended, and the Middle East has witnessed the signing of the Peace and Security Agreement.

America sits today as Queen among the nations, and her citizens dwell at ease, yet in one hour, her judgment shall come. Paul admonishes believers to be alert so that this day not overtake us unaware, as a thief, for we are not in darkness. Paul states clearly, the believers will be here to see the day when sudden destruction comes upon the world; otherwise, it could not overtake them. The true Church is not delivered out before the judgment, but is preserved through the judgment.

The Lord tells us our ways have warranted this judgment, and that it will be bitter, for it will reach to our very soul. Jeremiah laments for the pain in his heart; he can hear the trumpet of war sounding in the land, and he knows by the Spirit that God has decreed destruction upon destruction.

The whole land will be spoiled when sudden judgment comes in a moment in time. The prophet wonders, how long will he hear the trumpet sounds before the day is upon us? Like Jeremiah, I do not know the day nor the hour of the judgment to come upon America, but there is not much time left, for the Spirit of God testifies to me even now, *"It is at the door."* People wake up. Wake from your sleep. This message did not come from man, but from the Lord Jesus Christ.

"Thy way and thy doings have procured these things unto thee; this is thy wickedness, because it is bitter, because it reacheth unto thine heart. My bowels, my bowels! I am pained at my very heart; my

*heart maketh a noise in me; I cannot hold my peace, because thou
has heard, O my soul, the sound of the trumpet, the alarm of war.
Destruction upon destruction is cried; for the whole land is spoiled:
suddenly are my tents spoiled, and my curtains in a moment. How
long shall I see the standard, and hear the sound of the trumpet"*
(Jeremiah 4:18-21)?

The Lord then tells the prophet to go through the city, and see if
anyone executes judgment and walks in righteousness. Though all
the people speak in the name of the Lord, everyone speaks falsely.

*"Run ye to and fro through the streets of Jerusalem, and see now,
and know, and seek in the broad places thereof, if ye can find a
man, if there be any that executeth judgment, that seeketh the truth;
and I will pardon it. And though they say, The LORD liveth; surely
they swear falsely"* (Jeremiah 5:1-2).

THE LEADERS OF THE PEOPLE
HAVE FORSAKEN THE TRUTH

Jeremiah decides to go and speak to the leaders of the people, the
great men, for they have known the word of the Lord. The prophet
expects the religious leaders will hear the word, for they should
know the judgments of the Lord, yet they, also, are corrupted. Today, in most of the churches of America, the leaders who claim to
know His word cannot recognize the hour of judgment is at hand.
The lion and the leopard in the following passage refer to spiritual
forces about to be unleashed upon their cities because the people
are breaking God's laws and are full of backsliding.

*"I will get me unto the great men, and will speak unto them; for
they have known the way of the LORD, and the judgment of their
God: but these have altogether broken the yoke, and burst the
bonds. Wherefore a lion out of the forest shall slay them, and a wolf
of the evenings shall spoil them, a leopard shall watch over their cities: every one that goeth out thence shall be torn in pieces: because
their transgressions are many, and their backslidings are increased"* (Jeremiah 5:5-6).

THE PEOPLE SPEAK OF PEACE WHEN THERE IS NONE

The people have spoken falsely of the Lord, proclaiming no evil
shall come upon them. Jeremiah finds the nation hardened in sin,

and embracing a false prophecy of peace. Today's churches fill to overflowing to hear the pillow prophets teach the gospels of prosperity, while the voices declaring the impending judgment of our God are ignored. The great deception of the pre-tribulation rapture has cast a deep sleep over the Church, and they cannot see these events are being fulfilled before their eyes. This great deception will be discussed in detail in the chapter 11, *"First there shall come an Apostasy."*

"They have belied the LORD, and said, It is not he; neither shall evil come upon us; neither shall we see sword nor famine: And the prophets shall become wind, and the word is not in them: thus shall it be done unto them" (Jeremiah 5:12-13).

"FEAR YE NOT ME?" SAITH THE LORD

The Lord confronts the people, asking them, *"Will you not fear me?"* Indeed, when the judgment falls, everyone will fear the Lord but the people are full of evil and rebellious hearts, and they are revolted and gone from the Lord. They can no longer hear His voice, nor do they any longer fear Him. The Lord declares that among *"My people,"* in the household of God, the Church, are wicked men who lay wait and set snares for each other.

They are pictured as a cage full of birds, and houses full of deceit. Scripture speaks symbolically of birds as evil spirits. These are demonic powers, which have gained influence over the majority of the men in the Church. What is the result of all their wickedness? They have become rich, and in their wealth, they think themselves blessed of God. Their prophets also speak falsehoods, and their leaders rule by their own judgment, and not of the Lord. And the people love it this way, but what will you do, when the Lord brings about the end of these things?

"Fear ye not me? saith the Lord: will ye not tremble at my presence.... But this people hath a revolting and a rebellious heart; they are revolted and gone. Neither say they in their heart, Let us now fear the LORD our God, that giveth rain, both the former and the latter, in his season: he reserveth unto us the appointed weeks of the harvest. Your iniquities have turned away these things, and your sins have withholden good things from you. For among my people are found wicked men: they lay wait, as he that setteth snares; they

set a trap, they catch men. As a cage is full of birds, so are their houses full of deceit: therefore they are become great, and waxen rich.

"They are waxen fat, they shine: yea, they overpass the deeds of the wicked: they judge not the cause, the cause of the fatherless, yet they prosper; and the right of the needy do they not judge. Shall I not visit for these things? saith the LORD: shall not my soul be avenged on such a nation as this? A wonderful and horrible thing is committed in the land; The prophets prophesy falsely, and the priests bear rule by their means; and my people love to have it so: and what will ye do in the end thereof" (Jeremiah 5:22-31)?

THE LAODICEAN CHURCH IS BLIND AND NAKED

The Church in America is the Church of Laodicéa Jesus spoke of in the book of Revelation. This last day's Church thinks itself rich and in need of nothing. Jesus declares that it is wretched, miserable, poor, blind and naked. This church is also deaf, unable to hear the word of the Lord. This is the Church in America, full of wealth and in its own mind in need of nothing, yet in reality, oblivious to what the Lord is about to do in this land. Dear reader, do you have ears to hear what the Spirit is saying to the Church? If you cannot hear the Lord, it is because you are not close to Him! It is that simple. His word declares His sheep hear His voice. If you cannot hear Him, then what are you? And what is the chaff to the wheat?

I speak to the little ones, who tremble at the word of the Lord.

Do not fear, if you haven't heard His voice, believe Him and begin praying and fasting. This is the day the Lord spoke of, *"And it shall come to pass, that whosoever shall call on the name of the LORD shall be delivered..."*[49]

The Lord is standing outside of the Church of Laodicéa and knocking at the door. Who will open the door and let Jesus come in as Lord? Whoever opens the door to Christ, they shall be saved! Many are called, but few are chosen. Fear not little flock, only repent and return to the Lord.

"And unto the angel of the church of the Laodiceans write.... I know thy works, that thou art neither cold nor hot: I would thou wert cold or hot. So then because thou art lukewarm, and neither cold nor hot,

I will spue thee out of my mouth. Because thou sayest, I am rich, and increased with goods, and have need of nothing; and knowest not that thou art wretched, and miserable, and poor, and blind, and naked" (Revelation 3:14-17).

The prophet wonders, to whom can he speak? Who will listen to the true word of the Lord that they may give heed to the warnings of the Spirit? Behold, these people hold the true word of God as a reproach, as that which is disgraceful. They will no longer listen to the truth of the Scripture, but rather they follow that which seems right in their own eyes.

"In those days there was no king in Israel: every man did that which was right in his own eyes." (Judges 21:25).

"To whom shall I speak, and give warning, that they may hear? behold, their ear is uncircumcised, and they cannot hearken: behold, the word of the LORD is unto them a reproach; they have no delight in it" (Jeremiah 6:10).

THE PEOPLE REJECT THE TRUE WORDS OF GOD

Because the people will not receive the word of correction, but hold the truth of God as a reproach, the Lord declares he will pour out His judgment on all of them. *"Righteousness exalteth a nation: but sin is a reproach to any people."*[50]

"Therefore I am full of the fury of the Lord; I am weary with holding in: I will pour it out upon the children abroad, and upon the assembly of young men together: for even the husband with the wife shall be taken, the aged with him that is full of days. And their houses shall be turned unto others, with their fields and wives together: for I will stretch out my hand upon the inhabitants of the land, saith the LORD" (Jeremiah 6:11-12).

The Lord declares all of these people are full of covetousness. Each of them lusts after material gain. All of them love riches, and deal falsely. They lie and speak falsehoods one to another, and they heal the hurts of the people falsely, giving soft words of peace when there is no peace coming. Is this not the Church of today, with its peace and prosperity teachings, and full of the lust of the eyes and the pride of life? The message of false peace is the pre-tribulation rapture fable, and the Day of Judgment draws nigh.

> *"For from the least of them even unto the greatest of them every one is given to covetousness; and from the prophet even unto the priest every one dealeth falsely. They have healed also the hurt of the daughter of my people slightly, saying, Peace, peace; when there is no peace"* (Jeremiah 6:13-14).

> *"The Lord God of their fathers sent to them by his messengers... because he had compassion on his people.... But they mocked the messengers of God, and despised his words, and misused his prophets, until the wrath of the LORD arose against his people, till there was no remedy"* (2 Chronicles 36:15-16).

> *"He, that being often reproved hardeneth his neck, shall suddenly be destroyed, and that without remedy"* (Proverbs 29:1).

> *"The days of visitation are come, the days of recompense are come; Israel shall know it: the prophet is* (considered) *a fool, the spiritual man is* (thought to be) *mad, for the multitude of thine iniquity, and the great hatred"* (Hosea 9:7).

THE LORD PLEADS WITH HIS PEOPLE TO SEEK THE ANCIENT PATH

The Lord continues to plead with the people to stand in His ways and to see, and to seek the old path where is the good way. This is the path of faith and obedience, and of holiness unto the Lord, but the people refuse to walk in His ways. The Lord also declares He has set watchmen to tell the people, *"listen to the sound of the trumpet,"* warning of the impending judgment, but the people refuse to listen to the warnings, being hardened in their self-will and rebellion. Today, this is the state of America as watchmen all over the land, from David Wilkerson, Dumitru Duduman, Kato Mivule and others, are blowing the trumpet, yet the church refuses to wake from her sleep.

> *"Thus saith the LORD, Stand ye in the ways, and see, and ask for the old paths, where is the good way, and walk therein, and ye shall find rest for your souls. But they said, We will not walk therein. Also I set watchmen over you, saying, Hearken to the sound of the trumpet. But they said, We will not hearken"* (Jeremiah 6:16-17).

THE PROPHET CONFRONTS THE PEOPLE
WITH THE TRUTH

The prophet confronts the people: *"Why do you say you are wise, and that you know the ways of God and His law is with you? You claim to have His covenant but you do not keep the law of the Lord nor honor His covenant."* Therefore the wise men shall be ashamed! When the day of His visitation comes upon our nation, they will all be ashamed. We claim to have His New Covenant, but the majority in the Church no longer obeys the Lord, nor honors His Law. Jesus said, *"If ye love me, keep my commandments."*[51]

Our nation is full of professing Christians, who assume they will go to heaven, yet the Lord declares that many on that day will be cast out! *"Not every one that saith unto me, Lord, Lord, shall enter into the kingdom of heaven; but he that doeth the will of my Father which is in heaven. Many will say to me in that day, Lord, Lord, have we not prophesied in thy name? and in thy name have cast out devils? and in thy name done many wonderful works? And then will I profess unto them, I never knew you: depart from me, ye that work iniquity."*[52]

These poor souls were converted, and some had even done miracles in His name, yet they never knew Him. Dear reader, ask the Lord to test your heart. Do you know Him? Does His word abide in you? Are you abiding in Him? Do not trust in the mere confession of faith, but see if you have the love of the Father in your heart and the evidence of salvation, which is the desire to please and obey Him as Lord. His sheep hear His voice. Can you hear Him speaking through the words in this book?

> *"How do ye say, We are wise, and the law of the LORD is with us?.... The wise men are ashamed, they are dismayed and taken: lo, they have rejected the word of the LORD; and what wisdom is in them? Therefore will I give their wives unto others, and their fields to them that shall inherit them: for every one from the least even unto the greatest is given to covetousness, from the prophet even unto the priest every one dealeth falsely. For they have healed the hurt of the daughter of my people slightly, saying, Peace, peace; when there is no peace.*

"Were they ashamed when they had committed abomination? nay, they were not at all ashamed, neither could they blush: therefore shall they fall among them that fall: in the time of their visitation they shall be cast down, saith the LORD. I will surely consume them, saith the LORD.... Why do we sit still? assemble yourselves, and let us enter into the defenced cities, and let us be silent there: for the LORD our God hath put us to silence, and given us water of gall to drink, because we have sinned against the LORD. We looked for peace, but no good came; and for a time of health, and behold trouble" (Jeremiah 8:8-15)!

SUMMER IS ENDED, AND WE ARE NOT SAVED

The Lord asks in the above verse, "Why do we sit still?" He then directs His people who are listening to *"assemble yourselves"* and go into the *"defensed cities"* for the time of judgment is at hand. We are then given a prophetic clue of the timing of the judgment: *"The harvest is past, the summer is ended, and we are not saved."*[53]

The Feast of Pentecost inaugurated the outpouring of the Holy Spirit, and the beginning of the New Covenant, which gave birth to the church age. Pentecost occurs at the beginning of summer and marks the start of the wheat harvest of Israel. The Feast is celebrated with two loaves of bread, which contain leaven. The bread is placed in the fire until the leaven is purged. The wheat harvest is a picture of the judgment of God: His people are the wheat, and they are judged first.

The judgment of the Church will occur during the time of the wheat harvest, which is during the season of summer. And it will be obvious you did not get saved, for by the end of a soon summer, the Church in America will have gone into captivity, to the detention camps, as the nation goes under martial law. This is not the start of the Great Tribulation, or the end of the age. This is just the beginning of the judgment upon the household of God, a judgment that must come first.

THE PROPHET WISHES TO HIDE IN THE WILDERNESS

Jeremiah laments, wishing he had a place to hide in the wilderness so that he might leave his people, for they are an assembly of adulterers and treacherous, deceitful men. The Lord adds the final words stating, *"they proceed from evil to evil, and the people do not know me."* These people do not know the Lord. Jesus will say of them, *"And then will I profess unto them, I never knew you: depart from me, ye that work iniquity."*[54]

> *"Oh that I had in the wilderness a lodging place of wayfaring men; that I might leave my people, and go from them! for they be all adulterers, an assembly of treacherous men.... they proceed from evil to evil, and they know not me, saith the LORD"* (Jeremiah 9:2-3).

The Lord warns us to beware of our neighbor and to not trust our brothers in the Church, *"for every brother will utterly supplant, and every neighbor will walk with slanders."* The Hebrew for "supplant" is *aqab*[55] (aw-kab'); which means to seize by the heel, to circumvent and to restrain. The Hebrew word for "slanders" is *rakiyl* (raw-keel'); which means a scandalmonger, carry tales, a talebearer. The Lord is warning His remnant, which are surrounded by brothers who will attempt to trip them, and restrain them.

These so-called brothers also will talk and create scandal regarding the remnant, who appear to those in darkness as if they have lost their minds, for they are building an ark before it rains. Therefore, the Lord says He will melt them by a judgment with fire. Jesus himself warns us that before the Great Tribulation *"Then shall they deliver you up to be afflicted, and shall kill you: and ye shall be hated of all nations for my name's sake. And then shall many be offended, and shall betray one another, and shall hate one another."*[56]

The Lord tells us clearly that persecution shall first come in all nations, and when it comes, the majority will be offended and betray one another. This persecution precedes the revealing of the Antichrist, and the beginning of the Great Tribulation; it is the next immediate event in the United States, and when it comes, it will be sudden and devastating to the sleeping Church in America.

> *"Take ye heed every one of his neighbour, and trust ye not in any brother: for every brother will utterly supplant, and every neighbour will walk with slanders. And they will deceive every one his neighbour, and will not speak the truth: they have taught their*

tongue to speak lies, and weary themselves to commit iniquity. Thine habitation is in the midst of deceit; through deceit they refuse to know me, saith the LORD. Therefore thus saith the Lord of hosts, Behold, I will melt them."[57]

THE LORD ASKS WHO IS WISE THAT UNDERSTANDS?

The Lord then asks, *"Who is the wise man, that may understand this? And who is he to whom the mouth of the LORD hath spoken, that he may declare it"* (Jeremiah 9:12)? Who has wisdom? Who understands what is happening in the land? Who has heard the words of the Lord, that they might declare them? Only the poor in spirit, and the brokenhearted can hear the Lord. Only these humble souls will be able to discern this word. *"Many shall be purified, and made white, and tried; but the wicked shall do wickedly: and none of the wicked shall understand; but the wise shall understand."*[58]

> *"Who is the wise man, that may understand this? and who is he to whom the mouth of the LORD hath spoken, that he may declare it... the land perisheth and is burned up like a wilderness, that none passeth through?... Because they have forsaken my law which I set before them, and have not obeyed my voice.... But have walked after the imagination of their own heart.... I will scatter them... and I will send a sword after them, till I have consumed them"* (Jeremiah 9:12-16).

The Lord declares that after the judgment, the people will forsake the land, and they will be cast out of their homes. Their bodies shall fall as the dung in the open fields, and their dead shall lie littered upon the ground and no one shall even bury them! When the final judgment comes, the dead will greatly outnumber the living. The few souls saved will leave and forsake the land, and no one will bury the dead in America.

> *"For a voice of wailing is heard out of Zion, How are we spoiled!... For death is come up into our windows, and is entered into our palaces, to cut off the children from without, and the young men from the streets.... Thus saith the LORD, Even the carcases of men shall fall as dung upon the open field, and as the handful after the harvestman, and none shall gather them"* (Jeremiah 9:19-22).

Then the Lord admonishes those to whom His mysteries are revealed, that they should not glory in their wisdom, but let them glory that they know the Lord. The Lord is a God who loves mercy, justice and righteousness! Let all the earth fear before Him!

> *"Thus saith the LORD, Let not the wise man glory in his wisdom, neither let the mighty man glory in his might, let not the rich man glory in his riches: But let him that glorieth glory in this, that he understandeth and knoweth me, that I am the LORD which exercise lovingkindness, judgment, and righteousness, in the earth: for in these things I delight, saith the LORD. Behold, the days come, saith the LORD, that I will punish all.... the house of Israel are uncircumcised in the heart"* (Jeremiah 9:23-26).

LEARN NOT THE CUSTOMS OF THE HEATHEN

The Lord then commands the people not to engage in the customs of the heathen. The Lord specifically points to the pagan festival of Saturnalia, which is the birthday of Tammuz, the sun god of ancient Babylon who is a type and a shadow of the anti-Christ. *"The basis of this celebration can be traced back to the kingdom of Nimrod (Ancient Babylon)."*[59] The heathen have celebrated this pagan holiday for over 3,000 years. This is the modern holiday of Christmas.

The reference even describes the tradition of cutting down and decorating trees for the feast of Tammuz on December 25th. *"There are many features of Christmas that can be traced back to pagan worship such as Christmas trees, yule logs, mistletoe and other things."*[60] The early Americans refused to allow the pagan holidays of Christmas and Halloween; both were illegal in America in the first fifty years. Many people who love the Lord cherish these pagan rituals, which are now absorbed into the apostate Church.

In their ignorance, they are celebrating the birthday of the Antichrist. God forgives so many sins we commit in ignorance, but when He exposes the sin, He demands that we repent and change. Today, the majority of the people in America do not care what the word of God declares. They esteem it a reproach; they prefer their tradition to obedience by faith. Thus, the judgment will be just upon the disobedient that cry, *"Lord, Lord"* but will not obey Him.

They refuse to honor Him as Lord, seeking rather to please themselves by doing that which is right in their own eyes. Truly, these people are following the imaginations of their own heart!

> *"Hear ye the word which the LORD speaketh unto you, O house of Israel: Thus saith the LORD, Learn not the way of the heathen, and be not dismayed at the signs of heaven; for the heathen are dismayed at them. For the customs of the people are vain: for one cutteth a tree out of the forest, the work of the hands of the workman, with the axe. They deck it with silver and with gold; they fasten it with nails and with hammers, that it move not"* (Jeremiah 10:1-4).

The Lord then speaks of the people of the earth, calling them gods who did not create the earth. This speaks of the time that would come, when the people would think themselves gods. The New Age movement teaches exactly that. These false teachers and their deceived followers shall soon perish from the earth! This section of Scripture tells us we are dealing with the end of the world, not an ancient judgment upon Israel, for at this time the heathen who think themselves gods shall perish from the earth. This prophecy is not speaking of the destruction of ancient Israel, but of the heathen nations; this is an end time prophecy of the judgment of the entire world!

> *"And the nations shall not be able to abide his indignation. Thus shall ye say unto them, The gods that have not made the heavens and the earth, even they shall perish from the earth, and from under these heavens. He hath made the earth by his power, he hath established the world by his wisdom, and hath stretched out the heavens by his discretion"* (Jeremiah 10:10-12).

THE LORD DECLARES THE JUDGMENT MUST COME

The Lord tells us why the judgment must come. God rose early and pleaded with His people, demanding them to obey His voice, but they refused. The people committed three sins against the Lord for which the nation will be destroyed:

1. The disobeyed God's laws.
2. They refused to listen to God's voice.
3. Each of them walked after the imagination of their own hearts.

"For I earnestly protested unto your fathers in the day that I brought them up out of the land of Egypt, even unto this day, rising early and protesting, saying, Obey my voice. Yet they obeyed not, nor inclined their ear, but walked every one in the imagination of their evil heart: therefore I will bring upon them all the words of this covenant, which I commanded them to do; but they did them not. And the LORD said unto me, A conspiracy is found among the men of Judah, and among the inhabitants of Jerusalem.

"They are turned back to the iniquities of their forefathers, which refused to hear my words; and they went after other gods to serve them: the house of Israel and the house of Judah have broken my covenant, which I made with their fathers. Therefore thus saith the LORD, Behold, I will bring evil upon them, which they shall not be able to escape; and though they shall cry unto me, I will not hearken unto them" (Jeremiah 11:7-11).

Is this not the condition of the Church and our nation today? How many of the people who profess the name of Jesus truly seek to obey him? How many can hear His voice speaking to them? Almost no one can hear the Lord today. They all claim to follow Him, yet the word of God testifies, the people are actually walking in the way that seems right in their own eyes. They are not hearing the Lord at all, but are following the imagination of their own hearts, even as the ancient Israelites did before judgment. Woe unto us, for the summer is coming, and we are not saved!

MANY PASTORS HAVE DESTROYED GOD'S PEOPLE

The Lord then declares that many pastors have destroyed His people. When the Lord uses the word many, He means the majority of them. The Lord declares that no man understands or ponders this truth. Only a small remnant, which God is now restoring to His true covenant, can recognize that the pastors in America have deceived and destroyed the people of God. Ancient Israel erred, seeking a king to rule over them, and turned from the Lord. The church has committed the same act of treason before God, turning to the pastors for guidance, and forsaking the Lord. How have the pastors deceived the people? These blind guides of the blind have been teaching another gospel! This is the gospel of the last days' apostasy, and it is built upon four pillars of falsehood:

1. Conversion without true repentance
2. Faith without heart-felt obedience to the Lord
3. Discipleship without the cross and death to self
4. Religious works without true holiness

Where are the tears of repentance today? Where is the prayer and fasting among God's people? How many spend quiet time in devotions with God each day? Where is the compassion and the *agape* love which is the witness of the fruit of the Spirit? Today we find wealth, and vanities filling the churches, which are called by His name.

"Many pastors have destroyed my vineyard, they have trodden my portion under foot, they have made my pleasant portion a desolate wilderness. They have made it desolate, and being desolate it mourneth unto me; the whole land is made desolate, because no man layeth it to heart" (Jeremiah 12:10-11).

THE PEOPLE WILL BE CARRIED AWAY INTO CAPTIVITY

The prophet declares he is weeping because the people will be carried away into captivity. As Jeremiah, we who have heard this message from the Lord have also spent many days weeping for our families and friends, for the people we love shall all go into captivity, even as Israel went into slavery under judgment. The Church in America will soon go into captivity, enduring the hardships of slave labor in the death camps of the prince. Yet the people are asleep, having turned away from sound doctrines to falsehoods and fables.

"If ye will not hear it, my soul shall weep in secret places for your pride; and mine eye shall weep sore, and run down with tears, because the LORD'S flock is carried away captive. Say unto the king and to the queen, Humble yourselves, sit down: for your principalities shall come down, even the crown of your glory. The cities of the south shall be shut up, and none shall open them: Judah shall be carried away captive all of it, it shall be wholly carried away captive. Lift up your eyes, and behold them that come from the north.... Wherefore come these things upon me?

"For the greatness of thine iniquity are thy skirts discovered, and thy heels made bare. Can the Ethiopian change his skin, or the leop-

ard his spots? then may ye also do good, that are accustomed to do evil.... This is thy lot, the portion of thy measures from me, saith the LORD; because thou hast forgotten me, and trusted in falsehood" (Jeremiah 13:17-25).

THE FALSE PROPHETS ARE CRYING "PEACE, PEACE"

Next Jeremiah complains that the false prophets are telling the people they will have peace, and will not see the sword or famine. The Lord replies that these prophets are speaking lies. Dear reader, today's teachers of the pre-tribulation rapture are spreading the same deadly false prophecy. This false teaching has deceived the church, telling them they will never see the day of evil. These false teachers are also teaching lies! Notice what the Lord says will happen to these false teachers, and those who listen to them. The sword will consume them all.

"Then said I, Ah, Lord GOD! behold, the prophets say unto them, Ye shall not see the sword, neither shall ye have famine; but I will give you assured peace in this place. Then the LORD said unto me, The prophets prophesy lies in my name: I sent them not, neither have I commanded them, neither spake unto them: they prophesy unto you a false vision and divination, and a thing of nought, and the deceit of their heart. Therefore thus saith the LORD concerning the prophets that prophesy in my name, and I sent them not, yet they say, Sword and famine shall not be in this land; By sword and famine shall those prophets be consumed. And the people to whom they prophesy shall be cast out in the streets of Jerusalem because of the famine and the sword; and they shall have none to bury them, them, their wives, nor their sons, nor their daughters: for I will pour their wickedness upon them" (Jeremiah 14:13-16).

THE FALSE PROPHETS OF THE LAST DAYS

If you are tempted to think this is not a last days' warning, look at Jeremiah chapter 23 where the Lord declares the same word against these false prophets, telling us that in the last days we would understand perfectly what He is saying. The last days false prophecy of peace, when there will be no peace, is the pre-tribulation rapture. This false doctrine is a fable, a bedtime story for people who can no longer endure sound doctrine. Paul writes Timothy warning him that in the last days, the Church would no

longer want to hear the truth of Scripture, but would turn to stories and fables which had been invented in imaginations of men.

*"For the time will come when they will not endure sound doc-
trine; but after their own lusts shall they heap to themselves
teachers, having itching ears; And they shall turn away their
ears from the truth, and shall be turned unto fables."*[61] The Lord
declares he will destroy His people, His Christian nation, because
they refuse to repent, and will not turn from their own ways to
serve God as He commands. Rather they continue in their rebellion, and their disobedience, under the deception of false prophets.
Oh, My people, why do you perish?

*"Thou hast forsaken me, saith the LORD, thou art gone backward:
therefore will I stretch out my hand against thee, and destroy thee;
I am weary with repenting. And I will fan them with a fan in the
gates of the land; I will bereave them of children, I will destroy my
people, since they return not from their ways"* (Jeremiah 15:6-7).

THE LORD PROMISES DELIVERANCE
TO ALL WHO RETURN TO HIM

In the midst of the word of judgment, the Lord continues to promise His people *"If you will return to me... I will deliver you out of
the hand of the terrible!"*[62] Brethren, we must return to the Lord
with our whole heart, and to our first love, for the backslider and
the hypocrite will be judged! *"But know that the LORD shath set
apart him that is godly for himself: the LORD will hear when I
call unto him. Stand in awe, and sin not: commune with your
own heart upon your bed, and be still. Selah. Offer the sacrifices
of righteousness, and put your trust in the LORD."*[63] The Lord
then declares that He has taken away the peace of this people, and
they will not even be buried. After the initial judgment on the
Church, the Lord will turn and judge the entire nation. America
will suffer both biological and nuclear destruction, and the people
won't even bury the dead!

*"For thus saith the LORD, Enter not into the house of mourning, nei-
ther go to lament nor bemoan them: for I have taken away my
peace from this people, saith the LORD, even lovingkindness and
mercies. Both the great and the small shall die in this land: they*

shall not be buried, neither shall men lament for them, nor cut themselves, nor make themselves bald for them" (Jeremiah 16:5-6).

THE LORD PRONOUNCES JUDGMENT ON THE PASTORS

The Lord then pronounces judgment upon the many pastors who have destroyed His flock with their false teachings. The Lord will replace them with new shepherds, who will teach the truth. When King Balac wished to curse Israel, he hired Balaam the prophet. Balaam was a prophet for profit. He was motivated by money. When he inquired of the Lord, the Lord told him He would not curse Israel. Balaam, being cunning and knowing the ways of God, told Balac if he could get Israel to break God's laws, only then would the Lord curse His people.

Jesus warns the last days Church in Revelation: *"But I have a few things against thee, because thou hast there them that hold the doctrine of Balaam, who taught Balac to cast a stumblingblock before the children of Israel, to eat things sacrificed unto idols, and to commit fornication."*[64] These modern-day Balaams who are in the church are *prophets for profit* as well. They teach to sell the truth like merchandise. With their false teachings, they, like Balaam, have caused the people of God to stumble. How have they done this?   Revelation 2:14

They have done two things: They have turned the people to idolatry by bringing paganism into the Church and with it all forms of idolatry which include the lust of this life, and the love of money and pleasures. Second, by this idolatry they have turned the people to fornication. This speaks of both literal sexual disobedience and spiritual fornication, where the people have left the worship of the true God and are turned to idols, loving their money and their pleasures more than the Lord!

"Woe be unto the pastors that destroy and scatter the sheep of my pasture! saith the LORD. Therefore thus saith the LORD God of Israel against the pastors that feed my people; Ye have scattered my flock, and driven them away, and have not visited them: behold, I will visit upon you the evil of your doings, saith the LORD. And I will gather the remnant of my flock out of all countries whither I have driven them, and will bring them again to their folds; and they

shall be fruitful and increase. And I will set up shepherds over them which shall feed them: and they shall fear no more, nor be dismayed, neither shall they be lacking, saith the LORD" (Jeremiah 23:1-4).

The Lord also promises He will set up new shepherds over his sheep who will feed them the true word of God. As for the false shepherds, they will be judged first. The pastors will be the first ones taken into captivity. This is always the case. One day soon, the majority of the pastors in America will be arrested in the middle of the night. This will be the first day the darkness falls in America. The following Sunday, a new pastor will stand among the people declaring, *"God has moved your former pastor to a new calling. Today I am pleased to introduce myself as your new pastor."* These new pastors in the government churches will be the servants of the prince! Do you think the elders will object to this? No, they will all be arrested too.

This is exactly what happened in Russia, and many other countries, as they fell under tyranny. At this point, the true church will no longer meet in the government assemblies, but will be found in the homes. In most congregations, they will not even be missed, for only one or two will silently stop attending after being told by the Lord not to go back to church. The Lord will appoint His own pastors over His little flock in that day. They will have His heart for the people, and they will feed His sheep the truth.

Again, the Lord declares that the nation is full of adulterers, from the top elected officials in the land to the least of them, and because of swearing, the taking of the Lord's name in vain, the land mourns and is under judgment. The Lord declares both the prophet and the priest are profane, and unclean before Him. Yes, in His house, the church, is all of this wickedness found! Therefore, their way shall become slippery and they shall fall therein. The Lord shall bring evil upon them, even their year of visitation.

The Lord tells us these false prophets are actually prophesying under the influence of demons. They have caused the people to err; they have not exposed the sin of the people, but have lied, promising peace when there is none! Further, these false prophets commit adultery, and being full of deceit, they walk in lies. They also help other evildoers and therefore none of them returns from his wickedness. The Lord says these people remind him of Sodom and Gomorrah, and from these false prophets profanity has filled the entire nation. Therefore, the Lord will judge them.

"For the land is full of adulterers; for because of swearing the land mourneth; the pleasant places of the wilderness are dried up, and their course is evil. for both prophet and priest are profane; yea, in my house have I found their wickedness, saith the LORD. Wherefore their way shall be unto them as slippery ways in the darkness:... for I will bring evil upon them, even the year of their visitation, saith the LORD. And I have seen folly in the prophets of Samaria; they prophesied in Baal, and caused my people Israel to err.... they strengthen also the hands of evildoers, that none doth return from his wickedness: they are all of them unto me as Sodom, and the inhabitants thereof as Gomorrah" (Jeremiah 23:10-14).

IN THE LAST DAYS YOU WILL UNDERSTAND PERFECTLY

The Lord tells us *"do not listen to the false prophets who bring a message of peace"* by telling the people of God they will not see the day of evil. They are lying! The modern day false prophets are the mainstream Christian pastors who teach the pre-tribulation rapture doctrine. In addition, the Lord says they speak to a people who despise Him. How do the people despise the Lord? These refuse to obey His word, and continue in their sins. The Lord then asks, "Who has stood in His counsel, and heard His word?"

The ones who are declaring, "A whirlwind is about to fall in America," and it will not return until "He has executed!" What do you think He means by "executed"? When does this message apply? Jeremiah tells us clearly, for *"in the latter days you shall consider (understand) it perfectly."*

"Thus saith the LORD of hosts, Hearken not unto the words of the prophets that prophesy unto you: they make you vain: they speak a vision of their own heart, and not out of the mouth of the LORD. They say still unto them that despise me, The LORD hath said, Ye shall have peace; and they say unto every one that walketh after the imagination of his own heart, No evil shall come upon you. For who hath stood in the counsel of the LORD, and hath perceived and

heard his word? who hath marked his word, and heard it? Behold, a whirlwind of the LORD is gone forth in fury, even a grievous whirlwind.... The anger of the LORD shall not return, until he have executed.... in the latter days ye shall consider it perfectly" (Jeremiah 23:16-22).

CHAPTER 4

"THE DAY OF THE LORD IS AT HAND"
Isaiah 13:6

For thousands of years the prophets of God testified that a day would come when the Lord would judge the entire earth. Unlike His judgments in the past, which were upon various nations, and at various times, this day would be like none other. This will be the Day of the LORD, and it will come upon the entire earth, as a day of destruction for all the enemies of God. It will also be a day of deliverance for those abiding in Jesus Christ in holiness and purity. Jesus Christ will save His small remnant as He comes in judgment to lay the mountains low, and He will tread the nations in the winepress of His wrath. Having done all He could to save mankind in His death on the cross of Calvary, Jesus Christ now comes as Judge, with the full fury of the wrath of God.

IT SHALL COME AS DESTRUCTION FROM THE ALMIGHTY

What exactly do the prophets say about the Day of the LORD? First, it comes as destruction from the Almighty! This day comes from the Lord, and though He uses men as instruments of His judgment, God does these things. The Lord declares, *"Every one of them shall be faint, and all their hearts shall melt, and they shall be afraid!"* I trembled for seven days after I saw the Day of the LORD. One of my friends said to me *"We don't know if you have heard from God, or if you had a breakdown."*

I told him, it is both. God spoke and I broke. I shook like a frightened sinner, found guilty before the Judge of the whole earth. You can't even imagine the emotions that will run through your mind when they take your wife and your children from your side. If you stand there, as I did, you will know what the Lord meant when He said *"They will be amazed when they look at each other, for their faces will appear as if on fire."*

> *"And they shall be afraid: pangs and sorrows shall take hold of them; they shall be in pain as a woman that travaileth: they shall be amazed one at another; their faces shall be as flames"* (Isaiah 13:8).

Dear reader, the present age is drawing to a close. Its end will be with pain and anguish unseen before in the history of man. However, the Lord will be a shield to His remnant that return to Him with their whole hearts. To those who will forsake their sins, and who stop serving the gods of the Americans: the promise God made to our father Abraham is to us as well, *"Fear not... I am thy shield, and thy exceeding great reward."*[1]

The Lord Jesus Christ delights in mercy and His mercy triumphs over judgment. That is why during these 7 years following the 70th Jubilee of Israel, the Lord held back His judgment, and He has sent this true word to His people, that those who would turn with their whole hearts and repent of the apostasy might be delivered. I pray for you, that as the Father said of Jesus, *"This is my beloved Son: Hear him!"*[2] We must be able to hear from the Lord in this hour.

THE DAY OF THE LORD COMES WITH WRATH

The Lord tells us the day will come with intense stress upon all the nations! The Day of the LORD will bring destruction to the kingdom of sin, and to the peoples of this world, who walk in darkness and follow the prince of the air.

> *"Howl ye; for the day of the LORD is at hand; it shall come as a destruction from the Almighty. Therefore shall all hands be faint, and every man's heart shall melt: And they shall be afraid: pangs and sorrows shall take hold of them; they shall be in pain as a woman that travaileth: they shall be amazed one at another; their faces shall be as flames. Behold, the day of the LORD cometh, cruel both*

with wrath and fierce anger, to lay the land desolate: and he shall destroy the sinners thereof out of it.

"For the stars of heaven and the constellations thereof shall not give their light: the sun shall be darkened in his going forth, and the moon shall not cause her light to shine.

"And I will punish the world for their evil, and the wicked for their iniquity; and I will cause the arrogancy of the proud to cease, and will lay low the haughtiness of the terrible. I will make a man more precious than fine gold; even a man than the golden wedge of Ophir. Therefore I will shake the heavens, and the earth shall remove out of her place, in the wrath of the LORD of hosts, and in the day of his fierce anger" (Isaiah 13:6-13).

God says He will make man more rare than the golden wedge of Ophir. The wedge of Ophir was a myth. God is saying that, in the Day of the LORD, he will make man more precious than a myth! This is a complete destruction, which has been determined by the Lord.

"Enter into the rock, and hide thee in the dust, for fear of the LORD, and for the glory of his majesty. The lofty looks of man shall be humbled, and the haughtiness of men shall be bowed down, and the LORD alone shall be exalted in that day. For the day of the LORD of hosts shall be upon every one that is proud and lofty, and upon every one that is lifted up; and he shall be brought low" (Isaiah 2:10-12).

NOW WILL I RISE, NOW WILL I BE EXALTED

The prophet Isaiah testifies about the day of the *LORD*; *"Now will I rise, saith the Lord, now will I be exalted; now will I lift up myself."*[3] The Lord will stand to judge the people and in that day, He will perform His "strange work," and bring to pass His "strange act"— the work of judgment! God calls this his "strange work," because He does not take pleasure in the destruction of the wicked, nor in the judgment which must come upon the apostate Church. The Lord warns the people, *"Do not mock this word of warning, unless you want the bands that bind you to be made stronger."*[4]

Isaiah declares that he has heard from the Lord of a complete destruction, and a total consumption has been determined upon the whole earth for the Day of the LORD is at hand.

> *"For the LORD shall rise up as in mount Perazim, he shall be wroth as in the valley of Gibeon, that he may do his work, his strange work; and bring to pass his act, his strange act. Now therefore be ye not mockers, lest your bands be made strong: for I have heard from the Lord GOD of hosts a consumption, even determined upon the whole earth"* (Isaiah 28:21-22).

> *"And the loftiness of man shall be bowed down, and the haughtiness of men shall be made low: and the LORD alone shall be exalted in the day. And the idols he shall utterly abolish. And they shall go into the holes of the rocks, and into the caves of the earth, for fear of the LORD, and for the glory of his majesty, when he ariseth to shake terribly the earth"* (Isaiah 2:17-19).

The prophet Joel also spoke about the day of the LORD, declaring that it would be a day of darkness, and of thick darkness. All the inhabitants of the land will tremble. We are commanded to *"blow the trumpet in Zion"* to warn the people the day is at hand. *"Alas for the day! for the day of the LORD is at hand, and as a destruction from the Almighty shall it come."*[5] *"Blow ye the trumpet in Zion, and sound an alarm in my holy mountain let all the inhabitants of the land tremble: for the day of the LORD cometh, for it is nigh at hand; A day of darkness and of gloominess, a day of clouds and of thick darkness."*[6]

The Lord shall speak as a roaring lion on that day and His voice will *"thunder from Zion."* God will speak with such power, that *"the heavens and the earth will shake"* and everyone will panic. Fear will strike them all, save His remnant people. Of them, the Lord says *"the Lord will be the hope of His people and the strength of Israel."* Jesus told us when we see these things coming to pass to look up for in this day, the Lord is the only hope of His people. We have no other. He alone is our Hope. **God is my salvation, I will trust and not be afraid, for the Lord even Jehovah, He is my strength and my song.** All the songs and verses of Scripture we have learned will take on new meaning in that day.

"Multitudes, multitudes in the valley of decision: for the day of the LORD is near in the valley of decision. The sun and the moon shall be darkened, and the stars shall withdraw their shining. The LORD also shall roar out of Zion, and utter his voice from Jerusalem; and the heavens and the earth shall shake: but the LORD will be the hope of his people, and the strength of the children of Israel" (Joel 3:14-16).

Jesus spoke prophetically of this day, looking forward to the time of judgment, declaring that He will come forth *"to cast fire upon the earth."* This is the second half of His ministry, but first He would have to complete His mission as the Holy Lamb of God. Then, He would come again as a Lion, with fire before Him! Did Jesus come to bring peace and unity? *"I tell you, no, but rather division."* Thereby we know this move to a one-world church is a deception. And these supposed Christian leaders, who are now embracing the religions of darkness in unity and in the so-called *"doctrine of tolerance,"* are actually servants of the dragon. *"I have come to cast fire upon the earth; and how I wish it were already kindled! But I have a baptism to undergo, and how distressed I am until it is accomplished! Do you suppose that I came to grant peace on earth? I tell you, no, but rather division."*[7]

THOU ART MY BATTLE AXE AND WEAPON OF WAR

"The portion of Jacob is not like them; for he is the former of all things: and Israel is the rod of his inheritance: the LORD of hosts is his name. Thou art my battle axe and weapons of war: for with thee will I break in pieces the nations, and with thee will I destroy kingdoms; And with thee will I break in pieces the horse and his ride; and with thee will I break in pieces the chariot and his rider.... With thee also will I break in pieces man and woman; and with thee will I break in pieces old and young; and with thee will I break in pieces the young man and the maid; I will also break in pieces with thee the shepherd and his flock; and with thee will I break in pieces the husbandman and his yoke of oxen; and with thee will I break in pieces captains and rulers. And I will render unto Babylon and to all the inhabitants of Chaldea all their evil that they have done in Zion in your sight, saith the LORD. Behold, I am against thee, O destroying mountain, saith the LORD, which destroyest all the earth: and I will stretch out mine hand upon thee, and roll thee down from

the rocks, and will make thee a burnt mountain. And they shall not take of thee a stone for a corner, nor a stone for foundations; but thou shalt be desolate for ever, saith the LORD" (Jeremiah 51:19-26).

The prophet Amos also declares the day of the LORD will be a day of judgment where none can escape. *"Woe unto you that desire the day of the LORD! to what end is it for you? the day of the LORD is darkness, and not light. As if a man did flee from a lion, and a bear met him; or went into the house, and leaned his hand on the wall, and a serpent bit him."*[8] The Day of the LORD will be the Day of Judgment, and what measure we have used, will be measured back unto us. Therefore, dear remnant, choose mercy and extend forgiveness to everyone.

If we measure others with mercy, we can hope to receive mercy from God, and to escape these things, which shall surely come to pass. *"For the day of the LORD is near upon all the heathen: as thou hast done, it shall be done unto thee: thy reward shall return upon thine own head."*[9]

The Day of the LORD is near. During the writing of this book, the Lord said to me, *"It is at the door."* God declares He will bring distress upon all men, and they will walk like blind men, because they have sinned against the Lord. Let us repent, therefore, while it is still day, for the night is coming when no man can work. Only the Lord will be able to work in the night that is coming.

> *"The great day of the LORD is near, it is near, and hasteth greatly, even the voice of the day of the LORD: the mighty man shall cry there bitterly. That day is a day of wrath, a day of trouble and distress, a day of wasteness and desolation, a day of darkness and gloominess, a day of clouds and thick darkness, A day of the trumpet and alarm against the fenced cities, and against the high towers. And I will bring distress upon men, that they shall walk like blind men, because they have sinned against the LORD: and their blood shall be poured out as dust, and their flesh as the dung. Neither their silver nor their gold shall be able to deliver them in the day of the LORD'S wrath; but the whole land shall be devoured by the fire of his jealousy: for he shall make even a speedy riddance of all them that dwell in the land"* (Zepheniah 1:14-18).

"Therefore wait ye upon me, saith the LORD, until the day that I rise up to the prey: for my determination is to gather the nations, that I may assemble the kingdoms, to pour upon them mine indignation, even all my fierce anger: for all the earth shall be devoured with the fire of my jealousy. For then will I turn to the people a pure language, that they may all call upon the name of the LORD, to serve him with one consent.... I will also leave in the midst of thee an afflicted and poor people, and they shall trust in the name of the LORD. The remnant of Israel shall not do iniquity, nor speak lies; neither shall a deceitful tongue be found in their mouth: for they shall feed and lie down, and none shall make them afraid. Sing, O daughter of Zion; shout, O Israel; be glad and rejoice with all the heart, O daughter of Jerusalem. The LORD hath taken away thy judgments.... The LORD thy God in the midst of thee is mighty; he will save, he will rejoice over thee with joy; he will rest in his love, he will joy over thee with singing. I will gather them that are sorrowful for the solemn assembly, who are of thee, to whom the reproach of it was a burden. Behold, at that time I will undo all that afflict thee: and I will save her that halteth, and gather her that was driven out; and I will get them praise and fame in every land where they have been put to shame. At that time will I bring you again, even in the time that I gather you: for I will make you a name and a praise among all people of the earth, when I turn back your captivity before your eyes, saith the LORD" (Zepheniah 3:8-20).

"Behold, the day of the LORD cometh, and thy spoil shall be divided in the midst of thee. For I will gather all nations against Jerusalem to battle; and the city shall be taken, and the houses rifled, and the women ravished; and half of the city shall go forth into captivity, and the residue of the people shall not be cut off from the city" (Zechariah 14:1-2).

"Behold, God is exalted in His power; who is a teacher like Him?... Behold, God is exalted, and we do not know Him; The number of His years is unsearchable.... He covers His hands with the lightning, And commands it to strike the mark. Its noise declares His presence; the cattle also, concerning what is coming up. At this also my heart trembles, And leaps from its place. Listen closely to the thunder of His voice, And the rumbling that goes out from His mouth. Under the whole heaven He lets it loose, And His lightning to the

ends of the earth. After it, a voice roars; He thunders with His majestic voice; And He does not restrain the lightnings when His voice is heard. God thunders with His voice wondrously, Doing great things which we cannot comprehend" (Job 36:22-37,37:1-5 NAS).

"For, behold, the LORD cometh forth out of his place, and will come down, and tread upon the high places of the earth. And the mountains shall be molten under him, and the valleys shall be cleft, as wax before the fire, and as the waters that are poured down a steep place" (Micah 1:3-4).

"And of the children of Issachar, which were men that had understanding of the times, to know what Israel ought to do; the heads of them were two hundred; and all their brethren were at their commandment" (1 Chronicles 12:32).

CHAPTER 5

"REMOVE OUT OF THE MIDST OF BABYLON"
Jeremiah 50:8

One of the mysteries of Bible prophecy surrounds the identity of the end-time nation called *"Mystery Babylon"* whose destruction is foretold in the book of Revelation. As we have seen in chapter two of Daniel, all the ruling kingdoms of the earth are revealed as part of one empire—the kingdom of Satan, who himself is the prince of this present world. Each of these ruling empires is part of the same system, Mystery Babylon. As we have seen, Mystery Babylon is both a political power and a religious system. In this chapter, we shall review the prophecies surrounding the nation state revealed in Scripture as Mystery Babylon the Great. *"And there followed another angel, saying, Babylon is fallen, is fallen, that great city, because she made all nations drink of the wine of the wrath of her fornication."*[1]

In ancient times, cities identified nation states, as well as their capital. Ancient Babylon, in the time of king Nebuchanezzar, was both a great city and the capital of the nation-state ruling the earth of that time. The same is true of Rome, which was both a city and a nation state. In the modern era, Bible scholars debate the identity of the end-time nation "MYSTERY, BABYLON THE GREAT."

MYSTERY BABYLON THE GREAT

In Revelation 17 we are given several clues to the identity of Babylon. *"And there came one of the seven angels which had the seven vials, and talked with me, saying unto me, Come hither; I will show unto thee the judgment of the great whore that sitteth upon many waters: With whom the kings of the earth have committed fornication, and the inhabitants of the earth have been made drunk with the wine of her fornication.... And upon her forehead was a name written, MYSTERY, BABYLON THE GREAT, THE MOTHER OF HARLOTS AND ABOMINATIONS OF THE EARTH.... And the woman which thou sawest is that great city, which reigneth over the kings of the earth."*[2]

These are the clues to the identity of the woman Mystery, Babylon the Great:

1. She is referred to as a great whore, a prostitute.
2. She is seated upon many waters.
3. The rulers of the earth have engaged in illicit relations with her.
4. She has polluted the inhabitants of the earth with her idolatry, making them drunk.
5. She is the mother of all falsehood and abominations upon the earth at that time.
6. She is the great nation that rules over all of the kings of the earth.
7. She is called Mystery Babylon for her true identity is a secret.

IDENTIFYING THE WOMAN RIDING THE BEAST

First, this nation is identified as a whore. Matthew Henry's commentary offers insight into the meaning of the name Mystery Babylon, the Mother of Harlots.

> *"This is a name of great infamy. A whore is one that is married, and has been false to her husband's bed, has forsaken the guide of her youth, and broken the covenant of God. She had been a prostitute to the kings of the earth, whom she had intoxicated with the wine of her fornication. The appearance she made: it was gay and gaudy, like such sort of creatures: She was arrayed in purple, and scarlet color, and decked with gold, and precious stones, and pearls, Here were all the allurements of worldly honour and riches, pomp and pride, suited to sensual and worldly minds.*

> *"Her principal seat and residence—upon the beast that had seven heads and ten horns; that is to say, Rome, the city on seven hills, infamous for idolatry, tyranny, and blasphemy. Her name, which*

was written on her forehead. It was the custom of impudent harlots to hang out signs, with their names, that all might know what they were. Now in this observe, She is named from her place of residence—Babylon the great. But, that we might not take it for the old Babylon literally so called, we are told there is a mystery in the name; it is some other great city resembling the old Babylon."[3]

From the description of Babylon as a whore, we note that this nation was at one time married to the true God of Heaven but has turned a harlot and has gone whoring after other gods. Thus we know Mystery Babylon was at one time a godly nation but has now turned from the true God to the worship of idols and falsehood. She is an apostate!

Second, we are told this nation is seated upon many waters. This reference is both literal and symbolic. The modern nation Babylon physically possesses a land that is seated on many oceans, rivers and great lakes. This also speaks symbolically that she rules many peoples (waters refers to the nations) and has many diverse peoples as citizens or subjects.

Third, we are told this nation has engaged in illicit or immoral acts with the rulers of the other nations of the earth. Modern Babylon has political or economic ties to the rest of the planet through which she has spread her apostasy. Mystery Babylon is also the author of the last days' ecumenical movement through which the one-world religion of the beast will subdue the earth.

Fourth, we are told Babylon has polluted the earth with her idolatry and fornication, which is the worship of false gods. Babylon has exported her carnal idolatry to all of the other nations, corrupting them with the same idolatry with which she herself is polluted.

Fifth, modern Babylon is the mother of all falsehood and abominations on the earth in the last days, again referring to her export of her lewd and apostate culture and idolatry. She is the leader or mother of all the nations, which will be deceived by the little prince.

Finally, her identity is clearly revealed. We are told she is the great nation-state, which rules the kings of the earth in the last days. Can there be any doubt of which this prophecy speaks?

AMERICA—THE DAUGHTER OF BABYLON

Today there is only one nation that fits this prophetic picture and has fulfilled it literally: The United States of America. First, America was founded as a Christian nation under God, the only republic founded for the purposes of God aside from Israel herself. Israel was God's nation under the Old Covenant. The Lord called America forth, to be established under the New Covenant. Modern America has turned into a harlot, having become an apostate from the truth of God. Today, America worships the gods of money, fame and the pleasures of immorality. Thus, America fulfills the prophetic type of a whore perfectly.

Second, America is seated upon many waters both literally and symbolically. America physically sits on the Atlantic and Pacific oceans, the Great Lakes and many great rivers, while her influence covers the globe. Symbolically, she sits or rules over many nations through her leadership of the world during the twentieth century. America also has a population from all over the earth. People everywhere dream of the day they, too, can come to the great land of America. She is the pride of the whole earth.

Third, America is responsible for the United Nation's plan for a New World Order, having financed and promoted this plan to conquer the earth for the rich men. Her form of government, a union of independent states, is the model for the One World government of the prince who is to come, a United States of the World under the UN. The great seal of the US declares this in Latin, "Announcing the birth of the New World Order."

Forth, America has polluted the world with her idolatry. The world has gone into debt with American money from American banks, smokes American cigarettes, buys American weapons, has imported America's abortion policies called family planning, and is following the American-sponsored UN. The world watches American movies, buys American pornography, listens to American music, and idolizes the American culture of materialism and hedonism. America truly has polluted the earth with her filth.

Fifth, America is the mother of the falsehood of the earth at the time of the end. Her gospel of materialism and secular democracy has deceived the earth into embracing the one-world system of the

Anti-messiah. America is also the mother of the great last days' apostasy of the true faith of Jesus Christ—the one-world false religion of the beast which is the global ecumenical movement being organized under the World Council of Churches. America is also the mother of the final deception of the Church, the pre-tribulation rapture fable! All of this falsehood came out of America!

Finally, America is the reigning super power over the earth in these last days. The 20th century has been referred to as the American century. America has led the so-called free world, since the 1945 post war era. The Scripture is clear; the end-time nation called Mystery Babylon is the United States of America! Weep America, for your hour of judgment has come, and no one can deliver you. *"Come out from her My people"* says the Lord.

THE VOICES OF MEN OF WISDOM

Many other men of wisdom have given witness that the United States of America is the end time nation Mystery Babylon: David Wilkerson, Dumitru Duduman, among others have all confirmed this word. David Wilkerson, in, *Set the Trumpet to Thy Mouth*, declares: *"I believe modern Babylon is present-day America, including its corrupt society and its whorish church system. No other nation fits the description of Revelation 18.... America is going to be destroyed by fire! Sudden destruction is coming and few will escape. Unexpectedly, and in one hour, a hydrogen holocaust will engulf America—and this nation will be no more.... God is going to judge America for its violence, its crimes, its backslidings, its murdering of millions of babies, its flaunting of homosexuality... its corruption, its drunkenness and drug abuse, its form of godliness without power, its lukewarmness toward Christ.... Judgment is at the door! Our days are numbered! The Church is asleep, the congregations are at ease, and the shepherds slumber. How they will scoff and laugh at this message. Theologians will reject it... Pillow prophets of peace and prosperity will publicly denounce it.... I am blowing the Lord's trumpet with all my might.... Perhaps only the overcomers will accept and hear the sound of this trumpet blast, but I proceed with these warnings because God called me to be a watchman."*[4]

Dumitru Duduman is another of the men of wisdom, whom the Lord sent to warn the United States. Dumitru is from Romania. He smuggled Bibles into Russia for 15 years and then was arrested and severely tortured for five months. While they were attempting to kill him, the angel of the Lord appeared to him, telling him, "Plead the Blood of Jesus" and that he would be delivered and sent to America. He was sent to Fullerton in Southern California. There, the angel came to him again to show him what would come in America. Listen to Dumitru in his own words: *"If until now we have lived the way we wanted to, now the time has come when we must stop. It is enough that in the past we did what the world asked us to do. Some lived in wickedness. Others in abominations. We must put an end to all these things and return to God so that in the day of trouble, God would save us. I was awake as I am now... I was sitting outside my apartment, and I saw a light coming towards me... the light surrounded me. It was the same angel. He said Dumitru, 'I brought you to this country because this country will burn.' He showed me all of California. 'Do you see what I have shown you? This is as Sodom and Gomorrah. Their sins have reached unto God, and God has decided to punish them by fire. In one day it will burn.' He then showed me Las Vegas, New York, and Florida. Again he said 'This is as Sodom and Gomorrah. In one day it will burn.' I asked how will America burn? 'When America thinks it has peace and quiet, and they rule the world, then from the oceans, and from Cuba, Nicaragua, and Central America they will bomb America.' But what will you do with your Church? 'Many churches have left me.' What do you mean? "Do you not have people here? 'Tell them this: People glorify people. The honor that Christ deserves men take upon themselves. In the Church there is divorce, adultery, sodomy, abortion and all kinds of wickedness. Christ does not live in sin. Christ lives in holiness. Tell them to stop sinning and repent because God never stops forgiving. And all those who stop sinning and repent, God will save them in the day of trouble. 'As I saved Daniel from the lions, this is how I will save them. As I saved the three young ones from the furnace, this is how I will save them.' The word of God says 1,000 will fall at your side, and 10,000 at your right hand, but you will be protected by the power of God. I told the angel if you are truly the angel of God, everything must be written in the Bible. 'Have you read Jeremiah 51?' I answered, it speaks of old Babylon. 'Read again. Read again. It speaks of America not Babylon of old. Have you read Revelation 18? I will open your mind and you will understand.' American brothers, wake up, wake up. Wake from your sleep and repent and return to God. The day of wrath is near."⁵*

The Lord has raised up many other voices in this last hour. American brothers and sisters, listen to the word of the Lord. This is the final warning. There is precious little time left.

Mike McQuiddy has also spoken and written much on the soon judgment in America:

"In all of man's history on earth there has never been any society, country or people that survived if they allowed either one of two sins to continue—first, the killing of babies, abortion; second, homosexuality! America has both." Mike testifies the Lord spoke to him saying, *"America cannot stop the bleeding! America will be cut down like a corn field - flattened. They won't accept My grace, so now they will have to accept my law! The law demands blood restitution. America will bleed to death. The angel of death is coming. Pride comes before the fall. America says she sits like a queen on a throne—prideful. Now comes the fall. It's midnight and mankind doesn't know it! Judgment stalks the land! Warn the people!"⁷*

God has given visions to others, calling them also to warn America. One such man is Henry Gruver: "I began to see all of these submarines emerging from under the surface. I was surprised by how close they were to our borders. Then I saw missiles come out of them. They hit eastern coastal cities of the United States. I looked across the country... over in the northwest side and I saw the submarines. I saw missiles coming out and hitting the western coastal cities. I cried out "Oh God! Oh God! When will this be, and what shall be the sign of its coming?" I heard an audible voice speak to me and say, "When Russia opens her doors and lets the masses go. The free world will occupy themselves with transporting, housing, feeding, and caring for the masses, and will let down their weapons and cry peace and safety. Then sudden destruction will come. Then is when it will come."⁸

THE JUDGMENT OF AMERICA BABYLON

Scripture refers to America in Jeremiah 50 as the daughter of Babylon. *"Behold, a people shall come from the north, and a great nation, and many kings shall be raised up from the coasts of the earth. They shall hold the bow and the lance: they are cruel, and will not show mercy: their voice shall roar like the sea, and they shall ride upon horses, every one put in array, like a man to the battle, against thee, O daughter of Babylon."*9 America is called the daughter because she was born a direct descendent of the final king of Babylon.

We shall see in later chapters the final king of Babylon will come to power from England, for England is the king of the final beast empire, and America is his daughter. She is the Queen among the nations. And her symbol is the wings of the eagle spoken of in of Daniel.

Need I remind you of the Statue of Liberty standing in the harbor? Is this not the symbol of the great lady, the Queen of the nations? We refer to her as Lady Liberty. What will become of her promise of freedom? Having turned the harlot, she will now be destroyed and her people will go into slavery.

Now let us examine what the Scripture says of the judgments upon the United States.

Our first references come from the book of Jeremiah, in chapters 50-51. First, the Lord tells us an assembly of nations will destroy America. Only the Medes and Persians destroyed ancient Babylon. This is our first proof that this section of Scripture does not, and cannot, be fulfilled by ancient Babylon. These prophecies speak of one of the descendent empires of Babylon.

> *"For, lo, I will raise and cause to come up against Babylon an assembly of great nations from the north country: and they shall set themselves in array against her; from thence she shall be taken: their arrows shall be as of a mighty expert man; none shall return in vain."*10

The Lord tells us a great nation from the north, along with many kings, will make war against the daughter of Babylon. If you go north from the United States, over the pole you will find Russia.

Even now, the world's intelligence services are all reporting of the formation of an anti-American alliance by many nations, being led by Russia. *"Behold, a people shall come from the north, and a great nation, and many kings shall be raised up from the coasts of the earth."*[11]

Many kings are aligning themselves against America Babylon. Only two kings, the Medes and the Persians, attacked ancient Babylon. The judgment of America will follow soon after the judgment begins in the Church of God.

The Lord makes His word very clear: He is commanding His people to leave Babylon. They are to flee, and deliver their lives for this is the time of the Lord's vengeance. *"Flee out of the midst of Babylon, and deliver every man his soul: be not cut off in her iniquity; for this is the time of the Lord's vengeance; he will render unto her a recompense."*[12] The Day of the LORD is about to begin in the land of America Babylon.

AMERICA WILL BE JUDGED
FOR HER SIN OF COVETING

God says He will judge Babylon by the measure of her covetousness. *"O thou that dwellest upon many waters, abundant in treasures, thine end is come, and the measure of thy covetousness."*[13] Anyone who has lived outside of the United States will comprehend the level of idolatry and covetousness in America.

"How much she hath glorified herself, and lived deliciously, so much torment and sorrow give her: for she saith in her heart, I sit a queen, and am no widow, and shall see no sorrow. Therefore shall her plagues come in one day, death, and mourning, and famine; and she shall be utterly burned with fire: for strong is the Lord God who judgeth her."[14] To this degree, she will be judged!

The Lord even names the ancient kingdoms that will attack America including Iraq, Iran and the other Arab nations. *"Set ye up a standard in the land, blow the trumpet among the nations, prepare the nations against her, call together against her the kingdoms of Ararat, Minni, and Ashchenaz."*[15] Ararat is in the land that is now Iraq. To point out the obvious, Iraq is the nation where ancient Babylon stood. It is also interesting that the Lord mentions Iraq first, for it is Iraq that has been receiving all of the press from the conflict in the Persian Gulf. Remember Saddam Hussein declared this would become the *"Mother of all great battles."* He was not joking, and the war America started with Islam is far from over.

The American people sleep securely, unaware of the enemies slipping into their country under the cover of darkness. The prophet Ezekiel speaks of the plot against America, *"And thou shalt say, I will go up to the land of unwalled villages; I will go to them that are at rest, that dwell safely, all of them dwelling without walls, and having neither bars nor gates."*[16]

This attack on the people who dwell in the land of unwalled cities occurs at the same time as the next Middle East war, when Russia and the Arab alliance attack Israel. The people who live in unwalled villages are the Americans! God, speaking of the nuclear destruction of the coastlands of America says, *"I will send a fire on Magog, and among them that dwell carelessly in the isles: and they shall know that I am the LORD."*[17]

The word for "isles" is *'iy*[18] (ee), which means a habitable spot, dry land, a coast, or an island. This prophecy speaks of the Americans who dwell carelessly in the distant coastlands. Ancient Babylon was conquered in the middle of the night. When the people woke up in the morning, it was over. So, too, it shall be in America. One Sunday morning, you will awaken and it will be all over for America. Why do I mention Sunday? Remember, the Lord said he would tell us all things in advance. The judgment on the United States occurs on a Sunday. All the great defeats of America have occurred on the day of her sun god. Pearl Harbor and the Alamo both occurred on a Sunday. America will burn on a Sunday!

AMERICA SHALL BE SURPRISED
AND DESOLATE FOREVER

The Lord tells us Babylon, once destroyed, will be desolate forever. Ancient Babylon could not fulfill this prophecy, for once the daughter of Babylon is destroyed, she must remain desolate forever. The Medes occupied ancient Babylon. The people continued to dwell there under the new rulers. Therefore, the daughter Babylon in the last days must be a different nation! The last days' daughter of Babylon will be left desolate! *"Then shalt thou say, O*

LORD, thou hast spoken against this place, to cut it off, that none shall remain in it, neither man nor beast, but that it shall be desolate for ever."[19]

The biological and nuclear weapons used on her soil will contaminate the land for 5,000 years. They shall all depart! It is over, America. Your hour is at hand. Repent or perish!

We are told Babylon, whose power was as a hammer over the earth, will be destroyed with a great destruction, and that she will be taken unaware. The citizens and the leaders of Babylon will be totally surprised by her sudden and complete destruction. *"A sound of battle is in the land, and of great destruction. How is the hammer of the whole earth cut asunder and broken! how is Babylon become a desolation among the nations! I have laid a snare for thee, and thou art also taken, O Babylon, and thou wast not aware: thou art found, and also caught, because thou hast striven against the LORD.*"[20] Her fall was symbolized by the sinking of the Titanic. No one believes it is even possible.

God identifies Babylon as the most proud of all of the nations, and that the Lord Himself will fight against her on the day of her judgment. *"Behold, I am against thee, O thou most proud, saith the Lord GOD of hosts: for thy day is come, the time that I will visit thee.*"[21]

God tells us He will burn the cities of America. *"And the most proud shall stumble and fall, and none shall raise him up: and I will kindle a fire in his cities, and it shall devour all round about him.*"[22] This is consistent with the prophecies of Dumitru Duduman and David Wilkerson among others, which have seen the nuclear destruction of America. Ancient Babylon was not burned, nor devoured. It was overrun in one night while the people slept. In the morning when they awoke it was over. The fall of America will be as sudden, but unlike ancient Babylon, America will burn!

We are also told the nation will suffer a drought as a prelude to the destruction of the land. *"A drought is upon her waters; and they shall be dried up: for it is the land of graven images, and they are mad upon their idols.*"[23] Today, the weather in America is out of control. El Nino has produced flooding conditions in one part of the country, and drought in others. The prophecy reveals our nation will be in drought conditions as the hour of destruction draws near.

This summer should evidence extreme drought conditions, if the judgment of America is to come this fall. This is the warning to the remnant that it is time to flee. During a future summer, the Lord will destroy the summer harvest. The Lord is so rich in His mercy; He provides us a clear warning of when these things will come to pass. Watch the weather reports across the country, and don't expect the media to draw a lot of attention to the truth.

AMERICA SHALL BE JUDGED AS SODOM AND GOMORRAH

Again the Lord compares the total destruction of Sodom to what will befall America. *"As God overthrew Sodom and Gomorrah and the neighbour cities thereof, saith the LORD; so shall no man abide there, neither shall any son of man dwell therein."*[24] Ancient Babylon was not destroyed as Sodom and Gomorrah, but was overthrown by the Medes. America, however, will burn like Sodom. If you do not have the Lord as your shield on that day, you will be destroyed. In addition, if God is speaking to you about leaving, you had better obey Him!

We are told the whole earth will be shaken, and the nations will mourn, when they see America destroyed. *"At the noise of the taking of Babylon the earth is moved, and the cry is heard among the nations."*[25] The destruction of America will throw the entire world into crisis. The world's economy will collapse as the dollar becomes worthless. The largest import market in the world will be destroyed in one hour. Fear and panic will cover the nations of earth in that day. If the great Babylon can fall in one hour, who can stand?

THE LORD WILL NOT FORSAKE HIS REMNANT

The Lord promises that He will not forsake his true remnant, which have repented and returned unto Him. Though we have also sinned against the Lord, He is merciful to forgive us even at this late hour. Our God is a God of great mercy and His loving kindness extends forever to His chosen bride. *"For Israel hath not been forsaken, nor Judah of his God, of the LORD of hosts; though their land was filled with sin against the Holy One of Is-*

rael. Flee out of the midst of Babylon, and deliver every man his soul: be not cut off in her iniquity; for this is the time of the LORD'S vengeance; he will render unto her a recompense."[26] The Lord patiently repeats His instructions to His remnant to flee Babylon America. They are to leave, and deliver every one their soul, from the hour of God's judgment of America.

AMERICA WILL BE FILLED WITH FOREIGN SOLDIERS

Jeremiah tells us that God will fill America with men who will lift up a shout against her. *"The LORD of hosts hath sworn by himself, saying, Surely I will fill thee with men, as with caterpillars; and they shall lift up a shout against thee."*[27] Today, over one million foreign soldiers are on our soil as part of the plan for a UN occupation of America, which is called Operation Cable Splicer. This prophecy is being fulfilled literally as the Lord fills America with foreign soldiers, who will soon raise a shout against us.

THE PEOPLE SHALL LABOR FOR FIRE

God tells us the people of America will labor in the last days in vain. *"Thus saith the LORD of hosts; The broad walls of Babylon shall be utterly broken, and her high gates shall be burned with fire; and the people shall labor in vain, and the folk in the fire, and they shall be weary."*[28] They shall be weary from their long hours serving the gods of wood and stone, which their hands have made. Today we find Americans working harder than ever to fill up their 401(k) accounts, and to pay for their luxurious lifestyles. It will all be in vain, as the nation is destroyed in one hour!

Revelation 18:21 speaks of the judgment upon America: *"And a mighty angel took up a stone like a great millstone, and cast it into the sea, saying, Thus with violence shall that great city Babylon be thrown down, and shall be found no more at all."* Modern Babylon will never rise again!

"And Jeremiah said to Seraiah, When thou comest to Babylon, and shalt see, and shalt read all these words; Then shalt thou say, O LORD, thou hast spoken against this place, to cut it off, that none shall remain in it, neither man nor beast, but that it shall be desolate for ever. And it shall be, when thou hast made an end of reading this book, that thou shalt bind a stone to it, and cast it into the midst of Euphrates: And thou shalt say, Thus shall Baby-

lon sink, and shall not rise from the evil that I will bring upon her: and they shall be weary. Thus far are the words of Jeremiah."[29] These prophecies will be fulfilled in America very soon.

THE LORD COMMANDS HIS PEOPLE TO LEAVE THE COUNTRY

The Lord tells the leaders of His people *"Remove out of the midst of Babylon, and go forth out of the land of the Chaldeans, and be as the he goats before the flocks."*[30] In simple terms—leave the country! Today, so many who have heard the sound of the trumpet are praying and asking God what to do.

Read the word! I asked the Lord the same question. He told me, *"Search the Scriptures. The detailed instructions for this hour are in the word."* I do not intend to get into a debate on Bible translations, but many of these modern versions completely mistranslate the key instructional prophecies for this hour while the King James Version has the true message for the remnant; a coincidence? I think not. These new Bibles also omit many of the references to prayer and fasting, deleting the word "fasting."

In the prophecy of Joel, the Lord instructs us, *"Sanctify ye a fast, call a solemn assembly, gather the elders and all the inhabitants of the land into the house of the LORD your God, and cry unto the Lord; Alas for the day! for the day of the LORD is at hand, and as a destruction from the Almighty shall it come."*[31]

All of us should be fasting and praying as the hour draws near. Many within the remnant are fasting each Thursday of the week to pray for the deliverance of God's remnant. Dear friend, you might also consider reading a Bible that was not published by a company owned by the Illuminati. Remember, Jesus warned us the deception in the last days would be great. It is everywhere around you. Turn off your television, and get into the word of God.

> *"The voice of them that flee and escape out of the land of Babylon, to declare in Zion the vengeance of the LORD our God, the vengeance of his temple."*[32] We are reminded that the destruction of Babylon will be sudden! *"Babylon is suddenly fallen and destroyed: howl for her; take balm for her pain, if so be she may be healed."*[33]

We are told that Babylon is a nation abundant in wealth and great treasures. *"O thou that dwellest upon many waters, abundant in treasures, thine end is come, and the measure of thy covetousness."*34 The Scripture tells us America won't get a shot off in her defense; her destruction will be so sudden and complete she won't even defend herself. In one day, dear reader, all you see around you in America will be gone. *"The mighty men of Babylon have forborne to fight, they have remained in their holds: their might hath failed; they became as women: they have burned her dwelling places; her bars are broken."*35

A TIME OF HARVEST WILL COME
AFTER HER JUDGMENT

Here we have the first indication that after the time of judgment, the time of threshing, there will be a harvest in her as well. *"For thus saith the LORD of hosts, the God of Israel; The daughter of Babylon is like a threshingfloor, it is time to thresh her: yet a little while, and the time of her harvest shall come."* 36

The survivors in America will witness a great turning to the Lord of those left alive after the destruction of the nation. *"How is Sheshach taken! and how is the praise of the whole earth surprised! How is Babylon become an astonishment among the nations!"*37 Again, the reference is to a sudden and surprising destruction of the greatest nation on earth, and how astonished the other nations will be at the judgment of America.

THE LORD REPEATS HIS WARNING
STAND NOT STILL

Again, the Lord instructs His people to leave her, and to deliver themselves. *"My people, go ye out of the midst of her, and deliver ye every man his soul from the fierce anger of the LORD. And lest your heart faint, and ye fear for the rumor that shall be heard in the land; a rumor shall both come one year, and after that in another year shall come a rumor, and violence in the land, ruler against ruler."*38

Here specific action is required, that of leaving the country. God also tells us that rumors shall be in the land, first in one year and then another, then violence in the land, and ruler against ruler. This last reference speaks of the civil war which will occur in the

US as the United Nations-controlled central government attempts to impose its tyranny on the individual states. Many groups will raise opposition to the planned takeover of the US. They will not succeed, for all of the nations fall under the dominion of the prince, save Edom and Moab.

The Lord again reminds His people to leave, go away, do not stand still! *"As Babylon hath caused the slain of Israel to fall, so at Babylon shall fall the slain of all the earth. Ye that have escaped the sword, go away, stand not still: remember the LORD afar off, and let Jerusalem come into your mind."*39 Where are they to go? God says let Jerusalem come to mind, think about Jerusalem and the land of Israel.

THE MERCHANTS OF THE EARTH SHALL WEEP AND MOURN

We are told that after the fall of America Babylon, the world's economic powers will weep, for they have lost their principal export market, and no one buys their goods anymore. *"And the merchants of the earth shall weep and mourn over her; for no man buyeth their merchandise any more."*40 Only America could fit this prophecy.

If you are unclear about the status of America as the world's principal export market, think about which nation runs the world's largest trade deficit. It is not Europe or Japan. It is not China or South America. It is certainly not Iraq! The merchants of the earth all sell to America. Moreover, when she burns, they will all weep, and no one will buy their merchandise anymore. The world-wide economic collapse, which will follow the fall of America, will be devastating. The US dollar will be worthless, and US Treasury Bonds will be thrown in the streets.

Most of the nations of the earth have substantial investments in the United States. In one hour, these will all be vaporized, and the rest of the world will collapse in a global depression of unprecedented scale. The nations of the earth will all weep, and no man will buy their goods anymore!

"And saying, Alas, alas, that great city, that was clothed in fine linen, and purple, and scarlet, and decked with gold, and pre-

cious stones, and pearls! For in one hour so great riches is come to naught.

"And every shipmaster, and all the company in ships, and sailors, and as many as trade by sea, stood afar off, And cried when they saw the smoke of her burning, saying, What city is like unto this great city!"[41] Our trading partners will stand afar off, afraid to come near the US, for fear of the plagues, the biological weapons, the radiation, the riots and the civil war that will fall on our land at the same time!

THE REMNANT WILL RETURN TO ZION

When America is finally destroyed, the remnant, which shall be spared, will then ask the way to Zion. They will recognize the only place of safety now is in the land of Israel, and the sanctuary of Edom. Notice though, they will weep as they ask the way to Zion, for they will seek to find a way in a very difficult time.

"In those days, and in that time, saith the LORD, the children of Israel shall come, they and the children of Judah together, going and weeping: they shall go, and seek the LORD their God. They shall ask the way to Zion with their faces thitherward, saying, Come, and let us join ourselves to the Lord in a perpetual covenant that shall not be forgotten."[42]

The Lord gives to those who are spared, including His remnant, the assurance that He will forgive their sins in that hour. *"In those days, and in that time, saith the LORD, the iniquity of Israel shall be sought for, and there shall be none; and the sins of Judah, and they shall not be found: for I will pardon them whom I reserve."*[43]

Dear reader, the time is indeed short. I encourage you, repent of all of your sins, and turn back to the Lord Jesus Christ with all of your heart. Great is our God, and mighty is His arm to save all those who are walking with Him in obedience. I encourage each of you to pray to the Lord Jesus Christ about when you should leave this land.

Remember the warnings of our God. They shall all depart. No man shall dwell there anymore.

Babylon the Great is fallen, fallen, and she will never rise again!

CHAPTER 6

"THE REMNANT SHALL RETURN"
Isaiah 10:21

Throughout the word of God, the Lord declares in the last days He will again gather His Holy remnant back to the land of Israel. The prophet Isaiah was used by the Lord to speak the word of God to ancient Israel about the coming of the Messiah Jesus Christ. Contained in this book of the Bible are prophecies of both the First Coming and the Second Coming of the Lord. Isaiah's prophecies describe the return of the Lord at the end of the age, and the judgments, which shall come at that time. He also unveils the deliverance plan for the remnant, which shall be saved in the last days.

THE REMNANT SHALL BE FEW AND VERY SMALL

The promises of our Lord speak of a great deliverance in this hour of testing, the day of vengeance of our God. The word makes it clear that the remnant be few and very small in number. *"Except the LORD of hosts had left unto us a very small remnant, we should have been as Sodom, and we should have been like unto Gomorrah."*[1]

Let us fear the Lord for the greatness of His judgments and the mercy He has shown unto us whom He has quickened in this hour. The Lord speaks of the last days as a time when children will oppress the people, and women will act as rulers among the people. *"As for my people, children are their oppressors, and women rule over them. O my people, they which lead thee cause thee to err, and destroy the way of thy paths."*[2]

148

SEAL THE LAW AMONG MY DISCIPLES

We are instructed not to walk as the nations walk, nor to fear what they fear, but to fear only the Lord. The law which is the Torah, is to be sealed among the disciples of the Lord. To seal the law is to preserve and protect it. The true disciples will have the law sealed in their hearts, and if any one speaks not according to the law, and the testimony of the prophets, then we know there is no light in them.

> *"The LORD spoke to me... and instructed me that I should not walk in the way of this people.... neither fear ye their fear, nor be afraid. Sanctify the LORD of hosts himself; and let him be your fear, and let him be your dread. And he shall be for a sanctuary; but for a stone of stumbling and for a rock of offence.... And many among them shall stumble, and fall, and be broken, and be snared, and be taken. Bind up the testimony, and seal the law among my disciples. I will wait upon the LORD, that hideth his face from the house of Jacob, and I will look for him. Behold, I and the children whom the LORD hath given me are for signs and for wonders in Israel from the LORD of hosts, which dwelleth in mount Zion....To the law and to the testimony: if they speak not according to this word, it is because there is no light in them. And they shall pass through it, hardly bestead and hungry: and it shall come to pass, that when they shall be hungry, they shall fret themselves, and curse their king and their God, and look upward. And they shall look unto the earth; and behold trouble and darkness, dimness of anguish; and they shall be driven to darkness."[3]*

The remnant is described as those that *"escape"*[4] and we are told, *"The remnant shall return, even the remnant of Jacob, unto the mighty God. For though thy people Israel be as the sand of the sea, yet a remnant of them shall return: the consumption decreed shall overflow with righteousness."*[5] The Lord has decreed a great consumption; only a remnant shall return. We should greatly fear the Lord, for we are sinners, even as those that are going to the sword.

THE SECOND RECOVERY OF THE LAND OF ISRAEL

The second recovery of the nation of Israel back to their land began in the early 1900's. The remnant are described as *"the outcasts of Israel"* and *"He shall set up an ensign for the nations, and shall assemble the outcasts of Israel, and gather together the dispersed of Judah from the four corners of the earth."*[6] They are the true spiritual nation, comprising both Jews and Gentiles, who are found written in the Book of Life. They are worthy to be able to stand, and endure the hour of testing.

> *"And it shall come to pass in that day, that the remnant of Israel, and such as are escaped of the house of Jacob, shall no more again stay upon him that smote them; but shall stay upon the LORD, the Holy One of Israel, in truth. The remnant shall return, even the remnant of Jacob, unto the mighty God. For though thy people Israel be as the sand of the sea, yet a remnant of them shall return: the consumption decreed shall overflow with righteousness"* (Isaiah 10:20-22).

The Lord also reveals that His remnant will be gathered from the four corners of the earth, and they will lay their hands upon Edom and Moab, and the children of Ammon shall obey them. They shall also possess the land of Edom and Moab. This area of southern Jordan is actually part of greater Israel, and part of the Promised Land given to the descendents of Abraham. If we are of true Israel, it is also our land.

> *"And it shall come to pass in that day, that the Lord shall set his hand again the second time to recover the remnant of his people.... he shall set up an ensign for the nations, and shall assemble the outcasts of Israel, and gather together the dispersed of Judah from the four corners of the earth. The envy also of Ephraim shall depart, and the adversaries of Judah shall be cut off: Ephraim shall not envy Judah, and Judah shall not vex Ephraim. But they shall fly upon the shoulders of the Philistines toward the west; they shall spoil them of the east together: they shall lay their hand upon Edom and Moab; and the children of Ammon shall obey them"* (Isaiah 11:11-14).

EVERYONE THAT IS FOUND
SHALL BE THRUST THROUGH

The Lord commands us to hide ourselves, for this is the hour of His indignation. He also tells us that everyone will turn to his own people, and flee back to his own land.[7] When the Lord comes in final judgment of the earth, everyone that is found will be *"thrust through,"* and their children will be *"dashed to pieces"* and their wives *"ravished."* He also declares the beautiful cities of America Babylon will be judged like Sodom, torched! *"And Babylon, the glory of kingdoms, the beauty of the Chaldees' excellency, shall be as when God overthrew Sodom and Gomorrah."*[8] This is a reference to the coastal areas of California, Florida and New York. These are the beauty of Babylon's excellence, and the pride of America Babylon. They will all burn in one hour!

> *"And it shall be as the chased roe, and as a sheep that no man taketh up: they shall every man turn to his own people, and flee every one into his own land. Every one that is found shall be thrust through; and every one that is joined unto them shall fall by the sword. Their children also shall be dashed to pieces before their eyes; their houses shall be spoiled, and their wives ravished. Behold, I will stir up the Medes against them, which shall not regard silver; and as for gold, they shall not delight in it. Their bows also shall dash the young men to pieces; and they shall have no pity on the fruit of the womb; their eye shall not spare children. And Babylon, the glory of kingdoms, the beauty of the Chaldees' excellency, shall be as when God overthrew Sodom and Gomorrah"* (Isaiah 13:14-19).

THE REMNANT SHALL TAKE CAPTIVE
THE ENEMIES OF ISRAEL

The Lord will establish Israel in their own land; the Scripture declares everyone flees to their own land. The strangers that cleave unto Israel will be their servants, and Israel shall take captive those who once held them captive—this is Edom and Moab, who at one time captured Israel as they fled.

> *"For the LORD will have mercy on Jacob, and will yet choose Israel, and set them in their own land: and the strangers shall be joined with them, and they shall cleave to the house of Jacob. And the people shall take them, and bring them to their place: and the house of Israel shall possess them in the land of the LORD for servants and handmaids: and they shall take them captives, whose captives they were; and they shall rule over their oppressors."*[9]

Those who hold the false doctrines of replacement theology will dispute that these Scriptures apply to the Gentile believers, yet God only has one people—true Israel.

The Word shows that the *"lamb"* is to be sent *"to the ruler of the land from Sela"* (which is Petra) to the wilderness unto the mount of the daughter of Zion. Petra is next to mount Hor, where Moses and Aaron went up to meet the Lord, while the children of Israel waited in the valley below. This is the same wilderness area, which the Lord is preparing right now for His remnant to possess, even Edom and Moab. The lamb is the remnant who are to be protected during the Great Tribulation.

Moab will provide a covering to the outcasts of Israel from the face of the spoiler. The spoiler is the Antichrist. The sinners and the evil men are the extortioners, who are at their end, for the oppressors are about to be consumed out of the land.

> *"Send ye the lamb to the ruler of the land from Sela to the wilderness, unto the mount of the daughter of Zion. For it shall be, that, as a wandering bird cast out of the nest, so the daughters of Moab shall be at the fords of Arnon. Take counsel, execute judgment; make thy shadow as the night in the midst of the noonday; hide the outcasts; betray not him that wandereth. Let mine outcasts dwell with thee, Moab; be thou a covert to them from the face of the spoiler: for the extortioner is at an end, the spoiler ceaseth, the oppressors are consumed out of the land"* (Isaiah 16:1-4).

THE REMNANT SHALL BE
AS A GLEANING IN THE LAND

Damascus is to be destroyed during the battle of Ezekiel 38, and the Lord describes His remnant as a gleaning in the land. This is from the harvest law of the gleaning. The harvest was to be performed only once. Whatever crop was missed was to be left for the poor in the land. This is a picture of the remnant, which will be left. The few that are left will have respect for God, and not the work of their hands, their money or idols.

> *"The burden of Damascus. Behold, Damascus is taken away from being a city, and it shall be a ruinous heap.... And in that day it shall come to pass, that the glory of Jacob shall be made thin, and the fatness of his flesh shall wax lean. And it shall be as when the*

harvestman gathereth the corn, and reapeth the ears with his arm;
and it shall be as he that gathereth ears in the valley of Rephaim.
Yet gleaning grapes shall be left in it, as the shaking of an olive tree,
two or three berries in the top of the uppermost bough, four or five
in the outmost fruitful branches thereof, saith the LORD God of Is-
rael. At that day shall a man look to his Maker, and his eyes shall
have respect to the Holy One of Israel. And he shall not look to the
altars, the work of his hands, neither shall respect that which his
fingers have made, either the groves, or the images" (Isaiah 17:1-8).

The Lord speaks of the mountain in the wilderness where He will
prepare a feast for His people. There He will take away the veil
that is blinding the eyes of the people. The veil is sin and unbelief
in the word of God. This veil blinds the heart of man to the truth of
God. The Lord also states again that this mountain is where His
hand will rest; He is taking it for His people, and as a result Moab
shall be trodden down. Praise God for His plan!

"For thou hast been a strength to the poor, a strength to the needy in
his distress, a refuge from the storm, a shadow from the heat, when
the blast of the terrible ones is as a storm against the wall. Thou
shalt bring down the noise of strangers, as the heat in a dry place;
even the heat with the shadow of a cloud: the branch of the terrible
ones shall be brought low. And in this mountain shall the LORD of
hosts make unto all people a feast of fat things, a feast of wines on
the lees, of fat things full of marrow, of wines on the lees well re-
fined. And he will destroy in this mountain the face of the covering
cast over all people, and the vail that is spread over all nations. He
will swallow up death in victory; and the Lord GOD will wipe away
tears from off all faces; and the rebuke of his people shall he take
away from off all the earth: for the LORD hath spoken it. And it
shall be said in that day, Lo, this is our God; we have waited for
him, and he will save us: this is the LORD; we have waited for him,
we will be glad and rejoice in his salvation. For in this mountain
shall the hand of the LORD rest, and Moab shall be trodden down
under him, even as straw is trodden down for the dunghill" (Isaiah
25:4-10).

COME MY PEOPLE, AND HIDE FOR A LITTLE MOMENT

The Lord commands us to hide ourselves in our chambers, and to shut the door, as He hid Noah in the ark. Indeed, the Lord shut the door behind Noah. The Lord will also be our rear guard and our defense, if we obey Him. *"Come, my people, enter thou into thy chambers, and shut thy doors about thee: hide thyself as it were for a little moment, until the indignation be overpast. For, behold, the LORD cometh out of his place to punish the inhabitants of the earth for their iniquity: the earth also shall disclose her blood, and shall no more cover her slain."*[10] The Scripture here is speaking about the time of the end, when the Lord comes to punish the inhabitants of the earth. We do well to obey His commands, for everyone that is found will be killed with the sword.

THE LORD WILL RISE AND STAND IN JUDGMENT

The Lord tells us He will rise to stand in judgment. This is the same word the Lord spoke to me declaring; *"The Lord God Almighty is standing now ready to judge the entire earth!"*

The Lord always stands to judge the people. The Lord shall be angry when He comes to do *"His strange act, His strange work."* He describes His judgment as a strange work, a work the people do not expect or understand. It is also a strange act, for the Lord takes no delight in the judgment of man. Our God delights in mercy, justice and loving-kindness, but God is also a God of righteousness and judgment. He has decreed that He will judge the whole earth. The Lord has appointed the sword for judgment. This sword will bring His people to true repentance, and destroy the wicked. Our God is a consuming fire; let us fear Him and Him alone.

"For the LORD shall rise up as in mount Perazim, he shall be wroth as in the valley of Gibeon, that he may do his work, his strange work; and bring to pass his act, his strange act. Now therefore be ye not mockers, lest your bands be made strong: for I have heard from the Lord GOD of hosts a consumption, even determined upon the whole earth" (Isaiah 28:21-22).

THE LEADERS OF THE PEOPLE
ARE UNABLE TO UNDERSTAND

The Lord tells us the leaders and the prophets can't read His word, and they are unable to understand it, because they are not seeking Him with their hearts, only with their lips, Again, the Lord reiterates the marvelous solution he has planned; He will destroy the wisdom of those wise in their own eyes!

"For the LORD hath poured out upon you the spirit of deep sleep, and hath closed your eyes: the prophets and your rulers, the seers hath he covered. And the vision of all is become unto you as the words of a book that is sealed, which men deliver to one that is learned, saying, Read this, I pray thee: and he saith, I cannot; for it is sealed: And the book is delivered to him that is not learned, saying, Read this, I pray thee: and he saith, I am not learned. Wherefore the Lord said, Forasmuch as this people draw near me with their mouth, and with their lips do honor me, but have removed their heart far from me, and their fear toward me is taught by the precept of men: Therefore, behold, I will proceed to do a marvelous work among this people, even a marvelous work and a wonder: for the wisdom of their wise men shall perish, and the understanding of their prudent men shall be hid" (Isaiah 29:10-14).

WOE TO THOSE WHO GO DOWN UNTO EGYPT

In Chapter 30 we are warned against turning to the world for help or deliverance. The world (Egypt) cannot help us, and will only bring shame and confusion.

"Woe to the rebellious children, saith the LORD, that take counsel, but not of me; and that cover with a covering, but not of my spirit, that they may add sin to sin: That walk to go down into Egypt, and have not asked at my mouth; to strengthen themselves in the strength of Pharaoh, and to trust in the shadow of Egypt! Therefore shall the strength of Pharaoh be your shame, and the trust in the shadow of Egypt your confusion" (Isaiah 30:1-3).

THE PEOPLE SHALL BE AS THORNS
CUT UP AND BURNED IN THE FIRE

The Lord speaks of standing in judgment, and describes the people as *"thorns cut up"* and *"they shall be burned in the fire."* The people are described as *"thorns"* for they are unfruitful, having failed to abide in Him. These branches have withered, having failed to produce true fruit in the spirit. These are the persecuted believers of America. The Lord spoke of this judgment on the believers who would not abide in Him: *"I am the true vine, and my Father is the husbandman. Every branch in me that beareth not fruit he ta-keth away: and every branch that beareth fruit, he purgeth it, that it may bring forth more fruit.... If a man abide not in me, he is cast forth as a branch, and is withered; and men gather them, and cast them into the fire, and they are burned."*[11] Those who will not abide and walk in His spirit will be literally gathered up by men, and cast into the fire! These are the martyrs, who will be *"as thorns cut up,"* and their bodies will burn in the fire. After they are killed, the martyrs will be cremated in the death camps of the prince.

Who will be found among the remnant? Only those who walk in righteousness. Their place of safety will be the munitions or rocks. The word for munitions is *"metsad"* [12] (mets-ad') and is found only in this verse. It means a covering from an ambush, a castle, a stronghold and a covering from an ambush. The Hebrew word for rocks is *"cela"*[13] (seh'-lah) which is Petra in the Greek, and it means a fortress or stronghold of rocks. The Lord spells out the place where the remnant will be defended: the place of safety is the mountain of Petra, in the land of Edom and Moab! This is the place spoken of in Revelation 12, where the woman flees. God himself prepares this place for her.

It is beautiful. I have seen it with my own eyes. There are seven springs of pure water there, the air is pure, and there is a highway there, called the King's Highway. May the Lord grant us the faith to hear and believe and to submit to His plan, and not to rely on our own understanding, nor to go and hide in the shadow of Pharaoh. The ambush will soon snare the people of the earth, and where will you be found, dear reader?

> *"Now will I rise, saith the LORD; now will I be exalted; now will I lift up myself. Ye shall conceive chaff, ye shall bring forth stubble: your breath, as fire, shall devour you. And the people shall be as the burnings of lime: as thorns cut up shall they be burned in the fire. Hear, ye that are far off, what I have done; and, ye that are near,*

acknowledge my might. The sinners in Zion are afraid; fearfulness hath surprised the hypocrites. Who among us shall dwell with the devouring fire? who among us shall dwell with everlasting burnings? He that walketh righteously, and speaketh uprightly; he that despiseth the gain of oppressions, that shaketh his hands from holding of bribes, that stoppeth his ears from hearing of blood, and shutteth his eyes from seeing evil; He shall dwell on high: his place of defence shall be the munitions of rocks: bread shall be given him; his waters shall be sure. Thine eyes shall see the king in his beauty: they shall behold the land that is very far off" (Isaiah 33:10-17).

THE WILDERNESS SHALL BE GLAD FOR THEM

The Lord speaks of the wilderness being glad for His people and describes it as a solitary place. The scriptures reveal that God has provided one place for the remnant as a shelter from the storm. One of the prophets, when shown by God of the destruction of America asked the Lord, *"What about the believers in America?"* The Lord responded, *"I have not reserved America for the believer, but I do have a promise to keep to Judah!"*

I believe this means we have not been promised safety in this country, for we are aliens here, but the Lord has made a promise to Judah. This is a promise to all the remnant of Israel. This promise is a place of safety, where we can rest without fear, beyond the reach of the destroyer, who will conquer many nations. This place of safety is Petra!

"The wilderness and the solitary place shall be glad for them; and the desert shall rejoice, and blossom as the rose. It shall blossom abundantly, and rejoice even with joy and singing: the glory of Lebanon shall be given unto it, the excellency of Carmel and Sharon, they shall see the glory of the LORD, and the excellency of our God" (Isaiah 35:1-2).

The Lord describes the highway that will be found in this wilderness, for it is the way of holiness. The highway, which runs through Petra, is named *"The King's Highway."* This is the way He would have us walk—in holiness and truth. All who are found on this highway will walk as He walked.

"And a highway shall be there, and a way, and it shall be called The way of holiness; the unclean shall not pass over it;

but it shall be for those: the wayfaring men, though fools, shall not err therein. No lion shall be there, nor any ravenous beast shall go up thereon, it shall not be found there; but the redeemed shall walk there: And the ransomed of the LORD shall return, and come to Zion with songs and everlasting joy upon their heads: they shall obtain joy and gladness, and sorrow and sighing shall flee away" (Isaiah 35:8-10).

The Lord speaks again about the wilderness, and the highway the redeemed of the Lord will walk upon, for it is a straight road called The way of holiness. We had better straighten our hearts, for He will dwell among His remnant in holiness even as He dwelt among the children of Israel after they left Egypt. The exodus of Israel was a foreshadow of this very hour, and we are going to the same place, to wait for Him, even as they waited. How awesome is our God, how marvelous are His ways, and His wonders to perform. Who is wise that can discern these things of the Spirit? Let him declare it! Who hears from God? Let him speak.

"Comfort ye, comfort ye my people, saith your God. Speak ye comfortably to Jerusalem, and cry unto her, that her warfare is accomplished, that her iniquity is pardoned: for she hath received of the LORD'S hand double for all her sins. The voice of him that crieth in the wilderness, Prepare ye the way of the LORD, make straight in the desert a highway for our God" (Isaiah 40:1-3).

THE GOD OF ISRAEL WILL NOT FORSAKE THEM

The Lord describes the changes He will make in the wilderness, providing both water and plantings for His people, to provide for their needs. Little flock, don't be fearful, your Father knows of your needs, and He has promised to provide for you. You must do your part; obey and fear only Him.

"When the poor and needy seek water, and there is none, and their tongue faileth for thirst, I the LORD will hear them, I the God of Israel will not forsake them. I will open rivers in high places, and fountains in the midst of the valleys: I will make the wilderness a pool of water, and the dry land springs of water. I will plant in the wilderness the cedar, the shittah tree, and the myrtle, and the oil tree; I will set in the desert the fir tree, and the pine, and the box tree together" (Isaiah 41:17-19).

The Lord is doing a new thing now. He has held His peace a long time, but now He will destroy the wicked, and bring His people in paths they have not known. Behold, you who are reading these words, will you be found among those waiting for Him on that day? Repent, and turn with your whole heart, and you may find grace and mercy from Him.

Our God is a God of great mercy, desiring mercy and obedience before sacrifice.

"Behold, the former things are come to pass, and new things do I declare: before they spring forth I tell you of them. Sing unto the LORD a new song, and his praise from the end of the earth, ye that go down to the sea, and all that is therein; the isles, and the inhabitants thereof. Let the wilderness and the cities thereof lift up their voice, the villages that Kedar doth inhabit: let the inhabitants of the rock sing, let them shout from the top of the mountains.Let them give glory unto the LORD, and declare his praise in the islands. The LORD shall go forth as a mighty man, he shall stir up jealousy like a man of war: he shall cry, yea, roar; he shall prevail against his enemies. I have long time holden my peace; I have been still, and refrained myself: now will I cry like a travailing woman; I will destroy and devour at once. I will make waste mountains and hills, and dry up all their herbs; and I will make the rivers islands, and I will dry up the pools. And I will bring the blind by a way that they knew not; I will lead them in paths that they have not known: I will make darkness light before them, and crooked things straight. These things will I do unto them, and not forsake them" (Isaiah 42:9-16).

FEAR NOT, I WILL BRING MY SONS FROM FAR

The Lord tells us all of the people will be brought back, *"even every one that is called by my name."* Stating the obvious, when the Lord speaks of *everyone*, He means everyone! Again, he says, *"let the people be assembled"* and to those that escape to come near together, assemble and to come. *"Assemble yourselves and come; draw near together, ye that are escaped of the nations: they have no knowledge that set up the wood of their graven im-*

age, and pray unto a god that cannot save."[14] Let us come, for the time is at hand.

> *"Fear not: for I am with thee: I will bring thy seed from the east, and gather thee from the west; I will say to the north, Give up; and to the south, Keep not back: bring my sons from far, and my daughters from the ends of the earth; Even every one that is called by my name: for I have created him for my glory, I have formed him; yea, I have made him. Bring forth the blind people that have eyes, and the deaf that have ears. Let all the nations be gathered together, and let the people be assembled: who among them can declare this, and show us former things? let them bring forth their witnesses, that they may be justified: or let them hear, and say, It is truth"* (Isaiah 43:5-9).

> *"Remember the former things of old: for I am God, and there is none else; I am God, and there is none like me, Declaring the end from the beginning, and from ancient times the things that are not yet done, saying, My counsel shall stand, and I will do all my pleasure: Calling a ravenous bird from the east, the man that executeth my counsel from a far country: yea, I have spoken it, I will also bring it to pass; I have purposed it, I will also do it"* (Isaiah 46:9-11).

GO FORTH FROM BABYLON, FLEE THE LAND OF THE CHALDEANS

The Lord tells His people to flee from the land of Babylon and the Babylonian system of religion. He sends this message to *"the end of the earth."* *"Go ye forth of Babylon, flee ye from the Chaldeans, with a voice of singing declare ye, tell this, utter it even to the end of the earth; say ye, The LORD hath redeemed his servant Jacob."*[15] The people must leave the kingdom of the prince and go to the fortress among the rocks, to Petra. The Lord then compares this redemption to the deliverance from Egypt, when He led His people through the deserts.

"And they thirsted not when he led them through the deserts: he caused the waters to flow out of the rock for them: he clave the rock also, and the waters gushed out. There is no peace, saith the LORD, unto the wicked."[16] We will go out even as they went out, for great is the Lord Who saves us. The above verse also speaks of the way in the wilderness prepared for God's people.

HE THAT HAS MERCY ON THEM SHALL LEAD THEM

The Lord promises to have mercy upon His remnant; and to lead them home, they will neither hunger nor thirst, for the Lord will meet their needs. Truly, the Lord will comfort His people who trust in Him and walk before Him in obedience and holiness.

"They shall not hunger nor thirst; neither shall the heat nor sun smite them: for he that hath mercy on them shall lead them, even by the springs of water shall he guide them. And I will make all my mountains a way, and my highways shall be exalted. Behold, these shall come from far: and, lo, these from the north and from the west; and these from the land of Sinim. Sing, O heavens; and be joyful, O earth; and break forth into singing, O mountains: for the LORD hath comforted his people, and will have mercy upon his afflicted" (Isaiah 49:10-13).

Praise the Lord for His goodness unto us whom He is delivering. The Lord will lift up His hand to the Gentiles, *"and they shall bring my sons in their arms, and thy daughters shall be carried upon their shoulders. And kings shall be thy nursing fathers... they shall bow down to thee with their face toward the earth."* God promises to protect the children of His remnant and the kings of the gentiles will provide for His people. Is there anything to hard for the Lord? I think not!

"Thy children shall make haste; thy destroyers and they that made thee waste shall go forth of thee. Lift up thine eyes round about, and behold: all these gather themselves together, and come to thee.... The children which thou shalt have, after thou hast lost the other, shall say again in thine ears, The place is too strait for me: give place to me that I may dwell. Then shalt thou say in thine heart, Who hath begotten me these, seeing I have lost my children, and am desolate, a captive, and removing to and fro? And who hath brought up these? Behold, I was left alone; these, where had they been? Thus saith the Lord GOD, Behold, I will lift up mine hand to the Gentiles, and set up my standard to the people: and they shall bring thy sons in their arms, and thy daughters shall be carried upon their shoulders. And kings shall be thy nursing fathers, and their queens thy nursing mothers: they shall bow down to thee with their face toward the earth, and lick up the dust of thy feet; and thou

shalt know that I am the LORD: for they shall not be ashamed that wait for me. Shall the prey be taken from the mighty, or the lawful captive delivered? But thus saith the LORD, Even the captives of the mighty shall be taken away, and the prey of the terrible shall be delivered: for I will contend with him that contendeth with thee, and I will save thy children" (Isaiah 49:17-25).

In the midst of the Great Tribulation, the Lord says He will make the wilderness like Eden, and joy and gladness shall be found there.

"For the LORD shall comfort Zion: he will comfort all her waste places; and he will make her wilderness like Eden, and her desert like the garden of the LORD; joy and gladness shall be found therein, thanksgiving, and the voice of melody" (Isaiah 51:3).

DEPART, DEPART AND GO OUT
AND TOUCH NO UNCLEAN THING

The Lord again tells the people it is time to leave. It is time to depart, and touch nothing that is unclean. You must cleanse your hearts, and your hands, if you want to stand on the day that the sign of the Son of man appears in the heavens.

"Depart ye, depart ye, go ye out from thence, touch no unclean thing; go ye out of the midst of her; be ye clean, that bear the vessels of the LORD. For ye shall not go out with haste, nor go by flight: for the LORD will go before you; and the God of Israel will be your reward" (Isaiah 52:11-12).

The Lord declares that Gentiles who join Israel to serve the Lord, and who love the name of the Lord, will also be brought to the holy mountain, which is the wilderness of Petra. And every one of them who is spared, will honor and keep the law of the Lord.

"Also the sons of the stranger, that join themselves to the LORD, to serve him, and to love the name of the LORD, to be his servants, every one that keepeth the Sabbath from polluting it, and taketh hold of my covenant; Even them will I bring to my holy mountain, and make them joyful in my house of prayer: their burnt offerings and their sacrifices shall be accepted upon mine altar; for mine house shall be called an house of prayer for all people. The Lord GOD which gathereth the outcasts of Israel saith, Yet will I gather

others to him, beside those that are gathered unto him" (Isaiah 56:6-
8).

THEY SHALL BUILD THE OLD WASTE CITIES

The Lord speaks about His Second Coming and that His people
shall rebuild the desolate places. This speaks of the ships, which
will evacuate people out of the USA from the coastal areas of
Texas, and the islands of Central America, where the remnant will
rest on their way home. Even now, these refuge stations are being
prepared for the people.

*"Surely the isles shall wait for me, and the ships of Tarshish first, to
bring thy sons from far, their silver and their gold with them, unto
the name of the LORD thy God, and to the Holy One of Israel, because he hath glorified thee. And the sons of strangers shall build up
thy walls, and their kings shall minister unto thee: for in my wrath I
smote thee, but in my favor have I had mercy on thee"* (Isaiah 60:9-
10).

The prophecy of the Messiah in Isaiah 61 also declares the remnant shall build the old waste places, and raise up the former desolations:

*"The Spirit of the Lord GOD is upon me; because the LORD hath
anointed me to preach good tidings unto the meek; he hath sent me
to bind up the brokenhearted, to proclaim liberty to the captives,
and the opening of the prison to them that are bound; To proclaim
the acceptable year of the LORD, and the day of vengeance of our
God; to comfort all that mourn.... And they shall build the old
wastes, they shall raise up the former desolations, and they shall
repair the waste cities, the desolation's of many generations. And
strangers shall stand and feed your flocks, and the sons of the alien
shall be your plowmen and your vinedressers"* (Isaiah 61:1-5).

WHO IS THIS THAT COMES FROM EDOM?

The Lord asks, *"Who is this that cometh from Edom?"* This is the
Second Coming of the Lord. He first returns to Edom, to recover
His remnant that are waiting for Him there, and His angels will
gather the rest of His elect from the four corners of the earth.
These are His army, who were sent to fight the dragon and to wit-
ness of the Lord in the kingdom of darkness.

"Who is this that cometh from Edom, with dyed garments from Boz-rah? this that is glorious in his apparel, travelling in the greatness of his strength? I that speak in righteousness, mighty to save. Wherefore art thou red in thine apparel, and thy garments like him that treadeth in the winefat? I have trodden the winepress alone; and of the people there was none with me: for I will tread them in mine anger, and trample them in my fury; and their blood shall be sprinkled upon my garments, and I will stain all my raiment. For the day of vengeance is in mine heart, and the year of my redeemed is come" (Isaiah 63:1-4).

The Lord again declares His remnant shall be found in a cluster, in a group, and goes on to declare that they shall inherit His mountains, and His servants shall dwell there. *"Thus saith the LORD, As the new wine is found in the cluster, and one saith, Destroy it not; for a blessing is in it: so will I do for my servants' sakes, that I may not destroy them all. And I will bring forth a seed out of Jacob, and out of Judah an inheritor of my mountains: and mine elect shall inherit it, and my servants shall dwell there."*[17]

The deliverance plan of the remnant returning to Israel, and to the land of Edom and Moab, is not exclusive to the book of Isaiah. In the book of Daniel, chapter 11, the Lord declares Edom and Moab will not fall under the control of the prince. *"He shall enter also into the glorious land, and many countries shall be overthrown: but these shall escape out of his hand, even Edom, and Moab, and the chief of the children of Ammon."*[18] The chief of the children of Ammon refers to the royal family of Jordan, who will also escape.

In the book of Habakkuk, the prophet declares that his vision is for an appointed time, which is the time of the end. The prophet is also told the people would be unable to hear the truth: *"Behold ye among the heathen, and regard, and wonder marvellously: for I will work a work in your days, which ye will not believe, though it be told you."*[19] The prophet is instructed to make his vision plain, so that all who read it could clearly understand the message. Run! *"I will stand upon my watch, and set me upon the tower, and will watch to see what he will say unto me, and what I shall answer when I am reproved. And the LORD answered me, and said, Write the vision, and make it plain upon tables, that he may run that readeth it. For the vision is yet for an appointed time, but at the end it shall speak, and not lie: though it tarry, wait for it; because it will surely come, it will not tarry."*[20]

THEY THAT ESCAPE SHALL ESCAPE

Exekiel also tells us that those who escape *"shall escape."* They will have to *"run"* as Habakkuk declares, and they will *"hide them-selves."* They will be found *"on the mountains,"* each mourning for his own sins. As the remnant witness the judgments on the earth, and on the Church, they will weep for their iniquities, for only by the mercy of Jesus Christ and His loving kindness, have they been spared.

> *"But they that escape of them shall escape, and shall be on the mountains like doves of the valleys, all of them mourning, every one for his iniquity. All hands shall be feeble, and all knees shall be weak as water. They shall also gird themselves with sackcloth, and horror shall cover them; and shame shall be upon all faces, and baldness upon all their heads"* (Ezekiel 7:16-18).

Revelation 12 contains a specific prophecy of the place of safety prepared by God where the Lord will fulfill his promise to Judah, and to the remnant of Israel. The dragon will be enraged that he cannot reach the people in Edom, so he will turn and go to make war with those who dwell in the other parts of the earth. If you plan on continuing to live in the other areas of the world, such as the US, you can be certain that the prince will conquer this nation, and you will have to make war with the dragon personally. If you are called to this ministry, may God bless and protect your life.

> *"And to the woman were given two wings of a great eagle, that she might fly into the wilderness, into her place, where she is nourished for a time, and times, and half a time, from the face of the serpent. And the dragon was wroth with the woman, and went to make war with the remnant of her seed, which keep the commandments of God, and have the testimony of Jesus Christ"* (Revelation 12:14-17).

Again in Amos, the Lord provides a last days' prophecy of his people possessing the remnant of Edom. *"That they may possess the remnant of Edom... saith the LORD that doeth this. Behold, the days come, saith the LORD, that the plowman shall overtake the reaper, and the treader of grapes him that soweth seed; and the mountains shall drop sweet wine, and all the hills shall melt. And*

I will bring again the captivity of my people of Israel, and they shall build the waste cities, and inhabit them.... And I will plant them upon their land, and they shall no more be pulled up out of their land which I have given them, saith the LORD thy God."[21]

I WILL SURELY GATHER THE REMNANT OF ISRAEL

In Micah, the Lord declares that He will again assemble all of Jacob, and that He will gather the remnant of Israel together. He will put them together as the sheep of Bozrah. Bozrah is in the land of Edom! In addition, they shall make a great noise because there is such a large multitude gathered. Praise the Lord that He has prepared a place of safety for us to hide in—while His men of war fight the dragon in the cities, which were conquered by the prince. *"I will surely assemble, O Jacob, all of thee; I will surely gather the remnant of Israel; I will put them together as the sheep of Bozrah, as the flock in the midst of their fold: they shall make great noise by reason of the multitude of men. The breaker is come up before them: they have broken up, and have passed through the gate, and are gone out by it: and their king shall pass before them, and the LORD on the head of them."*[22]

Again, the Lord declares His remnant will spoil Moab, and the remnant of My people shall possess the land of Moab. This has not yet been fulfilled, but the day is at hand. *"And the coast shall be for the remnant of the house of Judah... the LORD their God shall visit them, and turn away their captivity. I have heard the reproach of Moab, and the revilings of the children of Ammon, whereby they have reproached my people, and magnified themselves against their border. Therefore as I live, saith the LORD of hosts, the God of Israel, Surely Moab shall be as Sodom, and the children of Ammon as Gomorrah...the residue of my people shall spoil them, and the remnant of my people shall possess them."*[23]

The Lord says the people of the nations will cling to the Jews for they will know the Lord is with them. The Lord humbled the Jews by sending the Gentiles to preach the word of the Lord to them. Now He will humble the Gentiles, by sending an anointed army of Jews to deliver them from the beast. They will take hold of the coat of a Jew, saying, *"let us go with you, for we know God is with you."*

"Thus saith the LORD of hosts; Behold, I will save my people from the east country, and from the west country; And I will bring them, and they shall dwell in the midst of Jerusalem: and they shall be my people, and I will be their God, in truth and in righteousness.... And it shall come to pass, that as ye were a curse among the heathen, O house of Judah, and house of Israel; so will I save you, and ye shall be a blessing: fear not, but let your hands be strong.... Thus saith the LORD of hosts; In those days it shall come to pass, that ten men shall take hold out of all languages of the nations, even shall take hold of the skirt of him that is a Jew, saying, We will go with you: for we have heard that God is with you."[24]

Again, in the book of Numbers the Lord repeats this prophecy of the possession of Edom.

"He hath said, which heard the words of God, and knew the knowledge of the most High, which saw the vision of the Almighty, falling into a trance, but having his eyes open: I shall see him, but not now: I shall behold him, but not nigh: there shall come a Star out of Jacob, and a Sceptre shall rise out of Israel, and shall smite the corners of Moab, and destroy all the children of Sheth. And Edom shall be a possession, Seir also shall be a possession for his enemies; and Israel shall do valiantly."[25]

OVER EDOM HAVE I CAST MY SHOE

The Lord declares that Edom and mount Seir will become the possession for their enemies, which is Israel. Two years ago, the Lord spoke to the remnant who are preparing Edom, telling them to take a shoe, and cast it over Mount Hor. They did not understand this commandment, but two men of God took a Shofar and a shoe and ascended the mountain. The Jordanian army guards this mountain, and when they threw the shoe and blew the Shofar, they had to run from their pursuers.

The Lord then showed them this prophecy, for the Lord has redeemed this land for the remnant, and over Edom He cast His shoe. The Lord has cast His shoe as the kinsman redeemer over the land of Edom, which had been given unto the curse. The Scripture then reveals prophetically the question: *"Moab is my washpot; over Edom will I cast out my shoe.... Who will bring me into the strong city? who will lead me into Edom?"*[26]

The prophet Amos speaks of the Day of the Lord as the time that the tabernacle of David is raised up. The Lord speaks again of the remnant possessing Edom. *"In that day will I raise up the tabernacle of David that is fallen, and close up the breaches thereof; and I will raise up his ruins, and I will build it as in the days of old: That they may possess the remnant of Edom, and of all the heathen, which are called by my name, saith the LORD that doeth this."*[27]

The Lord declares His judgment upon Edom again in the prophecies of Obadiah and declares that the remnant shall possess the possessions of Edom. *"Shall I not in that day, saith the LORD, even destroy the wise men out of Edom, and understanding out of the mount of Esau?... For thy violence against thy brother Jacob shame shall cover thee, and thou shalt be cut off for ever.... For the day of the Lord is near upon all the heathen: as thou hast done, it shall be done unto thee.... But upon mount Zion shall be deliverance, and there shall be holiness; and the house of Jacob shall possess their possessions."*[28]

Many of the words established by God are repeated and fulfilled twice. The Lord repeats the prophecy of the redemption of Edom again in Psalm 108. *"Moab is my washpot; over Edom will I cast out my shoe; over Philistia will I triumph. Who will bring me into the strong city? who will lead me into Edom?"*[29]

The Lord speaks through Micah, telling His little flock, *"Arise ye, and depart; for this is not your rest: because it is polluted, it shall destroy you, even with a sore destruction."*[30] The Lord is saying, *"Move on children, for this land is no longer a place of rest. The land wherein you dwell has now become defiled before Me, and I stand now ready to judge this wicked nation. You must move on, to the place, which I have prepared for your rest. Follow me, and do not fear, for I the Lord will go before you, and I shall be your rear guard."*

"I will surely assemble, O Jacob, all of thee; I will surely gather the remnant of Israel; I will put them together as the sheep of Bozrah, as the flock in the midst of their fold: they shall make great noise by reason of the multitude of men."[31]

Oh, the manifold wisdom of God! Who can hear His voice? Who can discern what the Spirit is saying to the bride? *"I am full of power by the Spirit of the Lord, and of judgment, and of might, to declare unto Jacob his transgression, and to Israel his sin."* For the Spirit of the Holy Lord says now to His true bride. *"Come and enter your chambers, my people and I will close the door behind you. Rest in me for a little while, and wait for me while I judge my enemies. For the desolation which is coming shall shortly pass."*

"I said, Hear, I pray you, O heads of Jacob, and ye princes of the house of Israel; Is it not for you to know judgment? Who hate the good, and love the evil.... Then shall they cry unto the LORD, but he will not hear them: he will even hide his face from them at that time, as they have behaved themselves ill in their doings. Thus saith the LORD concerning the prophets that make my people err... and cry, Peace; and he that putteth not into their mouths.... Therefore night shall be unto you, that ye shall not have a vision; and it shall be dark unto you, that ye shall not divine; and the sun shall go down over the prophets, and the day shall be dark over them. "Then shall the seers be ashamed, and the diviners confounded: yea, they shall all cover their lips; for there is no answer of God. But truly I am full of power by the spirit of the LORD, and of judgment, and of might, to declare unto Jacob his transgression, and to Israel his sin" (Micah 3:1-8).*

THERE IS A REMNANT ACCORDING TO THE ELECTION OF GRACE

"Esaias also crieth concerning Israel, Though the number of the children of Israel be as the sand of the sea, a remnant shall be saved: For he will finish the work, and cut it short in righteousness: because a short work will the Lord make upon the earth. And as Esaias said before, Except the Lord of Sabaoth had left us a seed, we had been as Sodoma, and been made like unto Gomorrha" (Romans 9:27-29).

"Even so then at this present time also there is a remnant according to the election of grace" (Romans 11:5).

May the God of Israel, even our Father in heaven, open our eyes to see that everyone who is the bride of Christ is the true seed of

Abraham. They are grafted into the true vine, which is Yeshua, the Messiah of Israel. They share these precious promises of a great deliverance. May we have eyes of faith to trust God and obey His word and to no longer rely on the world, or the nations of the world for our safety. The Lord alone is our salvation. Let us submit to His will and surrender to His plan.

CHAPTER 7

"HERE IS THE MIND WHICH HAS WISDOM"
Revelation 17:8

The apostle John in the book of Revelation, Chapter 17, states that he sees a picture of the woman called, Mystery Babylon, seated upon many waters and riding the beast. This vision is one of the tests of the men of wisdom. Those who have the true understanding of God can both identify, and reveal the mystery of the woman, and the beast on which she rides.

I WILL TELL YOU THE MYSTERY OF THE WOMAN

"There came one of the seven angels which had the seven vials, and talked with me saying unto me, Come hither; I will show unto thee the judgment of the great whore that sitteth upon many waters: With whom the kings of the earth have committed fornication, and the inhabitants of the earth have been made drunk with the wine of her fornication. So he carried me away in the spirit into the wilderness: and I saw a woman sit upon a scarlet coloured beast, full of names of blasphemy, having seven heads and ten horns" (Revelation 17:1-3).

The woman, Mystery Babylon, is clothed with royal clothing signifying her honor and authority over all of mankind. In the eyes of the world, she is rich and wealthy, covered with gold and precious stones. To those who dwell in darkness, Mystery Babylon is admired and worshipped. She is the pride of the whole earth. People from all the nations of the world come unto her, seeking pleasures in the life of this present age from the wealth which is in her hand.

Her great riches are the splendor of her glory. Mystery Babylon is also the false religious system of man and the mother of apostate Christianity. The nations of the earth have been deceived by her spiritual immorality. Those who are perishing, who have been deceived by her false doctrines and damnable heresies, worship her.

In the eyes of God, she is full of abominations, and the filth of her fornication and wickedness. She is the mother of all the harlots and abominations of the earth! Not only is she full of wickedness and sin, but also she leads the nations into the same abominations, and the whole earth has been deceived by her vainglory! She spreads her wickedness among the whole world, thereby corrupting the nations, and seducing them in her immorality. She has promised the nations freedom and happiness, all the while leading them into the slavery of sin! She claims to have the light of the gospel, and to be the bride of Christ, but in reality, she is the bride of Satan, the great deceiver of the nations.

"And the woman was arrayed in purple and scarlet colour, and decked with gold and precious stones and pearls, having a golden cup in her hand full of abominations and filthiness of her fornication: And upon her forehead was a name written, **MYSTERY, BABYLON THE GREAT, THE MOTHER OF HARLOTS AND ABOMINATIONS OF THE EARTH.**"[1]

John witnesses the woman is drunk, intoxicated, having lost her right mind, she is delirious, not from wine, but from blood— the blood of the saints of the Most High God. Mystery Babylon has persecuted and martyred the saints of the God of Heaven throughout the ages. Though her true nature is revealed to John, he, too, in his mortal mind wonders with great admiration at her beauty and her wealth. The angel then admonishes John, *"Why are you marveling? I will tell you the mystery of the woman and the beast that carries her."* The woman has no power of her own, for she is being carried and lifted up by the beast himself. She is his testament to the peoples of the world, who follow her in her carnality and are seduced by her immorality.

"And I saw the woman drunken with the blood of the saints, and with the blood of the martyrs of Jesus: and when I saw her, I wondered with great admiration. And the angel said unto me,

Wherefore didst thou marvel? I will tell thee the mystery of the woman, and of the beast that carrieth her, which hath the seven heads and ten horns" (Revelation 17:6-7).

THE BEAST WAS, AND IS NOT, AND SHALL ASCEND AGAIN

The angel then begins to reveal the mystery of the beast, *"who was, and is not."* At the time of this writing, the beast is no longer in power, but he shall come again, ascending out of the bottomless pit, only to go into perdition for eternity.

"The beast that thou sawest was, and is not; and shall ascend out of the bottomless pit, and go into perdition: and they that dwell on the earth shall wonder, whose names were not written in the book of life from the foundation of the world.... And here is the mind which hath wisdom. The seven heads are seven mountains, on which the woman sitteth, And there are seven kings: five are fallen, and one is, and the other is not yet come; and when he cometh, he must continue a short space. And the beast that was, and is not, even he is the eighth, and is of the seven, and goeth into perdition. And the ten horns which thou sawest are ten kings, which have received no kingdom... but receive power as kings one hour with the beast."[2]

This is the riddle of Revelation 17 which the men of wisdom can discern:

1. The meaning of the seven heads of the beast.
2. The meaning of the seven mountains on which the woman sits.
3. The identity of the seven kings, five of which have fallen.
4. The identity of the beast itself, which is the eighth king, and of the seven.
5. The meaning of the ten horns, which rule as kings for one hour with the beast.
6. The identity of the woman, Mystery Babylon.

THE GOD OF HEAVEN GIVES WISDOM UNTO THE WISE

This mystery has been revealed by the Lord Himself, for the mind of man has not revealed this matter. The seven heads of the beast are both governments and institutions used by the beast to exercise authority and dominion over the earth. In its manifest forms, the beast appears as both kings and mountains. These heads signify authority, one who is over, or above, in the seat of power. At the time of the writing of this prophecy, the sixth king sits in Rome, represented by the two legs of iron of Daniel's prophecy.

The legs of iron are also symbolic, for under the rule of Rome the beast transformed itself, and divided into two diverse institutions of power. The beast is the great deceiver, and it is always seeking to hide its true nature from mankind. From the time of the Roman Empire, the beast began operating through two diverse institutions, which are seen in the vision as kings and mountains. From these two bases of power, the beast will seek to subdue the people of the earth under its tyranny and depravity.

THE BEAST IN ITS VISIBLE FORM: KINGDOMS OF GOVERNMENT

The beast first appears as seven kings. They are the visible form of the beast, appearing as human governments. The word for king in the original Greek is *"basileus"* (bas-il-yooce'), which means a foundation of power, a sovereign or a ruler. The seven kings represent seven diverse empires or governments, which will rule over the entire earth. Through the thrones of these seven kings, the beast himself, who is the eighth king, exercises his authority as the supreme ruler over the political realm of mankind.

The seven kings who conquer the earth under the authority of the beast are:

1. Assyria
2. Egypt
3. Babylon of the Chaldeans
4. The Medes and Persians
5. Greece under Alexander
6. Rome
7. The New World Order of United Nations

The first five kingdoms had fallen by the writing of this prophecy. Rome, the sixth, was still in power. In addition, the other, which is not yet come, is the New World Order. This final kingdom shall only abide for a little while—42 months. Each of the kingdoms of the beast conquered the known world at that time. The first two had risen and fallen from power when Daniel was shown the prophetic revelation of what was yet to come. They were excluded from images of the king's dream, having already passed from the scene, yet these were also of the beast exercising his dominion in the political history of man. Though appearing as independent sovereigns, these kings are puppets of the beast. The seven kings sit upon the throne of the beast, and rule in his authority, over the political realm of mankind.

THE BEAST HIMSELF IS THE EIGHTH KING

We are told, "*The beast himself is the eighth king, and he is of the seven.*" This tells us the true nature of the seven, for the beast himself has been king in these empires all along.

The beast does not rule in his own right, or in his own name, but rather rules through these horns, which he has lifted up—his seven kings. The identity of the beast, which "*was, and is not, but shall ascend out of the bottomless pit*" is Satan, the great dragon.

We are told, "*He was, and is not*" for he "*was*" in authority over all the earth at one time, until Jesus Christ took the sins of the world upon Himself. In shedding His Precious Blood as a perfect sacrifice to God in His death on the cross, Jesus stripped the devil of his power, having canceled the accusations against us. Then the beast was cast down and now "*he is not*" in authority. All power and authority are now in the hands of Jesus Christ, and the Holy Spirit who restrains the beast, will allow him a little time to rule the kingdom of the earth once again, in the last half of the 70th week of Daniel.

Scripture testifies of this judgment on the prince of the world, the beast. "*Of judgment, because the prince of this world is judged.*"[3] He was judged at the cross, and then he was cast out of heaven into the bottomless pit. "*Now is the judgment of this world: now shall the prince of this world be cast out.*"[4] The chosen of the Lord now have the authority, because the beast is no longer the ruler of the earth. "*I beheld Satan as lightning fall from heaven. Behold, I give unto you power to tread on serpents and scorpions, and over all the power of the enemy: and nothing shall by any means hurt you.*"[5] Oh, what praise and thanksgiving should this truth generate in our hearts! Lord Jesus, thank You for suffering and dying for our sins. Thank You for the power of Your Blood as the Lamb of God, and for Your Word, which is our testimony, whereby we can overcome the dragon. We praise Your Name, Lord Jesus, for Your amazing grace and the riches of Your mercy. Open our eyes to see the incredible price You paid to redeem our lives. Help us, Lord, to live holy and pure lives in this present hour that we may give glory and honor to You. Lord, give us ears to hear, and hearts to obey You, that we might glorify and lift up Your Holy Name. Amen

In the present hour, the beast is not in authority! Praise God! Jesus Christ is Lord and the keys of death and Hades are in His hand, yet the beast continues to work, and await the day, which is coming soon, when he will be released for a short time. *"For the mystery of iniquity doth already work: only he who now letteth will let, until he be taken out of the way. And then shall that Wicked be revealed, whom the Lord shall consume with the spirit of his mouth, and shall destroy with the brightness of his coming."*[6]

The Scripture testifies the little prince will come after the working of Satan. *"Even him, whose coming is after the working of Satan with all power and signs and lying wonders, And with all deceivableness of unrighteousness in them that perish; because they received not the love of the truth, that they might be saved. And for this cause God shall send them strong delusion, that they should believe a lie: That they all might be damned who believed not the truth, but had pleasure in unrighteousness."*[7]

The prince is the seventh king of the beast. He will lead the seventh and final kingdom. The beast is himself the eighth king who works in his people. The sons of darkness abide in the beast, even as the true believers, the chosen elect of God, abide in Christ.

THE SEVEN TRUE SHEPHERDS OF ISRAEL

The seven kings of the beast are also a counterfeit of seven shepherds whom the Lord will raise up in the last days, as prophesied in the book of Micah, chapter 5. This prophecy contains details concerning the First and Second Coming of our Lord. Most people can identify the prophecies of the First Coming. We are told that the Messiah Who is to be ruler in all of Israel is He whose *"going forth is from everlasting."* The prophet declares that the Messiah is the Lord, for He comes forth from *"everlasting!"* Micah also prophesies that Jesus will come from Bethlehem.

> *"They shall smite the judge of Israel with a rod upon the cheek. But thou, Beth-lehem Ephratah, though thou be little among the thousands of Judah, yet out of thee shall he come forth unto me that is to be ruler in Israel; whose goings forth have been from of old, from everlasting."*[8]

All of these prophecies were fulfilled literally by Jesus Christ in His First Coming. The prophet then tells us from that time, which is the First Coming of Jesus, the Lord will give up His nation Israel until the time that she who is travailing has brought forth. The meaning of the travailing of Israel, and the last days' birth of the kingdom, will be discussed in chapter eight, *"The LORD will be the hope of His people."*

This is the time for Israel to give birth again and for the remnant to return to the land of Israel *"and they shall abide"* for *"he* (Jesus) *shall* (now) *be great unto the ends of the earth."* The power of Jesus Christ as LION OF JUDAH will be made manifest on this planet in greatness unseen in the history of man, and it will extend to the very ends of the earth! Oh, people of God, wait until you see what our Lord has planned! Do not fear, chosen ones, your God is coming again, just as He promised, and He will walk with you right through the fire! Micah then tells us, *"This man* (Jesus) *shall be the peace"* when the Assyrian shall invade the land, which is in the final battle of Ezekiel 38.

Then *"we* (Israel) *shall raise against him seven shepherds, and eight principal men."* These seven shepherds are the seven overseers appointed by the Lord as apostles to His remnant during the Tribulation. They are His seven kings, and He Himself is the eighth principal man. The seven kings of the beast, and the beast himself who is also the eighth, are just one more counterfeit of the true work of God.

> *"Therefore will he give them up, until the time that she which travaileth hath brought forth: then the remnant of his brethren shall return unto the children of Israel. And he shall stand and feed in the strength of the LORD, in the majesty of the name of the LORD his*

God; and they shall abide: for now shall he be great unto the ends of the earth. And this man shall be the peace, when the Assyrian shall come into our land: and when he shall tread in our palaces, then shall we raise against him seven shepherds, and eight principal men" (Micah 5:3-5).

And having raised up seven shepherds, the Lord uses them to waste the land of Assyria with the sword. *"And they shall waste the land of Assyria with the sword, and the land of Nimrod in the entrances thereof: thus shall he deliver us from the Assyrian, when he cometh into our land, and when he treadeth within our borders."*[9] These seven men shall lift their hands and pray. Then the sword will fall on the enemies of Israel.

These are but a few prophecies of the second 3-½ year ministry of Jesus Christ as the LION OF JUDAH. Read on in Micah chapter five, for the prophet reveals more about the mighty remnant, who will walk as lions in the anointing of the Lord Jesus during the last days.

The seven kings are an exact counterfeit of the true government God has established for His people in the last days of the tribulation, which are the seven shepherds.

THE SEVEN MOUNTAINS OF THE BEAST

The seven mountains are a counterfeit of another type. The Greek word for "mountain" is *"oros"* (or'-os), which means to rise, or to be lifted up, above the plain. This counterfeit lifts itself up in another realm, *outside of and separate* from the world of government. Again, the objective of the beast is the same. These mountains are of the beast kingdom in another form, manifesting his deception upon the souls of mankind. We are told that the mountains are the seven hills on which the woman sits. The city of seven hills is Rome.

At the time of the prophecy, Mystery Babylon had her seat of authority in Rome and the legs of iron were ruling the nations. This is when the beast divided his religious system from his political government. In all the prior kingdoms of Babylon, the religious institution and the king were united, for the emperor was a god. This is the first instance of the separation of the religion of Babylon from the state, for, during the rule of Rome, the secular institutions of church and state separated for the first time. These secular institutions are created by the beast and are used to deceive mankind.

With the beginning of the collapse of Rome, the emperor formally organized the political power of the state under a separate religious institution, which he called the Holy Roman Catholic Church. In Revelation 17, we are told Mystery Babylon has blasphemous names written on her. Blasphemy is to call that which is unholy, Holy. Thus, the very name of this religious branch of the Roman government is blasphemy.

Kings bear but a short life span, and then their kingdoms are given to another, whereas mountains endure throughout the millennium. They change not. Regardless of which king sits upon the throne of man, these mountains endure and are unchanging through the ages. They are not affected by the death of the monarch, for the mountain is an institution that is greater than the men who rule through her.

The exact word for "mountain" is to rise, to lift up above the plains. These mountains are the rulers of the false religions of man including apostate Christianity that began in Rome. The seven mountains are the apostate religions of the seven empires of beast. The mountains as religious institutions continue their power following the collapse of the Roman Empire. The ten toes, which survive the collapse of the Roman Empire, are divided under the two legs. Five toes now stand under each leg of the beast.

The five toes represent five religious institutions, which now rule over the five political areas that rose out of ancient Rome. They are all apostate perversions of the true gospel of Jesus Christ. The five institutions may comprise the following false churches:

1. The Roman Catholic Church
2. The Greek Orthodox Church
3. The English Anglican Church
4. The German Lutheran Church
5. The Russian Orthodox Church

Each of these churches was founded in the truth of the gospel, but became corrupted and fell into apostasy! Many true saints of the kingdom are still found within these false churches, ignorant of the deception into which they were born. Thus, the beast continues his rule over the people of the earth, now as the great deceiver, corrupting their souls. Each of these institutions martyred millions of believers who refused to deny the truth of Jesus Christ and His holy word.

Thus, we know that Mystery Babylon, which is the harlot, is both the government of this world, which is opposed to God, and the false religious system of the earth. She is indeed a mystery, for who could have known such deception would come?

THE MYSTERY OF THE TEN KINGS

The ten kings are descendants of the ten toes, which survive the collapse of the Roman Empire. These kings will come to power from within the beast political and religious institutions, which have ruled over the centuries. The founder of the Order of the Illuminati was a Jesuit priest named Adam Weishaupt. The small league he formed is an alliance between the royal families of Europe and the leaders of their false religions. The ten kings, who come to power with the beast for one hour, are the literal descendents of this small group of people who call themselves the Elite.

They are the political rulers in the last days who seize the kingdom by intrigue. This occurs at the end of the age, and the ten kings are the last days' rulers of the Order of the Illuminati, who bring the New World Order to power. Their purpose is to create the one world government, and to then give their power to the beast.

As they come to power, the ten kings shall turn and hate the woman. Their first act will be to destroy the woman. *"These have one mind, and shall give their power and strength unto the beast. These shall make war with the Lamb, and the Lamb shall overcome them: for he is Lord of lords, and King of kings: and they that are with him are called, and chosen, and faithful."*[10] In destroying the modern nation of Babylon, the United States of America, which rules the earth at the time of the end, they create the world crisis, which allows them to seize the throne.

They are responsible for World War III, after which the nations will surrender their sovereignty to the beast. When the ten kings seize the kingdom at the time of the end, Rome is no longer the ruling empire for Mystery Babylon has risen again, on a distant shore, far away over the great sea, in the new world called America. The angel tells John that modern Babylon is seated upon many nations, and peoples and tongues. This is America in the last days, before the rule of the Antichrist.

The rulers of the Illuminati hate America; they are even now planning to destroy her, to make her desolate, and naked, and to burn her cities with fire. *"The waters which thou sawest, where the whore sitteth, are peoples, and multitudes, and nations, and tongues. And the ten horns which thou sawest upon the beast, these shall hate the whore, and shall make her desolate and naked, and shall eat her flesh, and burn her with fire. For God hath put in their hearts to fulfil his will, and to agree, and give their kingdom unto the beast, until the words of God shall be fulfilled."*[11]

We are told Mystery Babylon is the great nation which rules the earth at the time of the end, immediately before the prince comes to power. *"And the woman which thou sawest is that great city, which reigneth over the kings of the earth."*[12] This is America, who is also called the daughter of Babylon, for she is a descendent of the final King of Babylon, who will rule the final one-world government from the throne of England.

LET HIM WITH WISDOM CALCULATE
THE NUMBER OF THE BEAST

The apostle John is shown the beast rising up out of the sea of humanity in Revelation 13. As the beast rises from the sea and comes to power, it has the head of a lion, the body of a leopard and the feet of a bear.

"And I stood upon the sand of the sea, and saw a beast rise up out of the sea, having seven heads and ten horns, and upon his horns ten crowns, and upon his heads the name of blasphemy. And the beast which I saw was like unto a leopard, and his feet were as the feet of a bear, and his mouth as the mouth of a lion: and the dragon gave him his power, and his seat, and great authority.... And he causeth all, both small and great, rich and poor, free and bond, to receive a mark in their right hand, or in their foreheads: And that no man might buy or sell, save he that had the mark, or the name of the beast, or the number of his name. Here is wisdom. Let him that hath

understanding count the number of the beast: for it is the number of a man; and his number is Six hundred threescore and six."[13]

The beast will require all the citizens of the earth who dwell within his kingdom to take a mark on their hand or forehead. This is the mark of the beast, and it is the number of his name, 666. The technology to imprint the mark was first developed in 1959. The Order introduced the first credit cards in the same year to begin the conditioning of the public. These last years the people have been made ready psychologically to accept the mark of the beast as an identity and financial tracking technology for security and convenience.

In 1979, I had a series of five interviews with IBM. In my last interview, I was with one of their senior executives. At the end of the interview he asked me the standard final question, *"Do you have any questions for me?"* *"I only have one. I have learned from five independent sources within your company, that IBM has developed an infrared laser tattoo device to imprint a laser tattoo on the hand or the forehead of every person, to identify them for the electronic money system which is coming, and that your company is presently storing these devices in warehouses in Europe and America, and that the identification mark is three sets of six digits. Is this true?"*

"That is old news" was his only reply. Everyone in the kingdom of the beast will bear the mark. That is why the remnant must flee to the wilderness prepared by God. You will neither be able to buy nor sell anything in the beast cities. They will hunt you, and seek to kill you, but if you have been chosen in His remnant, He will hide you, but you must soon leave the kingdom of the beast.

THE MYSTERY OF THE BEAST AND THE NUMBER OF HIS NAME 666

Prophecy often has both a literal and a symbolic application. The symbols used to describe the beast tell us about the nature of his actions and identify his throne of power. First, it has the head of a lion. This tells us the seat of authority of the beast will come out of England, which is symbolized by the lion. Second, it has the body of the leopard. The leopard comes from the Nazi empire pictured in Daniel's vision. The body of the beast symbolizes how the beast will operate. It moves with its body.

The beast empire shall be organized with a governmental system similar to the Nazi party, and will subdue the whole earth with the same lightening war tactics of Nazi Germany. Even now, the police state tactics and gun control laws being implemented in the USA are a carbon copy of those used in Nazi Germany. The recent gun control bill passed in the USA is an exact duplicate of the one that Nazi Germany passed following the Reichstag fire. The feet of the beast are from the bear. It will trample its subjects with the same brutal oppression of the Soviet empire. The beast will have its seat of power in the royal family of Windsor, while its tactics will be borrowed from the Nazi era and its brutality will be like unto the Soviet bloodshed of Stalin and Lenin. Lastly, the union of these three beasts is symbolic of the United Nations of the New World Order, which this beast will head. And America, pictured as eagles wings has been judged by the time the beast rises out of the sea of humanity.

THE HERALDIC BEAST OF THE HOUSE OF WINDSOR

There is also a literal fulfillment of this Scripture. Let us examine the symbol of the royal family of Windsor carefully. It is called the heraldic beast. It has the head of the lion, the body of the leopard and the feet of a bear. This is the exact picture in Revelation 13. The royal family of Windsor has been flying this flag for 500 years, and no one noticed! The Antichrist comes as a prince out of the house of Windsor.

When we are told to calculate the number of the beast, the true answer will be derived using the Hebrew gematria number system of assigning numbers to 22 letters, the length of the Hebrew alphabet. Let me present it as follows:

A	1	F	6	K	20	P	70	U	300
B	2	G	7	L	30	Q	80	V	400
C	3	H	8	M	40	R	90	W	0
D	4	I	9	N	50	S	100	X	0
E	5	J	10	O	60	T	200	Z	0

He is the most widely know politician in the world today. His face has been put in front of every nation on the globe every two weeks for the last fourteen years. You have seen him often. Daniel tells us he is *"the prince who shall come"* in his own name, representing his father, the Devil. He is the son of perdition and he makes his appearance as a prince.

PRINCE CHARLES OF WALES

(70+90+9+50+3+5)   (3+8+1+90+30+5+100)   (60+6)
(0+1+30+5+100) =

666

The name Charles means, *"man."* It is the number of a man; it is the number of a *"Charles."* Believers in Israel have translated the prince's name into Hebrew. The Hebrew name also totals 666. Others have run the calculation in Greek. Again, the answer is the same—666. English is the language of the modern world. Greek is the language of the ancient world. Hebrew is the language of the prophets themselves. In three languages, the prince is identified.

The symbol of Wales is the red dragon. At the prince's coronation, the queen pointed to the banners of the red dragon, which were flying over the assembly and said, *"This dragon has given you his power, his throne and his great authority."*[14] She quoted the verse in Revelation, which would be spoken of the beast. He responded by saying *"This day I have become your Lord man and am worthy of your earthly worship."*[15]

His mother the Queen has been quoted speaking of Charles saying, *"He is the chosen one."*[16] His coronation ceremony was taped and you can get a copy on the Internet if you wish to review this for yourself. The coat of arms for Prince Charles contains all the symbols of the Antichrist as revealed in the Scriptures.

He has ten heraldic beasts in this coat of arms. He is first monarch ever to have ten. He is the head of the Order of the Illuminati and is the head of world-wide Freemasonry. The family tree of Prince Charles shows him to be a descendant of King David of Israel. *"According to Anglo-Israelites, the queen descends from King David.... The queen's lineage, published in 1977 as 'The Illustrious*

Lineage of The Royal House of Britain' not only concurs, but depicts her household as 'The House of David—The Royal Line.'" [17]

He is the most popular international figure in Israel today. In late 1996, Israeli television ran a special on the prince. At the end of the show, they disclosed his lineage chart showing him to be the *"son of David"* and the rabbis left the viewers with the question—could he be the Messiah? No. He is the false messiah, the Antichrist. Let him who has wisdom count the number of the beast, for it is the number of a man. It is the number of a Charles. *"There is more evidence to prove that he (Prince Charles) is the anti-messiah than most people have to prove their own identity.*

"He has been involved in the occult.... He wants to be king of Europe. Is he the anti-messiah? I'll let the Lord reveal him at the abomination of desolation." [18] Is he involved with the Middle East Peace Accord? His personal attorney arranged the first meetings, which took place in Norway. Was he at Rabin's funeral to witness the confirming of the *"covenant with the grave?"* He sat in the first row in the seventh seat.

CHAPTER 8

"THE LORD WILL BE THE HOPE OF HIS PEOPLE"
Joel 3:16

The prophecies of the Bible are foundational to the faith of the people of the God. Over one-third of the Scripture is devoted to prophecy, much of which deals with the last days and the coming Great Day of the LORD. If the vision of prophecy is lost, the foundation is destroyed and the people soon fall into ruin. *"If the foundations be destroyed, what can the righteous do?"*[1] Scripture testifies to the importance of prophecy and its proper understanding. *"For through him we both have access by one Spirit unto the Father.*

> *"Now therefore ye are no more strangers and foreigners, but fellow citizens with the saints, and of the household of God; And are built upon the foundation of the apostles and prophets, Jesus Christ himself being the chief corner stone."*[2]

THE TESTIMONY OF JESUS IS THE SPIRIT OF PROPHECY

The message of all of the prophets is the revelation of Jesus Christ. They are His witness and the testimony that Jesus is the Messiah of Israel. He is our kinsman redeemer. He is both our peace and our salvation. The testimony of Jesus is the Spirit of all prophecy:

> *"I am thy fellow servant, and of thy brethren that have the testimony of Jesus: worship God: for the testimony of Jesus is the spirit of prophecy."*[3]

186

Those who ignore or dismiss prophecy, do so to their own harm, for the prophecies have been given as our instructions, and as a warning to us that we might take heed. Solomon writes in Proverbs 22:3 that the prudent, those with insight, who can see beyond the surface into what lies ahead, will hide themselves from the evil: *"A prudent man foreseeth the evil, and hideth himself: but the simple pass on, and are punished."*

NO PROPHECY IS OF PRIVATE INTERPRETATION

Many dismiss the study of prophecy based on an incomplete knowledge of Scripture. They have been taught no man can know the day or the hour, so they assume there is no value in watching, as the Lord commands. They also assume that prophecy is subject to various interpretations. It is not; there is one true interpretation, which is revealed by the Spirit. Many false teachers have come, just as Jesus warned, but those who have the Holy Spirit can discern the true from the false.

"We have also a more sure word of prophecy; whereunto ye do well that ye take heed, as unto a light that shineth in a dark place, until the day dawn, and the day star arise in your hearts: Knowing this first, that no prophecy of the scripture is of any private interpretation. For the prophecy came not in old time by the will of man: but holy men of God spake as they were moved by the Holy Ghost."[4]

THOSE THINGS, WHICH MUST SHORTLY COME TO PASS

The Revelation of John was given to show the bondservants of Jesus those things that must shortly come to pass. The message of the book was a specific prophecy to the remnant who are alive in the last days, and was meant for their specific instruction.

"The Revelation of Jesus Christ, which God gave unto him, to show unto his servants things which must shortly come to pass; and he sent and signified it by his angel unto his servant John." (Revelation 1:1).

THE PRUDENT SHALL KEEP SILENT IN THAT TIME

Prophecy is not only important; it is critical to the people to whom it was sent. Through prophecy, the Lord provides guidance and direction for these days. The prophet Amos speaks also of the time of judgment as a time when *"the prudent shall keep silence."* Why? Because the days are evil and they are hiding themselves.

They know from the prophecy it is a dangerous time, where one does not draw any unnecessary attention to oneself. Indeed, wisdom today is to do nothing but what the Lord commands. We should be praying about every decision, taking nothing for granted, for these days are full of great evil, and the time is very short.

Think not that the prudent will stop everyone they meet to warn them of the approaching lion, for they know better. The citizens of Babylon want nothing to do with this message. The Babylonians wish to continue sleeping, and simply enjoy the last days of their cruise on the great ship Titanic. Nor will they hear, for their hearts are hardened, so it is better to keep silent, and only speak when the Lord commands:

"Therefore the prudent shall keep silence in that time; for it is an evil time" (Amos 5:13). "Redeeming the time, because the days are evil. Wherefore be ye not unwise, but understanding what the will of the Lord is" (Ephesians 5:16-17).

Those who are prudent can foresee the day of evil and they will take note. Indeed, when you finally wake from your sleep, and recognize this is really happening, you will diligently seek the Lord, and ask Him what He calls you to do. In Jeremiah 4:7 we are told, *"the lion has come out of the thicket."*

The lion is no longer in hiding, but is clearly visible for the prudent to see. The verse continues *"and the destroyer of the gentiles is on his way."* This is the Antichrist, which is the destroyer of the Gentiles. He is the mouth of the Lion, the head of the beast.

THE WISE SHALL UNDERSTAND

The angel who answered Daniel at the end of his prophecy speaks of those who are prudent in the last days, those who can understand that the prophecies are being fulfilled saying, *"none of the wicked shall understand, but the wise shall understand."*[5] We are also told that at that time, many shall run to and fro, and the knowledge of mankind shall be greatly increased.

"But thou, O Daniel, shut up the words, and seal the book, even to the time of the end: many shall run to and fro, and knowledge shall be increased" (Daniel 12:4).

"And he said, Go thy way, Daniel: for the words are closed up and sealed till the time of the end. Many shall be purified, and made white, and tried; but the wicked shall do wickedly: and none of the wicked shall understand; but the wise shall understand" (Daniel 12:9-10).

MEN'S HEARTS SHALL FAIL THEM FOR FEAR

This chapter is written to the remnant, and those who are prudent, to encourage you to look to the Lord, for He is our hope and our peace. They are the wise that shall understand. The Lord knew these days would come, and told us in advance *"in the world ye shall have tribulation: but be of good cheer; I have overcome the world!"*[6]

We are supposed to be of good cheer. It is God's plan that we would rejoice as we see these things which will terrify the nations of the earth. We are to be a haven of rest and peace, as a witness to the people of the earth, that their hearts could find peace. Yet the events of the end of the age and the soon-coming of the Lord are fearful if seen only through the eyes of the natural man. Great and terrible judgments will soon fall upon our land, and then upon the entire earth. Jesus spoke of the things saying:

"And there shall be signs in the sun, and in the moon, and in the stars; and upon the earth distress of nations, with perplexity; the sea and the waves roaring; Men's hearts failing them for fear, and for looking after those things which are coming on the earth: for the powers of heaven shall be shaken. And then shall they see the Son of man coming in a cloud with power and great glory. And when these things begin to come to pass, then look up, and lift up your heads; for your redemption draweth nigh" (Luke 21:25-28).

In the Lord's own words, we know during the last days there will be signs in the sun, the moon and the stars, and great distress of nations, with perplexity. The heathen, who do not know the Lord, will have no idea what is happening as these signs begin to herald the soon-coming King! The sea in Scripture is symbolic of the people of the earth, and its waves will be roaring.

They will be crying out, gripped with fear such as they have never known. The hearts of the people will literally fail, and panic will seize the nations of the earth, as they see these things coming to pass. There shall be a great shaking upon the earth, and the very powers of heaven shall be shaken!

HIS THUNDER ANNOUNCES THE COMING STORM

A great storm is approaching our world. When a storm approaches, the first evidence is the sound of distant thunder. The coming storm is spiritual, and the thunder is the prophetic word of our God. *"His thunder announces the coming storm; even the cattle make known its approach."*[7] Just as cattle can sense a coming storm before humans, so to are the people of the Lord who can hear the prophetic word, and know the storm will soon be revealed.

The prophetic voice of the Lord announces the word of God as thunder. *"The voice of thy thunder was in the heaven: the lightnings lightened the world: the earth trembled and shook."*[8] The Lord uses His voice of thunder to announce the hour of judgment. *"Hast thou an arm like God? or canst thou thunder with a voice like him?"*[9] Today, all over America, the Lord is announcing the coming storm.

One of David Wilkerson's newsletters was aptly entitled *"The only Hope in the coming storm."* The storm is about to begin and the rain, which is now falling, is the word of the Lord. *"My doctrine shall drop as the rain, my speech shall distil as the dew, as the small rain upon the tender herb, and as the showers upon the grass."*[10]

The word of God is rain, and only those who can discern the Spirit can receive this latter-day rain. The Lord has been speaking His word of warning to America for years, but the people are all deaf, dumb and blind. The nation has come to the point of no return, and only a few recognize the hour is upon us. *"The days of visitation are come, the days of recompense are come; Israel shall know it: the prophet is a fool, the spiritual man is mad, for the multitude of thine iniquity, and the great hatred."*[11]

The proper meaning of this verse is the prophet is thought to be a fool, and the spiritual ones are seen as crazy! Why? Because the people are so backslidden and blinded by their sin, they cannot discern the word of God. *"Woe unto you America, and those who stand among you to mock My word, saith the Lord! Is not My word fire, declares the Lord! It shall burn all who have betrayed My holiness, and despised My grace."*

THEY SHALL SEE THE SON OF MAN COMING

Jesus is speaking of the tribulation period itself, when He says *"then shall they see the Son of man coming in a cloud with power and great glory"* This is a picture of the days immediately preceding the Second Coming of the Lord. Jesus tells his own, when you see these things come to pass, and the men of the earth who don't know the Lord are literally dying from fear, *"you lift up your heads for your redemption is drawing near!"*

Jesus tells us, His faithful remnant, to lift our heads, do not be downcast and full of fear like the heathen, for our redemption is coming. How will the bride of Christ be able to lift their heads in the midst of the most terrible time the world has even known? Only by looking to the Lord, keeping our eyes and faith upon Him, and by trusting His word. Dear reader, these days are described by the prophets as *"The Day of the LORD."*

It is His day, and none other! Jesus Christ will be in complete control of everything! We who know the Lord can rejoice, but we must learn to walk in faith, not trusting our own understanding, nor looking on the outward circumstances, but looking to His word and His precious promises to His faithful ones.

I WILL PROTECT THAT WHICH IS MINE

The Lord is coming to bring the final judgment and if you are not right with God, you have every reason to fear! Dear saint, if you know Him, and have opened the door of your heart to Him as Lord, you have no reason to fear anything but the Lord! *"And hereby we do know that we know him, if we keep his commandments. He that saith, I know him, and keepeth not his commandments, is a liar, and the truth is not in him. But whoso keepeth his word, in him verily is the love of God perfected: hereby know we that we are in him. He that saith he abideth in him ought himself also so to walk, even as he walked."*[12]

Understand this, to find Him you must first seek Him with your whole heart, and turn from your sins. The delivered remnant that will endure this hour must walk in obedience. If you have bowed in humble submission to the Lord, you have no reason to fear anything. Fear only the Lord, for this is the beginning of wisdom.

I was shown the Day of the LORD in the fall of 1996 and for seven days, the Spirit of the Lord burned upon my soul, with a fire I cannot describe. I spent hours each day weeping and crying out to the Lord. Every time I began to pray, I would fall to the ground on my face before my God. The Lord had shown me in the Spirit what would come.

I witnessed the severe judgment, which will first fall upon the church. I was caught up, in a vision, and I found myself standing in one of the detention camps, with my wife and children. In the process of separating from them, I experienced a level of heartbreak I could never have imagined exists on this earth. As the vision ended, I fell to the ground on my face screaming and weeping as I cried out, *"Lord, what must we do to be saved from these judgments?"* Jesus answered me in a clear audible voice saying, *"I will protect that which is mine, everything else will be destroyed."*

This, then, is the test, dear friend. Are you the Lord's, do you belong to Him? Does He own your life? Have you died to self, surrendering all to Him and His will? If you have, and you are His, you have nothing to fear. Only fear the Lord, for that is the beginning of wisdom. This is the very word Jesus spoke Himself in the gospel. How we failed to discern His true meaning: *"For whosoever will save his life shall lose it; but whosoever shall lose his life for my sake and the gospel's, the same shall save it."*[13]

IN THE FEAR OF THE LORD IS STRONG CONFIDENCE

I also asked the Lord what should we do specifically. He told me, *"Search the scriptures, for the detailed instructions for this hour are in the Word of God."* I remember feeling a sigh of relief, thinking, *"That's good, we can trust everything we find in the Word."* The Word of our God declares the starting point on the road to wisdom and understanding is the fear of the Lord. *"The fear of the LORD is the beginning of knowledge: but fools despise wisdom and instruction."*[14]

"The fear of the LORD is the beginning of wisdom: and the knowledge of the holy is understanding."[15] *"In the fear of the LORD is strong confidence: and his children shall have a place of refuge. The fear of the LORD is a fountain of life, to depart from the snares of death."*[16]

The Lord Jesus Himself had *"quick understanding in the fear of the Lord."* He is our example, and our king, and if He feared God, so should we. For if a man truly fears the Lord, he will fear nothing else, for our God is a sovereign king; He is the very King of the Universe and nothing can harm us without His consent.

> *"And there shall come forth a rod out of the stem of Jesse, and a Branch shall grow out of his roots: And the spirit of the LORD shall rest upon him, the spirit of wisdom and understanding, the spirit of counsel and might, the spirit of knowledge and of the fear of the LORD; And shall make him of quick understanding in the fear of the LORD: and he shall not judge after the sight of his eyes, neither reprove after the hearing of his ears: But with righteousness shall he judge the poor, and reprove with equity for the meek of the earth: and he shall smite the earth with the rod of his mouth, and with the breath of his lips shall he slay the wicked."*[17]

SEEK HOLINESS WITHOUT WHICH
NO MAN SHALL SEE GOD

The elect of God are distinguished by their holiness unto the Lord. *"Follow peace with all men, and holiness, without which no man shall see the Lord."*[18] Holiness means to be separated and set apart unto God. The holiness of the Lord is to be manifest in every area of our lives. Learning to submit to the Lord in obedience is the first step in our sanctification. The chosen have a choice. Will you allow Jesus to be Lord in your life?

The remnant delivered by the Lord walk before Him in holiness. Isaiah speaks of the path walked by the remnant, *"And an highway shall be there, and a way, and it shall be called The way of holiness; the unclean shall not pass over it; but it shall be for those: the wayfaring men, though fools, shall not err therein."*[19]

The holiness of the righteous is received by faith in Jesus Christ, but it must be received and appropriated into our lives. The perfect will of the Father is that we walk before Him in obedience and holiness, being sanctified from all dead works of the flesh, submitting all to His will, that His glory would be manifest in our lives. This is the heart of the Lord for His holy ones, whom He calls His remnant.

"Upon mount Zion shall be deliverance, and there shall be holiness; and the house of Jacob shall possess their possessions. And the house of Jacob shall be a fire, and the house of Joseph a flame, and the house of Esau for stubble, and they shall kindle in them, and devour them."[20] Mount Zion is the city of God, and the place where the Lord will dwell within His people. It is the spiritual temple built by the Lord Himself in the hearts of His chosen ones. All who are found in Zion in the last days walk in holiness.

Their hearts have been purged of the idolatry of the present age, and the lusts of the flesh, which have defiled the many who think themselves saved. *"Having therefore these promises, dearly beloved, let us cleanse ourselves from all filthiness of the flesh and spirit, perfecting holiness in the fear of God."*[21] The night is far spent, and the new day is dawning. It is time to focus on our total redemption, and to lay aside the works of the flesh, which so easily entangle us. *"Be ye holy; for I am holy."*[22]

The Lord is about to anoint again His holy people, who honor Him with their hearts, and not just their lips. If we wish to be found among the remnant, then we must cleanse our hearts, touch not the unclean thing, and return to the Lord. Repent, fast and pray, for the Lord is merciful, and He has promised to hear us. The day you seek Him with your whole heart, then you shall find Him.

"Holiness means to be set apart from the ordinary and the common. The chosen have a choice. The Holy Spirit is calling His chosen into a higher realm of spiritual reality and is revealing Himself through His Son, and awakening a holy and awesome revelation of His true holiness. There must be an opening of our spiritual eyes. When the high priest was dressed in his holy garments, the very last article to be placed upon his head was the holy crown. This crown had the engravings of the signet, Holiness to the Lord. The signet was a sign of the sealing of the mind of the priest."[23]

The Lord declares the way to life is straight and narrow, and very few find it. *"[S]trait is the gate, and narrow is the way, which leadeth unto life, and few there be that find it."*[24] The word for "narrow" is *"thlibo"*[25] (thlee'-bo) which means to afflict, trouble, suffer tribulation and narrow. It is through much tribulation that we enter the kingdom. The chosen ones are *"few."* The word means little. The chosen ones, who separate themselves from the company of the many who are called, are those who follow on to know the Lord at all costs. They are the remnant, and the little flock.

Jesus warned us to watch and pray that we may be included in the remnant that is accounted worthy to stand and endure the Tribulation. *"Watch ye therefore, and pray always, that ye may be accounted worthy to escape all these things that shall come to pass, and to stand before the Son of man."* (Luke21:36). The word "to stand" is *"histemi"*[26] (his-tay-mee), which means to literally abide, be appointed, continue, stanch, and to stand in the presence of the Lord. The word "before" is *"emprosthen"*[27] (em'-pros-then), which means in front of, in the presence of, or literally in place of. The word for the phrase "that ye may be accounted worthy" is *"katis-chuo"*[28] (kat-is-khoo'-o), which means to overpower and to prevail against. The word "to escape" is *"ekpheugo"*[29] (ek-fyoo'-go), which means to flee out and escape.

The remnant are those appointed to stand in His place during the last half of the 70th week. They are the overcomers to whom the seven promises of the book of Revelation apply:

"To him that overcometh will I give to eat of the tree of life, which is in the midst of the paradise of God.... He that overcometh shall not be hurt of the second death.... To him that overcometh will I give to eat of the hidden manna, and will give him a white stone, and in the stone a new name written, which no man knoweth saving he that receiveth it. And he that overcometh, and keepeth my works unto the end, to him will I give power over the nations: And he shall rule them with a rod of iron; as the vessels of a potter shall they be broken to shivers: even as I received of my Father. And I will give him the morning star. He that overcometh, the same shall be clothed in white raiment; and I will not blot out his name out of the book of life, but I will confess his name before my Father, and before his an-

gels.... *Him that overcometh will I make a pillar in the temple of my God, and he shall go no more out: and I will write upon him the name of my God, and the name of the city of my God, which is new Jerusalem, which cometh down out of heaven from my God: and I will write upon him my new name. To him that overcometh will I grant to sit with me in my throne, even as I also overcame, and am set down with my Father in his throne. He that hath an ear, let him hear what the Spirit saith unto the churches.*"[30]

"And I heard a great voice out of heaven saying, Behold, the taber-nacle of God is with men, and he will dwell with them, and they shall be his people, and God himself shall be with them, and be their God. And God shall wipe away all tears from their eyes; and there shall be no more death, neither sorrow, nor crying, neither shall there be any more pain: for the former things are passed away. And he that sat upon the throne said, Behold, I make all things new. And he said unto me, Write: for these words are true and faithful. And he said unto me, It is done. I am Alpha and Omega, the beginning and the end. I will give unto him that is athirst of the fountain of the water of life freely. He that overcometh shall inherit all things; and I will be his God, and he shall be my son" (Revelation 21:2-8).

HE HAS CHOSEN US IN HIM
BEFORE THE FOUNDATION OF THE WORLD

Before the foundations of the world, God established the covenant of faith, which was the promise to our father Abraham. This is the eternal covenant, for it spans both eternity past and future. *"Blessed be the God and Father of our Lord Jesus Christ, who hath blessed us with all spiritual blessings in heavenly places in Christ: According as he hath chosen us in him before the founda-tion of the world, that we should be holy and without blame be-fore him in love."*[31]

The true children of Abraham, who are the remnant of Israel, were predestined by God to participate in the holy covenant. From the beginning of eternity past, the Father chose us for adoption into His family through this covenant of faith. Having accepted us in the Beloved, God provided redemption through His own blood in the eternal covenant.

"Having predestinated us unto the adoption of children by Jesus Christ to himself, according to the good pleasure of his will, To the praise of the glory of his grace, Wherein he hath made us accepted in the beloved. In whom we have redemption through his blood, the forgiveness of sins, according to the riches of his grace; wherein he hath abounded toward us in all wisdom and prudence."[32] This was His promise to Abraham from the beginning. *"The Lord will provide himself a lamb."*

This is the mystery of our great salvation, and it was revealed in Jesus Christ. *"Having made known unto us the mystery of his will, according to his good pleasure which he hath purposed in himself: That in the dispensation of the fulness of times he might gather together in one all things in Christ, both which are in heaven, and which are on earth; even in him."*[33]

The promise of God to His elect was of an inheritance, and He has done this according to His own will. The evidence of the covenant in our lives is the promise of the Holy Spirit, which is the seal that we are God's own possession. *"In whom also we have obtained an inheritance, being predestinated according to the purpose of him who worketh all things after the counsel of his own will: That we should be to the praise of his glory, who first trusted in Christ.*

"In whom ye also trusted, after that ye heard the word of truth, the gospel of your salvation: in whom also after that ye believed, ye were sealed with that holy Spirit of promise, Which is the earnest of our inheritance until the redemption of the purchased possession, unto the praise of his glory."[34]

THE LORD SHALL ROAR FROM ZION

In the prophecies of Joel, we are given a picture of the multitudes, which will gather, in the valley of decision—the valley of Jezreel, where the final battle of Armageddon will be fought. The Lord will roar out of Zion, shaking the heavens and the earth with the sound of His voice! When the earth begins to shake, and the nations are gripped in fear, the Lord will be the only hope of His people.

He will become the strength of the children of Israel. Our only hope is in the Lord. We who are His faithful remnant will stand on His word, and we will stand in His strength and not in our own. *"Put ye in the sickle, for the harvest is ripe: come, get you down;*

for the press is full, the vats overflow; for their wickedness is great. Multitudes, multitudes in the valley of decision: for the day of the LORD is near in the valley of decision.

"The sun and the moon shall be darkened, and the stars shall withdraw their shining. The LORD also shall roar out of Zion, and utter his voice from Jerusalem; and the heavens and the earth shall shake: but the LORD will be the hope of his people, and the strength of the children of Israel."[35]

FEAR NOT SAYS THE LORD
FOR I WILL COME TO PROVE YOU

The promises of God are contained in the Holy Scriptures and the word of the Lord commands us to fear not what can man do unto us. Even in the midst of the fiery trial that faces us, fear the Lord and him alone. *"Is any thing too hard for the LORD?"*[36] Our God is a strong tower and the righteous run into Him and they are safe!

> *"And Moses said unto the people, Fear not: for God is come to prove you, and that his fear may be before your faces, that ye sin not"* (Exodus 20:20).

> *"Behold, the LORD thy God hath set the land before thee: go up and possess it, as the LORD God of thy fathers hath said unto thee; fear not, neither be discouraged"* (Deuteronomy 1:21).

THE COVENANT OF FAITH
WHICH WAS MADE BY THE LORD OUR GOD

If we are to survive the Great Tribulation, then we must understand our rights under the blood covenant of God. The word "covenant" is *beriyth*[37] (ber-eeth'), which means to cut a compact made by passing between pieces of flesh. The first covenant of Scripture was with Noah. The Lord said unto Noah, *"With thee will I establish my covenant; and thou shalt come into the ark, thou, and thy sons, and thy wife, and thy sons' wives with thee."*

"And God said, This is the token of the covenant which I make between me and you and every living creature that is with you, for perpetual generations: I do set my bow in the cloud, and it shall be for a token of a covenant between me and the earth. And it shall come to pass, when I bring a cloud over the earth, that the bow shall be seen in the cloud. And I, behold, I establish my cove-

nant with you, and with your seed after you,"[38] God's covenant is His word, and it stands eternal. *"God's covenants are established more firmly than the pillars of heaven or the foundations of the earth, and cannot be disannulled."*[39] It is the will of the Lord to keep and perform His holy covenants with His people. Do you doubt His strength to keep His covenant? Believe in Him. Trust Him. He has promised, if you called on His name in truth, He will hear from His holy temple.

"FEAR NOT MY CHOSEN ONES—I AM THY SHIELD"

The Lord entered into covenant with Abram when *"the word of the LORD came unto Abram in a vision, saying, Fear not, Abram: I am thy shield, and thy exceeding great reward."*[40] The Lord took Abram and said unto him *"Look now toward heaven, and tell the stars, if thou be able to number them: and he said unto him, So shall thy seed be. And he believed in the Lord; and he counted it to him for righteousness."*[41]

This covenant was by faith, for through believing what God said, it was counted to him for righteousness. This is the everlasting covenant and it was first revealed unto Abraham, *"I will establish my covenant between me and thee and thy seed after thee in their generations for an everlasting covenant, to be a God unto thee, and to thy seed after thee."*[42] David, who also inherited this covenant, said, *"he hath made with me an everlasting covenant, ordered in all things, and sure: for this is all my salvation, and all my desire."*[43]

The Lord declares, *"I have made a covenant with my chosen, I have sworn unto David my servant, Thy seed will I establish for ever, and build up thy throne to all generations."*[44] Praise the Lord, all you His chosen ones, for He has already done great things for you! *"O LORD God of Israel, there is no God like thee in the heaven, nor in the earth; which keepest covenant, and showest mercy unto thy servants, that walk before thee with all their hearts"* (2 Chronicles 6:14).

THE COVENANT THROUGH JESUS CHRIST

The covenant of faith, which Abraham received, was through Jesus Christ, and the many who have been grafted into Israel are the seeds of the promise, *"that the blessing of Abraham might come on the Gentiles through Jesus Christ; that we might receive the promise of the Spirit through faith."*[45]

The covenant was given to Abraham and his seed. To them alone was the promise of God by faith made, and this promise was hidden in Christ from the beginning. *"Now to Abraham and his seed were the promises made. He saith not, And to seeds, as of many; but as of one, And to thy seed, which is Christ."*[46] God the Father confirmed the covenant of faith through Jesus Christ, before the law was given to the children of Israel in the wilderness, therefore, the law could not disannul the covenant, for if the covenant was by the law, then it was not a promise by faith. *"And this I say, that the covenant, that was confirmed before of God in Christ, the law, which was four hundred and thirty years after, cannot disannul, that it should make the promise of none effect. For if the inheritance be of the law, it is no more of promise: but God gave it to Abraham by promise."*[47]

> *"And he said unto him, I am the LORD that brought thee out of Ur of the Chaldees, to give thee this land to inherit it. And he said, Lord GOD, whereby shall I know that I shall inherit it? And he said unto him, Take me an heifer of three years old, and a she goat of three years old, and a ram of three years old, and a turtledove, and a young pigeon."*[48]

This was the sacrifice, which evidenced the covenant of God with Abram our father and the certainty of God's promise to perform the covenant. *"And he said unto him, 'Take me an heifer of three years old, and a she goat of three years old, and a ram of three years old, and a turtledove, and a young pigeon. And he took unto him all these, and divided them in the midst, and laid each piece one against another: but the birds divided he not."*[49]

The cutting of the three-year-old heifer was symbolic of the death of our Lord. Under the temple worship, the altar must be first cleansed with the sacrifice of a three-year old heifer, thus this represented the altar which the Lord Himself would prepare on Calvary, for this symbolized the covenant by faith.

A SMOKING FURNACE AND A
BURNING LAMP PASSED BETWEEN

As night fell on the sacrifice Abram had made before God, the Lord began to perform the covenant He was making with Abram and all of his seed, the children of the promise. *"And it came to pass, that, when the sun went down, and it was dark, behold a smoking furnace, and a burning lamp that passed between those pieces. In the same day the LORD made a covenant with Abram, saying, Unto thy seed have I given this land, from the river of Egypt unto the great river, the river Euphrates."*[50]

Commentators teach that the smoking furnace signified the affliction of Abram's seed in Egypt, and the lamp symbolized their salvation.[51] This passage is literal. The smoking furnace is God our Father, and the burning lamp is His Son, Jesus, Who is the light of the world and the word of God. Our Father is a consuming fire, and His word is the lamp unto our feet. When the sun went down, and the darkness came, the smoking furnace and the burning lamp appeared literally before Abraham.

They passed between those pieces. The eternal covenant was forged in flesh, which was cut, and was consecrated in blood, which was poured out. Abram watched as God the Father and the Son walked in the holy covenant together. These symbols, which Abram saw, portrayed the covenant, which was performed by God in the heavens above that very day. This is the covenant of promise Abraham received from God which is inherited by faith. Jesus Christ entered into the blood covenant with the Father alone. Jesus stood in Abraham's place and for his seed to the last generation.

The Father and Jesus walked in a figure eight between the blood sacrifice. This signified the eternal nature of this covenant. The covenant was performed in the dark of night. This is symbolic of the night, which is coming, when the smoking furnace will again burn upon the earth, and the burning lamp that is the word of God will come and walk among us once again. *"For Zion's sake will I not hold my peace, and for Jerusalem's sake I will not rest, until the righteousness thereof go forth as brightness, and the salva-*

tion thereof as a lamp that burneth."[52] He has said, *"I will never leave you nor forsake you, even to the end of the age!"*

> *"The LORD said, Shall I hide from Abraham that thing which I do; Seeing that Abraham shall surely become a great and mighty nation, and all the nations of the earth shall be blessed in him? For I know him, that he will command his children and his household after him, and they shall keep the way of the LORD, to do justice and judgment; that the LORD may bring upon Abraham that which he hath spoken of him."*[53]

The Lord had literally become Abraham's shield. The Hebrew language does not contain the word covenant. The proper meaning is an alliance cut in blood. Under the terms of a blood covenant, if you fight with one of the members, you must fight with both of them unto all generations. All who would fight Abraham must first fight the Lord, and all who would oppose the Lord became the enemies of Abraham.

Under the terms of a blood covenant, both parties swear to protect the other to the death. Through this covenant, God literally said I will die for you, and no weapon formed against you shall prosper. For I shall protect you. Your enemies are now my enemies. You fight no one. I will defend you myself. Your enemies may come against you one way, but I will raise my hand against them, and they will flee seven ways before you.

The Lord promises that He will provide for us, and protect us Himself! He will guide us if we will just be obedient in thought, word and deed. The King of the Universe, The Ancient of Days Himself stands behind His promises and He will honor and do them! We have His promise if we will just obey Him! *"And I prayed unto the LORD my God, and made my confession, and said, O Lord, the great and dreadful God, keeping the covenant and mercy to them that love him, and to them that keep his commandments."*[54]

THE LORD CALLS YOU HIS DEARLY BELOVED

God called Abram his "friend," and the word He used is "ahab"[55] (aw-hab') which means to have strong affection for, to love dearly. This word for "friend" is only used in four places in the scripture, all of which refer to the Lord's great love for Abraham and his seed. In Proverbs the Lord speaks of His love for us, saying, *"there is a friend that sticketh closer than a brother."*[56] Truly the Lord is a closer friend than a brother, for these may betray and forsake, but the Lord will never forget His covenant with his beloved ones! Again, the Lord speaks to true Israel and Abraham their father, saying, *"But thou, Israel, art my servant, Jacob whom I have chosen, the seed of Abraham my friend."*[57]

The Lord also speaks of His faithfulness in wounding us to turn us from our transgression: *"Faithful are the wounds of a friend; but the kisses of an enemy are deceitful."*[58] In all other places in Scripture, the word used for "friend" is different. The most common is "reya"[59] (ray'-ah), which can be used for brother, companion, fellow, friend, husband, or neighbor. When speaking of His elect, the Lord speaks with strong affection declaring them to be, *"my dearly beloved."*

In ancient times, friends who were dearly beloved would enter into a blood covenant with each other, promising their faithful help to each other for their lives and their children's lives. This is our covenant with the Lord Jesus Christ.

THE ETERNAL COVENANT BETWEEN THE FATHER GOD AND HIS SON

A blood covenant must be tested to prove it is true. This is the work of the Messiah. He comes to confirm the covenant and prove it is true. This is the New Covenant, which our Father made with Jesus as our head, and it was confirmed in the blood of His Son. The new covenant is between the Father and the Son alone. You are only the prize, little flock. You are His reward. His faithful obedience to the Father earned Him the right to save you! You had nothing to do with the confirmation of this covenant. Enter into your rest.

Our great and awesome Lord did this all by Himself! The blood of the father is passed to his children, not the blood of the mother. The blood, which Jesus shed on the cross, was from our Father in heaven. When Jesus Christ died, the God of the universe died. We stand completely dependent upon the Lord for this covenant and for its saving power. We shall overcome by the Blood of the Lamb and the word of our testimony.

Jesus Christ fulfilled the Old Covenant of the law for us; everything Jesus did was done under the Old Covenant. Now Jesus Christ is preparing to fulfill the promise of the New Covenant, which is the salvation of those who are standing under it. In order to stand in this covenant, we must appropriate the Blood of the Lamb on our lives through faith, repentance and obedience. The Feast in which we celebrate this covenant is called Passover.

The obedient Israelites put the blood on their doors, and the angel of death had to pass over their homes. The Lord also commanded them to remove all leaven from their dwellings. They were to search even the corners of their rooms, so that no leaven would remain. Leaven is the symbol of sin. We, too, must search our hearts, and remove all the leaven through repentance, which is turning from our disobedience and surrendering to the Lord. The spiritual nation of Israel is composed of all the saints of God and includes everyone who has been adopted into the family of God, both Jew and Gentile.

We must understand this if we are to comprehend fully who we are in Him. We must repent and come under the covering of the Blood of the Lamb, the New Covenant of our Lord. The Great Tribulation is about to begin, but we have no reason to fear. If we are afraid, we have to ask ourselves where the fear is coming from—either the enemy or ourselves. How do we get rid of the fear? By drawing closer to the Lord and trusting in Him! I shall now reveal to you a mystery, hidden from the ages.

THERE APPEARED A GREAT WONDER IN HEAVEN

"And there appeared a great wonder in heaven; a woman clothed with the sun, and the moon under her feet, and upon her head a crown of twelve stars: And she being with child cried, travailing in birth, and pained to be delivered. And there appeared another wonder in heaven; and behold a great red dragon, having seven heads and ten horns, and seven crowns upon his heads. And his tail drew the third part of the stars of heaven, and did cast them to the earth: and the dragon stood before the woman which was ready to be delivered, for to devour her child as soon as it was born. And she brought forth a man child, who was to rule all nations with a rod of iron: and her child was caught up unto God, and to his throne. And

the woman fled into the wilderness, where she hath a place pre-
pared of God, that they should feed her there a thousand two hun-
dred and threescore days."[60]

The word used for "wonder" is *"semeion"*[61] (say-mi'-on), which
means a sign, which is ceremonial or supernatural. This woman in
travail is a sign of a great wonder, which will be revealed at the end
of the age. The woman is Israel, who will give birth to the Messiah,
the man-child who is to rule the nations with a rod of iron. She is
clothed with the sun, which represents the righteousness of Christ
received by her through faith.

She stands upon the moon, which is symbolic of Israel. All of the
pagan nations mark their calendar by the sun, while the times and
seasons of Israel are marked by the moon. The moon only reflects
the light of another greater body. Israel in all her greatness is only
reflecting the glory of the Lord. She is wearing a crown of twelve
stars representing the twelve tribes of the nation and the twelve
apostles of the New Covenant.

The woman is seen in travail, crying out and ready to give birth.
Some assume this speaks of the literal birth of the Messiah. This
prophecy is symbolic of the birth of the kingdom of God in the life
of the sanctified believer in the last days, prior to the tribulation.
The travail is the anguish, which comes upon these saints as their
old nature is finally crucified with Christ. As their old life is laid to
rest, the new creation is brought forth into this world.

Matthew Henry's commentary speaks to this passage clearly. *"She*
was safely delivered of a man-child, by which some understand
Christ... but others, with greater propriety, a race of true believ-
ers, strong and united, resembling Christ, and designed, under
him, to rule the nations with a rod of iron; that is, to judge the
world by their doctrine and lives now, and as assessors with
Christ at the great day."[62]

These believers, who give birth to the kingdom, do not just resem-
ble Christ, for we shall see from the Scripture that these sanctified
ones will be under the direct control of the Lord Himself. These
true Christians are the lions that are coming from Judah. And they
come to make war for the King! *"Christ came the first time with a*
birth, and He will come the second time with a birth. The differ-

ence between these two births is that the first birth was a physical birth, coming through physical Israel, while the second birth will be a spiritual birth coming through spiritual Israel."[63]

Jesus tells us, *"For whosoever shall do the will of my Father which is in heaven, the same is my brother, and sister, and mother."*[64] He is speaking of those who would surrender to Him fully and thus they will birth the kingdom of God in this world once again.

YOU SHALL WEEP... UNTIL A MAN IS BORN INTO THE WORLD

Jesus spoke of this mystery through a parable which He taught to the disciples: *"Do ye inquire among yourselves of that I said, A little while, and ye shall not see me: and again, a little while, and ye shall see me? Verily, verily, I say unto you, That ye shall weep and lament, but the world shall rejoice: and ye shall be sorrowful, but your sorrow shall be turned into joy. A woman when she is in travail hath sorrow, because her hour is come: but as soon as she is delivered of the child, she remembereth no more the anguish, for joy that a man is born into the world.... And in that day ye shall ask me nothing."*[65]

The Lord is speaking of His Second Coming, which will also begin with a birth. This is the mystery of the revelation of Jesus Christ, for He is about to be born in the lives of His chosen remnant. They shall walk in His power and authority, not as a lamb anymore, but as the LION FROM JUDAH!

HE THAT DWELLETH IN THE SECRET PLACE OF THE MOST HIGH

Jesus Christ opened up the way to enter the Holy of Holies. In His First Coming, Jesus tore the veil in two by His death on the cross. At the Second Coming, His remnant will be people who are found inside, hiding in the secret place of the Most High. The temple is a picture of the church. The outer court is the church assembly where the many who are called gather to hear the word of God proclaimed to the nations. The inner sanctuary is the place of the anointing of His Holy Spirit. Those who are chosen can enter in, and receive the baptism of His Spirit. Many mistake this for salvation, having never received the anointing. Most pastors and teachers in the church do not teach the believer the cleansing and puri-fying work of the Holy Spirit, called sanctification. Most believers are ignorant about the work of the cross that brings to death the carnal old nature.

Further, most pastors and teachers teach that the Lord no longer speaks to His people, for they themselves have never heard Him either. The Holy of Holies is the sacred place in the presence of God. If you enter therein, you can hear the Lord with your ears in an audible voice. The outer court will be destroyed during the tribulation, trodden under by the gentile nations, and burned to the ground. No one who continues to dwell there will survive what is coming. Do you want to be safe? Then follow Jesus into the most Holy Place!

> *"And there was given me a reed like unto a rod: and the angel stood, saying, Rise, and measure the temple of God, and the altar, and them that worship therein. But the court which is without the temple leave out, and measure it not; for it is given unto the Gentiles: and the holy city shall they tread under foot forty and two months"* (Revelation 11:1-2).

> *"He that dwelleth in the secret place of the most High shall abide under the shadow of the Almighty. I will say of the LORD, He is my refuge and my fortress: my God; in him will I trust. Surely he shall deliver thee from the snare of the fowler, and from the noisome pes-tilence. He shall cover thee with his feathers, and under his wings shalt thou trust: his truth shall be thy shield and buckler. Thou shalt not be afraid for the terror by night; nor for the arrow that flieth by day; Nor for the pestilence that walketh in darkness; nor for the de-struction that wasteth at noonday. A thousand shall fall at thy side, and ten thousand at thy right hand; but it shall not come nigh thee. Only with thine eyes shalt thou behold and see the reward of the wicked. Because thou hast made the LORD, which is my refuge, even the most High, thy habitation; There shall no evil befall thee, neither shall any plague come nigh thy dwelling. For he shall give his angels charge over thee, to keep thee in all thy ways"* (Psalm 91:1-11).

If you have never heard the voice of the Lord, it is because you have stayed in the outer court, and have never gone into His holy temple. You cannot speak with the Lord from the outside of His house. In the outer court are the many who have been called. The Lord sends His teachers and prophets to speak to the people in the outer court, bidding them to come into His sanctuary. But you must repent or you will not be allowed in. The Lord declares, *"and in that day there shall be no more the Canaanite in the house of the LORD of hosts."*[66] The word for "Canaanite" is "Kenaaniy"[67] (ken-ah-an-ee'), which means a merchant, or a trafficker.

The false prophets who have come in His name are spiritual Canaanites, and they traffic in the word of the Lord. They shall soon be cast out, and will no longer dwell in His house. Peter warned us these false prophets would come. *"There were false prophets also among the people, even as there shall be false teachers among you, who privily shall bring in damnable heresies, even denying the Lord that bought them, and bring upon themselves swift destruction. And many shall follow their pernicious ways; by reason of whom the way of truth shall be evil spoken of.*

"And through covetousness shall they with feigned words make merchandise of you."[68] They shall make merchandise of the people of God. Much of the false church is run as a business, by spiritual Canaanites who do not know the Lord. They have brought in damnable heresies, and lied to God's people.

In the Holiest place, the Lord Himself dwells with His people. He is our shield. He is our defense. By His power, His mighty army shall make war. The anointed remnant will soon appear before the nations, bursting upon the scene full of the power of the Lord. In terror, the children of men, the apostates and the tares, shall cry out before the anointed of the Lord.

The Lions from Judah are coming, and these anointed ones will hold the lightning sword of the Lord in their hands, and out of their mouth, the nations will hear the thunder of God's voice. They shall become terrified when they see the lions that are coming, and they shall cry out, *"Who are you? Who are you?"*

The anointed remnant will respond, I am the bow in His hand; His weapon prepared and fashioned for war! I have come to level the mountains and I shall break the nations in pieces, and cast down the kings from their thrones. I am full of the power of His Spirit, and I shall teach the people His truth. I will bring healing to His land. I am he whom they call, *"The Lord is my God!"*

The prophets speak of the holy remnant people. *"Thou art my battle axe and weapons of war: for with thee will I break in pieces the nations, and with thee will I destroy kingdoms; And with thee will I break in pieces the horse and his rider; and with thee will I break in pieces the chariot and his rider; With thee also will I break in pieces man and woman; and with thee will I break in pieces old and young.... I will also break in pieces with thee the shepherd and his flock... and with thee will I break in pieces captains and rulers. And I will render unto Babylon and to all the inhabitants of Chaldea all their evil that they have done in Zion in your sight, saith the Lord."*[69]

THE REMNANT SHALL RETURN
UNTO THE CHILDREN OF ISRAEL

Micah also prophesied of this sign: *"But thou, Beth-lehem Ephratah, though thou be little among the thousands of Judah, yet out of thee shall he come forth unto me that is to be ruler in Israel; whose goings forth have been from of old, from everlasting. Therefore will he give them up, until the time that she which travaileth hath brought forth: then the remnant of his brethren shall return unto the children of Israel. And he shall stand and feed in the strength of the LORD, in the majesty of the name of the LORD his God; and they shall abide: for now shall he be great unto the ends of the earth. And this man shall be the peace, when the Assyrian shall come into our land: and when he shall tread in our palaces, then shall we raise against him seven shepherds, and eight principal men."*[70]

The Lord will give up Israel, His people, until the time that the woman is ready to give birth. *"Then the remnant of his brethren shall return unto the children of Israel."* The remnant are those who are worthy to stand and endure the hour of testing, which will come upon the whole earth as a snare. The time of this prophecy is the Great Tribulation, and the prophecy is literal. The remnant will physically return to the land of Israel from all over the earth during the last days. They will flee the kingdom of darkness to the place of safety prepared by God in the wilderness. This prophecy is also symbolic.

The remnant will also return to the true vine, the New Covenant of Israel, into which they were grafted, by putting off the pagan teachings that have deceived apostate Christianity. Jeremiah also presents the travail of the woman Israel as a question in his prophecy of the time of Jacob's trouble: *"Ask ye now, and see whether a man doth travail with child? wherefore do I see every man with his hands on his loins, as a woman in travail, and all faces are turned into paleness? Alas! for that day is great, so that none is like it: it is even the time of Jacob's trouble; but he shall be saved out of it."*[71]

The prophet asks, *"Have you ever seen a man in travail with child before?"* You will. This prophecy has dual fulfillment. The unbelievers and the apostates will travail in fear, and will become like women. They will no longer have the strength of a man. The remnant will also be in travail, not in fear, but in the anguish of death, for they will put off their old nature and give birth to the kingdom of God.

THE DAY WHEN THE SON OF MAN IS REVEALED

This mystery of the last days' birth of the Messiah in Israel is revealed by the Lord Himself. In Luke's gospel, Jesus teaches us about the events of the Great Tribulation and His Second Coming. He says, *"Even thus shall it be in the day when the Son of man is revealed. In that day, he which shall be upon the housetop, and his stuff in the house, let him not come down to take it away: and he that is in the field, let him likewise not return back. Remember Lot's wife. Whosoever shall seek to save his life shall lose it."*[72]

In Matthew's account, Jesus speaks of the same day saying, *"When you see the abomination set up,"* which refers to the Antichrist being revealed. Now Jesus is referring to the day when the Son of man is revealed. This is the birth of the woman in travail. The day she gives birth, the Son of man will be revealed upon the earth once again, only this time in His children.

"And she brought forth a man child, who was to rule all nations with a rod of iron: and her child was caught up unto God, and to his throne."[73] His children will rule with a rod of iron. The iron

represents the absolute authority and the rule of God, which will be made manifest in the lives of these sanctified ones. They are pictured as caught up unto God and to His throne. The life they now live is hid in Christ, and it is He Who lives through them.

Jesus is seated upon the throne of God, and these, His remnant warriors, will walk in His power. These are the lions that will come forth from the remnant of Jacob. They will make war during the Great Tribulation. It is these men to whom the Lord is referring to when He speaks of *"the day when the Son of man is revealed."*

THE REMNANT OF JACOB SHALL BE AS LIONS AMONG THE SHEEP

"And the remnant of Jacob shall be in the midst of many people as a dew from the LORD, as the showers upon the grass, that tarrieth not for man, nor waiteth for the sons of men. And the remnant of Jacob shall be among the Gentiles in the midst of many people as a lion among the beasts of the forest, as a young lion among the flocks of sheep: who, if he go through, both treadeth down, and teareth in pieces, and none can deliver. Thine hand shall be lifted up upon thine adversaries, and all thine enemies shall be cut off." (Micah 5:7-9).

These are the lions of Judah. The prophet speaks of Israel as Jacob, referring to the people of God who walk in the flesh. The remnant people are distinguished for they shall be full of the Spirit. They are pictured as lions among the beasts of the forest. They will be more powerful that anything they face and they will walk among the people of this earth as a lion would walk through a flock of sheep or goats. The word used for "sheep" is *"tso'n"*[74] (tsone), which means a flock of sheep or goats and is figurative of men.

They will come to protect the sheep, and they will come to overthrow the goats. These lions from Judah will be able to pass through unhindered and unopposed. Those who do oppose them will be run over or be torn into pieces! If anyone comes against them, they have but to lift their hand, and God will cut off their enemies.

I HAVE CALLED MY MIGHTY ONES FOR MY ANGER

"Lift ye up a banner upon the high mountain, exalt the voice unto them, shake the hand, that they may go into the gates of the nobles. I have commanded my sanctified ones, I have also called my mighty ones for mine anger, even them that rejoice in my highness. The noise of a multitude in the mountains, like as of a great people; a tumultuous noise of the kingdoms of nations gathered together: the LORD of hosts mustereth the host of the battle. They come from a far country, from the end of heaven, even the Lord, and the weapons of his indignation, to destroy the whole land."[75]

These are the sanctified army of God, which will be sent into the world during the Great Tribulation. They are the host of the Lord and He musters them for battle. *"The LORD hath opened his armoury, and hath brought forth the weapons of his indignation: for this is the work of the Lord GOD of hosts in the land of the Chaldeans."*[76]

These men are His weapons to be used for His indignation, and they come to destroy the whole land. We are told they come from a far country, for the remnant will be among all the nations when they give birth to the kingdom. We are also told they come from the end of heaven, even the Lord. It is the Lord Himself revealed in these sanctified ones. The Lord is doing this work. They are merely servants executing the King's orders and they come to battle the dragon. These men are the holy army of God.

The storm clouds are rising and gathering as a *great storm* with a wind ready to destroy what ever it hits. In Scripture, they are called the Lord's nimbus clouds. *Webster's* defines a nimbus cloud as *"a cloudy luminescence enveloping a deity when on earth... a radiance or a bright circle appearing above the heads of saints, a heavy rain cloud."*[77]

These are His judgment clouds in the form of a man's hand, the ministry of His government. They will bring the judgment upon the peoples and all the sinners of Zion. They are the bow in His hand, and His arrow will be shot forth from His bow, which is Judah, His remnant. The bow is their mouth, and upon their lips, He will place His new threshing instrument. *"Behold, I will make thee a new sharp threshing instrument having teeth: thou shalt thresh the mountains, and beat them small, and shalt make the hills as chaff."*[78]

Their lips will hold the breath of God. They are in His hand—as an armory comprising the weapons of war! *"Thou art my battle ax and weapons of war: for with thee will I break in pieces the nations, and with thee will I destroy kingdoms."*[79] These of the Lord's camp are being mustered for spiritual combat for His purposes. They are well-trained and are experienced in the ways of their Captain.

Soon, they will be thrust forth to accomplish His ultimate purpose in the land as His weapons of war! Woe unto those who do not obey the Gospel of Jesus Christ the Messiah! Woe unto the shepherds that feed not the sheep! Woe unto the false prophets and teachers, for that day is upon us! *"I looked, and, behold, a whirlwind came out of the north, a great cloud, and a fire infolding itself, and a brightness was about it, and out of the midst thereof as the colour of amber, out of the midst of the fire."*[80] His Holy Presence is the fire, which is His Shekinah Glory manifest in the set-apart and consecrated army of the Lord.

> *"Thou shalt be visited of the LORD of hosts with thunder, and with earthquake, and great noise, with storm and tempest, and the flame of devouring fire."*[81] The prophet's vision was a people with the presence of the Lord radiating from them in judgment. His presence is as fire! *"Who maketh his angels spirits; his ministers a flaming fire."*[82]

The Lord himself is a *"consuming fire,"* He will manifest Himself, and His Shekinah Glory through a people prepared for His name! *"In that day* (the Day of the Lord) *will I make the governors of Judah* (His vanguard of the host of His army) *like an hearth of fire among the wood* (flesh), *and like a torch of fire* (God's Holy Presence) *in a sheaf* (a bundle of wheat representing the people); *and they shall devour all the people round about."*[83] *"Through the wrath of the Lord of hosts is the land darkened, and the people shall be as the fuel of the fire: no man shall spare his brother."*[84] The Lord is coming forth as a man of War![85]

THE LAMB WILL STAND
WITH 144,000 OF HIS ANOINTED ONES

The Lord will indeed come to your rescue! Do not fear! The beginning of the Great Tribulation opens with the Lamb standing on mount Zion, and with Him are 144,000 of His sanctified ones. We are told they are the first fruits of the Revelation of Jesus Christ!

> *"And I looked, and, lo, a Lamb stood on the mount Sion, and with him an hundred forty and four thousand, having his Father's name written in their foreheads. And I heard a voice from heaven, as the voice of many waters, and as the voice of a great thunder.... And they sung as it were a new song before the throne... and no man could learn that song but the hundred and forty and four thousand, which were redeemed from the earth. These are they which were not defiled with women; for they are virgins. These are they which follow the Lamb whithersoever he goeth. These were redeemed from among men, being the firstfruits unto God and to the Lamb. And in their mouth was found no guile: for they are without fault before the throne of God"* (Revelation 14:1-5).

Children, the LION FROM THE TRIBE OF JUDAH will come for you! He will be your rear guard, and He will go before you. You, who are His chosen remnant, the delight of His heart, He will surely not forsake you, nor will He turn His ear from your cries. Like King David and the prophets of old, you also will proclaim, *"The Lord is my Deliverer!"* Though the enemy of your soul plots to take your very life, both you and your family, do not fear! The Lord will remember His covenant with Israel. *"The secret of the LORD is with them that fear him; and he will show them his covenant."*[86] The covenant is by faith and is evidenced by the obedience of those covered therein.

"The mercy of the LORD is from everlasting to everlasting upon them that fear him, and his righteousness unto children's children; To such as keep his covenant, and to those that remember his commandments to do them."[87] Oh, let us give praise to His name, for His mercy endures forever! *"Say to them that are of fearful heart; Be strong, fear not: behold, your God will come with vengeance, even God with a recompense; He who will come and save you."*[88]

"Behold, the Lord GOD will come with His strong hand, behold his arm shall rule for him: and his reward is with him, and his work before him."[89] *"For, behold the LORD will come with fire, and with his chariots like a whirl-wind, to render his anger with fury, and his rebuke with flames of fire. For by fire and by his sword will the LORD plead with all flesh: and the slain of the LORD shall be many."*[90]

This is the army of God. They are 144,000-strong from the twelve tribes of Israel, and they are coming! They come from a far country but they will be gathered in Zion. They come from the end of heaven, even the Lord. This is the mystery of the revelation of Jesus Christ. These 144,000 are the LIONS FROM JUDAH! These are the chosen ones of whom the Lord says, *"I have commanded my sanctified ones, I have also called my mighty ones for my anger."*[91]

Some of the people in the faith have struggled with the thought that our God still makes war, and calls forth from among the people, men of war. Children, sit down and be silent before the Lord, for this is His hour. Do not raise your voice against the word of the Lord, or the messengers of His covenant. The Lord is restoring His order to all things. *"Delight is not seemly for a fool; much less for a servant to have rule over princes."*[92]

IN RIGHTEOUSNESS HE DOES JUDGE AND MAKE WAR

The war, which is about to be fought, is the final battle in 6000 years of conflict. This battle is the Lord's. *"The LORD your God which goeth before you, he shall fight for you, according to all that he did for you in Egypt before your eyes."*[93] *"And I saw heaven opened, and behold a white horse; and he that sat upon him was called Faithful and True, and in righteousness he doth judge and make war."*[94]

David says of the Lord, *"He teacheth my hands to war; so that a bow of steel is broken by mine arms."*[95] The prophet Zechariah speaks of the mighty men of God who are coming to fight this war, saying, *"And they shall be as mighty men, which tread down their enemies in the mire of the streets in the battle: and they shall fight, because the LORD is with them."*[96] Each of the men who is called and sanctified for this purpose will say, *"Blessed be the LORD my strength, which teacheth my hands to war, and my fingers to fight"*[97]

I remember when I was a youth, the Lord spoke to me for many years saying, *"When you turn forty, I am going to use you. I am making you into a weapon, and we will level the mountains!"* I used to wonder, *"What will happen when I turn forty?"* What could this mean, that one day I would become a weapon? What were these mountains, which would fall? Indeed, if a word is from God, then let the day declare it!

PROCLAIM AMONG THE GENTILES: PREPARE FOR WAR

"Proclaim ye this among the Gentiles; Prepare war, wake up the mighty men, let all the men of war draw near; let them come up: Beat your plowshares into swords, and your pruning hooks into spears: let the weak say, I am strong. Assemble yourselves, and come, all ye heathen, and gather yourselves together round about: thither cause thy mighty ones to come down, O LORD. Let the heathen be wakened, and come up to the valley of Jehoshaphat: for there will I sit to judge all the heathen round about. Put ye in the sickle, for the harvest is ripe: come, get you down; for the press is full, the vats overflow; for their wickedness is great. Multitudes, multitudes in the valley of decision: for the day of the LORD is near in the valley of decision. The sun and the moon shall be darkened, and the stars shall withdraw their shining."[98]

That day will soon be here. The words of the prophet Joel will now be fulfilled. The nations are all preparing for war, and the Lord is about to cause His mighty ones to come down!

THE LORD OUR GOD WILL BOW THE HEAVENS AND COME DOWN

"When the waves of death encompass me, and the floods of the ungodly men make me afraid; and the sorrows of hell surround me, in my distress I will call upon the Lord, and I will cry to my God: and he will hear my voice out of his temple, and my cry will enter into his ears. Then the earth will shake and tremble; the foundations of heaven will move and shake, because he will be wroth. There will go up a smoke out of his nostrils, and fire out of his mouth will devour;

coals will be kindled by it. He will bow the heavens also, and come down; with darkness under his feet.

"He will ride upon a cherub, and will fly: and he will be seen upon the wings of the wind. He will make darkness pavilions round about him, dark waters, and thick clouds of the skies. Through the brightness before him, the coals of fire are kindled. The Lord will thunder from heaven, and the most High will utter his voice. He will send out arrows, and scatter them; and His lightning will trouble them. The channels of the sea will appear, the foundations of the world will be discovered, at the rebuking of the Lord, at the blast of the breath of his nostrils.

"He will send from above, he will take me; and he will draw me out of many waters; He will deliver me from my strong enemy, and from them that hate me: for they are too strong for me. They prepared the day of my calamity: but the Lord will be my stay. He will bring me forth also into a large place: he will deliver me, because he delights in me. I am His beloved. The Lord will reward me according to my righteousness: according to the cleanness of my hands, he will recompense me, for I have kept the ways of the Lord, and have not wickedly departed from my God."[99]

MY MESSENGER SHALL COME, AND WHO CAN ABIDE IN THAT DAY?

"Behold, I will send my messenger, and he shall prepare the way before me: and the LORD, whom ye seek, shall suddenly come to his temple, even the messenger of the covenant, whom ye delight in: behold, he shall come, saith the LORD of hosts. But who may abide the day of his coming? and who shall stand when he appeareth? for he is like a refiner's fire, and like fullers' soap: And he shall sit as a refiner and purifier of silver: and he shall purify the sons of Levi, and purge them as gold and silver, that they may offer unto the Lord an offering in righteousness. Then shall the offering of Judah and Jerusalem be pleasant unto the LORD, as in the days of old, and as in former years. And I will come near to you to judgment; and I will be a swift witness."[100]

The messengers of the Lord, those who come in the office and anointing of Elijah, are also weapons of the Lord. They are His mighty ones, the lions from Judah, and they come forth from the

Lord Himself. *"And when ye see this, your heart shall rejoice, and your bones shall flourish like an herb: and the hand of the LORD shall be known toward his servants, and his indignation toward his enemies. For, behold, the LORD will come with fire, and with his chariots like a whirlwind, to render his anger with fury, and his rebuke with flames of fire.*

"For by fire and by his sword will the Lord plead with all flesh: and the slain of the Lord shall be many."[101] The word for "fire" is *"esh"*[102] (aysh) and means burning, fiery, and flaming hot. The Lord is speaking about the messengers of His covenant, whom He is sending before He appears. The word for "chariots" is *"cuwphah"*[103] (soo-faw') and means a hurricane, a tempest, and a whirlwind. These are His messengers and they come full of the wrath of the Lord. The word for "wrath" is *"chemah"*[104] (khay-maw') and means anger, furious, indignation, and rage.

These are the ones that the Lord has called forth to express His anger. The word used for "sword" is *"lahab"*[105] (lah'-hab), which means to gleam, a flash, a sharply polished blade or point of a weapon.

The Lord has determined to judge the people with fire, and who can abide in the day of His coming unto us in His mighty ones? *"Therefore shall the Lord, the Lord of hosts, send among his fat ones leanness; and under his glory he shall kindle a burning like the burning of a fire.*

"And the light of Israel shall be for a fire, and his Holy One for a flame: and it shall burn and devour his thorns and his briers in one day; and shall consume the glory of his forest, and of his fruitful field, both soul and body: and they shall be as when a standard-bearer fainteth. And the rest of the trees of his forest shall be few, that a child may write them. And it shall come to pass in that day, that the remnant of Israel, and such as are escaped of the house of Jacob, shall no more again stay upon him that smote them; but shall stay upon the LORD, the Holy One of Israel, in truth. The remnant shall return, even the remnant of Jacob, unto the mighty God."[106]

"And he shall pass over to his strong hold for fear, and his princes shall be afraid of the ensign, saith the LORD, whose fire is in Zion, and his furnace in Jerusalem" (Isaiah 31:9).

"But upon mount Zion shall be deliverance, and there shall be holiness; and the house of Jacob shall possess their possessions. And the house of Jacob shall be a fire, and the house of Joseph a flame, and the house of Esau for stubble, and they shall kindle in them, and devour them; and there shall not be any remaining of the house of Esau; for the LORD hath spoken it" (Obadiah 1:17-18).

THE LORD YOUR GOD IS HE
THAT GOES WITH YOU, FEAR NOT!

"And I say unto you my friends, Be not afraid of them that kill the body, and after that have no more that they can do. But I will forewarn you whom ye shall fear: Fear him, which after he hath killed hath power to cast into hell; yea, I say unto you, Fear him. Are not five sparrows sold for two farthings, and not one of them is forgotten before God? But even the very hairs of your head are all numbered. Fear not therefore: ye are of more value than many sparrows."[107]

"And shall say unto them, Hear, O Israel, ye approach this day unto battle against your enemies: let not your hearts faint, fear not, and do not tremble, neither be ye terrified because of them; For the LORD your God is he that goeth with you, to fight for you against your enemies, to save you."[108] *"Be strong and of a good courage, fear not, nor be afraid of them: for the LORD thy God, He it is that doth go with thee; he will not fail thee, nor forsake thee."*[109] *"And the LORD, he it is that doth go before thee; he will be with thee, he will not fail thee, neither forsake thee: fear not, neither be dismayed."*[110]

"And Joshua said unto them, Fear not, nor be dismayed, be strong and of good courage: for thus shall the LORD do to all your enemies against whom ye fight."[111] *"And I said unto you, I am the LORD your God; fear not the gods of the Amorites, in whose land ye dwell"*[112] *"The LORD said unto him, Peace be unto thee; fear not: thou shalt not die."*[113] *"And Samuel said unto the people, Fear not: ye have done all this wickedness: yet turn not aside from following the LORD, but serve the LORD with all your heart; And turn ye not aside: for then should ye go after vain things, which cannot profit*

nor deliver; for they are vain. For the LORD will not forsake his people for his great name's sake: because it hath pleased the LORD to make you his people. Moreover as for me, God forbid that I should sin against the LORD in ceasing to pray for you: but I will teach you the good and the right way: Only fear the LORD, and serve him in truth with all your heart; for consider how great things he hath done for you. But if ye shall still do wickedly, ye shall be consumed, both ye and your king."[114]

AND ELISHA PRAYED OPEN HIS EYES THAT HE MAY SEE

"And he answered, Fear not: for they that be with us are more than they that be with them. And Elisha prayed, and said, LORD, I pray thee; open his eyes that he may see. And the LORD opened the eyes of the young man; and he saw: and, behold, the mountain was full of horses and chariots of fire round about Elisha."[115] *"Say to them that are of a fearful heart, Be strong, fear not: behold, your God will come with vengeance, even God with a recompence; he will come and save you."*[116] *"For I the LORD thy God will hold thy right hand, saying unto thee, Fear not; I will help thee."*[117] *"Fear not, O land; be glad and rejoice: for the LORD will do great things."*[118]

"But now thus saith the LORD that created thee, O Jacob, and he that formed thee, O Israel, Fear not: for I have redeemed thee, I have called thee by thy name; thou art mine. When thou passest through the waters, I will be with thee; and through the rivers, they shall not overflow thee: when thou walkest through the fire, thou shalt not be burned; neither shall the flame kindle upon thee. For I am the LORD thy God, the Holy One of Israel, thy Saviour: I gave Egypt for thy ransom, Ethiopia and Seba for thee. Since thou wast precious in my sight, thou hast been honourable, and I have loved thee: therefore will I give men for thee, and people for thy life.

"Fear not: for I am with thee: I will bring thy seed from the east, and gather thee from the west; I will say to the north, Give up; and to the south, Keep not back: bring my sons from far, and my daughters from the ends of the earth; Even every one that is called by my name: for I have created him for my glory, I have formed him; yea, I have made him."[119]

A FLAME FOR GOD

There are many who have been called, but only a *"few"* were chosen. The chosen must submit to the final burning and purging away of the flesh, the carnal nature that resides in us from the original Adam. Those who are willing to be separated unto God are the first fruits of His choosing. The Lord will keep those who are predestined to become His *"flames of fire,"* His ministers of righteousness, and the plantings of the Lord. *"Seven days thou shalt make an atonement for the altar, and sanctify it; and it shall be an altar most holy: whatsoever toucheth the altar shall be holy."*[120]

These who are the remnant have placed their lives upon the altar of God. The man-child to be born in the Spirit are those who have come to maturity first, and they will be the full measure of the stature of the Christ. These are full-grown sons, who will go on to bear the rod of iron in the Spirit. The woman spiritual Israel is in travail, and is pained to be delivered of the child. This last generation will be given His authority and governmental power to rule the nations with a rod of iron.

Before their birth, these sons of the King have been hidden from the church and the world. The woman, who is true Israel, is about to persecuted in an unprecedented onslaught from the dragon, but God will protect her through the hands of the Jewish remnant that will come forth as the lions from Judah.

These are not defiled with women, for they have come out of the Babylonian system of religion, and are no longer defiled with the apostasy, which is known as American Christianity. The woman Babylon is both the Antichrist government of the nations, and the false Church, which claims His name, but does not obey His voice. They are the mixed multitude, lost in their sins, thinking themselves saved; they are drunk, having been intoxicated and deceived by the woman.

The remnant has come out of her as God commanded. The first fruits of the Lord are now receiving their marching orders from the General of the Host. The Holy One of Israel is His name, and they come in His power. They are sounding the trumpet, and proclaiming the voice of the Lord to the nations. These priests of the

Lord shall bring the pure "meat" offering without leaven. The word they have brought forth is without corruption. Those who are chosen have the seal of God on their shoulders, the seal of God in their hearts, and the seal of God on their foreheads.

This is the last and final sealing, which signifies those who have gone through the fire, and have been approved and accepted as the genuine seed and joint heirs to the Father's throne with Jesus Christ. The fire, which consumes the final offering of our lives, will set us free to walk in the victory. The remnant has laid their lives down, and turned from the pleasures of this world.

> *"In the day when the keepers of the house shall tremble, and the strong men shall bow themselves, and the grinders cease because they are few, and those that look out of the windows be darkened, And the doors shall be shut in the streets, when the sound of the grinding is low, and he shall rise up at the voice of the bird, and all the daughters of music shall be brought low; Also when they shall be afraid of that which is high, and fears shall be in the way, and the almond tree shall flourish, and the grasshopper shall be a burden, and desire shall fail: because man goeth to his long home, and the mourners go about the streets."*[121]

His first fruits almond trees are beginning to blossom, and soon the fruit will appear in all its glory. The almond trees shall flourish, while the desire of all flesh shall fail. And man shall go to his home, and the mourners shall fill the streets. *"A quick work is in progress, and I the Lord hasten to perform it. The rod of Aaron is beginning to bud and blossom, and these of My choosing shall be the instruments of My government upon the earth. Sons are coming forth into maturity."*

> *"As the days of Noah, so are the days of My return. The flood is coming, but only a few are preparing their ark. Come away with Me in the secret place and I will protect you. No evil shall befall you and no plague will come near your home. The lofty looks of man shall be humbled, and the haughtiness of men shall be bowed down, and the LORD alone shall be exalted in that day. For the day of the LORD of hosts shall be upon every one that is proud and lofty, and upon every one that is lifted up; and he shall be brought low."*[122]

"For thus saith the high and lofty One that inhabiteth eternity, whose name is Holy; I dwell in the high and holy place, with him also that is of a contrite and humble spirit, to revive the spirit of the humble, and to revive the heart of the contrite ones" (Isaiah 57:15).

"In flaming fire taking vengeance on them that know not God, and that obey not the gospel of our Lord Jesus Christ: Who shall be punished with everlasting destruction from the presence of the Lord, and from the glory of his power; When he shall come to be glorified in his saints, and to be admired in all them that believe (because our testimony among you was believed) in that day" (II Thessalonians 1:8-10).

MY WORD WILL COME FORTH
LIKE FIRE IN THAT DAY

"The prophetic signs are all in acceleration. The nations will tremble, and the kingdoms of man will all fall to the ground. The American dream will be shattered, and the New World Order will rise from the ruins. It will remain for only a short while, and then the Kingdom of God shall come. Fear not what you are about to see and hear.

"Focus your thoughts in the heavenly, and keep your eyes on Me. I the Lord will heal My people of their backsliding, and restore to them the years the locusts have taken from them. The soul is the battleground, and I will conquer the enemy for you. Remember, I have saved the best wine for last. I will give it unto you, and I shall pour out on My righteous ones My power, that you may do greater works than I. This is My word, and I shall bring it to pass.

"The mustering of the troops is underway, and I am calling even now for My sanctified ones, who rejoice in My holiness. I have numbered My own, they are all accounted for, fully arranged in order and rank. They know their identity, and are accounted worthy to stand in My presence, and will be given charge of My courts. They have been first called, and then approved in fire. I have chosen them from among the many.

"I have placed My seal of approval upon them, and with holiness I sanctify their lives. I shall write My name upon their foreheads. My chosen sons and daughters shall all bear My name, and they

shall glory in Me alone. My witnesses shall open the secret mysteries of My word to My people. My word will come forth in this season like fire, and many shall fall, but My righteous shall rejoice. Famine shall cover the land, but My anointed ones shall be full.

"The wise shall understand, and they will continue to watch, and keep their lamps trimmed with My holy oil. The vanguard of My host is ready. I shout to My chosen ones, and they all hear My voice. The coming days will bring many signs and wonders. My chosen ones will be noble warriors in that day, walking in My power and anointing. Distress among nations, and fearful signs shall come in the heavens, but be not dismayed at these signs. I the Lord have the dominion. The earth and the fullness thereof is mine and mine alone. Know and understand that I am sovereign, all things are under My control, for I am King who rules over His entire Kingdom. I say unto you, do not fear what is to come. Fear only Me.

"The barley harvest has begun, and I will soon gather My first fruits into My secret place. Then I will come and gather the wheat from among the tares. I shall purge My wheat with fire, to purify a people for Myself, and the tares shall be burned with unquenchable fire!

"As it was in the day of Pentecost, so it shall be again. The end of all flesh is at hand, and I will begin by purifying the minds of my chosen ones. I shall come again to Zion in the fullness of My Spirit and I will pour out My great glory upon My humble ones. Now gather yourselves together, and begin to fast and pray.

"The war, which is about to be fought, is spiritual, and I shall provide the weapons for this battle. I am raising up young lions from among My sheep. My hand will be lifted up against all My enemies. I come to make war on the earth, and I shall wage war in the heavens above. Make your shields ready, for I am coming as KING. I am standing now ready for battle.

Behold, My people shall rise up as a great lion, and as a young lion they will not lie down until they have seized the prey. And the slain of the Lord shall be many in that day."[123]

FEAR NOT LITTLE FLOCK

"Fear not, little flock; for it is your Father's good pleasure to give you the kingdom. Sell that ye have, and give alms; provide yourselves bags which wax not old, a treasure in the heavens that faileth not, where no thief approacheth, neither moth corrupteth For where your treasure is, there will your heart be also. Let your loins be girded about, and your lights burning; And ye yourselves like unto men that wait for their lord, when he will return from the wedding; that when he cometh and knocketh, they may open unto him immediately. Blessed are those servants, whom the lord when he cometh shall find watching: verily I say unto you, that he shall gird himself, and make them to sit down to meat, and will come forth and serve them."[124]

FEAR NOT, I AM THE FIRST AND THE LAST

"And when I saw him, I fell at his feet as dead. And he laid his right hand upon me, saying unto me, Fear not; I am the first and the last."[125] *"But fear not thou, O my servant Jacob, and be not dismayed, O Israel: for, behold, I will save thee from afar off, and thy seed from the land of their captivity; and Jacob shall return, and be in rest and at ease, and none shall make him afraid."*[126] *"Thou drewest near in the day that I called upon thee: thou saidst, Fear not. O LORD, thou hast pleaded the causes of my soul; thou hast redeemed my life. O LORD, thou hast seen my wrong: judge thou my cause. Thou hast seen all their vengeance and all their imaginations against me. Thou hast heard their reproach, O Lord, and all their imaginations"*[127]

TRUST IN THE LORD AND DO GOOD,
WAIT PATIENTLY FOR HIM

"Trust in the LORD, and do good; so shalt thou dwell in the land, and verily thou shalt be fed. Delight thyself also in the LORD; and he shall give thee the desires of thine heart. Commit thy way unto the LORD; trust also in him; and he shall bring it to pass. And he shall bring forth thy righteousness as the light, and thy judgment as the noonday. Rest in the LORD, and wait patiently for him: fret not thyself because of him who prospereth in his way, because of the man who bringeth wicked devices to pass. Cease from anger, and forsake wrath: fret not thyself in any wise to do evil. For evildoers

shall be cut off: but those that wait upon the LORD, they shall in- herit the earth. For yet a little while, and the wicked shall not be: yea, thou shalt diligently consider his place, and it shall not be. But the meek shall inherit the earth; and shall delight themselves in the abundance of peace.

"The wicked plotteth against the just, and gnasheth upon him with his teeth. The LORD shall laugh at him: for he seeth that his day is coming. The wicked have drawn out the sword, and have bent their bow, to cast down the poor and needy, and to slay such as be of up- right conversation. Their sword shall enter into their own heart, and their bows shall be broken. A little that a righteous man hath is better than the riches of many wicked. For the arms of the wicked shall be broken: but the LORD upholdeth the righteous. The LORD knoweth the days of the upright: and their inheritance shall be for ever.

"They shall not be ashamed in the evil time: and in the days of fam- ine they shall be satisfied. But the wicked shall perish, and the ene- mies of the LORD shall be as the fat of lambs: they shall consume; into smoke shall they consume away. The wicked borroweth, and payeth not again: but the righteous sheweth mercy, and giveth. For such as be blessed of him shall inherit the earth; and they that be cursed of him shall be cut off. The steps of a good man are ordered by the LORD: and he delighteth in his way.

"Though he fall, he shall not be utterly cast down: for the LORD up- holdeth him with his hand. I have been young, and now am old; yet have I not seen the righteous forsaken, nor his seed begging bread. He is ever merciful, and lendeth; and his seed is blessed. Depart from evil, and do good; and dwell for evermore. For the LORD loveth judgment, and forsaketh not his saints; they are preserved for ever: but the seed of the wicked shall be cut off. The righteous shall inherit the land, and dwell therein for ever. The mouth of the righteous speaketh wisdom, and his tongue talketh of judgment.

"The law of his God is in his heart; none of his steps shall slide. The wicked watcheth the righteous, and seeketh to slay him. The LORD will not leave him in his hand, nor condemn him when he is judged. Wait on the LORD, and keep his way, and he shall exalt thee to in- herit the land: when the wicked are cut off, thou shalt see it. I have seen the wicked in great power, and spreading himself like a green bay tree. Yet he passed away, and, lo, he was not: yea, I sought him, but he could not be found. Mark the perfect man, and behold the upright: for the end of that man is peace.

"But the transgressors shall be destroyed together: the end of the wicked shall be cut off. But the salvation of the righteous is of the LORD: he is their strength in the time of trouble. And the LORD shall help them, and deliver them: he shall deliver them from the wicked, and save them, because they trust in him."[128]

"Behold, the people shall rise up as a great lion, and lift up himself as a young lion: he shall not lie down until he eat of the prey, and drink the blood of the slain" (Numbers 23:24).

"Lo, these are parts of His ways: but how little a portion is heard of Him? but the thunder of His power who can understand" (Job 26:14)?

CHAPTER
9

"WE HAVE HEARD OF THE PRIDE OF MOAB"
Isaiah 16:6

The Lord declares in His word the curses that would come if His nation Israel refused to obey His voice, and followed their own ways into rebellion. America and her false religious systems have also refused to obey the Lord and have chosen their own way. The people of America are hardened in their rebellion. They shall witness these same curses poured out upon them.

"I am the LORD your God, which brought you forth out of the land of Egypt, that ye should not be their bondmen; and I have broken the bands of your yoke, and made you go upright. But if ye will not hearken unto me.... And if ye shall despise my statutes, or if your soul abhor my judgments, so that ye will not do all my commandments, but that ye break my covenant: I also will do this unto you; I will even appoint over you terror... and ye shall sow your seed in vain, for your enemies shall eat it.... and ye shall be slain before your enemies: they that hate you shall reign over you; and ye shall flee when none pursueth you.... And I will break the pride of your power.... And your strength shall be spent in vain.... I will also send wild beasts among you.... And I will bring a sword upon you, that shall avenge the quarrel of my covenant: and when ye are gathered together within your cities, I will send the pestilence among you; and ye shall be delivered into the hand of the enemy.... And I will make your cities waste, and bring your sanctuaries unto desolation.... And I will scatter you among the heathen, and will draw out

a sword after you: and your land shall be desolate, and your cities waste" (Leviticus 26:13-33).

THE SIN OF PRIDE GOES BEFORE THE FALL

The sin of pride is an abomination to the Lord. Everyone that is proud and exalted in his or her own eyes shall be brought down! *"The lofty looks of man shall be humbled, and the haughtiness of men shall be bowed down, and the LORD alone shall be exalted in that day. For the day of the LORD of hosts shall be upon every one that is proud and lofty, and upon every one that is lifted up; and he shall be brought low."*[1]

The exaltation of man in his arrogance receives a harsh rebuke from the Lord. The attitude and the speech of the proud men are detestable before our God. Throughout Scripture, the Lord repeats His admonition against pride, for God despises pride and its related sins of arrogance and all forms of boasting. He declares that He hates them. *"The fear of the LORD is to hate evil: pride, and arrogancy, and the evil way, and the froward mouth, do I hate."*[2] *"Pride goeth before destruction, and an haughty spirit before a fall."*[3]

The Lord spoke about the end of the world to Ezekiel declaring pride has budded!

"Moreover the word of the LORD came unto me, saying.... An end, the end is come upon the four corners of the land. Now is the end come upon thee, and I will send mine anger upon thee, and will judge thee according to thy ways, and will recompense upon thee all thine abominations. And mine eye shall not spare thee, neither will I have pity: but I will recompense thy ways upon thee, and thine abominations shall be in the midst of thee: and ye shall know that I am the LORD. Thus saith the Lord GOD; An evil, an only evil, behold, is come. An end is come, the end is come: it watcheth for thee; behold, it is come. The morning is come unto thee, O thou that dwellest in the land: the time is come, the day of trouble is near, and not the sounding again of the mountains. Now will I shortly pour out my fury upon thee, and accomplish mine anger upon thee: and I will judge thee according to thy ways, and will recompense thee for all thine abominations. And mine eye shall not spare, neither will I have pity: I will recompense thee according to thy ways and thine

abominations that are in the midst of thee; and ye shall know that I am the LORD that smiteth. Behold the day, behold, it is come: the morning is gone forth; the rod hath blossomed, pride hath budded."[4]

The Lord speaks in the book of Obadiah to the nation of Moab. *"The arrogance of your heart has deceived you, You who live in the clefts of the rock, In the loftiness of your dwelling place, who say in your heart, 'Who will bring me down to earth?' Though you build high like the eagle, though you set your nest among the stars, From there I will bring you down, declares the Lord."*[5]

America has committed the same sins as Moab. She also has set her throne on high as an eagle, and she will face the same judgment. The Lord declares even if you built your nest among the stars, from there I will bring you down. America and her space program may have reached to the stars, but from this great height, she will be brought down.

THE LORD WILL PUNISH THOSE WHO ARE STAGNANT IN SPIRIT

Zephaniah declares, in the Day of Judgment the Lord will go through the land and will search for those things hidden in the darkness. *"And it will come about at that time That I will search Jerusalem with lamps, and I will punish the men Who are stagnant in spirit, Who say in their hearts, 'The LORD will not do good or evil!' Moreover, their wealth will become plunder, And their houses desolate; Yes, they will build houses but not inhabit them And plant vineyards but not drink their wine."*[6]

The Lord will punish all those who are stagnant in their spirit. These men are neither hot nor cold, but are lukewarm. These men stagnant in spirit refuse to hear the prophetic message, and they say to themselves in their hearts, *"The Lord will do neither good nor evil."* These men walk as unbelievers, for they refuse to believe the Lord will intervene in the world. They reject the word of God's prophets, and even mock it within themselves. God says their wealth will become plunder, and their houses will be deserted. They will lose everything in the Day of Judgment, which they derided.

The prophet declares that the Lord will punish these stagnant ones at the time of the end of the age, for his words speak of The Day of the LORD: *"Near is the great day of the LORD, Near and coming very quickly; Listen, the day of the LORD! In it the warrior cries out bitterly. A day of wrath is that day, A day of trouble and distress, A day of destruction and desolation, A day of darkness and gloom, A day of clouds and thick darkness, A day of trumpet and battle cry, Against the fortified cities And the high corner towers.*

"And I will bring distress on men, So that they will walk like the blind, Because they have sinned against the LORD; And their blood will be poured out like dust, And their flesh like dung. Neither their silver nor their gold Will be able to deliver them On the day of the LORD'S wrath; And all the earth will be devoured In the fire of His jealousy, for He will make a complete end, Indeed a terrifying one, Of all the inhabitants of the earth."[7]

AMERICA HAS COMMITTED THE
SIN OF MOAB—GREAT PRIDE

"We have heard of the pride of Moab; he is very proud: even of his haughtiness, and his pride, and his wrath: but his lies shall not be so."[8] Moab was very proud and full of arrogance. America has committed the same sins before God. Our nation is like Moab, and the prophecies against her speak against America. *"Therefore shall Moab howl for Moab, every one shall howl: for the foundations of Kirhareseth shall ye mourn; surely they are stricken. For the fields of Heshbon languish, and the vine of Sibmah: the lords of the heathen have broken down the principal plants thereof, they are come even unto Jazer, they wandered through the wilderness: her branches are stretched out, they are gone over the sea."*[9] Who is wise in spirit that he may discern the hidden things in the Word?

THE SUMMER HARVEST SHALL FAIL
BEFORE THE JUDGMENT

The judgment on Moab began with the failing of a summer harvest. So, too, in America, the judgment of God will begin in the time of a future summer harvest season. The nation will be struck with heat and drought, and her summer harvest will fail. This is the sign to the remnant that the judgment is about to begin, and it is time to flee.

> *"Therefore I will bewail with the weeping of Jazer the vine of Sibmah: I will water thee with my tears... for the shouting for thy summer fruits and for thy harvest is fallen. And gladness is taken away, and joy out of the plentiful field; and in the vineyards there shall be no singing, neither shall there be shouting: the treaders shall tread out no wine in their presses; I have made their vintage shouting to cease."*[10]

When the judgment begins to fall, Moab shall come into his sanctuary to pray, but he will not prevail. *"And it shall come to pass, when it is seen that Moab is weary on the high place, that he shall come to his sanctuary to pray; but he shall not prevail. This is the word that the LORD hath spoken concerning Moab since that time."*[11]

America, too, once her judgment commences, will seek to pray for relief but it will not be granted her. This word has been spoken concerning Moab and the sins of Moab, which are the sins of national pride since that time. Every nation, which exalted itself as Moab, will be judged in the same fashion.

The Lord changes not. Every word He speaks shall come to pass. *"But now the LORD hath spoken, saying, Within three years, as the years of an hireling, and the glory of Moab shall be contemned, with all that great multitude; and the remnant shall be very small and feeble."*[12] The word also tells us the remnant of America, those who survive her judgment, will be very small and feeble. Only a small number of people will escape what is about to come to pass in America.

Lest we be doubters that these words have no bearing on the events of the end of the age, Isaiah immediately speaks of the destruction of Damascus, which will occur at the end of the age. *"The burden of Damascus. Behold, Damascus is taken away from being a city, and it shall be a ruinous heap."*[13] This is the destruction that will fall on Damascus following the next war in Israel, and Damascus will be no more!

Moab is warned to flee into the wilderness, for the spoiler will come upon every city. America has also been at ease from her youth. *"Flee, save your lives, and be like the heath in the wilderness. For because thou hast trusted in thy works and in thy treasures, thou shalt also be taken.... And the spoiler shall come upon every city, and no city shall escape....*

"Give wings unto Moab, that it may flee and get away: for the cities thereof shall be desolate, without any to dwell therein. Cursed be he that doeth the work of the LORD deceitfully, and cursed be he that keepeth back his sword from blood. Moab hath been at ease from his youth, and he hath settled on his lees, and hath not been emptied from vessel to vessel, neither hath he gone into captivity: therefore his taste remained in him, and his scent is not changed.

"Therefore, behold, the days come, saith the LORD, that I will send unto him wanderers, that shall cause him to wander, and shall empty his vessels, and break their bottles."[14] A generation of Americans has never known the judgment of the Lord, so they have settled on their lees, meaning, they have not been poured out and cleansed, but have the residue of sin within their hearts. Rather than cleaning these vessels, the Lord is going to shatter them.

America will be spoiled and everyone will flee out of her cities. Her young men are going to go down to the slaughter. *"Moab is spoiled, and gone up out of her cities, and his chosen young men are gone down to the slaughter, saith the King, whose name is the LORD of hosts. The calamity of Moab is near to come, and his affliction hasteth fast.*

"All ye that are about him, bemoan him; and all ye that know his name, say, How is the strong staff broken, and the beautiful rod!"[15] The calamity is near to come, and this great affliction hastens quickly upon our land. How is the strong staff broken! How the power of America is thrown down to the ground!

Again, the people are warned to leave the cities. Go up into the mountains and live among the rocks. *"O ye that dwell in Moab, leave the cities, and dwell in the rock, and be like the dove that maketh her nest in the sides of the hole's mouth. We have heard the pride of Moab (he is exceeding proud), his loftiness, and his arrogancy, and his pride, and the haughtiness of his heart.*

"I know his wrath, saith the LORD; but it shall not be so; his lies shall not so effect it."[16] We have heard of the pride of America, she is very proud and haughty in her heart. And she has great wrath, but she will not stand, says the Lord.

Again, we are reminded of the timing of the judgment, for it will begin when her summer fruit fails and the spoiler comes upon her summer harvest. *"O vine of Sibmah, I will weep for thee with the weeping of Jazer: thy plants are gone over the sea, they reach even to the sea of Jazer: the spoiler is fallen upon thy summer fruits and upon thy vintage."*[17] America will be judged shortly after the failure of her summer harvest in the season of fall.

CHAPTER 10

"BABYLON THE GREAT IS FALLEN, FALLEN"
Revelation 18:2

The book of Revelation contains a series of visions by John the Apostle of the events during the Great Tribulation. They are revealed one after another, yet they do not occur chronologically in time. These are a series of revelations, presented as visions, of what is to come upon the earth at the time of God's judgment of the world. Many scholars make the error of assuming the events are in sequential order—they are not.

THE LAMB STOOD ON MOUNT ZION
WITH HIS ANOINTED ONES

The beginning of the Judgment by God is contained within Chapter 14, which opens with the vision of the Lamb, Jesus Christ on mount Zion, and with him, 144,000 of his sanctified ones.

"And I looked, and, lo, a Lamb stood on the mount Sion, and with him an hundred forty and four thousand, having his Father's name written in their foreheads. And I heard a voice from heaven, as the voice of many waters, and as the voice of a great thunder: and I heard the voice of harpers harping with their harps: And they sung as it were a new song before the throne, and before the four beasts, and the elders: and no man could learn that song but the hundred and forty and four thousand, which were redeemed from the earth. These are they which were not defiled with women; for they are virgins. These are they which follow the Lamb whithersoever he goeth. These were redeemed from among men, being the firstfruits

unto God and to the Lamb. And in their mouth was found no guile: for they are without fault before the throne of God" (Revelation 14:1-5).

They are the army of God, which Isaiah chapter 13 speaks of entitled *"The burden of Babylon which Isaiah did see."* This army of 144,000 is seen gathered into the mountains of Jordan, which is Edom. This may be symbolic of these anointed ones standing with the Lamb or it may have a literal fulfillment, and just as the Lord 2,000 years earlier walked out of Jordan, so, too, His anointed ones may come from Edom. These are the *chosen men*, of whom the Lord says, *"I have commanded my sanctified ones, I have also called my mighty ones for my anger, even them that rejoice in my highness."*[1]

THE HOUR OF GOD'S JUDGMENT HAS COME

Immediately after the Lamb gathers His army, a voice thunders from heaven with the sound of many waters, declaring *"FEAR God, AND GIVE GLORY UNTO HIM; FOR THE HOUR OF HIS JUDGMENT HAS COME!"* This is the heavenly declaration of the commencement of the judgment of God; this scene takes place at the very start of God's judgment upon the earth. Immediately, a second angel declares *"Babylon is fallen, is fallen, that great city!"*

The fall of Babylon is the first event following the announcement of the hour of judgment by God. America Babylon is destroyed immediately before the Tribulation period, but she is not the final kingdom of Babylon—America is the daughter of Babylon and what will follow is the seventh kingdom of Babylon, in which Lucifer will rule the one world government of the New World Order in possession of the Antichrist. And he is the eighth king, and the final kingdom of the beast empire will manifest the full and uncensored evil of Lucifer himself. It, too, will fall in one hour— which lasts 42 months.

"And I saw another angel fly in the midst of heaven, having the everlasting gospel to preach unto them that dwell on the earth, and to every nation, and kindred, and tongue, and people, Saying with a loud voice, Fear God, and give glory to him; for the hour of his judgment is come: and worship him that made heaven, and earth, and the sea, and the fountains of waters. And there followed an-

other angel, saying, Babylon is fallen, is fallen, that great city, because she made all nations drink of the wine of the wrath of her fornication" (Revelation 14:6-8).

What is the hour of God's judgment? When the Lord speaks of timing, we know a day in His watch is a thousand years in our sight. If we divide 1,000 years by 24 hours, we get approximately 42 years, which is also the number of months of the Great Tribulation. The hour of God's final judgment of the earth is 42 months long. This hour is symbolic of the time the Lord has appointed to judge the earth.

This is the judgment of the heathen nations, for the judgment of the church has already begun in the persecution, which precedes the tribulation. Then the Lord turns to judge the nations, and He starts with the most proud—America Babylon, the reigning super power at the time of the end. The next event is a third angel pronouncing the wrath of God shall be upon all those who worship the beast, for this is God's final warning on the unsaved before they take the mark of the beast. The mark will follow shortly thereafter, in the first part of the 42-month tribulation.

"And the third angel followed them, saying with a loud voice, If any man worship the beast and his image, and receive his mark in his forehead, or in his hand, The same shall drink of the wine of the wrath of God, which is poured out without mixture into the cup of his indignation; and he shall be tormented with fire and brimstone in the presence of the holy angels, and in the presence of the Lamb: And the smoke of their torment ascendeth up for ever and ever: and they have no rest day nor night, who worship the beast and his image, and whosoever receiveth the mark of his name" (Revelation 14:9-11).

The patience of the saints is this knowledge: first, God shall judge those who worship the beast with righteousness and severity, and second, those who are faithful to the Lord, even in death, may rest from their labors and their faithful works follow after them. Then we are presented another picture of the judgment, which is a harvest, in which the earth will be reaped.

The wheat will be gathered into the Father's barn, as a chosen bride, and the tares, they, too, will be gathered—into bundles and burned with unquenchable fire—and their torment will ascend forever!

> *"Here is the patience of the saints: here are they that keep the com-mandments of God, and the faith of Jesus. And I heard a voice from heaven saying unto me, Write, Blessed are the dead which die in the Lord from henceforth: Yea, saith the Spirit, that they may rest from their labours; and their works do follow them. And I looked, and behold a white cloud, and upon the cloud one sat like unto the Son of man, having on his head a golden crown, and in his hand a sharp sickle. And another angel came out of the temple, crying with a loud voice to him that sat on the cloud, Thrust in thy sickle, and reap: for the time is come for thee to reap; for the harvest of the earth is ripe. And he that sat on the cloud thrust in his sickle on the earth; and the earth was reaped"* (Revelation 14:12-16).

Last, another angel with a sharp sickle thrusts his instrument into the winepress of the wrath of God, and the blood flow from the battle of Armageddon will be 1,600 furlongs, which is approxi-mately 200 miles. From the valley of Jezreel, 200 miles to the southeast lies the Arnon river, which is the outer edge of the sanc-tuary prepared for the remnant who at that time will have been fully re-gathered and safely hidden in the mountains of Petra.

> *"And another angel came out of the temple which is in heaven, he also having a sharp sickle. And another angel came out from the al-tar, which had power over fire; and cried with a loud cry to him that had the sharp sickle, saying, Thrust in thy sharp sickle, and gather the clusters of the vine of the earth; for her grapes are fully ripe. And the angel thrust in his sickle into the earth, and gathered the vine of the earth, and cast it into the great winepress of the wrath of God. And the winepress was trodden without the city, and blood came out of the winepress, even unto the horse bridles, by the space of a thousand and six hundred furlongs"* (Revelation 14:17-20).

From the Scriptures, we know that the judgment on America Babylon will occur at the start of the judgment by God upon the entire earth. This judgment will be sudden, for in a moment in time, she will fall; but how can this be? America is the greatest na-tion in the earth now, and who can resist her military might? Like the Titanic that sailed with the envy of the world almost 100 years ago, she too is unsinkable—at least in the minds of her passengers sleeping quietly below her decks.

Standing above, in the shadows of darkness, which have descended upon her as night falls, the watchmen of the Lord announce an iceberg larger in size than any could imagine, waiting in her immediate path. The watchmen sound the alarm, yet only a few will listen to their warning cry, *"A lion has emerged from the thicket and the destroyer of the nations is on his way!"* And he will destroy the *"mighty"* nation first, and then turn to *"make war"* on the saints.

THE PATTERN OF GOD'S JUDGMENT

The history of God's judgments contains a similar pattern each time; those who do not remember history are destined to repeat it. From the Lord's own words, we know the judgment at the time of the end of the age will be similar to the time of Noah: Noah found favor with the Lord, while the people of the earth were full of wickedness.

God sent His warnings to them for one hundred and twenty years, then sent a final warning as Noah entered the ark. In Sodom, the Lord removed the righteous before destroying the city. In the fall of Jerusalem at 70 AD, the Roman army pulled back for several days to allow the believers time to escape, and everyone else who stayed, thinking the city's walls would protect them, was destroyed or taken into slavery.

AMERICA WILL NOT BE ABLE TO STOP THE BLEEDING

The Lord has never allowed a society to promote homosexuality or abortion without bringing His judgment—ours is no different: America is even now under the judgment of the Lord. America will not be able to stop the bleeding; foreign armies will occupy this land. Behold, they are already among you, and you see them not. America has refused the Lord's grace, now she must accept His judgment:

1. Innocent blood has been spilled on the land and the land is now defiled.
2. The blood of over 50 million babies has been shed in this land.

3. The sin has reached unto the throne of the Holy One.
4. Judgment is now upon the land; it will tarry no longer.
5. The blood of the offender has to be appeased.
6. America rejected the Lord's grace, she will have to accept His judgment.[2]

IT'S MIDNIGHT AND MANKIND DOESN'T KNOW IT

As this hour of judgment draws near, and it will surely come, we must hide ourselves in the mercy of the Lord for only those who abide in the Lord, and are covered by the blood of Jesus, will be spared.

1. The angel of death is coming to America.
2. Pride comes before the fall; America says she sits as a queen enthroned, now her judgment is upon her and she will fall in one hour.
3. To the degree she lived luxuriously, she will receive double for her sins.
4. It is midnight, and mankind doesn't know it.[3]

America is in trouble because America forgot who she was. Our forefathers were men of prayer. The United States was built on the foundation of the word of God. The Lord does not do anything without first prophesying the word. God will use us in mighty ways if we will let him. History is about to be repeated. The Lord is always able to take care of the problem, but he will not do it if we are in the way. The Lord declares, *"Behold, to obey is better than sacrifice."*[4]

In Isaiah we are told, *"If ye be willing and obedient, ye shall eat the good of the land."*[5]

The word says that whoever sees his brother in need and does not meet the need, he does not have the love of God in his heart. We are going to have to watch out for each other. The Lord tells us to buy a sword in this hour. Jesus spoke prophetically of this hour saying, *"But now, he that hath a purse, let him take it, and likewise his scrip: and he that hath no sword, let him sell his garment, and buy one.*

"For I say unto you, that this that is written must yet be accomplished in me, And he was reckoned among the transgressors: for

the things concerning me have an end. And they said, Lord, behold, here are two swords. And he said unto them, It is enough."[6] The sword will not save us, but we must be obedient and follow His word in every detail. The Lord saved Hananiah, Mishael, and Azariah, when they were thrown down bound into the midst of the burning fiery furnace.

Then the King of Babylon answered and said, *"I see four men loose, walking in the midst of the fire, and they have no hurt; and the form of the fourth is like the Son of God."* Jesus Christ is going to save us, only Him and nothing else.

THE FALL OF JERUSALEM

"The siege of Jerusalem in 70 AD is symbolic of the judgment that will fall on America; the judgment came because the nation was in sin just like America. The reasons given in Scripture include the oppression of the poor, the land full of violence, false prophets crying peace and safety, and people relying on religion and not on God. The people refused to hear the truth, and they were rejecting God's laws, and were hard-hearted and full of sin."[7] The same is true of America today.

It is interesting that the people in Jerusalem thought God would never destroy the nation of Israel. The people in America today are trusting in their great wealth, which is actually great debt, and their strong military, while we are totally vulnerable to terrorism, and believe she is also invincible. In one hour she will burn!

Jesus prophesied the destruction of Jerusalem himself. *"O Jerusalem, Jerusalem, which killest the prophets, and stonest them that are sent unto thee; how often would I have gathered thy children together, as a hen doth gather her brood under her wings, and ye would not! Behold, your house is left unto you desolate: and verily I say unto you, Ye shall not see me, until the time come when ye shall say, Blessed is he that cometh in the name of the Lord."*[8]

Today many prophets have been raised up to warn of the destruction of America including Dumitru Duduman, David Wilkerson, and others who have seen the nuclear destruction on the coast lands of America following a civil war in the heartland. When the siege of Jerusalem started, the Roman army surrounded the city and then pulled back for several days to give those who would choose to escape an opportunity to leave, and those who fled were saved. Several men have spoken that the Lord will give a similar warning to the believers in America through a major sign, and then the remnant will have to flee.

GOD ALWAYS GIVES A FINAL WARNING

The judgments of the past all contained the following pattern:

1. The judgment is prophesied to the people as a warning.
2. The Lord always gives a final warning.
3. God's faithful and obedient people are always given the opportunity to flee.
4. Those who disobey and do not head the warnings are destroyed.
5. The judgment includes plagues, famine and the sword.
6. God always remembers His blood covenant and an obedient remnant is saved.
7. The Lord always gets the glory for saving His remnant.

The Word of God speaks of the fall of America Babylon. *"And after these things I saw another angel come down from heaven, having great power; and the earth was lightened with his glory. And he cried mightily with a strong voice, saying, Babylon the great is fallen, is fallen.... And I heard another voice from heaven, saying, Come out of her, my people, that ye be not partakers of her sins, and that ye receive not of her plagues."*[9]

THE LORD IS PREPARING HIS REMNANT

The Lord is now preparing a remnant people and is teaching them how to prepare for the great hour of testing that is quickly coming upon the entire earth. *"Because thou hast kept the word of my patience, I also will keep thee from the hour of temptation, which shall come upon all the world, to try them that dwell upon the earth."*[10]

In 1 Thessalonians 5:2-4, the word declares we should not be in the dark about the sudden coming of the Day of Judgment. *"For yourselves know perfectly that the day of the Lord so cometh as a thief in the night. For when they shall say, Peace and safety; then sudden destruction cometh upon them, as travail upon a woman with child; and they shall not escape. But ye, brethren, are not in darkness, that that day should overtake you as a thief.*" We should be able to see the signs and be preparing for the imminent judgment upon the entire earth.

THE SOON AND CERTAIN JUDGMENT UPON AMERICA

The Lord has revealed several things about the coming judgment upon America:

1. The Hebrew Year Ending in March of 1999 marked the end of 70th Jubilee. This has been followed by seven Sabbath years which were missed during the seven weeks of years, following the decree to rebuild Jerusalem. The 7th Sabbath ends in 2006.
2. We will witness the judgment of America Babylon begin in the near future.
3. Civil war will come to America at the beginning of the judgment.
4. In one day, America will burn and suffer massive losses.
5. The east and west coasts will be destroyed by nuclear fire.
6. Biological weapons will be used in the other major U.S. cities.
7. The U.S. will suffer a staggering loss of life in the tens of millions.
8. America as we know it is over, and nation will not survive following the judgments that are coming upon her.

The judgment is certain to happen, and we are responsible to prepare and take action; there are things you must do to prepare for the tough times immediately ahead. Before the Holocaust in Germany, the Lord sent people to warn the Jews to leave the country because a terrible thing was about to happen. Those who listened sold their possessions, converted them to diamonds, and fled.

They were obedient and saved both their lives and property. Others left at the last minute, and only saved their lives. The majority refused to hear and obey the message, and lost everything including their lives. Another greater holocaust is coming; we had better prepare for we stand right at the door. The land will witness civil war before the final judgment of fire! *"And lest your heart faint, and ye fear for the rumour that shall be heard in the land; a rumour shall both come one year, and after that in another year shall come a rumour, and violence in the land, ruler against ruler."*[11]

THE ONLY WAY OUT IS TO LEAVE EARLY

God always gives us a warning; we live under the rule of a sovereign king who loves us. Will you be ready for what is coming? You must take care of the spiritual needs first. You must be able to hear His voice, or you will be one of the frightened ones. What will you do when the panic hits your city? The only way out of the cities is to leave early! Everyone will flee the cities of America Babylon! *"Her cities are a desolation, a dry land, and a wilderness, a land wherein no man dwelleth, neither doth any son of man pass thereby."*[12]

The day will come when you must hear His still small voice, and when it's time to go, you must obey, or it will cost you everything. Remember, there never has been a time when the Lord did not deliver a remnant. You must learn the power of the name of Jesus Christ and the word of authority of divine command: the power to enforce the authority of the kingdom of God in our lives, our homes and our families.

1. You have to learn to stand your ground in His power and authority.
2. To do this, you must be grounded in the word of God.
3. Clean out your house, and deal with any area of sin in your life.
4. You must plead the Blood of Jesus Christ over your life, your loved ones and your property.

This is done verbally by faith. You have the right to claim the covering of the Blood of Jesus, so be obedient and pray! The prophecies of many of the men of God, David Wilkerson, Dumitru Duduman, and others proclaim the sudden destruction of the United States. The Lord told Duduman that *"the Church has left me."* We need to stop sinning and return to the Lord. If you don't, if you stay in your sin and rebellion, you will be destroyed.

THE LORD IS SENDING HIS PROPHETS
WITH HIS FINAL WARNING

The Lord is again sending His prophets with the final warning call pleading with the people to turn from their sin and repent before the hour of destruction is upon the land. The pattern is the same, the people are hardened in their sins and are choosing to listen to the false prophets who promise peace and safety through the pre-tribulation rapture, yet a remnant is hearing the word of the Lord, and they are preparing their hearts to meet the Lord and they are preparing an ark for safety.

"Even thus shall it be in the day when the Son of man is revealed. In that day, he which shall be upon the housetop, and his stuff in the house, let him not come down to take it away: and he that is in the field, let him likewise not return back. Remember Lot's wife. Whosoever shall seek to save his life shall lose it; and whosoever shall lose his life shall preserve it.

I tell you, in that night there shall be two men in one bed; the one shall be taken, and the other shall be left. Two women shall be grinding together; the one shall be taken, and the other left. Two men shall be in the field; the one shall be taken, and the other left. And they answered and said unto him, Where, Lord? And he said unto them, Wheresoever the body is, thither will the eagles be gathered together" (Luke 17:30-37).

The Lord tells us that the day the Son of man is revealed, we are to flee, and do not even go back into your house to get your things, but flee immediately. The reference to the day *"when the Son of man is revealed"* speaks of the remnant who will be sealed and the Lord Himself coming back into the world through His mighty ones to walk for 3½ years as THE LION FROM THE TRIBE OF JUDAH.

This occurs at the same time that the abomination occurs, for both princes now come forth revealed to mankind, to fulfill the last half of the covenant of their fathers. Notice this is not a reference to the Second Coming. We do not have to flee at that time. The Lord is referring to the revelation of His witnesses, the army of the 144,000 who will be anointed and revealed at the same time that *"the one who makes desolate is revealed"* and then the judgment will begin.

The reference to the ones taken speaks of those who will die in the judgment and the ones that are left are the remnant, for the apostles question Him, *"where Lord?"* asking where will they be taken to? His answer speaks of the death of the ones taken.

Remember, in Daniel we are told the prince will make war with the saints. *"I beheld, and the same horn made war with the saints,*

246 The Day of the LORD is at Hand *Second Edition* Benjamin Baruch

and prevailed against them."[13] Again, we are told the prince has power for only 3½ years: *"Thus he said, The fourth beast shall be the fourth kingdom upon earth, which shall be diverse from all kingdoms, and shall devour the whole earth, and shall tread it down, and break it in pieces.*

"And the ten horns out of this kingdom are ten kings that shall arise: and another shall rise after them; and he shall be diverse from the first, and he shall subdue three kings. And he shall speak great words against the most High, and shall wear out the saints of the most High, and think to change times and laws: and they shall be given into his hand until a time and times and the dividing of time."[14] The reference to wearing out the saints speaks of the slave labor camps, in which the believers will be held until their death as martyrs.

In Revelation 14:7-8 we read: *"Fear God, and give glory to him; for the hour of his judgment is come: and worship him that made heaven, and earth, and the sea, and the fountains of waters. And there followed another angel, saying, Babylon is fallen, is fallen, that great city, because she made all nations drink of the wine of the wrath of her fornication."* In Revelation 12:6 we are told this same 3-½ year period is the time of the flight of the woman, *"And the woman fled into the wilderness, where she hath a place prepared of God, that they should feed her there a thousand two hundred and threescore days."*

The world wide dominance of the prince is made clear in Revelation 13:7, *"And it was given unto him to make war with the saints, and to overcome them: and power was given him over all kindreds, and tongues, and nations."* One of the first acts of the prince is to destroy the mighty people. In Daniel 8:24 we read, *"And his power shall be mighty, but not by his own power: and he shall destroy wonderfully, and shall prosper, and practice, and shall destroy the mighty and the holy people."*

This reference is to the destruction of the mighty nation, which precedes his war on the holy people. This mighty nation—the U.S.A.—will fall immediately prior to the setting up of the one-world government.

In Revelation 17:15-18, *"And he saith unto me, The waters which thou sawest, where the whore sitteth, are peoples, and multitudes, and nations, and tongues. And the ten horns which thou sawest upon the beast, these shall hate the whore, and shall make her desolate and naked, and shall eat her flesh, and burn her with fire.*

For God hath put in their hearts to fulfil his will, and to agree, and give their kingdom unto the beast, until the words of God shall be fulfilled. And the woman which thou sawest is that great city, which reigneth over the kings of the earth." The city is a reference to the nation-state, which is reigning over the nations of the earth, at the time of the end, the one remaining super power, the U.S.A.

In Isaiah 47:5, the Lord describes the daughter of Babylon as the lady of kingdoms *"Sit thou silent, and get thee into darkness, O daughter of the Chaldeans: for thou shalt no more be called, The lady of kingdoms."* And again the Scripture reiterates in Isaiah 47:8-9 that the people of Babylon dwell *"carelessly."*

"Therefore hear now this, thou that art given to pleasures, that dwellest carelessly, that sayest in thine heart, I am, and none else beside me; I shall not sit as a widow, neither shall I know the loss of children: But these two things shall come to thee in a moment in one day, the loss of children, and widowhood: they shall come upon thee in their perfection for the multitude of thy sorceries, and for the great abundance of thine enchantments."

In Isaiah 13:19 the Lord states the beautiful parts of the Babylonian kingdom (the coastlands) will be overthrown and destroyed as Sodom: *"And Babylon, the glory of kingdoms, the beauty of the Chaldees' excellency, shall be as when God overthrew Sodom and Gomorrah."*

What evidence is there to confirm these things? More than you could ever review in 20 years' time, which is about how long I have been watching diligently! Here is a short summary—highlights of the news you probably did not hear about, or notice the significance of, while it occurred.

THE REPORT FROM IRON MOUNTAIN

The first public information revealed about the plans of the Illuminati for America began to surface in the public view in the 1960's. One of the most significant leaks was the *"Top Secret Report from Iron Mountain"* published by Dial Press in 1967.

"In 1961 the Kennedy Administration ordered a Top Secret study to determine the problems facing the United States if the world moved from an era of war to a Golden Age of Peace.... Their first and last meetings were held at a nuclear survival retreat called Iron Mountain. The study was concluded in 1966 and President Johnson gave the order that the report was never to be released. Due to the nature of the conclusions reached, one of the men involved in this study elected to release it to the public at great risk to himself under the name of John Doe. Dial Press published the Report from Iron Mountain in 1967. The establishment promptly renounced it as a hoax. It was no hoax. Iron Mountain is now hard to obtain, but many large libraries still have copies of it. This report looks deep into the soul of the New World Order. Iron Mountain is the covert agenda to bring the world and America under the control of the United Nations. The conclusions reached are now being implemented upon the American people without their knowledge or consent. It is real.... and no person in America is safe, because in spite of all the denials of authorities, it is real, and these plans are now coming to pass. Iron Mountain explains how the rich men of the earth are operating and why. Iron Mountain is a look into the soul of Lucifer, the Antichrist, long foretold by Jesus Christ, who warned us 2000 years ago, this was coming ...IT IS NOW HERE."[15]

U.S. STATE DEPARTMENT PUBLICATION 7277

In the same year, the United States Department of State issued Publication Number 7277, *Freedom from War: The United States Program for General Disarmament in a Peaceful World.* The introduction states, "the United States has introduced at the Sixteenth General Assembly of the United Nations a Program for General and Complete Disarmament in a Peaceful World.... it is based on three principles deemed essential to the achievement of practical progress in the disarmament field: First, there must be an immediate disarmament action....

"Second, all disarmament actions must be subject to effective international controls.... Third, adequate peace-keeping machinery must be established.... This can only be achieved through the progressive strengthening of international institutions under the United Nations and by creating a United Nations Peace Force to enforce peace as the disarmament process proceeds."[16]

"And through his policy also he shall cause craft to prosper in his hand; and he shall magnify himself in his heart, and by peace shall destroy many" (Daniel 8:25).

Publication Number 7277 includes a three-stage disarmament process, of which we are now in the last part of stage three; these include:

1. Stage One: provided that the nuclear threat would be reduced through weapons testing prohibitions, nuclear weapons would be limited, and the armed forces of the USSR and the USA would be reduced.

2. Stage Two: included further substantial reductions in national armed forces, establishment of a permanent international peace force within the UN, and the dismantling or conversion of military bases

3. Stage Three: provided the final steps whereby states would only retain those forces and non-nuclear armaments required for the purposes of maintaining internal order and provide agreed manpower for a UN peace force: manufacture of armaments would be prohibited except for those of agreed types and quantities to be used by the UN Peace Force. All other armaments would be destroyed or converted to peaceful purposes.

Thus, the *"peacekeeping"* capabilities of the United Nations would be sufficiently strong... as to assure peace and the just settlement of differences in a disarmed world.[17] Few Americans realized the US Department of State embarked on a mission to disarm America in the early 1960's and surrender her military might to a new central government of the world under the United Nations. This is the

New World Order and the citizens of America will be brought under its power without a vote or any awareness of this plan.

> *"And in the latter time of their kingdom, when the transgressors are
> come to the full, a king of fierce countenance, and understanding
> dark sentences, shall stand up. And his power shall be mighty, but
> not by his own power: and he shall destroy wonderfully"* (Daniel
> 8:23-24).

> *"He shall enter peaceably.... And such as do wickedly against the
> covenant shall he corrupt by flatteries: but the people that do know
> their God shall be strong, and do exploits. And they that understand
> among the people shall instruct many"* (Daniel 11:24, 32-33).

THE NEW WORLD ORDER IN THE YEAR 2000

In other published UN documents, we have learned the New
World Order and the one world government were to be established
by the year 2000. "The UN-funded commission of Global Governance has completed its three-year study, and has announced publicly its plans to implement global government by the year 2000.
They call for a World Conference on Global Governance by 1998
for the purpose of submitting to the world the necessary treaties
and agreements for the ratification and implementation by the
year 2000."[18]

The goal is to have the world enter the New Millennium under the
control of the final one-world empire of the beast. This is their
agenda, but God will allow it to come to pass in the hour He
chooses. Dear reader, any delay is God granting us more time to
get ready!

To establish a world empire the servants of the anti-christ must
first introduce a crisis in order to change the political system of the
United States of America. Other leaked intelligence confirms these
insiders have been instructed by Lucifer to cleanse the earth before the dawn of the so-called "New Age." To do this, they must
eliminate all of the believers who will not embrace their pagan
worldview, so that the earth might experience the next step in the
spiritual evolution of man. Little do they realize they are "*cleansing the earth*" and readying it for the true Millennium, which is
coming after Jesus Christ returns.

World leaders from all nations now are publicly acknowledging this reality. Norman Cousins, Under Secretary of State declared, "World Government is coming, in fact it is inevitable. No arguments for or against it can change that fact."[19]

President George Bush introduced the American people to the plan of a New World Order: *"What is at stake is more than one small country, it is a big idea, a New World Order, where diverse nations come together to achieve the universal aspirations of mankind... based on shared principles and the rule of law.... The illumination of a thousand points of light... the winds of change are with us now."*[20]

Pope John Paul II wrote, "By the end of this decade (AD 2000) we will live under the first one world government that has ever existed in the society of nations. One world government is inevitable."[21] His last statement is true; it is inevitable, for the Spirit of the Lord has prophesied these events. His first remarks are false; the world has lived under world government before, in all the prior kingdoms of Mystery Babylon.

THE FALSE MILLENIUM OF THE BEAST

This New World Order, which is about to come to power, is the false millennium, under the false messiah, after the counterfeit battle of Armageddon, which is about to be fought in the Middle East. Lucifer counterfeits everything God does. Here at the end of the age, his false messiah, the little prince, will appear before the world to bring *"peace and security"* after the destruction of America and the nuclear war which will come in the Middle East:

1. Top Intelligence agencies all confirm the Middle East is ready to explode.
2. The Arab nations including Syria and Iran have all signed a cooperation agreement to align in a joint war with Israel
3. The Israelis are planning for war and are readying their forces for inevitable conflict but are presently in a poor state of readiness, the Arabs know that in waiting they give the Israelis time to increase their strength.
4. The plan includes holding the U.S. hostage with the threat of domestic terrorist attacks using both biological and nuclear

weapons smuggled onto U.S. soil. These teams have been coming in for years, and are now fully in place.

5. This battle is the war of Ezekiel 38 & 39, where we know the Israelis will suffer substantial losses, but will emerge victorious. When they retaliate with their nuclear arsenal, the Scripture says in Ezekiel 39:6, "*and I will send fire on Magog, and among them that dwell carelessly in the distant (coastlands).*" This is a direct reference to the fall of America Babylon, which will take a massive nuclear strike on the east and west coasts.

6. The financial and political collapse, which will follow, will be absolute. Out of the ruins of the present world order, when the eagles wings are plucked, then the New World Order of the beast will be lifted up and given dominion over all the earth.

MASS DESTRUCTION TERRORISM IN THE UNITED STATES

The *Intelligence Digest* in a special report of terrorism stated that, "*The widening availability of the means to manufacture or acquire biological, chemical, and/or nuclear weapons; the proliferation of religiously inspired terrorist groups; and the failure to forge a permanent peace between the Arabs/Iran and Israel... has led to the increasing fear among western security experts that a terrorist attack using weapons of mass destruction is now a question of when, not if.*"[22] In their newsletter dated October 3, 1997 they state, "*the very point of the KGB's nuclear terror bombs was to explode them in an American city 'at the right moment'.... The crucial difference now is that the bombs are allegedly no longer under Russian control... and therefore the United States cannot threaten retaliation.... the revelation that KGB-designed, suitcase sized, nuclear terror bombs have gone missing is an important factor in assessing the likelihood and timing of the next Arab-Israeli war.*"[22] In one hour Babylon will burn!

THE GROWING RISK OF FAMINE IN AMERICA

"*Were looking at a very good chance of empty bins: for the first time there's a chance we may actually run out of corn and wheat.*"[23] "*There is a new crisis looming that could dwarf all the others. It is a global shortage of food: Drought and other abnormal weather conditions have all but wiped out the 1996 hard red winter wheat crop worldwide.... Perhaps the most disturbing aspect of this unacknowledged crisis is that our own government has given away our strategic food reserves to Russia and a host of other communist countries at a time when our own grain reserves are at a 50 year low."*[24]

THE IMPENDING STATE OF MARTIAL LAW IN THE US

The United States has been operating under a state of National Emergency since March 9, 1933 under the War Powers Act. Every President reinstated this status since Roosevelt. Under the Act, the President is vested with dictatorial Powers should he move to declare a national emergency and evoke the Executive Orders Provisions of the Act. Al Gore, writing in *Earth in the Balance*, says on page 48, *"There is a threshold coming, and when it is crossed a flood of dramatic change will occur all at once."* No doubt! President George Bush recently announced he may resort to a declaration of martial law in the event of a break out of the avian bird flu.

PRESIDENTIAL EXECUTIVE ORDERS

The President of the United States has quietly accumulated dictatorial powers under the guise of Presidential Executive Orders including the following:

10995 - Seizure of all communications media in the United States.
10098 - Seizure of all food supplies and resources, public and private, all farms and farm equipment.
11000 - Seizure of all American population for work forces under federal supervision, including dividing as necessary according to government plans.
11002 - Empowers the Postmaster General to register all men, women and children.
11004 - Seizure of all housing and finance authorities to establish Forced Relocation.

Notice these executive orders include the seizure of civilians including the division of families according to government plans. Where do you think they are planning on sending your divided family?

DETENTION CAMPS IN AMERICA

The United States Government has been quietly building detention camps on more than 100 U.S. Military bases for the alleged purposes of fighting the War on Drugs. Thus far, most of these facilities have limited or no inmates. Capacity of these camps is in the millions. Obviously, the government is planning to step-up the war on some group in the near future.

Senate Bill No. 269, 104th Congress, which passed on January 10, 1995 that included Sec. 152, approved this, "... *to determine the feasibility of the use of military bases available through the defense base closure and realignment process as detention centers.*" *Dept. of Army Civil Affairs Operations Manual FM 41-10 which includes a Destruction Notice on its cover reading "Destroy by any method that will prevent disclosure of contents or reconstruction of the document."*

The manual outlines procedures to be used for control of civilian populations within the United States including design and operations guidelines for detention camps for U.S. citizens.

All of these measures are ostensibly intended to be used in the war against terrorism; but who are the terrorists? Headline for the March 5, 1997 issue of U.S. Today states; "*FBI turns aggressive on terror.*" The accompanying table titled "*Number of Patriot groups rises*" further states, "*There are 857 active patriot groups in the USA up from 809 last year....*

"*The groups are defined as militias, common-law courts, churches, radio broadcasters, publishers and others who identify themselves as anti-government or as opposed to the New World Order.*"[25] When did churches become terrorist organizations? When did a political opinion in the United States become terrorism? People wake up! They have overrun our free institutions and are ready to dismantle our democratic republic, and with it your freedom and you don't even know it!

THE CHURCH OF JESUS CHRIST IS THE ENEMY NOW

In the 1990s a US Government official was interviewed on the CNN show, Larry King Live, when she discussed the need to crackdown on the terrorist elements including radical cults within

American society. King asked, *"Who are these radical cultists?"* The official responded, *"A cultist is one who has a strong belief in the Bible and the Second Coming of Christ; who frequently attends Bible study; who has a high level of financial giving to a Christian cause; who home schools his children; who has accumulated survival foods; who has a strong belief in the 2nd amendment and... a strong distrust of big government."*[26] You may find this unbelievable—I did as I sat and witnessed this interview myself.

I literally fell off the couch. During the time of this interview, I was still asleep as most Americans, oblivious to what was happening right under my nose, or in front of my eyes on TV. The Church of Jesus Christ is the enemy now. The agents of Lucifer, the Order of the Illuminati, have now gained control of our institutions of power. They seized the kingdom by *"intrigue and flatteries"* as Daniel said. In other words, they just walked right in while no one was watching, and set up shop for the prince of darkness.

Jesus said, *"You shall be hated by all nations"* and the time has come. Some have warned me not to write this book, fearing my life would be in danger. I thank them for their concern for my safety, but I must stand bold as our forefathers did and oppose the tyranny of our time regardless of the cost. *"To sin by silence when one should protest makes cowards of men."*—Abraham Lincoln. *"The so-called modern Communism is apparently the same hypocritical and deadly world conspiracy to destroy civilization that was founded by the secret order of the Illuminati in Bavaria on May 1, 1776.*

"The world revolution conspiracy appears to have been well organized as to be ever continuing, and ever on the alert to take advantage of every opportunity presenting itself or that the conspiracy could create."[27] *"We are on the verge of global transformation. All we need is the right major crisis and the nation will accept the New World Order."*[28]

THE MOVE TOWARDS A ONE-WORLD RELIGION

Nineteen ninety-three was a bad year for the people of this planet; for the pagans who worship the earth itself, the Gaia worshippers, it was a very good year. In 1993, darkness began to slowly fall upon the earth. One of the greatest examples of the growing evil is the UN Treaty titled the *"Convention on Biological Diversity."* President Clinton signed this UN Treaty and submitted it to Congress on November 20th, 1993.

Fortunately, Congress had the good sense to defeat this measure. It will be enacted under the power of Executive Orders during the state of martial law, which is coming soon. The Convention contains ten objectives listed below; read these ten carefully.

1. To make nature the central organizing principle. This places the creation above the creator. In the minds of these pagans, nature is God and man is subject to it.

2. To establish a legal regime that will utilize international treaties to control all policies, from the international level to the national and local levels. They plan to use this treaty, and the ones which will follow, to usurp the sovereignty of the regional governments of the world and impose their rule of law from the seat of power in the UN. *"The New World Order... must unite us all in a global partnership which... must recognize the transcending sovereignty of nature, of our only one Earth."*[29]

3. To make the use of natural resources a cost.

4. To promote the precautionary principle that scientific evidence is not necessary to implement radical environmental policies. *"Lack of full scientific certainty should not be used as a reason for postponing measures to avoid or minimize threats to biological diversity."*[30]

5. To inventory natural and human resources. You have now been reduced to the equivalent of a resource, of no greater value than the other assets in inventories of the one-world masters of the global village.

6. To make man equal to all other species. You have the same level of value in the New World Order as a cockroach, or a rat, or a germ for that matter. Actually, in the mind of these pagans, you are seen as the enemy of the earth, and above all others, you are the one species with which they will make war.

7. To classify people as the enemy. "The astounding success of the human species, its proliferation in numbers and in the scale and intensity of its activities, is threatening the future of

the Earth's life systems."[31] This is why the elite talk of reducing the earth's population by up to 95%; you and your family are the enemy of their planet, and they intend to do something about it—and do it soon. A new age is coming and those in this convention set the year 2000 as their completion date. Fortunately, their timetable has been frustrated, but they continue to pursue their evil plan, looking to hasten the day when the world will come under their new order. They arrogantly announced their plans to have the one world government in full power and to have the earth cleansed by that time. They boast that they will defeat their enemy, the people of the earth, especially the Christians and the Jews, in a series of attacks on our nation and the world.

8. To create areas devoid of human presence. This is referred to as re-wilding; the Nazi's promoted a similar program in forcing civilians out of entire regions of the countryside, this time the application will be far more lethal. Examples of this doctrine in present form include the Wildlands Project, National Wildlife Refuges, Wilderness Corridors and Buffer Zones, and, of course, UN Biosphere's. They all sound harmless enough—you need to read the fine print.

9. To make nature worship a state religion. "The transformation of our vision of a sustainable civilization into reality... will not occur without a major cultural transformation—a reorientation of the ethical, moral and spiritual values which provide the primary motivations for human behavior."[32] They are going all the way with this, not only are you a resource, equal to all other species, but your freedom of religious thought threatens their little world system so they are going to impose their faith on you, and if you don't like worshipping the earth and the beast—they have a solution.

10. To promote the traditional lifestyles, cultures, and beliefs of indigenous peoples. Stamping out the Christian heritage is not enough; they need to replace it with the ancient paganism practiced by indigenous peoples.[33] Friend, the hour is late, indeed.

AMERICA TURNS FROM THE TRUTH TO THE BIG LIE

TWA Flight 800, Oklahoma City, Ruby Ridge, Vincent Foster, and Ron Brown—these are some of the names from the events that will stand forever in time as the point in time where America turned from the truth to the big lie, and began the rapid descent from freedom to tyranny while the majority of the people looked the other way, or could care less. Examine the facts; if you care to look at the truth, the evidence is overwhelming.

"Our information is that TWA 800 was struck by an unarmed missile, fired from a US submarine or other submersible platform.... this theory is enhanced by the fact that the missile was seen streaking towards the plane by no fewer than 244 witnesses, including a National Guard helicopter pilot. But the FBI's James Kallstrom dismissed the testimony of the eyewitnesses claiming that 'Eyewitness testimony is not evidence' Preposterous! Informed sources tell Strategic Investments that Kallstrom told other investigators soon after TWA 800 went down, that 'this ain't going to be a missile.'

"Kallstrom reportedly explained that the American people would 'freak' if they knew the truth."[34] You have been lied to! Every last one of you will "freak" when you finally learn the truth! Jesus warned you, "Take heed that no man deceive you." One of the attorneys involved in the Oklahoma City independent investigation by the Governor stated, "One day when you know what I know, and what I have learned, and that day will come, you will never again look at the government of the United States in the same way."[35] That day is coming soon for America.

THE GLOBAL ETHIC TOWARDS
A ONE-WORLD RELIGION

On September 4, 1993, just nine days prior to the signing the covenant with death in Israel, the leaders of the World Parliament of Religions met in Chicago. Approximately 150 of the worlds best-known religious leaders met to sign a document called "The Global Ethic," better known as Ecumenicalism.

They included Christians, Muslims, Buddhists, Hindus, Zoroastrians (Luciferians), Janis, Jews, Neo-Pagans, Satanists, Wiccas (Witchcraft), Baha'I, Brahmans, Taoists, Sikhs, and Unitarians.

Within this document you will find the phrase "not authentically human," which refers to anyone who holds the archaic dogmas of the past—that their one God is the only God. This was the same rationale the Nazis used to legitimize the killing of the Jews—they weren't considered human.

It is not just the Jews this time, now it's all of us who believe in the God of Israel, and this time the biggest massacre will be in America. On unity and the spirit of Ecumenicalism, I bring Jesus as my sole witness against this deception and apostasy:

"Suppose ye that I am come to give peace on earth? I tell you, Nay; but rather division: For from henceforth there shall be five in one house divided, three against two, and two against three. The father shall be divided against the son, and the son against the father; the mother against the daughter, and the daughter against the mother; the mother in law against her daughter in law, and the daughter in law against her mother in law. And he said also to the people, When ye see a cloud rise out of the west, straightway ye say, There cometh a shower; and so it is. And when ye see the south wind blow, ye say, There will be heat; and it cometh to pass. Ye hypocrites, ye can discern the face of the sky and of the earth; but how is it that ye do not discern this time?" (Luke 12:51-56).

In spite of the Lord's own words that His truth would bring division, today we find the majority of the leaders in American Christianity embracing unity and tolerance and entering into covenants with all forms of religious darkness. This false religious covenant was signed just nine days before the political covenant of the beast.

The time is indeed late, please pray, test this word and seek the Lord that you may be hid in this hour of judgment. Where are our leaders coming from? Our own President in his last inauguration speech said, *"The wrong kind of faith leads to division and conflict. Prejudice and contempt cloaked in the presence of religion or political conviction are no different. These forces have nearly destroyed our nation in the past. We shall overcome them."*[36]

When did the wrong kind of faith almost destroy our nation? When did the government begin expressing an opinion on the kind of faith that is right? Listen to what your leaders are saying between the lines (lies) in their speeches!

THE GLOBALIST AGENDA FOR YOU
AND YOUR FAMILY

The Globalists themselves are more direct in their disclosures of what they are planning for you and your family. Ted Turner, speaking at the Gorbachev Forum in 1995 said, *"A total world population of 250-300 million people, a 95% decline from present levels would be ideal."* Dr. Jacques Cousteau is quoted as saying *"In order to stabilize world population, we must eliminate 350,000 people per day."*

The Orange County Register reported on August 4, 1996 *"In 1971, the United States quietly joined a UN program calling for the establishment of 'biosphere reserves' around the world, each surrounded by buffer zones devoid of human activities. Since that time, our federal government has classified 47 national parks as such sanctuaries without needing to consult congress. Today, these cover over 51 million acres."* Under these areas, the UN has complete domain. U.S. sovereignty has been completely compromised. Without a shot being fired, our nation is being dissolved and no one seems to care.

On June 29, 1993, the President by Executive Order #12852 established the Council on Sustainable Development to advise the President on matters pertaining to *"economic growth that will benefit present and future generations without detrimentally affecting the resources or biological systems of the planet."*37

Where did this concept of sustainable economic growth come from? It was lifted right out of the Constitution of the Union of Soviet Socialist Republics (1977), Chapter 2, and Article 18. The Elite have been working towards a world government for years, using a myriad of organizations including: The World Federalist Association, World Constitution and Parliament Association, The World Constituent Assembly, Gorbachev Foundation USA, Lucis Trust (formerly named The Lucifer Trust before 1923), The Trilateral Commission, The Council on Foreign Relations, to name just a few.

THE LUCIFER TRUST

The Lucis Trust (formerly the Lucifer Trust) is one of the first organizations to publicly disclose the satanic nature of this vast conspiracy. Part of this strategy is to move mankind towards worship of the beast itself. In a 1995 memo to friends of the Trust, they write, *"Since it was released in 1945... promotion of the Great Invocation has been a constant and central feature of the service activities of the Lucis Trust.... It expresses a vision of the oneness of life; it affirms the promise of the reappearance of Christ... (we) will evoke the recognition by people of goodwill everywhere that all formulations of truth and belief are only partial, formed to suit the psychology and conditions of a particular time and people.... This is the spiritual core of tolerance and it is significant that the United Nations has designated 1995 the Year for Tolerance. In this year of Emergence/Impact on Public Consciousness, is the three-year cycle of the group of world servers, an understanding of public consciousness, as the essence of true citizenship is urgently needed by humanity.... Humanity is at a turning point."*[38]

> *"And they worshipped the dragon which gave power unto the beast: and they worshipped the beast, saying, Who is like unto the beast? who is able to make war with him? And there was given unto him a mouth speaking great things and blasphemies; and power was given unto him to continue forty and two months.... And it was given unto him to make war with the saints, and to overcome them"* (Revelation 13:4-7).

The Lord spoke in his law that the penalty for disobedience to his truth would be severe: *"Thy sons and thy daughters shall be given unto another people, and thine eyes shall look, and fail with longing for them all the day long: and there shall be no might in thine hand. The fruit of thy land, and all thy labours, shall a nation which thou knowest not eat up; and thou shalt be only oppressed and crushed always: So that thou shalt be mad for the sight of thine eyes which thou shalt see"* (Deuteronomy 28:32-34).

America has thrown out God's law and with it her freedom. We are now in the final hour of the history of the America we know and love. Wake up, America, wake up, church of Jesus Christ, or the next sound you will hear will be the prison door slamming shut behind you and your family. I have seen the detention centers in a vision, I cried and trembled for seven days. This is real. Judgment is real. Sin is real and the consequences are real. We are not playing a game folks—this is life and death.

TRAGEDY AND HOPE

Dr. Carroll Quigley wrote the treatise on the operations of the Order, *Tragedy and Hope*, disclosing the secret activities of the Council on Foreign Relations during the early 1960's. This book has all but disappeared from American libraries. Most have lost their copy. I reviewed the text in the early 70's. Quigley's title is his message; the tragedy is that we are going to lose our national sovereignty and freedoms under the plans of the New World Order.

The hope is, that once in place, this super central government will ensure permanent peace. "He says in effect it is now too late for the little people to turn back the tide. In a spirit of kindness, he is therefore urging them not to fight the noose which is already around their necks."39

The Order uses the Hegelian principle of creating a problem and then proposing as the solution, the goals they wish to achieve. Why do we need this New World Order?

1.   To protect the environment.
2.   To deal with the "world debt" problem.
3.   To alleviate world hunger.
4.   To bring about a permanent and lasting peace.

The blind guides continue to stumble onward to the pit, while the sheep sleep in line, waiting their turn at the edge of the abyss. "'We're on the threshold of the first global civilization.... Spiritual unity fits the philosophy of our age: everything is changing, so compromise, cooperate, unify, and adapt' said Episcopal Bishop William A. Swing shortly before leaving on a world tour to build support for his dream: a United Religions, modeled after the UN."40 Compromise?

Why not just throw out the truth altogether and go down in flames; why pretend to be holy when you are headed for hell? You deceive more people when you show up as an angel of light. Read what another famous American TV preacher, who believes in the wide road that leads to heaven, said. *"I don't think anything has been done in the name of Christ and under the banner of Christianity that has proven more destructive to human personality and hence, counterproductive to the evangelism enterprise than the often crude, uncouth and un-Christian strategy of attempting to make people aware of their lost and sinful condition."*[41]

Sorry to shatter your dreams, but Jesus said only the straight gate leads to life.

> *"Enter ye in at the strait gate: for wide is the gate, and broad is the way, that leadeth to destruction, and many there be which go in thereat: Because strait is the gate, and narrow is the way, which leadeth unto life, and few there be that find it. Beware of false prophets, which come to you in sheep's clothing, but inwardly they are ravening wolves"* (Matthew 7:13-15). *"Mine eyes shall be upon the faithful of the land, that they may dwell with me: he that walketh in a perfect way, he shall serve me. He that worketh deceit shall not dwell within my house: he that telleth lies shall not tarry in my sight"* (Psalm 101:6-7).

Thomas Jefferson: *"I tremble for my country when I reflect that God is just and that His justice cannot sleep forever."*

WHAT DO WE DO NOW—A GUIDE TO PREPARATIONS

1. Begin with prayer. We are in a spiritual war and the weapons of our warfare are spiritual.
2. Food—begin to stockpile food, be careful not to be seen as hoarding because looting and seizure will be commonplace.
3. Water—this is the most critical need you face.
4. Other emergency preparedness edeas—Americans are the most heavily insured people on the planet, but they are 100% dependent on the system and its infrastructure. It will be turned off in the near future—and what are you going to do about it?

THE ENEMY

> *"For we wrestle not against flesh and blood, but against principalities, against powers, against the rulers of the darkness of this world, against spiritual wickedness in high places. Wherefore take*

unto you the whole armour of God, that ye may be able to withstand in the evil day, and having done all, to stand.

"Stand therefore, having your loins girt about with truth, and having on the breastplate of righteousness; And your feet shod with the preparation of the gospel of peace; Above all, taking the shield of faith, wherewith ye shall be able to quench all the fiery darts of the wicked.

"And take the helmet of salvation, and the sword of the Spirit, which is the word of God: Praying always with all prayer and supplication in the Spirit, and watching thereunto with all perseverance and supplication for all saints; And for me, that utterance may be given unto me, that I may open my mouth boldly, to make known the mystery of the gospel" (Ephesians 6:12-19).

Learn the art of spiritual warfare, taking authority in prayer and speaking aloud the name of JESUS CHRIST and the power of HIS BLOOD. Become cleansed and walk in true righteousness and holiness.

"And they overcame him by the blood of the Lamb, and by the word of their testimony; and they loved not their lives unto the death" (Revelation 12:11).

Take the offensive in prayer: Our God is the Awesome God, He reigns from heaven above with Wisdom, Power and Love, Our God is the Awesome God. There is none other!

CHAPTER 11

"FIRST THERE SHALL COME AN APOSTASY"
2 Thessalonians 2:3

Scripture contains many warnings regarding the last days, and the terrible times, which would come. *"This know also, that in the last days perilous times shall come. For men shall be lovers of their own selves, covetous, boasters, proud, blasphemers, disobedient to parents, unthankful, unholy, Without natural affection, truce-breakers, false accusers, incontinent, fierce, despisers of those that are good, Traitors, heady, highminded, lovers of pleasures more than lovers of God; Having a form of godliness, but denying the power thereof: from such turn away."*[1]

Men will be lovers of their own selves, consumed with pleasing and serving their own pleasures. The understanding of many will be darkened, and they will be absorbed in bondage to the kingdom of self, which is also the kingdom of sin and rebellion. These men will be high-minded, and proud to the point of arrogance, lovers of pleasure more than God, and despising that which is good and holy.

Thinking it right, they shall live life for the pursuit of their own fleshly happiness. Their minds will be absorbed with what they foolishly call *"their self esteem,"* which is self-worship. In the last days, the worship of self has become the national pastime, and all but the holy remnant are to be consumed by this spirit.

266 The Day of the LORD is at Hand *Second Edition* Benjamin Baruch

IN THE LAST DAYS SCOFFERS SHALL COME

The apostle Peter also gave us warning that in the last days scoffers would come, walking after their own lust, mocking the promise of the coming of our Lord. These scoffers are within the Church, and they mock the messengers, who are telling the people of God it is time to get ready for the return of the Lord.

These scoffers are ignorant of the long suffering of our God, nor do they know He made the heavens and the earth, for to the Lord one day is as a thousand years. And a thousand years upon the earth is but one day for God.

> *"Knowing this first, that there shall come in the last days scoffers, walking after their own lusts, And saying, Where is the promise of his coming? for since the fathers fell asleep, all things continue as they were from the beginning of the creation. For this they willingly are ignorant of, that by the word of God the heavens were of old, and the earth standing out of the water and in the water .... But, beloved, be not ignorant of this one thing, that one day is with the Lord as a thousand years, and a thousand years as one day"* (2 Peter 3:3-8).

In the last days, the people of God will no longer want to hear sound doctrine, and will turn their ears away from the truth. They will heap to themselves teachers who will teach pleasantries and the people shall be turned to fables: *"For the time will come when they will not endure sound doctrine; but after their own lusts shall they heap to themselves teachers, having itching ears; And they shall turn away their ears from the truth, and shall be turned unto fables"* (2 Timothy 4:3-4).

The modern Church has received these fables with open arms; having refused the true word of God, they have fashioned a gospel unto their own desires. And they have heaped upon themselves many teachers who proclaim these same words of error. This a very grave and sobering hour, and few realize the Great Tribulation and the Day of the LORD is fast upon us. *"Now the Spirit speaketh expressly, that in the latter times some shall depart from the faith, giving heed to seducing spirits, and doctrines of devils; Speaking lies in hypocrisy; having their conscience seared with a hot iron."*[2]

These wayward churches have fallen from the truth, and cannot hear the warnings of God. Many of the Lord's people in the religious system of man, have chosen men to rule over them just like ancient Israel; having rejected the Lord, they have turned to man. What happened to Israel in the natural is being fulfilled again in the Church in the spiritual. The people have sought falsehoods as a covering and chosen lies for a refuge. *"Because ye have said, We have made a covenant with death, and with hell are we at agreement; when the overflowing scourge shall pass through, it shall not come unto us: for we have made lies our refuge, and under falsehood have we hid ourselves."*3

The false gospel of the apostasy and the pre-tribulation rapture are these false coverings, and they are about to be revealed for what they truly are—covenants from hell. And because of this great evil, the Lord declares *"Judgment also will I lay to the line, and righteousness to the plummet: and the hail shall sweep away the refuge of lies, and the waters shall overflow the hiding place."*4

MY PEOPLE GO INTO CAPTIVITY
FOR LACK OF KNOWLEDGE

It is not going to be very pleasant for the pastors and teachers who have preached these lies. The day of playing church is over, dear reader, and we are about to see the judgment of God fall with such severity as has been unknown from the beginning of time until now. The Lord tells us the honorable men are famished, because they have no knowledge of the truth of the Lord.

Who are the honorable men within the Church—the pastors, teachers and the false prophets who teach lies, and their congregations are dried up with thirst, for they have not received the living water, but have been led to broken cisterns, which cannot hold water.

"Therefore my people are gone into captivity, because they have no knowledge: and their honourable men are famished, and their multitude dried up with thirst. Therefore hell hath enlarged herself, and opened her mouth without measure: and their glory, and their multitude, and their pomp, and he that rejoiceth, shall descend into it. And the mean man shall be brought down, and the mighty man shall be humbled, and

the eyes of the lofty shall be humbled: But the LORD of hosts shall be exalted in judgment, and God that is holy shall be sanctified in righteousness."5

*"The LORD'S voice crieth unto the city, and the man of wisdom shall see thy name: hear ye the rod, and who hath appointed it. Are there yet the treasures of wickedness in the house of the wicked, and the scant measure that is abominable? Shall I count them pure with the wicked balances, and with the bag of deceitful weights? For the rich men thereof are full of violence, and the inhabitants thereof have spoken lies, and their tongue is deceitful in their mouth."*6

The Lord speaks to the wicked city Babylon. The men of wisdom know your true name! Come and sit in the dust, daughter of the Chaldeans!

There are two principal errors which are deceiving the people of God in America today: The first of these errors is the new gospel of the carnal Christian, which teaches that we no longer have to obey the Lord, but only need to believe in His name. *"Know ye not, that to whom ye yield yourselves servants to obey, his servants ye are to whom ye obey; whether of sin unto death, or of obedience unto righteousness?* 7

Though we are saved by faith, and this alone, and our works cannot add to the righteousness which came by Jesus Christ through faith, yet they are the evidence of our salvation and are the way of sanctification. *"Many will say to me in that day, Lord, Lord, have we not prophesied in thy name? and in thy name have cast out devils? and in thy name done many wonderful works?*

*"And then will I profess unto them, I never knew you: depart from me, ye that work iniquity."*8 The second error is the pre-tribulation rapture deception, which I will uncover towards the end of this chapter.

STRIVE TO ENTER BY THE NARROW GATE

The word for "iniquity" in the original Greek is "adikia"9 (ad-ee-kee'-ah) which is from the word injustice (the act), which means moral wrongfulness (of character, life or act) and is translated as iniquity, unrighteousness, or lawlessness.

"Then said one unto him, Lord, are there few that be saved? And he said unto them, Strive to enter in at the strait gate: for many, I say unto you, will seek to enter in, and shall not be able. When once the master of the house is risen up, and hath shut to the door, and ye begin to stand without, and to knock at the door, saying, Lord, Lord, open unto us; and he shall answer and say unto you, I know you not whence ye are: Then shall ye begin to say, We have eaten and drunk in thy presence, and thou hast taught in our streets. But he shall say, I tell you, I know you not whence ye are; depart from me, all ye workers of iniquity. There shall be weeping and gnashing of teeth, when ye shall see Abraham, and Isaac, and Jacob, and all the prophets, in the kingdom of God, and you yourselves thrust out. And they shall come from the east, and from the west, and from the north, and from the south, and shall sit down in the kingdom of God. And, behold, there are last which shall be first, and there are first which shall be last" (Luke 13:23-30).

Matthew Henry's Commentary provides a great insight into this promise by the Lord: "(1) All that will be saved must enter in at the strait gate, must undergo a change of the whole man, such as amounts to no less than being born again, and must submit to a strict discipline. (2) Those that would enter in at the strait gate must strive to enter. It is a hard matter to get to heaven, and a point that will not be gained without a great deal of care and pains, of difficulty and diligence. We must strive with God in prayer, wrestle as Jacob, and strive against sin and Satan. We must strive in every duty of religion; strive with our own hearts, agonizesthe— 'Be in an agony; strive as those that run for a prize; excite and exert ourselves to the utmost.'"[10]

Note this is not outward works of religious observance, but obedience from the heart, and this obedience is to walk in holiness, seeking to deny ourselves and to love our neighbor as ourselves. If this causes you to fear, dear reader, you have heard well, for this is the beginning of the fear of the Lord. This is why we must be born again, for the old nature cannot please nor obey God.

"Woe unto you, scribes and Pharisees, hypocrites! for ye are like unto whited sepulchres, which indeed appear beautiful outward, but are within full of dead men's bones, and of all uncleanness. Even

so ye also outwardly appear righteous unto men, but within ye are full of hypocrisy and iniquity" (Matthew 23:27-28).

A GREAT APOSTASY SHALL
FIRST COME UPON THE CHURCH

Paul warns us specifically that there shall first come a great apostasy or falling away, a departure from the truth and from sound doctrine. The Greek word is *"apostasia"*[11] (ap-os-tas-ee'-ah), which means a defection from truth—a falling away, forsake.[12]

Matthew Henry's Commentary provides a further insight into this apostasy which would come in the last days, for it is the same spirit of rebellion which inspired the many defections witnessed among the people of God throughout the ages: "A general apostasy, there would come a falling away first... spiritual or religious matters, from sound doctrine... and a holy life.

"The apostle speaks of some very great apostasy, not only of some... should be very general, though gradual, and should give occasion to the revelation of the rise of antichrist, that man of sin. And let us observe that no sooner was Christianity planted and rooted in the world than there began to be a defection in the Christian church.

"It was so in the Old-Testament church... soon after the promise there was revolting; for example, soon after men began to call upon the name of the Lord all flesh corrupted their way,—soon after the covenant with Noah the Babel-builders bade defiance to heaven,—soon after the covenant with Abraham his seed degenerated in Egypt—soon after the Israelites were planted in Canaan... they forsook God and served Baal—soon after God's covenant with David his seed revolted, and served other gods—soon after the return out of captivity there was a general decay of piety... and therefore it was no strange thing that after the planting of Christianity there should come a falling away."[13]

Paul, writing to the Thessalonians, addresses a rumor which had come into the church that the Day of the LORD and the *"gathering"* of the church had already come. Paul seeks to beseech, to plead with them, that the Day of the LORD, and the gathering of the faithful to the Lord, which is the rapture of the Church, will not come until two things first come to pass:

1. A great apostasy or falling away from the truth would come.
2. The Antichrist will be revealed.

"Now we beseech you, brethren, by the coming of our Lord Jesus Christ, and by our gathering together unto him, That ye be not soon shaken in mind, or be troubled... that the day of Christ is at hand. Let no man deceive you by any means: for that day shall not come, except there come a falling away first, and that man of sin be revealed, the son of perdition; Who opposeth and exalteth himself above all that is called God, or that is worshipped; so that he as God sitteth in the temple of God, shewing himself that he is God.... And then shall that Wicked be revealed, whom the Lord shall consume with the spirit of his mouth, and shall destroy with the brightness of his coming: Even him, whose coming is after the working of Satan with all power and signs and lying wonders, And with all deceivableness of unrighteousness in them that perish; because they received not the love of the truth, that they might be saved. And for this cause God shall send them strong delusion, that they should believe a lie: That they all might be damned who believed not the truth, but had pleasure in unrighteousness" (2 Thessalonians 2:3-12).

AS IT WAS IN THE DAYS OF NOAH

Jesus also warned us of the last days. *"And as it was in the days of Noe, so shall it be also in the days of the Son of man.... Likewise also as it was in the days of Lot.... But the same day that Lot went out of Sodom it rained fire and brimstone from heaven, and destroyed them all. Even thus shall it be in the day when the Son of man is revealed. In that day, he which shall be upon the housetop, and his stuff in the house, let him not come down to take it away: and he that is in the field, let him likewise not return back. Remember Lot's wife. Whosoever shall seek to save his life shall lose it; and whosoever shall lose his life shall preserve it. I tell you, in that night there shall be two men in one bed; the one shall be taken, and the other shall be left.... And they answered and said unto him, Where, Lord? And he said unto them, Wheresoever the body is, thither will the eagles be gathered together."*[14] This is one of the most misunderstood Scriptures, for those taken are not raptured, but are taken into captivity!

Jesus tells us it would be like the days of Noah and the days of Lot. In the days of Noah, the earth was full of wickedness and every man did that which was right in his own eyes. *"By faith Noah, being warned of God of things not seen as yet, moved with fear, prepared an ark to the saving of his house; by the which he condemned the world, and became heir of the righteousness which is by faith."*[15]

Noah found righteousness with God by faith, and was warned by the Lord of the judgment that would come. Having heard God's warning, Noah believed and was moved with fear to prepare an ark for the saving of his house. Noah believed, even though that which God had spoken remained unseen at the time. It had never rained before on the earth. Brethren, when you finally understand that these days are coming soon, you, too, will be moved with fear. Remember—fear only the Lord!

Noah built his ark for one hundred and twenty years, enduring the mocking of scoffers who walked in that hour. Noah stood firm on the word He had heard from God. This was his only evidence of the judgment that was to come. Noah continued preparing for one hundred and twenty years having just a word from God. Everyone who heard and believed the warning took action, and all were saved in that hour.

All of the scoffers, who mocked the message, perished in the judgment, every one of them. Not one who mocked survived, and all who trusted and obeyed were preserved. This is a picture of the remnant, a small group of faithful people, warned by God of judgment to come and given instruction to prepare their house to endure. They all survived the hour. This word is being fulfilled again, and all over the earth, the humble and the poor in spirit are being alerted by the Lord to ready their house.

Yet they are a small remnant, even so this, too, is from the Lord. Lot also presents a picture of the rapture on the last day. The angels came and took them out *"and on the same day that Lot went out of Sodom it rained fire and brimstone from heaven, and destroyed them all. Even thus shall it be in the day when the Son of man is revealed."*

The same day the angels come to take the few faithful saints home, the *Noah Company* that heard the word and prepared, on that same day the fire will come and destroy everyone else. This is a picture of the rapture and it comes on the last day before the wrath of God is poured out upon the earth!

THE PRE-TRIBULATION RAPTURE DECEPTION

The majority of modern prophecy teachers embrace a theory which they call the pre-tribulation rapture. This great deception has entered the church at large and neutralized it. The church has been taught they will not see the final battle, but will be taken out beforehand. As a result, the church has adopted a position of neutrality, assuming they are not involved in this final battle.

This deception has rendered them useless, for they are not preparing spiritually or emotionally for the fight that is ahead. The Scripture is clear. We are staying here through the tribulation. We are not be raptured to safety until the last day. We must begin to prepare both our hearts and our homes to endure this hour of testing. There is no chance of a pre-tribulation rapture, none whatsoever!

Jesus Himself prayed for us saying, *"I pray not that thou shouldest take them out of the world, but that thou shouldest keep them from the evil."*[16] Jesus did not pray that the Father would take us out of the tribulation. There is not a single Biblical text that supports the theory of a rapture of the Church prior to the Great Tribulation.

The so-called proof texts are taken totally out of context, and used only as an inference of this great end-time fable. This is a relatively new dogma, and is held primarily in the Church in America. In the nations already witnessing the violent persecution, of which Jesus warned, this false doctrine is no longer held. If you tried to teach Christians in China that there would be rapture before the tribulation, they would perceive you to be insane. The Church in China is already in tribulation.

I HAVE DREAMED A DREAM AND SEEN A VISION

The pre-tribulation rapture theory was created from a vision of a thirteen-year-old girl, Margaret MacDonald, of Port Glasgow Scotland.[17] She had a vision in 1830 where she saw the last days of the earth before the Great Tribulation. Her vision was misinterpreted and the teaching of a pre-tribulation rapture began to spread until it became embraced by the mainline teachers of the day.

There is no Biblical basis for this teaching, none whatsoever! The Scripture warns us that in the last days the people of God, the church, will no longer want to hear sound doctrine but will turn instead to fables, and to stories made up in the imaginations of men. *"For the time will come when they will not endure sound doctrine; but after their own lusts shall they heap to themselves teachers, having itching ears; And they shall turn away their ears from the truth, and shall be turned unto fables."*[18] This false teaching is the fable. The Lord refers to it as *"The Great Deception."*

This false doctrine was created through deception, and then promulgated by the enemy of your soul. The Illuminati invested substantial resources in the promotion and publication of this false doctrine. The purpose was to disarm the Church, so they could slaughter the people of God. And the saints, now seeking to hear pleasant things, and no longer wishing to endure sound doctrine, bought the lie hook, line and sinker.

The Church in China and Russia and many other nations was decimated because the people had not prepared themselves for violent persecution. When the missionaries went back into China years after the Communist revolution, the few surviving believers asked, *"Why did you lie to us?"* This false doctrine is primarily held in the apostate nations of the West where real persecution has not yet reared its ugly head.

MARGARET MACDONALD'S VISION OF THE LAST DAYS

"It was first the awful state of the land that was pressed upon me. I saw the blindness and the infatuation of the people to be very great. I felt the cry of Liberty to be just the hiss of the Serpent, to drown them in perdition.... The people of God think they are waiting, but they know not what it is they wait for....

"Suddenly it burst upon the scene with a glorious light.... I saw the Lord Himself descending from heaven.... I saw the error of men who think this will be something seen by the natural eye, but

the kingdom of God is liken unto the ten virgins who went forth....
the oil the wise took is the light that they may discern, for the
kingdom of God cometh not with observation to the natural eye.
Only those who have the light of God within them will see the sign
of His appearance.

"Oh the glorious in breaking of God which is now about to burst
on this earth.... Oh what a holy, holy bride she must be.... now
shall the glorious mystery of God in our nature be known. The
Revelation of Jesus Christ has yet to be opened up. It is not
knowledge about God that it contains, it is an entering into God
which only those filled with the Spirit can see, those who have not
the Spirit could see nothing...

" I saw people of God in an awfully dangerous situation, and
many about to be deceived and fall. Now will the wicked one be
revealed, Oh it will be a fiery trial, and every soul will be shaken.
Now shall the awful sight of a false Christ be seen on the earth...
the trial of the Church is from the Antichrist. It is being filled with
the Spirit that we shall be kept. What had hindered the real life of
God from being received by His people, was their turning away
from Jesus.... they were all passing by the cross....

"I saw on that night, there will be such an outpouring of the Spirit
such as has never been, a baptism of fire... the servants of God
sealed in their foreheads, and His holy image seen in His peo-
ple."[19] This vision reveals the mystery of the Second Coming in the
lives of the holy remnant, and the teachers who created the false
doctrine of the pre-tribulation rapture did so out of their own
imagination!

WOE UNTO THE PASTORS WHO SCATTER MY FLOCK

The prophet Jeremiah spoke directly to the pastors who would
preach a false teaching in the last days, which presented a false
peace to the people, referring to them as destroying and scattering
His sheep. The Lord also says that at that time the people will no
longer speak of the deliverance from Egypt, which was the original
Exodus. Now the people will speak of this great last day's exodus
during the time of the Great Tribulation:

"Woe be unto the pastors that destroy and scatter the sheep of my pasture! saith the LORD. Therefore thus saith the LORD God of Israel against the pastors that feed my people; Ye have scattered my flock, and driven them away, and have not visited them: behold, I will visit upon you the evil of your doings, saith the LORD. And I will gather the remnant of my flock out of all countries whither I have driven them, and will bring them again to their folds; and they shall be fruitful and increase. And I will set up shepherds over them which shall feed them: and they shall fear no more, nor be dismayed, neither shall they be lacking, saith the LORD. Behold, the days come, saith the LORD, that I will raise unto David a righteous Branch, and a King shall reign and prosper, and shall execute judgment and justice in the earth. In his days Judah shall be saved, and Israel shall dwell safely: and this is his name whereby he shall be called, THE LORD OUR RIGHTEOUSNESS. Therefore, behold, the days come, saith the LORD, that they shall no more say, The LORD liveth, which brought up the children of Israel out of the land of Egypt; But, The LORD liveth, which brought up and which led the seed of the house of Israel out of the north country, and from all countries whither I had driven them; and they shall dwell in their own land" (Jeremiah 23:1-8).

Jeremiah continues to lament that his heart is broken and that he is like a man who is overcome with wine because of the Lord and the word of His holiness. Jeremiah understands the holiness of the Lord. He knows that the people are corrupt and have turned to lies. *"Both the prophet and the priest are profane, in my house I have found their wickedness,"* declares the Lord. These people, though they are in God's house, are full of wickedness, and they shall be driven to darkness.

"Mine heart within me is broken because of the prophets; all my bones shake; I am like a drunken man, and like a man whom wine hath overcome, because of the LORD, and because of the words of his holiness. For the land is full of adulterers; for because of swearing the land mourneth; the pleasant places of the wilderness are dried up, and their course is evil, and their force is not right. For both prophet and priest are profane; yea, in my house have I found their wickedness, saith the LORD. Wherefore their way shall be unto them as slippery ways in the darkness: they shall be driven on, and

fall therein: for I will bring evil upon them, even the year of their visitation, saith the LORD" (Jeremiah 23:9-12).

I HAVE SEEN THE FOLLY
IN THE PROPHETS OF SAMARIA

The Lord continues His rebuke of these false prophets declaring, *"they have prophesied in Baal."* These false prophets are actually under demonic deception, and through this deception they have led the people of God into error. The Lord then warns the people, *"Do not listen to these false teachers, for they speak a vision of their own imagination."*

The Lord then tells us, *"They are still teaching this false doctrine to the people who despise me."* This falsehood continues unto the present time. What is the false teaching? They tell the people, *"You shall have peace, and they teach everyone who walks after the imagination of their own hearts, no evil will come upon you!"*

> *"And I have seen folly in the prophets of Samaria; they prophesied in Baal, and caused my people Israel to err. I have seen also in the prophets of Jerusalem an horrible thing: they commit adultery, and walk in lies: they strengthen also the hands of evildoers, that none doth return from his wickedness: they are all of them unto me as Sodom, and the inhabitants thereof as Gomorrah. Therefore thus saith the LORD of hosts concerning the prophets; Behold, I will feed them with wormwood, and make them drink the water of gall: for from the prophets of Jerusalem is profaneness gone forth into all the land. Thus saith the LORD of hosts, Hearken not unto the words of the prophets that prophesy unto you: they make you vain: they speak a vision of their own heart, and not out of the mouth of the LORD. They say still unto them that despise me, The LORD hath said, Ye shall have peace; and they say unto every one that walketh after the imagination of his own heart, No evil shall come upon you"* (Jeremiah 23:13-17).

WHO HAS STOOD IN MY COUNSEL
AND HEARD MY WORDS?

"For who hath stood in the counsel of the LORD, and hath perceived and heard his word? who hath marked his word, and heard it? Behold, a whirlwind of the LORD is gone forth in fury, even a grievous

whirlwind: it shall fall grievously upon the head of the wicked. The anger of the LORD shall not return, until he have executed, and till he have performed the thoughts of his heart: in the latter days ye shall consider it perfectly" (Jeremiah 23: 18-20).

The Lord then declares, *"Who has stood in my counsel? Who has perceived and heard my words? Who has marked the proper scriptures which speak to the people of this hour, to those in the last days?"* The Lord Himself declares the truth! *"A whirlwind from the Lord is gone forth in fury! It will fall grievously upon the head of the wicked! And the anger of the Lord shall not return until He has executed those who hold his truth in contempt!"*

I heard the Lord myself, and His voice sounded like the sound of thunder when He said unto me, *"Do not tell them this is going to happen. Tell them this word has already gone forth, for it has already been spoken in heaven! The judgment is determined, and it will surely come! WARN THE PEOPLE!"* Upon hearing this I trembled with fear. This is precisely the word God spoke to Jeremiah as well, when He said, *"A whirlwind of the LORD is gone forth in fury!"*

The whirlwind had already gone forth in the heavens, and it would only be a short time before that word which had already been spoken was performed on the earth! The last statement the Lord makes in this section tells us the timing of this prophecy for He says, *"In the last days you shall understand this perfectly."* In the last days the true meaning of this prophecy would be perfectly understood, for this speaks of the final deception of the saints—the pre-tribulation rapture!

I HAVE NOT SENT THESE PROPHETS YET THEY RAN

The Lord then declares He did not send these false teachers, yet they spoke. The Lord says, *"I heard what these false prophets have said, these who teach lies in my name. They say, 'I had a dream, yet they are prophets only of the deceit which is in their own hearts."* *"What is the chaff to the wheat,"* declares the Lord! Do you not fear God? Who are you to declare His word? Did He appoint you a prophet or a teacher, or have you appointed yourself?

"Is not my word like fire?" declares the Lord. We should greatly fear before we are so presumptuous as to suppose we can teach the brethren, for everyone who is called to be a teacher shall receive the greater judgment. Pray for your author, dear reader, for I am compelled by the Spirit to dismiss these false teachings, and to publish the word of truth. I must therefore endure the greater judgment.

> *"I have not sent these prophets, yet they ran: I have not spoken to them, yet they prophesied. But if they had stood in my counsel, and had caused my people to hear my words, then they should have turned them from their evil way, and from the evil of their doings. Am I a God at hand, saith the LORD, and not a God afar off? Can any hide himself in secret places that I shall not see him? saith the LORD. Do not I fill heaven and earth? saith the LORD. I have heard what the prophets said, that prophesy lies in my name, saying, I have dreamed, I have dreamed. How long shall this be in the heart of the prophets that prophesy lies? yea, they are prophets of the deceit of their own heart; Which think to cause my people to forget my name by their dreams which they tell every man to his neighbour, as their fathers have forgotten my name for Baal. The prophet that hath a dream, let him tell a dream; and he that hath my word, let him speak my word faithfully. What is the chaff to the wheat? saith the LORD. Is not my word like as a fire? saith the LORD; and like a hammer that breaketh the rock in pieces?"* (Jeremiah 23:21-29).

EACH OF THEM STEALS MY WORDS FROM HIS NEIGHBOR

The Lord then declares these false teachers have deceived the people causing them to walk in error by their lies and by their lightness. These teachers have made the truth of God a light thing, deceiving the people, for the Lord Himself said *"Strive, agonize, and exert much effort to enter the straight gate."*

The truth of God is not a light thing at all! The Lord continues saying, *"I did not send these prophets, nor commanded them to speak, and they will be of no profit to my people."* And this pre-tribulation deception is of no profit. Rather it has put the people to sleep. Rather than preparing their house and hearts for the hour of testing, they have assumed they will escape it. Both student and teacher of this false doctrine will fall together into the ditch!

The Lord also declares that these false teachers *"steal my words from their neighbors."* These false teachers cannot hear from God, so they merely repeat the words spoken by another. Thus, many false witnesses mimic these false teachings. Terrible trouble and much woe will come upon them all!

> *"Therefore, behold, I am against the prophets, saith the LORD, that steal my words every one from his neighbour. Behold, I am against the prophets, saith the LORD, that use their tongues, and say, He saith. Behold, I am against them that prophesy false dreams, saith the LORD, and do tell them, and cause my people to err by their lies, and by their lightness; yet I sent them not, nor commanded them: therefore they shall not profit this people at all, saith the LORD. And when this people, or the prophet, or a priest, shall ask thee, saying, What is the burden of the LORD? thou shalt then say unto them, What burden? I will even forsake you, saith the LORD. And as for the prophet, and the priest, and the people, that shall say, The burden of the LORD, I will even punish that man and his house"* (Jeremiah 23:30-34).

JESUS SAID IMMEDIATELY AFTER THE TRIBULATION

Let us examine what the Scripture itself says regarding the rapture of the church. Jesus, after discussing the events of the Great Tribulation in Matthew chapter 24, says:

> *"Immediately after the tribulation of those days shall the sun be darkened, and the moon shall not give her light, and the stars shall fall from heaven, and the powers of the heavens shall be shaken: And then shall appear the sign of the Son of man in heaven: and then shall all the tribes of the earth mourn, and they shall see the Son of man coming in the clouds of heaven with power and great glory. And he shall send his angels with a great sound of a trumpet, and they shall gather together his elect from the four winds, from one end of heaven to the other. Now learn a parable of the fig tree; When his branch is yet tender, and putteth forth leaves, ye know that summer is nigh: So likewise ye, when ye shall see all these things, know that it is near, even at the doors"* (Matthew 24:29-33).

Notice the timing of these things, immediately after the tribulation. The tribulation has just ended, and then the sign of the Son of man shall appear in the heavens. All of those left standing upon the earth will see the sign of the Son of man, and then all of the people of the earth shall mourn, for they will know that this is Jesus Who is coming now to set up His kingdom. And Jesus will then send His angels with the sound of a great trumpet! When this final trumpet sounds after the Tribulation, then the angels will gather the elect from the four winds.

The four winds refer to the four corners of the earth, where the remnant army of God is stationed. The reference to *"from one end of heaven to the other"* speaks of the saints who have already died and been raised in the first resurrection. Some will dispute that this text speaks of believers being gathered from the earth.

The Lord gave the same discourse in Mark's gospel saying, *"And then shall he send his angels, and shall gather together his elect from the four winds, from the uttermost part of the earth to the uttermost part of heaven."*[20] Thus, it is clear that this reference speaks of the elect who are taken by the angels. This is the rapture, and it occurs *"immediately after the tribulation of those days."*

AT THE LAST TRUMPET WE SHALL ALL BE CHANGED

Paul also writes about the rapture, declaring, *"Behold, I show you a mystery; We shall not all sleep, but we shall all be changed, In a moment, in the twinkling of an eye, at the last trump: for the trumpet shall sound, and the dead shall be raised incorruptible, and we shall be changed."*[21]

The rapture occurs when the last trumpet sounds. When is the last trumpet? *"And the seventh angel sounded; and there were great voices in heaven, saying, the kingdoms of this world are become the kingdoms of our Lord, and of his Christ; and he shall reign for ever and ever."*[22] Jesus told us in Matthew 24 that after the tribulation of those days the angels will come with the sound of a great trumpet.

This last trumpet is blown after the Tribulation! Children, trust the Scriptures, not the teachings of men, who claimed to have dreamed a dream and seen a vision!

Again, Paul writes to dispel rumors that the day of the Lord had already come. Notice he also says *"and our gathering together unto him."* This gathering is the rapture and it comes at the last trumpet.

The rapture is the final Day of the LORD! Notice Paul also says that *"our gathering to the Lord"* cannot happen until first two things occur. First, there must come a great falling away, which is the last days' apostasy covered in chapter 11.

Second, the son of perdition will be revealed. This is the Antichrist, who is revealed at the start of the Tribulation. Clearly, the saints will be on the earth when the tribulation begins for this must happen first before *"our gathering unto him."*

> *"Now we beseech you, brethren, by the coming of our Lord Jesus Christ, and by our gathering together unto him, That ye be not soon shaken in mind, or be troubled, neither by spirit, nor by word, nor by letter as from us, as that the day of Christ is at hand. Let no man deceive you by any means: for that day shall not come, except there come a falling away first, and that man of sin be revealed, the son of perdition; Who opposeth and exalteth himself above all that is called God, or that is worshipped; so that he as God sitteth in the temple of God, showing himself that he is God. Remember ye not, that, when I was yet with you, I told you these things? And now ye know what withholdeth that he might be revealed in his time. For the mystery of iniquity doth already work: only he who now letteth will let, until he be taken out of the way. And then shall that Wicked be revealed, whom the Lord shall consume with the spirit of his mouth, and shall destroy with the brightness of his coming"* (2 Thessalonians 2:1-8).

THE DAY SHOULD NOT OVERTAKE YOU AS A THIEF

Paul also admonishes that *"the day of the Lord will come as a thief in the night,"* but we are not of darkness so the day should not overtake us unaware. This day is the beginning of the tribulation and the believer is not to be taken by surprise. Look at the signs the Lord has given us. This is obvious if you are watching. Remember, Jesus commanded us to watch! He didn't suggest that we watch; this was His commandment!

"But of the times and the seasons, brethren, ye have no need that I write unto you. For yourselves know perfectly that the day of the Lord so cometh as a thief in the night. For when they shall say, Peace and safety; then sudden destruction cometh upon them, as travail upon a woman with child; and they shall not escape. But ye, brethren, are not in darkness, that that day should overtake you as a thief" (1 Thessalonians 5:1-4).

THESE ARE THEY WHICH CAME OUT OF THE GREAT TRIBULATION

Many scholars argue the Church is not in the book of Revelation and therefore must have been raptured out before hand. Look at chapter seven. This great multitude is the faithful Church and they came out of the Great Tribulation.

"After this I beheld, and, lo, a great multitude, which no man could number, of all nations, and kindreds, and people, and tongues, stood before the throne, and before the Lamb, clothed with white robes, and palms in their hands; And cried with a loud voice, saying, Salvation to our God which sitteth upon the throne, and unto the Lamb. And all the angels stood round about the throne, and about the elders and the four beasts, and fell before the throne on their faces, and worshipped God, Saying, Amen: Blessing, and glory, and wisdom, and thanksgiving, and honour, and power, and might, be unto our God for ever and ever. Amen. And one of the elders answered, saying unto me, What are these, which are arrayed, in white robes? and whence came they? And I said unto him, Sir, thou knowest. And he said to me, These are they which came out of great tribulation, and have washed their robes, and made them white in the blood of the Lamb" (Revelation 7:9-14).

The Church is also mentioned in Revelation chapter 17, for by the time of the end, she has become an apostate. This is the Church of Laodicea, and Jesus tells us He is standing at the door outside, knocking and seeking to come in. *"As many as I love, I rebuke and chasten: be zealous therefore, and repent. Behold, I stand at the door, and knock: if any man hear my voice, and open the door, I will come in to him, and will sup with him, and he with me. To him that overcometh will I grant to sit with me in my throne, even as I also overcame, and am set down with my Father in his throne. He that hath an ear, let him hear what the Spirit saith unto the churches.*"[23]

Daniel was also told about the Antichrist *"I beheld, and the same horn made war with the saints, and prevailed against them; Until the Ancient of days came"*[24] How could the Antichrist make war with the saints if they had been taken out before he comes to power? The word is clear! I rest my case on the words of Jesus, Paul and John the apostle. The modern teachers are deceived and continue this deception out of ignorance! These men are God-fearing, but in this critical doctrine, they are themselves deceived and their flocks are headed for destruction!

JUDGMENT IS COMING AND THE CHURCH IS ASLEEP

Judgment is coming and the pre-tribulation rapture message has lulled the church to sleep. There is no precedent for the Lord removing His people before the problem. The Lord prepares His people and preserves them in the midst of the fire. Mankind lives by the pleasure of God's word. Man, whether he likes it or not, lives by the word of God. Mankind, whether we like it or not, is bound by what God says. In the days ahead, the Lord is going to test His people to see what is in their hearts.

If it is what the Lord placed there, we are going to receive promises and power beyond what we believe—this is a heart issue and we must be hidden in His hands. We must learn to hear from the Lord ourselves, through the word, and not to rely on our leaders to teach us His Word.

History always proves the Lord's word comes to pass exactly as He spoke it, every time. God has always protected a remnant in every time of judgment. Jesus told us he did not come to abolish the law, but to fulfill it. We are under both covenants; He fulfilled the old (obedience) and added the new (grace and truth).

This is a time when many will become tempted to fear. We must memorize these verses: I John 4:18 *"There is no fear in love; but perfect love casteth out fear."* 2 Timothy 1:7 *"For God hath not given us the spirit of fear; but of power, and of love, and of a sound mind."* We must understand that fear does not come from God; God says DO NOT FEAR!!

In Revelation 21:8 He says, *"But the fearful, and unbelieving, and the abominable, and murderers, and whoremongers, and sorcerers, and idolaters, and all liars, shall have their part in the lake which burneth with fire and brimstone: which is the second death."* We must not fear; this is an issue of obedience.

Look at the history of God's judgments. Did He ever rapture His people out before the problem? No, He has never done so in the past and He won't do it now. Jesus prayed not to take us out but to deliver us in this hour, for this is the greater miracle! Our deliverance is based on our obedience; if the children of Israel hadn't put the blood of the lamb on their doors, they would not have been delivered. We must get ready physically and spiritually, not fearing but drawing closer and closer to the Lord. We must learn to pray, listen and then do.

We have the promises of God, the same promises He gave to the children of Israel in the wilderness; if we are obedient, He promises deliverance and safety, if not, we can expect the sword.

"And it shall come to pass, if thou shalt hearken diligently unto the voice of the LORD thy God, to observe and to do all his commandments which I command thee this day, that the LORD thy God will set thee on high above all nations of the earth: And all these blessings shall come on thee, and overtake thee, if thou shalt hearken unto the voice of the LORD thy God. Blessed shalt thou be in the city, and blessed shalt thou be in the field. Blessed shall be the fruit of thy body, and the fruit of thy ground, and the fruit of thy cattle, the increase of thy kine, and the flocks of thy sheep. Blessed shall be thy basket and thy store. Blessed shalt thou be when thou comest in, and blessed shalt thou be when thou goest out. The LORD shall cause thine enemies that rise up against thee to be smitten before thy face: they shall come out against thee one way, and flee before thee seven ways. The LORD shall command the blessing upon thee in thy storehouses, and in all that thou settest thine hand unto; and he shall bless thee in the land which the LORD thy God giveth thee. The LORD shall establish thee an holy people unto himself, as he hath sworn unto thee, if thou shalt keep the commandments of the LORD thy God, and walk in his ways. And all people of the earth shall see that thou art called by the name of the LORD; and they shall be afraid of thee." (Deuteronomy 28:1-22)

The promise also contains a curse for disobedience. *"But it shall come to pass, if thou wilt not hearken unto the voice of the LORD thy God, to observe to do all his commandments and his statutes which I command thee this day; that all these curses shall come upon thee, and overtake thee: Cursed shalt thou be.... The LORD shall smite thee with a consumption, and with a fever, and with an inflammation, and with an extreme burning, and with the sword, and with blasting, and with mildew; and they shall pursue thee until thou perish."*

Here we have the words of God, His promise of blessings and protection if we are obedient, or cursing if we chose disobedience, and everyday we chose the blessing or the curse. If you will obey the Lord, you can be certain of His blessing! The sovereign Lord says, *"Know for certain, you are in my hands. Relax in me. If you will be obedient in thought, word and deed, I will certainly deliver you from this hour."*[25]

"The organized churches of our day have produced congregations of spiritually malnourished people, who are so weak in spirit, that they cannot recognize truth when they see it. Thankfully a small remnant has always been saved in spite of organized religion. In addition to idolatry, apostasy and witchcraft entering in, the secret societies and lodges of the Grand Orient began to take over in organized religion.

"Then came rock music and entertainment. It was not long until sin was no longer sin. Thus, the very agency that was supposed to fight Satan and his entire dark kingdom became a cleverly disguised agency for the Illuminati of the last days to bring about the New World Order. We also have men such as Dr. Robert Schuller, who in his 'Institute for Successful Church Leadership' which was held at the Crystal Cathedral, trained over 80 gay and lesbian pastors and lay leaders."[26] "Sodom and Gomorrah had come under a Crystal roof."[27]

We have the current outcry of the coming revival, which will bring the wayward factions of the body of Christ into unity, and will usher in the *'great outpouring of the latter rain,'* which will produce great signs and supernatural wonders within our church services that will cause the unsaved to come flocking in.

Could this be why we are experiencing a famine of the word of God in our churches today? Could it be that most cannot, and will not, tolerate the truth when they hear it? *"Wonder; cry ye out, and cry: they are drunken, but not with wine; they stagger, but not with strong drink. For the Lord hath poured out upon you the spirit of deep sleep, and hath closed your eyes: the prophets and your rulers, the seers hath he covered."* [28]

Lest the conservative advocates of the 'great escape' deny this... because he is, in his own mind, not prophesying, as he assures his followers of their peace and eternal security, let them also consider *"All the sinners of my people shall die by the sword, which say, The evil shall not overtake nor prevent us."* [29] *"One form of lie is no different than another in God's eyes, if it is used to deceive His people into apathy and complacency."* [30]

> *"Son of man, the house of Israel is to me become dross: all they are brass, and tin, and iron, and lead, in the midst of the furnace; they are even the dross of silver. Therefore thus saith the Lord GOD; Because ye are all become dross, behold, therefore I will gather you into the midst of Jerusalem. As they gather silver, and brass, and iron, and lead, and tin, into the midst of the furnace, to blow the fire upon it, to melt it; so will I gather you in mine anger and in my fury, and I will leave you there, and melt you. Yea, I will gather you, and blow upon you in the fire of my wrath, and ye shall be melted in the midst thereof."* [31]

The word for "dross" is *ciyg* [32] (seeg) which means refused and scorned. The word is derived from *cuwg* [33] (soog) a primitive root, which means to flinch, to go back, literally to retreat, or figuratively to apostatize, a backslider. The Lord has declared His people, who are called by His name, are all backsliders, and they have been refused and scorned.

THE WORD OF THE LORD

"Far from Me are the hearts of many who claim to be mine. Their iniquity is greater than their love for me. Many have departed from Me. Though they still speak My name with their lips, yet their hearts are far from Me. There are many religious, but not many righteous. Many imagine they will live with Me for eternity, and they imagine they abide in Me now. I say they imagine

in their hearts, but they do not abide in Me. They only delude themselves. They cannot see.

"Their iniquity and their pride have blinded their eyes and they cannot see. They cannot hear. They imagine I no longer speak to my chosen ones for they cannot hear. They follow the imaginations of their own heart to destruction! Under the shadow of death, they run to hell. They cannot see where they are going.

"They go their own way, and they run to folly. They think they are wise, but how great will their fall be! What they seek and look for, they seek in another. They do not seek Me. I tell you the truth, the time is close at hand when man shall be no more, and only My righteous ones shall stand.

"The hour of testing which I have prepared is close at hand. A time as never before is about to break out upon the earth. This is the hour when I separate the precious from the vile. I will soon pour out my judgments on the whole earth. I show forth my power. No man will be able to stand in that day, but I shall save My holy remnant by My power. When the waves of judgment roll in, many men will be washed away with the tide.

"Those who are religious and who only know My name shall all be swept away, yet the righteous who know Me shall all be purified with fire! I will soon release the floods of my judgments and the mass multitudes of those religious shall perish. Helpless and hopeless, they shall perish. The time of the Gentiles is soon over, and then My angels will come and seal My holy ones. The devastation, which is coming, shall cover the whole earth, and only those who abide in Me will be spared. My true people, whom I call Yisrael, shall all be saved. Each and everyone of them over whom I rule.

"I speak to those who are My own. It is now time to get ready. Draw closer to Me than ever before. The day is coming and no one can stop it! The time is short. The time is now to repent, and touch not the unclean thing. The time is close at hand when I will take vengeance upon all of My enemies. The mountains and the hills will come down and only My holy mountain will remain. There is little time to prepare, for the time of preparation is al-

most over. *The time is far spent, and My indignation is coming very soon.*

"*I say it is come. It is here. Be quiet and be still. Listen to Me when I speak to you. I say listen, for the time is at hand. I tell all of my people, go to My holy mountain, and I will meet you there. Do not fear what is coming, fear only Me. For the fear of the Lord is the beginning of all wisdom, and by My wisdom is the house built upon a sure foundation. And if anyone builds without Me, I will cast that house down.*

"*Liars have taught My people lies in hypocrisy. These deceivers shall wax worse and worse, deceiving and being deceived. These preach another gospel for those who do not love My truth. Each of them who follows the imagination of their own heart shall be turned over to strong delusions and they shall believe a lie.*

"*But I the Lord shall raise up holy shepherds, and they shall teach My people the truth. I say unto the liars who have lied to My people, I shall bring them down from their thrones. They thought they would reign forever, but I say that I am the Living God and I shall bring them down. I will separate them from My people and the separation is final. Wait and see the recompense of the wicked! Wait and see what will come of the proud, and the liars, and those who walk in disobedience yet claim they know Me. They know Me not, they only know My name. The devils know My name and they tremble! Soon, the wicked shall all tremble as well.*

"*To My holy remnant, I say learn to live in Me now. Learn to walk in Me. Learn to train your thoughts on Me. Learn to stay close to Me. Learn to refresh your souls and drink the water of life. Walk in the water, and let Me fill you to overflowing. Come into your prayer closets, and learn to stay close to Me. Learn to hear My voice. Learn to watch and pray. Learn to fast and pray, so that your lamps may be lit with My holy oil.*

"*Do not listen to man. I speak to My chosen ones who are faithful and true. Separate yourselves from the filthiness which now covers the earth and walk before Me in holiness and humility. I will walk with you, and I will do mighty works through you. My light is about to be revealed in you, and it will hurt their eyes. My light will make them angry and upset, for My light is bright. My light will irritate all who do not walk with Me. The whole world shall go into confusion soon but I will lead thee forth into an ark of safety.*

"I desire a pure people, a people who will be Mine alone. I will protect My holy remnant in the day of My anger, but destruction awaits the wicked."

CHAPTER 12

"RETURN OH LORD, HOW LONG?"
Psalm 90:13

The coming of the Messiah of Israel has been the hope of God's people from the time of Moses. His First Coming as the Holy Lamb of God, to be slain for the sins of the world on the Feast of Passover, was missed by the religious leadership of that day. They had been instructed in the prophecies, and told to watch for One Who would come. The Lord Himself in Revelation also commands us to watch, or we will find that He has come upon us as a thief in the night and in an hour we did not know:

> "Remember therefore how thou hast received and heard, and hold fast, and repent. If therefore thou shalt not watch, I will come on thee as a thief, and thou shalt not know what hour I will come upon thee."[1]

Jesus, when teaching His disciples about His Second Coming, tells that the events of the end of the age will come as a snare upon everyone who dwells on the face of the earth. A snare is an unseen trap, which captures its prey suddenly. Again, in the Gospels, He commands us to *"Watch... and pray always, that ye may be accounted worthy to escape all these things that shall come to pass, and to stand before the Son of Man."*[2]

WHY CAN'T YOU TELL THE SIGNS OF THE TIMES?

Jesus also rebuked the Pharisees and Sadducees who came seeking a sign from heaven. His rebuke contains a message: you can tell the signs of the weather; why can you not tell the signs of the times? *"The Pharisees also with the Sadducees came, and tempt-*

ing desired him that he would show them a sign from heaven. He answered and said unto them, When it is evening, ye say, It will be fair weather: for the sky is red.

"And in the morning, It will be foul weather today: for the sky is red and lowering. O ye hypocrites, ye can discern the face of the sky; but can ye not discern the signs of the times?"[3] Jesus was referring to the signs in the prophecies, which pointed clearly to the time He would come and the many works He would do to fulfill the Word of God. Yet, they in their blindness could see none of this. Dear reader, can you see?

The Lord, speaking through the prophet Jeremiah, laments that the animal kingdom knows their appointed times, but the people of God do not know the time which has been appointed for their visitation and judgment. *"Even the stork in the heavens knows her appointed times; and the turtledove, the swift, and the swallow observe the time of their coming. But My people do not know the judgment of the LORD."*[4]

The modern Church in America is about to make the same mistake, with disastrous effects, and this even after they have been commanded to watch and have the warning of Israel's missing their first visitation. *"Who is the wise man who may understand this? and who is he to whom the mouth of the Lord has spoken, that he may declare it? Why does the land perish and burn up like a wilderness, so that no one can pass through?"*[5]

What do we know in the Scriptures about the return of the Lord? Skeptics will no doubt quote the verse, *"No man knows the day or the hour,"* dismissing any attempt to gain insight into the time of the Lord's coming. However, this was not the meaning of the Lord's statement. This phrase is a Hebrew idiom, and refers to the new moons and feasts of Israel where no man knew the exact day or hour, and had to await the sign of the new moon.

Likewise, in the Second Coming, no one will know the exact day or hour, but we are given many signs of the impending judgment, which will precede His physical return to the earth. Throughout the Scriptures, we are commanded to watch, and the Lord expects us to obey Him. The word of God contains many passages which provide us insight into the season of the beginning of God's judgment upon the earth. The first prophetic witness is found in the beginning, for in the story of creation, the Lord has told us about the timing of the end of the age!

DECLARING THE END FROM THE BEGINNING

"I am God, and there is none like me, Declaring the end from the beginning, and from ancient times the things that are not yet done, saying, My counsel shall stand, and I will do all my pleasure: Calling a ravenous bird from the east, the man that executeth my counsel from a far country: yea, I have spoken it, I will also bring it to pass; I have purposed it, I will also do it" (Isaiah 46:9-11).

The Lord tells us that He has declared the end from the beginning! The Lord is referring to the story of creation, which gives us the prophetic picture for the seven millenniums of mankind upon the earth. They are presented to us in the seven days of creation. Each day represents 1,000 years of human history.

Remember, to the Lord a day is 1,000 years, and 1,000 years is but a day. The modern church has lost sight of many Biblical truths, this being one of them. The scholars at the time of Jesus knew the meaning of this promise by God, and that is one of the reasons they rejected Jesus as Messiah. They erred as well, for He would come twice, first at the beginning of the fifth day and then again at the start of the seventh day.

THE MESSAGE OF THE FIRST DAY

In the first day, God created light and darkness, and God separated the light from the darkness. In the first 1000 years of the history of man, God created Adam, and Adam sinned and was separated from God, and died just before the end of 1000 years. God told Adam, the day you eat of this fruit, you shall die. Adam died at the age of 930 years near the end of the first day, just as God had said.

THE MESSAGE OF THE SECOND DAY

In the second day, God created the waters, and divided the waters from the heavens. In the second 1000 years, Noah was saved when God judged the earth by water. The Lord divided the righteous from the wicked though the waters of judgment.

"And the LORD said, My spirit shall not always strive with man, for that he also is flesh: yet his days shall be an hundred and twenty years. The earth also was corrupt before God, and the earth was filled with violence. And God looked upon the earth, and, behold, it was corrupt; for all flesh had corrupted his way upon the earth. And God said unto Noah, The end of all flesh is come before me; for the earth is filled with violence through them; and, behold, I will destroy them with the earth."[6]

The water is also a symbol of the Spirit of God. And at the last day, the Spirit will again divide mankind, and those without His Spirit will be cast out of the kingdom.

THE MESSAGE OF THE THIRD DAY

In the third day, God created the dry land, and the plants yielding fruit and seed after their own kind. At the start of the third 1000 years, God called Abraham and gave him the promise of the seed, which would come. This is the covenant of faith, which God planted into the hearts of the true sons of Israel. Notice, the seed produces after its own kind. This is one of God's laws of creation. That which is sown in the flesh produces after its own kind, and that which is sown into the spirit produces fruit unto eternal life.

THE MESSAGE OF THE FOURTH DAY

In the fourth day, God created the lights in the heavens to be signs for seasons and for days and for years. *"It is he that buildeth his stories in the heaven, and hath founded his troop in the earth; he that calleth for the waters of the sea, and poureth them out upon the face of the earth: The LORD is his name."*[7]

During the fourth 1000-year period, God began to send His prophets as lights unto the people to show them the signs of the seasons and to reveal to them those things which God had decreed must be. Isaiah, Jeremiah and the other prophets of Israel all came in the 1000 years before the Messiah.

THE MESSAGE OF THE FIFTH DAY

In the fifth day, God created the living creatures, and He blessed them, saying, *"Be fruitful and multiply and fill the waters and the earth."* At the beginning of the fifth day, 2000 years ago, God sent Jesus Christ, the Messiah, to bring the new creation to mankind.

Jesus is our redeemer and our deliverer from our sins; through His shed blood, we can be born again as a new creation before God.

THE MESSAGE OF THE SIXTH DAY

In the sixth day, *"And God said, Let us make man in our image, after our likeness.... So God created man in his own image, in the image of God created he him; male and female created he them."* (Genesis 1:26-27). And God blessed them and told them to be fruitful and multiply, and to fill the earth and have dominion over it. Notice, God refers to Himself as *"us"* speaking of a plurality, for the Lord is One, and He is also Father, Son and Holy Spirit. In the last 1000 years, mankind has multiplied his knowledge and dominion of the earth.

Man has even mounted unto the heavens, having now walked upon the moon. The late 1990's were the end of the sixth day. Man has fulfilled his purpose given to him by God and now mankind stands on the threshold of the seventh day of creation, which is the Day of the LORD.

THE MESSAGE OF THE SEVENTH DAY

The seventh day is The Day of the LORD. In the seventh day God ended His work, which He had made, and He rested. God blessed the seventh day, and sanctified it. God declares, *"I am the Lord of the Sabbath,"* and the seventh day is the Sabbath Day. The Sabbath Day is a picture of the Messiah and His rule. In the seventh 1000 years of the history of man upon the earth, God will bring the rule of His Messiah, and restore His Kingdom upon the earth. This is the millennium, which is to come, and it begins with the judgment of God. In Hebrew, it is called Yom Hadeen, The Day of Justice.

THE SIX THOUSAND YEARS
OF MANKIND UPON THE EARTH

The ancient scholars taught the 6,000 years doctrine, and it was widely held from the time of the first prophets. The Lord would make a quick work on the earth and all would be fulfilled within 6,000 years. The Lord declares mankind *"is flesh: yet his days shall be an hundred and twenty years."* The reference to the days of man being 120 years is also prophetic of the 120 Jubilees which the earth shall observe, and then the end of all flesh shall come. Noah spent one hundred and twenty years building the ark, and then the judgment came. Moses lived one hundred and twenty years, and then he died. *"And Moses was an hundred and twenty years old when he died: his eye was not dim, nor his natural force abated."*[8]

This is one of the reasons why the religious leaders in Jesus' day rejected Him: because he did not fulfill the prophecies regarding the Messiah as they were expecting. One of these was the 6,000-year doctrine, and only then after the 6000 years would the Messianic kingdom come. They concluded Jesus could not be Messiah, for He came at the beginning of the fifth day. But they were ignorant of the truth: He would come twice. First as the Lamb of God, then again at the end of the age, as the Lion from the Tribe of Judah.

Thus the oldest Biblical prophecy, which is the story of creation, points to the soon coming of our Great King. Today, the calendars we use are in error. The Jewish calendar is wrong. Modern scholars believe the year count is off by 240 years, resulting from an error made after the first Babylonian exile. They estimate the proper year count to be 5,998. We know from prophecy that the year of Jubilee ended on March 18, 1999.

There shall be one hundred and twenty Jubilees in creation; therefore, we may conclude the correct year count is Adar 26, 6000. It is midnight, and mankind does not know it! While all of humanity is looking for peace and safety, sudden destruction is coming very soon.

THE FEASTS OF ISRAEL

The seven feasts of Israel all point to different works of the Messiah. The feasts are prophetic of the work of the Messiah, and the progressive revelation of God's truth to His people Israel. Jesus Christ fulfilled all of the spring feasts in His First Coming. Many of the famous words and works of Jesus occurred at the various feast days of Israel. This is one more example of the great falling away from the truth which has occurred here in these last days.

Most of the church is ignorant of the feasts of the Lord, while they celebrate what are historically pagan holidays, which now are overlaid with a pretense of Christianity. But the truth of Jesus has nothing to do with these pagan days, regardless of the façade in which they are now draped. The Truth of the Lord does not change to please the tradition of men. Jesus Christ is the King of the Jews, and He will fulfill the fall feasts in His Second Coming.

THE SPRING FEASTS OF ISRAEL
THE FIRST COMING OF THE LORD

In His First Coming, Jesus fulfilled all three spring feasts literally. The harvest season began with the spring feasts of Israel, and the first crop which was reaped was the barley, beginning with the Passover.

Jesus was the Passover Lamb Who was slain, and He died precisely on the Feast of Pesach, which is Passover. The celebration of the feast to remember the deliverance from ancient Egypt was symbolic of the Lord delivering us from the bondage of sin. During the seven days which follow Passover, all of Israel was commanded to eat nothing but unleavened bread. This seven-day feast of unleavened bread symbolized the sanctification of the true believer in the Spirit. The word "sanctify" means to set apart from the world, and to set apart unto God. The sanctification under the New Covenant is in the Spirit.

Jesus warned us to beware of the leaven of the Pharisees. This is the leaven of false religious works, of hypocrisy, iniquity, legalism, and the doctrines of men. Jesus called these *"dead works."* As believers under the New Covenant, we must empty ourselves of the leaven of religion, and keep the feast of unleavened bread in the spirit. *"Purge out therefore the old leaven, that ye may be a new lump, as ye are unleavened. Or even Christ our Passover is sacrificed for us: Therefore let us keep the feast, not with old leaven, neither with the leaven of malice and wickedness; but with the unleavened bread of sincerity and truth."*[9]

The unleavened bread of the New Covenant is holiness and truth in the inner man. The remnant is to be purged of the leaven of sin, false religion, and the lust of the world. The chosen ones walk before the Lord in holiness and truth. These are the true worshippers of which Jesus spoke: *"But the hour cometh, and now is, when the true worshippers shall worship the Father in spirit and in truth: for the Father seeketh such to worship him. God is a Spirit: and they that worship him must worship him in spirit and in truth."*[10] Those who survive and endure to the end of the seventieth week will be found without leaven, for only the pure will be counted worthy to stand before the Son of man in His coming!

THE FIRST FRUITS HARVEST OF THE LORD

Three days after the Passover lamb was slain, the priests would wave a sheaf of barley before the Lord on the feast day of First Fruits. This was the celebration of the first fruits of the harvest, which was to come. The waving of the sheaf was done in the sign of the cross. Jesus rose from the dead while the priests waved the first fruits of the barley harvest before the Lord. The barley sheaf was waved in celebration, and to give thanks to God for the abundant harvest which was to come. Jesus rose as the First Fruits of the resurrection of Israel, symbolizing the harvest which would come through His name.

The barley is a picture of the remnant. They are called the First Fruits of Jesus Christ in the Revelation. These chosen ones walk the straight and narrow way that leads to a life of fullness in the Lord. The very nature of Jesus Christ will radiate from these people. The elect found among the remnant are the barley harvest, and upon these sanctified saints rests the high favor of God. They are the most holy of His little flock. They walk in the light of the Lord, and He shines His face upon them. These are the humble and contrite ones, in whom the Lord delights. Their sole desire is to serve and please the Lord. The Lord has chosen them as the First Fruits of the harvest of Israel. They are the barley, the handful of corn, which is reaped first, before the wheat harvest of Pentecost. *"There shall be an handful of corn in the earth upon the top of the mountains; the fruit thereof shall shake like Lebanon: and they of the city shall flourish like grass of the earth."*[11]

THE HOLY SEED SHALL BE HIS

This handful of *"corn on top of the mountains"* is the people who will come to maturity first. This small group of believers has been selected from among all the elect of God. They will be winnowed, and separated from all that is chaff, and set apart from the false doctrines of the apostate church. This holy seed will bear His name and His nature. In the days immediately ahead, they will manifest His love, for they are the praise of His glorious grace! The holy remnant shall do His will on earth, as it is done in heaven above.

The holy seed shall destroy the works of the devil. It is for them that Zion travails. In sorrow and anguish they will be born, a remnant seed of the woman Israel.[12] They shall walk in the anointing and the power of Elijah, for in their hearts, the Holy Spirit of the King will dwell. In their lives, His mighty power will be revealed! The holy seed are His first fruits, a tithe from among the people given by the Father as a special gift to the Son. They shall be cleansed from all sin and guile. It is to them the bridegroom cries, *"Come away my beloved!"*

Christ is foreshadowed as our first fruit in the feast that followed Passover. After the death of our Savior, at dusk, the priests cut down a sheaf of barley, the first ripe standing grain. *"[Y]e shall bring a sheaf of the first fruits of your harvest."*[13] The sheaf was called an omer, which meant a handful. The sheaf is representative of the first fruits of Jesus Christ. These are mentioned in Revelation.

> *"These are they which were not defiled with women; for they are virgins. These are they which follow the Lamb whithersoever he goeth. These were redeemed from among men, being the firstfruits unto God and to the Lamb. And in their mouth was found no guile: for they are without fault before the throne of God."*[14]

The remnant people of God who survive the tribulation are the first fruits of the harvest of God, being the first grain to ripen. *"The ears of the barley were brought into the court of the Temple and threshed... this was done so that the grain was not crushed. The grain was then ready... to be torched with fire, and finally exposed to the wind. It was then ground and sifted.... The tithe portion was an exact omer, a tenth of an ephah. It was offered in the Temple."*[15]

The barley sheaf contained no leaven. It was a pure offering before the Lord. This foreshadowed the chosen ones, who would be *"the first fruits unto God and to the Lamb."*

The holy remnant follows the Lamb wherever He goes. And in their mouth is found no guile. The holy remnant has no false doctrines, nor do they speak words of guile against the truth of the Lord or the covenant of God.

They are described as virgins, for they are not defiled with the apostate worship of the religion of Mystery Babylon, and her great apostasy, which has deceived the Church at large. The first fruits of Jesus are pure and without fault before the Lord.

Malachi speaks of the remnant whom God shall spare during the tribulation: *"Then they that feared the LORD spake often one to another: and the LORD hearkened, and heard it, and a book of remembrance was written before him for them that feared the LORD, and that thought upon his name. And they shall be mine, saith the LORD of hosts, in that day when I make up my jewels; and I will spare them, as a man spareth his own son that serveth him. Then shall ye return, and discern between the righteous and the wicked, between him that serveth God and him that serveth him not."*[16]

These lowly saints fear the Lord. They tremble before Him, and they speak often one to another. They have been rejected by the Church, who cannot hear the word which they have received, so they speak to each other, and share the mysteries, which God has hidden within His word.

The Lord hearkens as His little ones speak in fear of His name. These are the saints in travail about to give birth to the kingdom. They weep, and cry out in anguish, to be delivered from the sin within them. They fear the Lord, and they know the fierce judgment, which must come. Like Noah, this little remnant has been shown the time and manner of judgment, which will come. The Lord will save each one of them, as a man who spares his own son who labors for him. They are the holy seed that do the will of the Father.

They are found laboring for the Lord. Because they fear His name, and have put their trust in no other, the Lord will have compassion upon them. The Lord will give His commandment to save them, and His angels will be given charge to deliver them!

"In You, O Lord, I put my trust; let me never be put to shame. Deliver me in Your righteousness, and cause me to escape; incline Your ear to me, and save me. Be my strong refuge, to which I may resort continually; you have given the commandment to save me, for You are my rock and my fortress. Deliver me, O my God, out of the hand of the wicked, out of the hand of the unrighteous and cruel man."[17]

Oh, the praise His little remnant shall bring as an offering to the Lord, for in His mercy, He has commanded His angels to save them in this hour! The word used for "save" is *"yasha`"* (yaw-shah') and it is the name of the Savior Himself, Yeshua. It means to be free, to be safe, to avenge, defend, and deliver, to help, preserve, to rescue, and to receive the victory. Yeshua is His name, and it will be written upon the foreheads of each one of the holy seeds whom He saves in that hour.

The remnant is likened unto Jeremiah, for they have the very words of God in their mouth. *"For You are my hope, O Lord God; you are my trust from my youth. By You I have been upheld from birth; you are He who took me out of my mother's womb. My praise shall be continually of You. I have become as a wonder to many, but You are my strong refuge."*[18]

As the prophets of old, God took the seed forth from the womb, and they are a wonder to many. The word for "wonder" is *"mowpheth"*[19] (mo-faith') and means a miracle, a token or an omen. The salvation of the remnant is a miracle, and they are the token of His grace, the first fruits of His resurrection.

When you see the armies which have assembled against the Church, you will understand the miracle of the Lord that any are spared. They are the gleaning, which is left in the land, for they are hidden in the secret hiding place of Most High God. And Yeshua will become their salvation.

"For the upright shall dwell in the land, and the perfect shall remain in it. But the wicked shall be cut off from the earth, and the transgressors shall be rooted out of it."[20] The word used for "shall

dwell" is *"shakan"*[21] (shaw-kan'), which means to reside or permanently stay, to abide, and to continue, to remain, and to rest.

At the time of the end, the remnant, which continues to "dwell" in the land, will have learned to abide in the Sabbath rest of the Lord. They will have continued on to follow the Lord to the cross and will have died to self. They will have ceased from their own works, and now found in Him, are therefore worthy to escape all these things. The word used for the "perfect" is *"tamiym"*[22] (tawmeem'), which means moral integrity, truth, without blemish, complete, full of sincerity, without spot, undefiled, upright, and perfect.

These *"perfect"* ones shall remain in the land. These are the righteous ones whom the Lord deems worthy to escape all these things and to stand before Him at the Second Coming. The word for "shall remain" is *"yathar"*[23] (yaw-thar'), which means to remain or be left behind; to preserve a remnant.

This proverb is a prophecy of the remnant. They walk before the Lord in moral integrity and truth. In the eyes of the Lord they are without blemish, undefiled and upright. This holy remnant abides in Jesus Christ. They have continued on to the cross and have surrendered to Jesus as Lord. They are His precious ones, His dearly beloved and He will protect His own! They *"shall remain."*

This word means they will be left behind while the others are taken into captivity. They are the gleaning left in the land, which was hidden by the Lord during the harvest judgment. He will preserve them as His remnant. The definition of the remnant of the Lord, the First Fruits of Jesus Christ, is those who remain. *"Watch ye therefore, and pray always, that ye may be accounted worthy to escape all these things that shall come to pass, and to stand before the Son of man."*[24]

COUNT THE DAYS FROM THE OMER

The leaders among the remnant are called the "Vanguard." A vanguard is defined as the foremost position in an army, or the leading position in a movement. The movement of God in this hour is with an army, and the following prophecy was spoken of the Vanguard He has appointed as leaders in these last days.

"The Vanguard is readied as of now, and in these advance troops there is a megaton of truth, which has not been known openly before. They, who are of this company are known by their depth of perception, by their understanding of hard sayings, and by their conformity to the Anointed One.

"They have been hidden away until the time of their coming forth.... They shall burst upon the scene and open up the way whereby many others follow through. They have written and are writing, and their message of truth, as composition, will come into being. Twofold is their purpose, to manifest the Living One of Israel, and to lead the people into their inheritance. As they burst upon the scene, they also burst the bondages.

"Moreover, they loose the time of fullness. They reveal the mysteries, and show them openly in an understandable manner, for the wise shall understand. Count now therefore, from the time the sickle is put to the corn, for then is the moving forth that no man can hinder."[25]

The sickle is put to the corn in the latter rain season of the first month of the sacred calendar. The reaping takes place after the *"almond"* trees have bloomed. *"And it came to pass, that on the morrow Moses went into the tabernacle of witness; and, behold, the rod of Aaron for the house of Levi was budded, and brought forth buds, and bloomed blossoms, and yielded almonds."*[26] The almond tree is the first to bloom in the land, and represents the anointed leadership appointed by the Lord.

"He spake unto Korah and unto all his company, saying, Even to morrow the LORD will show who are his, and who is holy; and will cause him to come near unto him: even him whom he hath chosen will he cause to come near unto him."[27] During the Great Tribulation, the Lord will again show who are His first fruits and who are holy unto Him. Those who have raised themselves up within His church shall be cut down as Korah from among the people.

The corn represents the first fruits of barley. The word used is *"bar"*[28] (bawr), which means a winnowing of grain of any kind, even while standing in the field. The corn in the above prophecy refers to the barley which was cut for the Feast of Unleavened

Bread. *"And as soon as the commandment came abroad, the children of Israel brought in abundance the firstfruits of corn, wine, and oil, and honey, and of all the increase of the field; and the tithe of all things brought they in abundantly."*[29]

All of Israel is commanded to count the time from when the sickle is put to the corn, which is the omer of the Passover. This is the time of the latter day rains and the barley harvest, which are the first fruits of the Lord. The remnant will know to gather during the omer of the Jubilee year, all of them together in one accord.

There they will await the fire of the Lord. Count the days, for after seven Sabbath weeks, on the fiftieth day, the fire will fall once again. *"The thing that hath been, it is that which shall be; and that which is done is that which shall be done: and there is no new thing under the sun."*[30] As in the day the one hundred and twenty gathered in the upper room, so shall it be again. The end of all flesh is at hand.

For the remnant, it will begin with the end of the mind of flesh. God's pattern never changes, and to those who see in the Spirit, with the mind of truth, the count of the omer has begun. A great cleansing of the presence of the Lord is coming to His chosen ones. We are to pray, *"Ask ye of the LORD rain in the time of the latter rain; so the LORD shall make bright clouds, and give them showers of rain, to every one grass in the field."*[31] The word for "bright clouds" is "*chaziyz*"[32] (khaw-zeez'), which means a flash of lightning or bright cloud. The clouds are the anointed messengers who are coming in His power, full of His Shekinah Glory.

The end of the age is a time when all men shall become afraid, and fear shall be in the streets. *"When they shall be afraid of that which is high, and fears shall be in the way, and the almond tree shall flourish, and the grasshopper shall be a burden, and desire shall fail: because man goeth to his long home, and the mourners go about the streets."*[33] In that same day, the anointed leadership of the Lord, the almond tree, shall flourish once again.

Jeremiah was shown an almond tree in the spirit, to confirm his appointment by the Lord. *"See, I have this day set thee over the nations and over the kingdoms, to root out, and to pull down, and to destroy, and to throw down, to build, and to plant. Moreover the word of the LORD came unto me, saying, Jeremiah, what seest thou? And I said, I see a rod of an almond tree."*[34]

As an appointed leader by the Lord, he is given authority and power to pull down and destroy nations. Jeremiah's prophecies fulfilled this commission. In these last days, the anointed almond trees of the Lord shall literally fulfill this mission, for they shall bring the judgment of God upon the nations of the earth.

"The adversaries of the LORD shall be broken to pieces; out of heaven shall he thunder upon them: the LORD shall judge the ends of the earth; and he shall give strength unto his king, and exalt the horn of his anointed."[35] The word for "shall he thunder" is *"ra `am"*[36] (raw-am'), which means: to be violently agitated, a crash of thunder, to irritate with anger, to make to trouble.

These messengers of the Lord Jesus Christ, who are His vanguard, will speak with *"thunder."* They will violently oppose all forms of darkness, and will be violently agitated against the enemies of God. They will also irritate their apostate listeners, who cannot tolerate the bright light of the words of God. *"The voice of thy thunder was in the heaven: the lightnings lightened the world: the earth trembled and shook."*[37]

The thunder of God is His prophetic voice, and it will be revealed through these anointed ones. The verse declares that God's prophetic voice is *"in the heavens."* The word for "heavens" is "galgal"[38] (gal-gal'), which actually means a whirlwind from heaven. The prophetic thunder of God's messengers will be the prophetic declaration of the whirlwind to come from the Lord! The thunder is contrasted with God's *"lightnings,"* which will enlighten the world. The word for "lightnings"[39] is "'owr" (ore), which means to be luminous, as the break of day, glorious, and to kindle and set on fire, to be enlightened and to shine. The word used for "lightened" the world is *"baraq"*[40] (baw-rawk') which means a flashing sword, or a bright glittering sword, full of lightning. The anointed remnant will bring the whirlwind to pass, they will hold the flashing sword of the Lord in their hands, and with it they shall kindle a fire upon the nations!

These are the Lions from Judah, God's anointed remnant, and they will cause the earth to *"tremble."* The word for "tremble" is "*ragaz*"[41] (raw-gaz'), which means to quiver with a violent emotion, especially anger or fear, and to be afraid, to stand in awe, to provoke, to trouble, and be wroth. The message of God's judgment will initially provoke the heathen and the apostates to anger against the word of the Lord and the messengers of His covenant.

As the Lord, Himself, begins to thunder, His word will be revealed upon the earth in the fire He kindles. The word will come with a whirlwind, and soon the apostates and the heathen will be filled with fear, for the judgment will begin to be poured out. His messengers will be as coals of fire burning the ground and ears around them.

The voice of God's prophets will thunder from the heavens. His word will be manifest in the whirlwind, which is about to fall upon the earth. With a flashing sword, "*the lightnings*" of the word of the Lord will be revealed to all flesh. The fire of His lightening will kindle upon the whole world, and all the people of the earth shall tremble and shake.

They will stand in awe before thee, and will be overcome with fear of the Lord. They shall be troubled, and will shake with fear when the prophecies of these messengers begin to be fulfilled. "*Who hath divided a watercourse for the overflowing of waters, or a way for the lightning of thunder?*"[42] The word used for "thunder" in this passage is "*qowl*"[43] (kole), meaning to call aloud, a voice or sound, to cry out, to proclaim, thundering, and to yell.

THE FEAST OF SHAVUOT

The Israelites were to count seven Sabbaths from the day of Passover, and then on the following fiftieth day, they were to observe the feast of Shavuot, which is called Pentecost. The law was given unto Moses on the Feast day of Shavout, and it foreshadowed the day when the Lord would fulfill His promise to give a New Covenant to Israel. This was the day that the Lord came down, when the mountain burned.

> "*And the LORD said unto Moses, Go unto the people, and sanctify them to day and tomorrow, and let them wash their clothes, And be ready against the third day: for the third day the LORD will come down in the sight of all the people.*"[44]

The third day is time of the Second Coming, which will occur during the third day of creation, following the death of the Messiah. *"After two days will he revive us: in the third day he will raise us up, and we shall live in his sight."*[45]

Following the death of the Passover Lamb of God, the law of the Spirit was written upon the hearts of men just as He promised His people through Jeremiah 500 years earlier. The outpouring of the Spirit under the New Covenant followed the Passover by fifty days exactly.

Shavuot marks the beginning of the wheat harvest of Israel. The wheat represents the people of God, and the last days' harvest of the earth begins with the Church. *"Now therefore stand and see this great thing, which the LORD will do before your eyes. Is it not wheat harvest today? I will call unto the LORD, and he shall send thunder and rain; that ye may perceive and see that your wickedness is great, which ye have done in the sight of the LORD.... and all the people greatly feared the Lord."*[46]

The Lord allowed leaven to be used in the two loaves presented at Shavuot. This foreshadowed the church of Jews and Gentiles, who would be brought into spiritual Israel. The leaven represented the evil, which would be found within a compromising church. The two wave loaves are symbolic of the leaven or evil in the church, and therefore the loaves are baked.

The compromising church will be placed within an oven and burned in the fire once again at the end of the age, during the Great Tribulation. *"And the people shall be as the burnings of lime: as thorns cut up shall they be burned in the fire. Hear, ye that are far off, what I have done; and, ye that are near, acknowledge my might.*

"The sinners in Zion are afraid; fearfulness hath surprised the hypocrites."[48] Those cut up like thorns, and burned in the fire of the Great Tribulation have leaven in their hearts, therefore they are to be cut off and burned, to purify them for the wedding feast. The sinners in His house will all become afraid and fear will surprise the hypocrites! *"Knowing therefore the terror of the Lord, we persuade men."*[49]

"May we be accounted worthy to be one of these whom the Lord chooses as His ripe fruit in the field. In the mind of God the Father, all has been predestined and settled."[50]

These seven Sabbath weeks, which occur between Passover and Shavuot, are the same period of seven weeks which Daniel prophesied would occur before the Second Coming. *"Seven weeks shalt thou number unto thee: begin to number the seven weeks from such time as thou beginnest to put the sickle to the corn. And thou shalt keep the feast of weeks unto the LORD thy God with a tribute of a freewill offering of thine hand, which thou shalt give unto the LORD thy God, according as the LORD thy God hath blessed thee."*[51]

The Feast of Passover symbolized the First Coming of the Lord as the Lamb of God. The Feast of Shavuot is symbolic of the final Jubilee in which Israel will celebrate the deliverance of the people. The seven weeks of Daniel's prophecy have now concluded, followed by the final 70th Jubilee. Soon after, God will again pour out his Holy Spirit upon His people before the Day of the LORD. We have now waited seven Sabbath years which were required under the law, and these will conclude in 2006.

The feast of Pentecost is symbolic of the Jubilee, and following this last Jubilee, the remnant shall be anointed with power from on high. Then, after the anointing of the remnant, the Day of the LORD will begin.

"I saw four angels standing on the four corners of the earth, holding the four winds of the earth, that the wind should not blow on the earth, nor on the sea, nor on any tree. And I saw another angel ascending from the east, having the seal of the living God: and he cried with a loud voice to the four angels, to whom it was given to hurt the earth and the sea, Saying, Hurt not the earth, neither the sea, nor the trees, till we have sealed the servants of our God in their foreheads."[52]

THE FALL FEASTS OF THE SECOND COMING

Jesus will fulfill the fall feasts of Israel in the Second Coming. The fall feasts are preceded by the time of Teshuvah, the days of repentance, which is the forty days before Yom Kippur. These include the Feast of Trumpets, which is Rosh HaShanah.

The Feast of Trumpets begins Yom Shoffar, which is the holy convocation for the people to repent during the ten Days of Awe before Yom Kippur, the Day of Atonement. Following Yom Kippur is the last feast of Israel, which is known as the Feast of Tabernacles or Sukkot.

The civil new year of Israel is announced by the blowing of the Shofar, on the first day of the seventh month of the religious calendar. The trumpets announce the beginning of the ten Days of Awe, which precede the Day of Atonement. The trumpets are a prophetic announcement in the spirit of the coming Day of the LORD.

This is the last day, when the resurrection of the believers and the rapture of the remnant will occur. Solomon's temple was completed in the seventh month, and is a picture of the completed spiritual temple of the Lord, which will also be finished during the fall feasts of Israel.

Yom Kippur represents the Day of the LORD and is a picture of how we are to approach the judgment by God. It is a day of fasting and mourning, for God takes no joy in the judgment of the wicked. Therefore, we, His people are, to be silent and abstain from all pleasure on this day as a reminder to us.

Yom Kippur also marks the day of proclaiming the Year of Jubilee. Only after the atonement, could the forgiveness and redemption begin.

Lastly, Yeshua will fulfill the Feast of Tabernacles. This is the seventh feast and will be fulfilled with His actual Second Coming. Do we know the day or hour? No. For in the Feast of Tabernacles, the people wait in tents to enter the Promised Land.

So, too, we among God's remnant who are counted worthy to stand on the final Feast of Tabernacles will wait, while the sign of the Son of Man appears in the sky. And then every eye shall see Him, and all the families of the earth will mourn; even so, come Jesus. Amen!

The beginning of the Great Tribulation, which commences the Day of the LORD, is the Feast of Purim, celebrated at the end of winter. Purim represents God's deliverance of Israel from the Antichrist.

The Great Tribulation will begin around the Feast of Purim and on a Sabbath day at the end of winter. Then the great judgment of the Lord will begin.

THE PARABLE OF THE FIG TREE

Jesus commanded us to learn the meaning of *"The Parable of the Fig Tree,"* which is Israel. When she puts forth her branches again, you will know that summer is near. The spiritual meaning of this parable is that when you see Israel begin to shoot forth her leaves, then you know the generation which witnesses this restoration of the nation shall see the fulfillment of all these things, which were written.

The Lord said we would know *"summer is near,"* and the Lord doesn't waste words. He chose "summer" as a warning. For the judgment upon the Church in the last days begins in the season of summer.

> *"Now learn a parable of the fig tree; When his branch is yet tender, and putteth forth leaves, ye know that summer is nigh: So likewise ye, when ye shall see all these things, know that it is near, even at the doors. Verily I say unto you, This generation shall not pass, till all these things be fulfilled"* (Matthew 24:32-34).

HIDDEN PROPHECIES IN THE PSALMS

> *"Hear this, all ye people; give ear, all ye inhabitants of the world: Both low and high, rich and poor, together. My mouth shall speak of wisdom; and the meditation of my heart shall be of understanding. I will incline mine ear to a parable: I will open my dark saying upon the harp. Wherefore should I fear in the days of evil, when the iniquity of my heels shall compass me about?"*[53]

In Psalm 49 David tells us he will open up a *"dark saying upon the harp"*; David will reveal a secret or *"dark"* saying upon his harp, which would be written into one of the psalms. David has revealed that the Lord has hidden a secret in one of the psalms. This secret is the mystery of a parable. The psalm also speaks prophetically of the men of wisdom who would listen and understand, and then open this dark saying giving understanding to the many: *"I will incline mine ear to a parable, I will open my dark saying."*

Which parable? The only parable we were told and instructed to study and learn the meaning of by Jesus was the parable of the Fig Tree.

This *"dark saying"* was placed in psalm 90. This is the only Psalm written by Moses, and the dark saying is the mystery of the 80 years, which would mark the life of the re-birthed nation of Israel in the last days. This is the length of the generation about which Jesus told us and the mystery of the parable we were instructed to learn. This generation would witness the judgment of God. In Psalm 90, Moses questions God regarding the return of the Lord, saying, *"Return, Oh LORD, How long?"*

Bible scholars for the most part have completely missed the significance of this text, yet it reveals the approximate time of the beginning of the judgment by our God. At the beginning of the psalm, Moses declares that from the beginning of time, before the mountains were brought forth, or even the creation of the earth itself, from eternity past, THE HOLY ONE OF ISRAEL is the King of the Universe. He alone is God. Blessed are the ones who come in the name of the Lord Adonai!

Moses declares God has established the secret mysteries of the times, for a thousand years in his sight, are but one day. And when the days are done, then the Lord will carry them away with a flood. The ones carried away are those who are spiritually asleep. In the morning they grow up like the grass, but soon the sun rises, and in the heat of the day they dry up and are withered and are all blown away.

> *"Before the mountains were brought forth, or ever thou hadst formed the earth and the world, even from everlasting to everlasting, thou art God. Thou turnest man to destruction; and sayest, Return, ye children of men. For a thousand years in thy sight are but as yesterday when it is past, and as a watch in the night. Thou carriest them away as with a flood; they are as a sleep: in the morning they are like grass which groweth up"* (Psalm 90:2-5).

TEACH US TO NUMBER OUR DAYS

Moses then asks the Lord, teach us to count the number of our days, that we might know wisdom; how long will it be unto Your return, Lord? He continues asking the Lord to repent concerning His servants; to repent of destroying them along with all the others who have been appointed to be judged in the last hour.

*"So teach us to number our days, that we may apply our hearts unto wisdom. Return, O LORD, how long? and let it repent thee concerning thy servants."*54 The Spirit reveals the answer to this prayer of Moses, that we might know the time of His coming: *"The days of our years are threescore years and ten; and if by reason of strength they be fourscore years, yet is their strength labour and sorrow; for it is soon cut off, and we fly away."*55

Thus we are told the years of the last days' nation Israel will be eighty, and then we are soon cut off, and we fly away. Shortly after the end of the eightieth year, Israel shall be *"cut off"* in the destruction of the Great War. Now, what does this mean to us? Everything! Remember, the word of our Lord, the word of truth must be confirmed with two or more witnesses. This is what Torah requires for us to receive a word of testimony. There must be two confirmations or we cannot be lawfully certain of a matter.

When did Israel put forth her leaves? The prophet Haggai gives us the date which began the first recovery to the land in the time of Nehemiah, for on the 24th day of the 9th month, the cornerstone was set for the rebuilding of the temple. Haggai tells us to consider it. This is the day we are told to watch, on this same day, the second restoration would begin.

On December 19, 1917, which was the 24th day of the 9th month in the Hebrew calendar, General Allenby conquered Jerusalem for the British Empire, and shortly thereafter, the British issued the Balfour Declaration, allowing for the immigration of Jews back to the land for the first time in 2000 years. The mountains of Israel began to put forth their leaves on this day. Consider it.

These events in 1917 signify the shooting forth of the leaves. Ezekiel provides the key to this part of God's great hidden secret, which has remained hidden within the Scriptures.

"Consider now from this day and upward, from the four and twentieth day of the ninth month, even from the day that the foundation of the LORD'S temple was laid, consider it. Is the seed yet in the barn? yea, as yet the vine, and the fig tree, and the pomegranate,

and the olive tree, hath not brought forth: from this day will I bless you."[56] *"But ye, O mountains of Israel, ye shall shoot forth your branches, and yield your fruit to my people of Israel; for they are at hand to come."*[57]

Notice, the mountains shoot forth their branches, for the people are at hand to come. They are ready to begin coming home. And in 1917 under the Balfour Declaration, they did begin to come home to the Land, the Blessed Land of my beloved Eretz Yisrael.

Baruch Hashem! If this is the proper day to begin the countdown for the 80 years, we should see confirmation on the other significant years which follow: 30, 50, 70 and 80. Thirty is the number of Maturity, thus, after 30 years we should see the land mature. Fifty is the Jubilee number, and we should see the completion of the restoration at the 50-year mark.

Seventy marks the time of trouble, so we should see problems in the land at the 70-year point. Eighty marks the fulfillment, thus, this should also be a significant year for the nation. Notice, the psalm says and then soon we are cut off, so the judgment on Israel begins soon after the end of the 80th year. The judgment follows the 80th year. Remember the Lord has appointed the days of mankind according to the sacred calendar of Israel, which begins in the March/April months.

Does the history of the land confirm this is the proper starting point? Let me present the answer in a table:

- **1917** On December 9, 1917 the land is opened again, the fig tree puts out her leaves. The count begins. The first year ends in March of 1918.

- **1947** In November of 1947, the United Nations formally declares a Jewish Homeland partitioning Palestine and creating the State of Israel... 30 years is a maturity cycle, thus the maturing of the Land has been accomplished and the newborn Israel now stands up among the nations.

- **1967** This is a Jubilee period, being 50 years. This year is not a Jubilee, for the land was restored in 1948 during a Jubilee. This is only a Jubilee cycle from 1917. Under the law of the Jubilee, all lands that were foreclosed or lost had to be returned to the original tribe which owned them, and all debts had to be forgiven. Thus, Israel is returned: Jerusalem, her capital, and Samaria and the West Bank of the Jordan Valley, which is also rightfully hers. Thus, this countdown fits perfectly. Where were the prophecy teachers 30 years ago? They thought the countdown started in 1948! Also ignorant of the secrets of Psalm 90, they thought a generation was 40 years, which it is not. It is 80 years.

- **1987** This is the 70th year for Israel, and in 1987 the Intifada rebellion of the Palestinians began. This is the time of trouble spoken in the psalm.

- **1997** The year 1997 on the secular calendar, or the year which began on April 8, 1997 on the sacred calendar, is Israel's 80th year and it ended on March 28, 1998. Soon *"they are cut off and they fly away."* Thus, the 80-year count is fulfilled and the judgment will follow soon after the end of the 80th year.

Thus from Psalm 90, we know that Israel will be destroyed in part, judged by God in the battle of Ezekiel 38, some time after the end of the 80th year which ended in March, 1998. Now if this is a true revelation of God's timing, opened to us at the very time of the end, then there should be confirmation from the other prophecies which also tell us when the judgment will begin. These include Daniel's seventy weeks prophecies and the words of Jesus Himself regarding His anointing and His coming unto us in the Year of Jubilee.

THE SEVENTY WEEKS OF DANIEL

Daniel's prophecy of the seventy weeks includes the prophecy that from the decree to rebuild Jerusalem the second time, unto Messiah as Prince there would be seven weeks. Thus, there shall be forty-nine full Jewish years from the decree to rebuild Jerusalem until Messiah comes as Prince. These are forty-nine Hebrew years and they represent seven Sabbath-year cycles. Every seven years, Israel is to have a Sabbath year, and after seven Sabbath years, which is forty-nine years, we have the Jubilee, which is the time of restoration.

The command to restore Jerusalem was issued shortly after Israel declared independence in May of 1948. It occurred in the Jewish year ending in March 1949 on the sacred calendar. The first year, in which Israel was restored to its land as a Sovereign nation, was itself a Jubilee Year. The Jubilee cycle requires seven Sabbath years until the next Jubilee. Thus in 1949, the 49-year cycle began, which takes us to March of 1998, the same date as Psalm 90. Both the seven weeks of Daniel and the 80th year of Psalm 90 precede the final Jubilee of Israel. The word of truth is confirmed with two or more witnesses. The judgment of the Lord is to follow the final Jubilee, which began on March 28, 1998 and will end March 18, 1999. This is the year which follows the 80 years of Psalm 90 and the seven weeks of Daniel. This year is the final Jubilee of the Lord. Let all the earth fear and be silent before Him! Truly, the Spirit of the Lord has spoken, *"The Day of the LORD is at Hand!"*

THE JUBILEE OF THE LORD

The word "Jubilee" in Hebrew is *"yovel"*, which means to be "jubilant" and to "exult." The Jubilee year is announced with the blowing of the Shofar on the Day of Atonement, which is Yom Kippur. *"And thou shalt number seven sabbaths of years unto thee, seven times seven years; and the space of the seven sabbaths of years shall be unto thee forty and nine years.*

"Then shalt thou cause the trumpet of the jubile to sound on the tenth day of the seventh month, in the day of atonement shall ye make the trumpet sound throughout all your land. And ye shall hallow the fiftieth year, and proclaim liberty throughout all the land unto all the inhabitants thereof: it shall be a jubile unto you; and ye shall return every man unto his possession, and ye shall return every man unto his family."[58] The Jubilee of Israel is set in remembrance of the deliverance from the slavery of Egypt.

The Exodus was the first Jubilee. After Israel had entered the land, the Lord established the Jubilee as a memorial to the deliverance of the people from their slavery in Egypt. The Jubilee is a year in which to proclaim freedom and deliverance throughout all the land. Individuals who had incurred debts and had sold themselves as slaves or servants to others were released from their debts and were set at liberty. Like the Sabbatical years, the Year of Jubilee was a year for neither sowing nor reaping. The Jubilee was a special year of God's mercy. *"The sabbatical year and presuma-*

bly the Year of Jubilee were also characterized by instruction in the Law. In this way the people learned that God's demand to love and obey Him was directly related to his concern for the welfare of all the people of Israel."[59] *"The Year of Jubilee was a special year in family renewal. A man who was bound to another as a slave or indentured servant was set free and returned to his own family. If any members of his family were also bound, the entire family was set free. Houses and lands could also be redeemed in the Year of Jubilee. If they were not redeemed within a year, however, they became the permanent possession of the previous owner."*[60]

The Jubilee is the *"Favorable Year"* of the Lord, the year God extended mercy to all the inhabitants of the land. Thus, the date count of both Psalm 90, and Daniel's final seven weeks' prophecy, both end at the beginning of the last Jubilee of Israel. The Lord declares His mercy triumphs over judgment, and thus, as we stand at the end of the age, the Lord gives one last great Jubilee, for this was the final Jubilee of Israel.

THE 70th JUBILEE

This past Jubilee, which ended March 18, 1999, was the 70th Jubilee of Israel. The nation was restored 50 years ago in 1948 during the 69th Jubilee. If we trace the calendar back we find that Jesus was born during the 30th Jubilee in 2 BC. David was made king over all of Israel during the 10th Jubilee. God raised Gideon up as a warrior immediately after the 7th Jubilee. The Exodus from Egypt was the first Jubilee.

Today we enjoy the fruits of the 70th Jubilee. Thus, the last half of the 70th week of Daniel is to be completed following the 70th Jubilee. Oh, the wonder and the wisdom of God! How marvelous are His ways, His wonders to observe. The Lord began His ministry in Nazareth when He stood up and opened the Torah to Isaiah 61; He read only part of the prophecy of the Messiah, stopping mid-sentence at *"the acceptable year of the Lord."* The acceptable year of the Lord is the Jubilee. Jesus did not read *"and the Day of Vengeance of our God"* for this will be fulfilled at the Second Coming. Jesus was in Nazareth to fulfill the meaning of the Jubilee, to redeem that which had been lost, and to free those in slavery to Satan.

"The Spirit of the Lord GOD is upon me; because the LORD hath anointed me to preach good tidings unto the meek; he hath sent me to bind up the brokenhearted, to proclaim liberty to the captives, and the opening of the prison to them that are bound; To proclaim the acceptable year of the LORD, and the day of vengeance of our God."[61]

The Lord then closed the book and told the people *"these words are fulfilled in your hearing."* He did not read the second half of the prophecy at that time, because it was not time to fulfill the day of vengeance. The day of vengeance would have to wait until the Jubilee, which would follow Daniel's prophecy of the seven weeks. That time has now come. *"The day of vengeance, the Day of the LORD is at hand."* Isaiah prophesied both in Chapter 61, But look closer, Isaiah is actually telling us the Day of the Lord must occur during or immediately after a Jubilee Year, for both must be fulfilled in the Second Coming in the order spoken by Jesus: "To proclaim the Jubilee year of the LORD, and the day of vengeance of our God."

Now, as we learned from the above, the 49 years which follow the year of Israel's restoration ended in March of 1998, and then we entered the 70th Jubilee. The Day of the LORD will begin during or shortly after the 70th Jubilee, which ended on March 18, 1999.

In Isaiah 61, speaking of the Second Coming, the Lord is declaring both, a final Jubilee and *"The Day of Vengeance."* The next major war in the Middle East, and the judgment on America Babylon, will begin following the end of the 70th Jubilee, which ends on March 18, 1999.

The events of the Great Tribulation must therefore follow after the completion of the seven weeks prophecy and after the birth of the man-child company, the 144,000 sealed servants of the book of Revelation. According to this understanding, the man-child must be born during 2006, which concludes the end of the eighth week, for the Messiah the Prince comes after seven weeks and not after eight.

"Know therefore and understand, that from the going forth of the commandment to restore and to build Jerusalem unto the Messiah the Prince shall be seven weeks."[62]

Thus, the return of Jesus Christ, begins through the birth of the man-child, the 144,000 who are the Elijah company of the last hour, walking in the power and authority of the Lord. The birth of the man-child should therefore occur before 2007, which would be the end of the eighth week following the command to restore Jerusalem in June of 1948. Truly, we are at the door. People, wake up. Remnant saints, stand up your hour is come!

Please bear with me and open your hearts and minds to understand this mystery. In the first coming, Jesus Christ was born in the flesh in Bethlehem. All of Israel was looking for the coming of the Messiah. And after he was born into the world, the nation did not see him for 30 years, as he lived and matured in Nazareth. So too the birth of the man-child company may not coincide immediately, with their being revealed unto the nation in the beginning of their ministry for they too may spend a season maturing under the hidden hand of the Lord. Nevertheless, the scripture is clear. Following the birth of the man-child, the dragon shall then turn and begin to persecute the woman who gave birth to the child and the remnant of her seed, who keep the testimony of Jesus. Therefore, we should expect that if the man-child is born into the world in 2006, then a world-wide persecution against the true believers should break out almost immediately.

The Yom Kippur War in Israel was a foreshadow of these events. The war, which occurred in October 1973, was at the exact midpoint of the Jubilee cycle. In Israel, the number 25 is referred to as half a Jubilee. The Yom Kippur War is a sign of the other half of the proclamations and the prophecies surrounding the 70th Jubilee, for it inaugurates the last half of the 70th week of Daniel. The proclamation of Jesus in Isaiah 61 contains two parts; the final Jubilee comes after the 7 weeks of Daniel and immediately before the end of the 70th week itself, which is the Day of The LORD!

Indeed, proclaiming the 70th Jubilee of the Lord, and the end of the 70th week, we are entering the day of vengeance of our God

THE SIGNS IN THE SUN, THE MOON AND THE STARS

God told us that in the fourth day of creation He created the lights in the heavens for signs of the seasons and the times of mankind. Jesus also told us that we would see specific signs in the heavens as evidence that the events of the end of the age were upon us.

"And there shall be signs in the sun, and in the moon, and in the stars; and upon the earth distress of nations, with perplexity; the sea and the waves roaring" (Luke 21:25).

In the prophecies of Joel, the Lord declares that He will show us signs in the heavens and the earth before the beginning of the Great Day of The LORD.

"And I will show wonders in the heavens and in the earth, blood, and fire, and pillars of smoke. The sun shall be turned into darkness, and the moon into blood, before the great and the terrible day of the LORD come. And it shall come to pass, that whosoever shall call on the name of the LORD shall be delivered: for in mount Zion and in Jerusalem shall be deliverance, as the LORD hath said, and in the remnant whom the LORD shall call" (Joel 2:30-32).

The witness of Psalm 90, Daniel's seven weeks, and the statements by the Lord Himself regarding the Fig Tree, and His announcing the year of Jubilee and then the year of Justice, are all consistent and confirm this present hour. What confirmation do the signs in the heavens and upon the earth provide? If this interpretation of prophecy is correct, we should also find signs in the heavens above and upon the earth below.

The scientific community has been observing our sun with great interest in the modern era. The exploration of space and the use of satellites for communications have required extensive monitoring of the sun. Today, you can access the space weather on the Internet, and the activities of the sun are under scrutiny.

The sun itself moves through an eleven-year solar cycle. The activities in the sun are becoming much more volatile. Solar flares have the capability to reach millions of miles into space. These flares have become far more dangerous, with a massive explosion last year that damaged several key communications satellites, almost interrupting the long distance phone service in the US.

The sun's ultraviolet radiation is lethal to life on the earth. This planet is protected from these deadly rays by the both the magnetic field and the ozone layer. The magnetic poles of the earth are now destabilizing and beginning to wobble. Magnetic north is shifting from a historically normal 12° to 14° to now as much as 28°.

This is occurring because the molten iron core of the planet is now shifting. These changes in the magnetic field may portend a change in the level of radiation on the surface of the earth.

The ozone layer itself is also severely damaged and has two large holes, one in the southern hemisphere, which rotates around the South Pole passing over southern Chile and Argentina and New Zealand. The other hole is in the northern hemisphere over the northern pole.

SIGNS IN THE MOON

Signs in the moon represent events affecting Israel, while signs in the sun speak of the nations. The nations of the earth all use a solar calendar, while Israel alone uses the moon to mark her times. The moon has been producing signs since 1996:

Israel witnessed the first of a series of four blood-red lunar eclipses on Passover in April of 1996. A full eclipse was visible from Jerusalem as the blood-red moon rose over the Temple mount. Passover is the first feast of Israel. It is in remembrance of the deliverance of the nation from Egypt, when the angel of death came into the land and passed over those whose lives were covered by the blood of the lamb.

This first eclipse lasted exactly 70 minutes over Jerusalem. The 70 minutes are for the 70 weeks of Daniel, which concluded. It also foretold the 70th Jubilee, which precedes the end of all these things.

The next blood-red moon occurred on the Feast of Sukkot, which is Tabernacles, in September of 1996. Sukkot is the seventh and last feast of Israel and celebrates the people waiting to enter the Promised Land. This last feast is symbolic of our waiting for the kingdom of our Lord to be restored on this earth. At the high point of the eclipse, the planet Saturn was 3° from the moon. Saturn represents the Sabbath or the seventh day.

The first two blood-red moons appeared on the first and the last feasts of Israel. They speak of deliverance from slavery and waiting to enter the Kingdom. They also speak of Jesus Christ, Who says of Himself, *"I am the First and the Last."* The second eclipse on the seventh feast is also symbolic of the seven weeks of Daniel, which concluded in the same year of 1997, and the seventh day of creation, which is about to begin.

The third blood-red moon occurred on the next Biblical feast, which was Purim in March of 1997. This is the feast to celebrate the deliverance from Haman, a type of the antichrist. All of these signs in the moon point to the ending of the 70th week of Daniel, and to the conclusion of the seven weeks which precede the Second Coming. They also symbolize the proclamation by our Lord of the coming 70th Jubilee of Israel, and then the coming of the great and terrible Day of The LORD. These three blood-red moons occurred on the only three Biblical feasts which fall on full moons. The three lunar eclipses fell on three consecutive Biblical feasts in a row. Eighteen months after the first lunar eclipse, the fourth occurred during the *"Days of Teshuvah,"* which are called the Days of Repentance. The fourth blood-red moon occurred on September 16, 1997. These four eclipses preceded the start of the 70th Jubilee of Israel exactly. Are you getting this picture yet? The biggest event in the history of the earth is coming upon us and the Lord is broadcasting His warnings using all available means.

SIGNS IN THE STARS

In February 1997 the Comet Hale-Bopp began to appear to the visible eye for the first time. The course of Hale-Bopp is of interest to us for it paints a picture of what is shortly to come. Hale-Bopp begins its journey through the sky passing through the right hand of the constellation of the Cross. Hale-Bopp then rides across the constellation Pegasus, the horse, signifying the four horsemen of Revelation, which are about to ride.

Photographs of the comet reveal seven tails behind her path. In the year before Hale-Bopp, the earth was visited by another comet called Hyakutake near the time of the first lunar eclipse on Passover. This comet was pale green in color—the color of the fourth horse of the Apocalypse.

In 1993, the earth witnessed the first planetary impact in history as Comet Shoemaker-Levy 9 broke up into 21 pieces and slammed into the planet Jupiter. These 21 fragments are symbols of the 21 judgments, which will fall during the tribulation. Jupiter is the symbol of the king of Babylon, who is also about to be judged.

A further sign was evidenced in the heavens in September of 1996. The Lord created the signs in the stars to communicate with mankind the story of the Messiah. The great deceiver, seeking to hide this truth in the stars, created astrology as a counterfeit of the true message of God.

In September, the constellation of Bethulah, the virgin, was in position above the moon, symbolic of the woman in Revelation 12, who is seen standing upon the moon. Over the top of Bethulah was the constellation Bernice's Hair, which represents the crown of 12 stars. Standing next to Bethulah was the constellation Draco, which is the Dragon who awaits the birth of the man-child he is seeking to devour.

This is the exact picture presented in chapter 12 of the book of Revelation. This arrangement of stars has never happened before, nor will it ever again.[63] This is an exact picture of the world waiting for the start of the Great Tribulation, and the Lord has displayed it in the heavens as a giant post-it note for the whole earth to read. This is also a sign to the remnant, which the Lord will awaken, that the time to flee is soon at hand.

SIGNS UPON THE EARTH

Jesus also told us there would be signs upon the earth including floods, droughts, famines, earthquakes and volcanoes. Joel spoke of signs of blood, fire and pillars of smoke. Today, El Nino is producing both floods and droughts, causing a massive shift in the normal weather patterns of the world. And the fires of Malaysia, Mexico and Brazil as the fires across the U.S. are becoming more intense. The smoke from these fires could be seen from the space shuttle. Of course, the violent storms and the raging waves of the sea are another sign Christ spoke of.

Many of the worlds volcanos are also beginning to evince activity as we race toward the end of this last Jubilee and headlong into the beginning of the end of the 70th week of Daniel. The prophecy warns us before the judgment begins, we will witness heat and drought in the land.

The US News and World Report cite these recent warming of the earth. "It just keeps getting hotter.... There is no sign the trend is easing. The years 1990, 1995, and 1997 in particular were the hottest. February of this year, reports the Climate Predictions Center, was a whopping 3.2 degrees Fahrenheit above the average during the last 30 years.... It is by far the most extreme monthly temperature rise ever seen.... The analysis supports, in unprecedented detail, existing conclusions by United Nations-based climate reports that the recent warmth is not only extreme but is rising ever faster."[64] The signs upon the earth, and in the stars, the sun and the moon, all confirm the Day of the LORD is at hand!

JESUS IS LORD AND HE IS COMING SOON

The remnant is the Lord's portion, His tithe of the whole body. They are the omer, the handful of corn, which will dwell upon the top of the mountains. These true sons and daughters are the plantings of the Lord who can hear with a spiritual ear, a people called out of the world of religious confusion.

They are the outcasts of Israel and are not known by the titles of man. The wilderness journey has done its work, and they have come out leaning upon their Beloved. The Lamb has chosen a Bride, and she has made herself ready. Before the storm breaks forth in all its fury, His chosen remnant will be joined together in unity of mind and spirit. No man will have anything to do with this gathering by the Spirit.

None will be missing and each will find their place in rank. The seed of David through Christ is being called to a place of high authority. They shall sit upon thrones of judgment. They shall strike through kings in the day of His power! He is restoring His people and causing them to return to Him. These set-apart ones are called to an inheritance incorruptible, and undefiled, reserved in heaven for them. They are kept by the power of God, and are ready to be revealed in the last time.

He is collecting His troops, and calling them now into their ranks. Soon the tares will be removed, for the time of their maturity is at hand. These are the sons of the wicked one, wild wheat and noxious weeds that give off poison. The tares will be bundled and burned as briars and thorns. The remnant are being kept by His hand.

It is the Father's pleasure to refine each of us and purify our faith that we faint not in the day of trouble. He is faithful Who called you. He chose you in the furnace of affliction for Himself and His purpose. The perfecting of His vessels has been necessary to complete His work. Through life's wrenching circumstances, their soul has been wounded almost beyond measure. The six thousand years are upon us. Only the wise will understand, for the wicked will continue to do wickedly.

> *"The Lord, in His mercy, has set watchmen upon the walls to sound the trumpet to warn of the impending sword. Judgment awaits the unrepentant and the lukewarm."*[65]

HE SHALL COME TO BE GLORIFIED IN HIS SAINTS

The Lord is fast coming upon the world and the wayward churches that have fallen from the true purposes of the Father for His people. The Lion is beginning to roar from His habitation, for His camp is very great and there is a sound going forth that will awaken His people to the time of battle! Many of the Lord's people in the religious system of man's order have made kings to rule over them, just as the children of Israel did in the time of Samuel.

> *"My people are destroyed for lack of knowledge: because thou hast rejected knowledge, I will also reject thee, that thou shalt be no priest to me: seeing thou hast forgotten the law of thy God, I will also forget thy children. As they were increased, so they sinned against me: therefore will I change their glory into shame.... My people ask counsel at their stocks, and their staff declareth unto them: for the spirit of whoredoms hath caused them to err, and they have gone a whoring from under their God. They sacrifice upon the tops of the mountains, and burn incense upon the hills, under oaks and poplars and elms, because the shadow thereof is good: therefore your daughters shall commit whoredom, and your spouses shall commit adultery."*[66]

They have taken coverings of strange trees; the standing images (men's idols today), in the likeness of male and female, which God forbids in His word. The people would have it so, but as we can see, we are living out a repeat of history. People take counsel from their stocks, the standing images of the Church. The Lord of Hosts is getting ready to do some awesome breaking with His sword, His Word.

The religious kingdoms of man's order are about to be shaken to the core, nothing will be left standing for she, and all of her harlots, will be burned with fire! This religious order of Babylon is of man's making and appointment, and their voices of confusion will not be able to stand for they have taken men of their choosing for their foundational stones.

Many of the Lord's people have not the slightest desire to hear from God directly. There are so many that allow someone else to do all their studying for them. The Lord calls them dull of hearing.

God's people have been fed so much mixture of truth and error by their pastors that they would not even recognize Jesus if He walked into their very midst. The day of playing church is over, my friends, and we are about to see destruction in the land the likes of which man has never beheld with his eyes.

The pastors and teachers and the people have no true knowledge of God or His ways. The leaders are famished for the true Word, and their people are dried-up for thirst. There is no water, no true, living life-sustaining bread to nourish the flock. The true voice of God is no longer in their midst. No prophetic word and no vision restores the people back to God.

The Spirit is telling the remnant to awaken, to see and open our eyes, and to loose ourselves from all that would hinder us from the Lord's purposes. The hour is late! The Father's true sons and daughters have been in the wilderness to humble them and to prove them and to know what was in their hearts, whether they would keep His word or not.

JESUS CHRIST SHALL BE THE HEAD OVER THEM

There is only one head over the Lord's remnant people, and that is Jesus Christ. *"Then shall the children of Judah and the children of*

Israel be gathered together, and appoint themselves one head, and they shall come up out of the land: for great shall be the day of Jezreel."[67] The remnant has been hidden away under the shadow of His hand. Soon they will come forth as clean and pure vessels and as the weapons of the Lord's indignation.

The man-child of Revelation is about to be born, and they are the remnant that will be in the full image of Christ, possessing His nature, with His character sealed in their foreheads, holiness to the Lord. They are the final work of the Father, and they will manifest His presence among the people.

> *"And to you who are troubled rest with us, when the Lord Jesus shall be revealed from heaven with his mighty angels, In flaming fire taking vengeance on them that know not God, and that obey not the gospel of our Lord Jesus Christ: Who shall be punished with everlasting destruction from the presence of the Lord, and from the glory of his power; When he shall come to be glorified in his saints, and to be admired in all them that believe (because our testimony among you was believed) in that day."*[68]

They are the bright clouds *"Ask ye of the LORD rain in the time of the latter rain; so the LORD shall make bright clouds, and give them showers of rain, to every one grass in the field."*[69] They are coming to pour out the living water of His word, to the very dry ground of His people.

> *"My doctrine shall drop as the rain, my speech shall distil as the dew, as the small rain upon the tender herb, and as the showers upon the grass.*[70]

There is a remnant, but it is made up of a few, a *"handful"* of corn on top of the mountains. They are the "omer" and the tithe from the body, the Lord's portion and His first fruits of the resurrection. We are to die to our self and press on to the mark of the high calling of God. That high calling is the full redemption of the spirit, soul and body preserved blameless unto the coming of our Lord.

> *"For I reckon that the sufferings of this present time are not worthy to be compared with the glory which shall be revealed in us. For the earnest expectation of the creature waiteth for the manifestation of the sons of God.*[71]

They are the first ripe grain of the field, the first fruits of the harvest, and are pure of any defilement. These will be hated and rejected by the Church, and will have all manner of evil spoken of them. They also have the favor of the Lord, and therefore the world and the compromised Church will reject them.

These are the "Joseph Company" of the Lord, and the elder leadership of the Church will hate them, even as his brethren hated Joseph. These are the weapons of the Lord.

"A fire is kindled in mine anger, and shall burn unto the lowest hell, and shall consume the earth with her increase, and set on fire the foundations of the mountains.... If I whet my glittering sword, and mine hand take hold on judgment; I will render vengeance to mine enemies, and will reward them that hate me. I will make mine arrows drunk with blood, and my sword shall devour flesh; and that with the blood of the slain and of the captives, from the beginning of revengers upon the enemy. Rejoice, O ye nations, with his people: for he will avenge the blood of his servants, and will render vengeance to his adversaries, and will be merciful unto his land, and to his people."[72]

"For all people will walk every one in the name of his god, and we will walk in the name of the LORD our God for ever and ever. In that day, saith the LORD, will I assemble her that halteth, and I will gather her that is driven out, and her that I have afflicted; And I will make her that halted a remnant, and her that was cast far off a strong nation: and the LORD shall reign over them in mount Zion from henceforth, even for ever. And thou, O tower of the flock, the strong hold of the daughter of Zion, unto thee shall it come, even the first dominion; the kingdom shall come to the daughter of Jerusalem."[73]

The remnant will walk in the name of the Lord alone. They have been outcasts from the assembly, and rejected by the people. The word for "halted" is *tsala`*[74] (tsaw-lah'), which means to limp. These of the remnant have been limping; they have been wounded in the house of their friends. The word for "outcast" is *"nadach"*[75] (naw-dakh'), which means literally to expel, strike, inflict, cast down, drive away, outcast.

They are the afflicted of the Lord, the lowly ones, whom the Lord has been preparing in the fires of His judgment. The word for "afflicted" is *ra ` a* [76] (raw-ah'), which means to break down in pieces, to do evil, do harm, hurt, and to punish. The remnant has known many afflictions by the Lord. They are the outcasts of the assembly who have been mistreated by the people, even as his own brethren betrayed Joseph.

The word for "remnant" is *she'eriyth* [77] (sheh-ay-reeth'), which means a remainder or residual, the surviving final portion, those who are left and remain. The remnant shall be given the first dominion of the kingdom. The word for "dominion" is *memshalah* [78] (mem-shaw-law'), which means to rule, or power to rule, those who possess sovereign authority. These are the outcasts of Israel.

These are the saviors, who come up on mount Zion to judge the mount of Esau. They will posses the land of Edom, and through their hand, the Lord will judge the nations. They are referred to as saviors, for through their hand the Lord will bring His deliverance to His people. They are described, as *"a fire"* for the presence of God shall burn within the remnant.

> *"But upon mount Zion shall be deliverance, and there shall be holiness; and the house of Jacob shall possess their possessions. And the house of Jacob shall be a fire, and the house of Joseph a flame, and the house of Esau for stubble, and they shall kindle in them, and devour them; and there shall not be any remaining of the house of Esau; for the LORD hath spoken it. And they of the south shall possess the mount of Esau; and they of the plain the Philistines: and they shall possess the fields of Ephraim, and the fields of Samaria: and Benjamin shall possess Gilead. And the captivity of this host of the children of Israel shall possess that of the Canaanites, even unto Zarephath; and the captivity of Jerusalem, which is in Sepharad, shall possess the cities of the south. And saviours shall come up on mount Zion to judge the mount of Esau; and the kingdom shall be the LORD'S."* [79]

HIS GOING FORTH IS FROM ETERNITY

> *"But thou, Bethlehem Ephratah, though thou be little among the thousands of Judah, yet out of thee shall he come forth unto me that is to be ruler in Israel; whose goings forth have been from of old,*

from everlasting."[80] *"For behold, the LORD is coming forth from His place. He will come down and tread on the high places of the earth. The mountains will melt under Him, And the valleys will be split, Like wax before the fire, Like water poured down a steep place."*[81] *"And I saw when the Lamb opened one of the seals, and I heard, as it were the noise of thunder, one of the four beasts saying, Come and see. And I saw, and behold a white horse: and he that sat on him had a bow; and a crown was given unto him: and he went forth conquering, and to conquer."*[82] *"When I have bent Judah for me, filled the bow with Ephraim, and raised up thy sons, O Zion, against thy sons, O Greece, and made thee as the sword of a mighty man."*[83]

THE HOUR OF HIS JUDGMENT IS COME

"The final Jubilee is at hand, and it shall overlap into the full fury of the Lord's judgment upon the earth. This is the 120th Jubilee of the earth, and the 70th Jubilee of Israel. The end of all flesh is at hand. This is the day of My vengeance saith the Lord, and the year of my redeemed has come! My sanctified remnant has now been approved. They have passed through the wilderness of testing, and judgment in fire, and now are being restored by My mighty hand. This is the year, which I have appointed, and the great and awesome day is at hand. My indignation shall come upon all nations, and My righteous anger shall now be revealed. This is the year of My visitation, with the thunder of My prophetic word, I shall cut down the mountains. With the storm, the tempest, and a devouring fire I shall plead with all flesh. And the slain of the Lord shall be many.

"Behold, I the Lord shall come with FIRE, and with My chariots of FIRE like a whirlwind, to render My recompense to the nations, and My judgment in Israel. Woe, I say, Woe unto the dull of hearing and slothful. Woe unto the foolish ones who know not My ways of righteousness. The midnight hour is upon you and where will you hide in the day of My indignation? You have rejected the words of My messengers, and have not heeded My correction, nor have you received My counsel. Why do you think I will save you in the day of My wrath? My warnings have gone forth, yet there are very few that hear and take My words to heart. This is a nation of people who do not obey the Lord, nor will they receive

correction from their God. Therefore I shall number you among the slain, and I shall turn My ear from your cries.

"Neither will I pity, nor spare, but I shall bring upon you the fruit of your ways, and pour upon you My wrath, for you refused in the day I called.

"To My remnant I say come unto Me and hide yourself for a moment while My indignation passes through your land. Come and join yourselves to Me in a perpetual covenant. I will bring you again unto My holy mountain, and you shall live in My sight.

"My holy remnant are prepared, and they carry My weapons for war. Many kings shall fall in their sight, and My wrath shall be poured out through their hands. The time to thresh has come My people. The Day of vengeance is in My heart.

Flee out of the false churches who do not know me. Flee out the great harlot Babylon, for the hour of her judgment is come. My sword is drawn and ready for the battle, and I shall destroy Babylon in one hour. Her princes and wise men shall all fall in the day of My judgment.

"The false preachers and false prophets have taught lies to My people, and they shall all fall says the Lord. To My remnant, I say watch, and stay awake for the hour of My judgment is come! I shall spare My chosen ones and show them My everlasting loving kindness. I shall reveal My great mercy, favor and compassion because they have chosen to follow Me fully. The nations shall all recognize My chosen ones.

"Those that afflicted you in the past shall come bowing before you. I will take away all of your judgments. Your brethren that hated you, and cast you out for My name's sake shall all know that I have chosen you and appointed you as My witness to the nations.

"I, the Lord, shall appear to your glory, and all those who stood against you shall be ashamed. Hear and know that I have spoken to you My word. You know who you are. This is the day you have long waited for.... This is the beginning of the end, and the new dawn has come! Rejoice and be glad, for I am the Lord and My great day is at hand!"[84]

"For the Lord takes pleasure in His people; he will beautify the humble with salvation. Let the saints be joyful in glory; let them sing aloud on their beds. Let the high praises of God be in their mouth, and a two-edged sword in their hand, To execute vengeance on the nations, and punishments on the peoples; To bind their kings with chains, and their nobles with fetters of iron; To execute on them the written judgment—this honor have all His saints. Praise the Lord" (Psalm 149:4-9 NKJV).

"The LORD reigneth; let the earth rejoice; let the multitude of isles be glad thereof. Clouds and darkness are round about him: righteousness and judgment are the habitation of his throne. A fire goeth before him, and burneth up his enemies round about. His lightnings enlightened the world: the earth saw, and trembled.

The hills melted like wax at the presence of the LORD, at the presence of the LORD of the whole earth" (Psalm 97:1-5).

THUS SAITH THE LORD OF HOSTS

I will surely save My people
from the land of the east and from the west
and I will bring them back, to live in their own land
and they will be my people,
and I will be their God in truth and righteousness!
I, the Lord, will arise, and in that hour, my enemies will scatter,
Let victory be your cry, Israel
Let the joy of the Lord be my people's strength
For I come as Messiah and the hope of all Israel!
Sing and rejoice and be glad, daughter of Zion
For I am coming in you as KING!
I will dwell in your midst,
and you will know that I am the LORD of Hosts
Let your hands be strong, oh Zion,
Do not fear, all Israel!
For, behold, I am your King and I am coming
and salvation I will bring.
The day of vengeance is in My heart,
and the year of My redeemed has come.
Truly your redemption draweth nigh!
Lift up your heads, Zion, I come and shall reveal My glory!

**Shema Yisrael
Hashem Elkokeynu
Hashem Echad**

**"Hear O Israel
The Lord our God
The Lord is one"**

FINAL WORDS

"In Returning And Rest Shall Ye Be Saved"
Isaiah 30:15

Seven years passed since the fall of 1996 when the Lord revealed unto me that the Day of the LORD was at hand; I witnessed the soon and certain judgment which is coming upon America. Writing this book has been a great blessing, and this second edition offers me the opportunity to share some of the things that the Lord has revealed in the years which have followed. My prayer is that the Lord will be gracious and once again anoint my words to share with you, for the time for the fulfillment of all things is now at hand.

I HAVE DREAMED A DREAM

In the summer of 2001, I had a dream. I was driving in my truck along the coast of northern California. I stopped in front of a house on the beach, and as I got out, I heard the roar of a jet above me. The sound was louder than any jet I had ever heard before and it startled me. Looking up a United Airlines 767 raced overhead at low altitude and at a very high rate of speed. The sound of the engines scared me. I had never heard a jet fly at such high speed while at low altitude before.

Its engines were screaming as if on full throttle. The jet crossed the sky in a few moments of time, and was gone. Suddenly, another jet appeared, this time, an American 767 roaring across the sky and I wondered if the second plane was chasing the first. It, too, disappeared over the horizon as I stood and watched. Suddenly two more jets, another American and United plane, came screaming back from the opposite direction. I hurried inside the house where a group of people had gathered; a brother who was on the Internet looked up and said, *"Benjamin, I am so glad you are here.*

"I have a question I need to ask you." I said, *"Wait, I need to show you something first, come outside."* Then I thought to myself, this is *apriori* knowledge; he is going to ask me when the war is going to start, and I am going to show him the answer, for these four jets are the beginning of the war.

We walked outside and the jets were gone. The sky had turned dark gray, and in the distance, large white clouds touched the ground. I wondered why the clouds were on the ground, and then I looked up, and saw six or seven mushroom clouds hundreds of miles wide. Ashes began to then fall from the sky. I held my hands out and began to catch them.

They were large, thick and appeared as if they were chips of paint, whitish with yellow colors mixed in. I awoke in the middle of the night knowing I had just been shown a prophetic dream. I could not go back to sleep so got on the Internet and found a friend online who was a military analyst. I shared with him the dream, and he said to me, *"Have you ever seen fallout before?" "No."* *"Well, that is exactly what fallout looks like."*

I asked him, *"Do you think planes that look like commercial aircraft could bomb us?"* He said, *"No, I don't think so."* *"Well"* I told him, *"I don't understand it, but we are going to be attacked by United Airlines."* He responded by telling me *"Benjamin, that sounds crazy, how could we be attacked by United Airlines?"*

Over the next few weeks that passed, I shared this dream with many of my friends. Then, on September 11th, 2001, my phone rang off the hook all morning. The events of that morning are the beginning of World War III, and they will culminate in the battle of Ezekiel 38 and global thermonuclear exchange.

THE FIRST FOUR JUDGMENTS ARE READY TO BEGIN

In late 1999, I was speaking to a group of believers who had gathered outside a church called Rock Harbor, to hear me share the message of my book. I began to tell them a summary of the word the Lord had revealed. At first I fumbled with the message, struggling to make sense of this incredible revelation in a few brief sentences. I mentioned the coming terrorism, the financial collapse, the martyrdom of the church in the death camps of the prince, and the ultimate nuclear war which would come as judgment upon America. As I spoke, I could discern the group, mostly young people in their early 20's, were filled with disbelief as they smirked at my message and laughed at me under their breath. Suddenly the Holy Spirit fell on me, and I heard the Lord say unto me, "I will take this conversation from here." I thought to myself, "That's good, I really don't know what to say anyway." The topic immediately changed, only now I spoke in a loud voice and with authority as I declared:

**"THE FIRST FOUR JUDGMENTS ARE READY
TO BEGIN, AND THEY ARE READY TO
BREAK FORTH UPON YOU EVEN NOW!"**

Then I walked into the crowd and got right into the face of one of the young men, and grabbing him by the arm, I said:

**"AND IT IS GOING TO BE JUST LIKE ON
YOUR ARM BROTHER! THE FIRST FOUR
JUDGMENTS ARE READY TO BEGIN, JUST
LIKE ON YOUR ARM!"**

He turned and ran and a friend chased after him. I continued speaking to the crowd and minutes later, the friend came back and interrupted me saying, "How did you know about his arm?" I didn't recall doing this so I answered, "Excuse me, I don't know what you are talking about?" "You said the first four judgments were ready to begin and they would be just like on his arm. How did you know?" At that point I could remember doing this. I responded, "Oh yes, I did say that, but I don't know anything about his arm." "Well, he is sitting in his car so scared he cannot drive, and he asked me; 'How did this guy know about my arm? I have never seen this guy before.'" I answered him, "Look, I don't know anything about his arm." "Well, he has a tattoo of the four horsemen of the book of Revelation on his arm." At this point the smirking faces in the crowd grew long. In the back of the audience, a young man raised his hand and began to speak saying, "I am a Navy Seal, and I have been in the military for eight years." Then he began to break down and weep, as he shouted, "And everything this man said is true!" The Torah tells us every word of truth will be confirmed by two or more witnesses. That morning the Lord sent two witnesses, the first by His Spirit, and the second, a Navy Seal.

IT IS TIME FOR THE LIGHT OF THE MORNING TO BREAKTHROUGH

As I began to write these new chapters for the second edition of this book, in March of 2003, the Lord sent word to me in the morning. As I awoke, I heard two angels speaking audibly in my room. Their voices sounded like trumpets; in perfect and beautiful harmonic tones. I have never heard anything like these voices before and could never have imagined anything like the sound of these two angels.

The first angel stood on my left side asked the question which is on many of our hearts: *"Do you know what time it is?"* Then another angel standing on my right answered in a loud voice: *"It is time for the light of the morning to breakthrough!"* We should all be Bereans and study these words carefully, for they have truly come from the Lord.

Do you know what time it is? It is time. It is now. The judgment is about to come and is ready to begin. The night of unbelief is almost over. The light of the bright and shining morning star is about to break out upon the earth. The phrase *"the light of the morning"* appears in Scripture in one place, speaking of the authority of God.

> *"The God of Israel said, the Rock of Israel spake to me, He that ruleth over men must be just, ruling in the fear of God. And he shall be as the light of the morning, when the sun riseth, even a morning without clouds; as the tender grass springing out of the earth by clear shining after rain. Although my house be not so with God; yet he hath made with me an everlasting covenant, ordered in all things, and sure: for this is all my salvation, and all my desire, although he make it not to grow."*[1]

The Lord Himself is the Light of the morning. *"We have also a more sure word of prophecy; whereunto ye do well that ye take heed, as unto a light that shineth in a dark place, until the day dawn, and the day star arise in your hearts."*[2] Now is the time for the Day Star to arise in the hearts of the chosen ones who are called faithful and true. The Church today stands at the threshold of a new day, a day which will witness the outpouring of the power of God in ways unimaginable. The night is almost over, and the blessed day is about to dawn.

This is the third day following the resurrection of our Lord and the beginning of the seventh day of creation. The long-awaited Sabbath in which no man can work is about to begin. For the world, a time of great darkness is coming; for the body of true believers, the light of God's glory is about to break forth as the light in the morning. Jesus prophesied of this hour in which darkness will fall upon the planet in which no man can work: *"I must work the works of him that sent me, while it is day: the night cometh, when no man can work."*3 Yet, in this night, which is coming, God can and will work, and those of us who are walking in the Spirit at that time will do the greater works, which were prophesied to come.

In the Hebrew calendar, the day begins at sundown. We read in Genesis that the evening and the morning were the measure of the day. In an earlier chapter of this book, I discussed the Jubilee count, which concluded that the seventh day began on Nissan one, in the year 1999 following the seventieth Jubilee. Many questioned the accuracy of that word when the years passed and nothing seemed to occur in the natural.

Yet we know, a new day begins in a time of darkness or evening. Now the morning light is about to break through, with judgment falling upon the nations. Yet, the Day of the LORD has already begun, not with thunder, nor with lighting, but with a gentle rain of sound doctrine. God speaks to His people in the time of darkness through the sure word of prophecy, and then when the light of day breaks, He speaks to the nations through His judgments.

We often approach the Scripture with so many preconceptions and assumptions that many times the true meaning is missed. The beginning of the Day of the LORD is no exception. The average student of Bible prophecy has been taught and assumes the day begins with a massive event, which will change the planet. But nowhere in Scripture does it say anything of the sort. Actually, the word declares that the Lord first comes as thief in the night, breaking in while we all sleep.

And a night intruder comes silently, not making a sound in order to avoid waking anyone. The First Coming of the Messiah is another example of this. When Jesus was born into the world, scarcely anyone noticed. Yet the understanding of that time was that as soon as the Messiah appeared, He would deliver them from the Romans. Nothing could have been further from the truth. Today in these last days, the end-time believers have made many similar errors in their thinking, overlaying their understanding of the Scriptures with their own opinions and ideas.

Margaret McDonald's vision addressed the secret beginning of the Day of the LORD with the Lord breaking in upon us all as a thief in the night:

"It was first the awful state of the land that was pressed upon me. I saw the blindness and the infatuation of the people to be very great. I felt the cry of Liberty to be just the hiss of the Serpent, to drown them in perdition.... The people of God think they are waiting, but they know not what it is they wait for...

"Suddenly it burst upon the scene with a glorious light.... I saw the LORD himself descending from heaven... I saw the error of men who think this will be something seen by the natural eye. Oh the glorious in breaking of God which is now about to burst on this earth.... Oh what a holy, holy bride she must be.... now shall the glorious mystery of God in our nature be known. The Revelation of Jesus Christ has yet to be opened up.

"It is not knowledge about God that it contains, it is an entering into God which only those filled with the Spirit can see, those who have not the Spirit could see nothing.... I saw people of God in an awfully dangerous situation, and many about to be deceived and fall. Now will the wicked one be revealed, Oh it will be a fiery trial, and every soul will be shaken. Now shall the awful sight of a false Christ be seen on the earth.... the trial of the Church is from the Antichrist.

"It is being filled with the Spirit that we shall be kept. What had hindered the real life of God from being received by His people, was their turning away from Jesus... they were all passing by the

cross.... I saw on that night, there will be such an outpouring of the Spirit such as has never been, a baptism of fire... the servants of God sealed in their foreheads, and His holy image seen in His people."

Another misconception is that the Day of the LORD begins with the Great Tribulation. Again, this is a misconception, and based solely upon the opinions of men and not the word of God. No, the Day of the LORD begins in ways unseen by the natural eye. For a new day under God's calendar begins at twilight and in the gathering darkness, and only when the morning light comes, can the world begin to see.

Let me explain this clearly. The seventieth Jubilee ended in 1999. The seven weeks of years following the second command to rebuild Jerusalem have now ended and we have passed over into the eighth week following the command to rebuild Jerusalem. And the Lord, who is referred to as Messiah the Prince in Daniel's seventy weeks prophecy, must now come after the seventh week or during the eighth week.

The seventh week ended in 1998 and was followed by the seventieth Jubilee of Israel and the hundred and twentieth Jubilee of creation. What has followed has been the eighth week, a time of new beginnings, which will end in 2006. Based upon a literal fulfillment of Daniel's prophecy, the Messiah the Prince must therefore come before the end of the eighth week in order to fulfill the Scripture perfectly, for He comes after seven weeks (and therefore during the eighth week) and not after eight weeks.

Please understand, this is the in-breaking of the Lord, the coming of Messiah to complete the second half of His seven year ministry upon the earth and it is not the literal Second Coming, for that will await the conclusion of the Great Tribulation. Rather, the coming of the Messiah in the ministry of the anointed messengers of God will occur by 2006. This coming is the birth of the man-child of book of Revelation.

In order to alleviate any misunderstanding, let me clarify the timing of these events. Daniel writes *"Know therefore and understand, that from the going forth of the commandment to restore and to build Jerusalem unto the Messiah the Prince shall be seven weeks, and threescore and two weeks: the street shall be built again, and the wall, even in troublous times. And after threescore and two weeks shall Messiah be cut off."*[4]

The coming of Messiah the Prince occurs after seven weeks following the command to rebuild Jerusalem. This is the Messiah coming as a ruling Monarch, not as a suffering servant. The sixty-two weeks is the period of the First Coming. Sir Isaac Newton understood this difference and accurately tied the sixty-two weeks to the date of the order to rebuild Jerusalem and the birth of the Messiah in 2 BC.

The seven weeks is the compass of time for the Second Coming, and this time the Messiah comes as a ruling Monarch, and as the Lion from the Tribe of Judah. His second appearance occurs seven weeks or forty-nine years following a second command to rebuild Jerusalem.

Isaac Newton spent his life studying this prophecy, and possessed a far greater mind than the majority of the biblical scholars of today. He was also 300 years closer to the actual events, and personally learned ten ancient lost languages in order to read the historical texts to confirm these dates. I was given this revelation directly by the Lord before I read Newton's account.

I thought to myself, Isaac Newton got it right, I can only wonder if he reasoned the conclusion or if he was shown this by the Lord. The second command to rebuild Jerusalem was given in May of 1948, following the declaration of independence of the state of Israel. The seven weeks of years then concluded with the 70th Jubilee of Israel in 1999. We are now in the eighth week, which will not end until 2006, and by then, Messiah the Prince will have been born again among us, only this time through His people.

The First Coming of the Lord was in the natural and began with a supernatural birth. A virgin was with child. The Second Coming begins in the same mysterious way, with a birth, not in the natural but in the spirit.

The Second Coming of the Lord, when every eye shall see Him, is preceded by a supernatural birth in the spirit in which the Lion of Judah is born again within a holy remnant who walk in the full power of His holy anointing during the time of tribulation. This is the second half of the ministry of the Messiah, for it is He who confirms and fulfills the covenant, which His father made with Israel, for seven years.

Having finished the first half Himself as a man, He now completes the second half of His ministry through the Holy Spirit through the lives of His anointed remnant as the Lion of Judah. Luke describes this in his account of the Second Coming, only the true meaning of his message was hidden from our eyes all of these years. This is the point of Margaret McDonald's prophecy.

> *"Even thus shall it be in the day when the Son of man is revealed. In that day, he which shall be upon the housetop, and his stuff in the house, let him not come down to take it away: and he that is in the field, let him likewise not return back."*[5]

This is the same warning that Jesus mentioned in Matthew 24.

> *"When ye therefore shall see the abomination of desolation, spoken of by Daniel the prophet, stand in the holy place, (whoso readeth, let him understand): Then let them which be in Judaea flee into the mountains: Let him which is on the housetop not come down to take any thing out of his house: Neither let him which is in the field return back to take his clothes.... For then shall be great tribulation, such as was not since the beginning of the world to this time, no, nor ever shall be."*[6]

The Scripture is referring to the same day in both texts. The day that the Son of man is revealed is the same day that the abomination of desolation is revealed. Remember, where sin abounds, grace abounds more.

The word of God is always true and the final hour of sin upon the earth, when sin will abound as never before, will also be the hour of the greatest outpouring of Holy Spirit in all of history, for the Lord Himself shall first appear in His people. *"Christ in you, the hope of glory."*[7] This is the beginning of the Great Tribulation in which Jesus Christ begins to fulfill the second half of His seven-year ministry upon the earth, not as a lamb anymore, but as the Lion of the Tribe of Judah.

Dear saints, this is the final day, and the last hour of the history of man, and in this hour, the Son of man, Jesus Christ, will be revealed. The tribulation does not start with the disappearance of the saints in a pre-tribulation rapture, but rather with the revelation of Jesus Christ in the 144,000 witnesses, which He Himself shall appoint. Scripture also tells us where the Lord will begin His judgment of the earth: from the river Euphrates, which is in Iraq.

> *"When its limbs are dry, they are broken off; Women come and make a fire with them. For they are not a people of discernment, Therefore their Maker will not have compassion on them. And their Creator will not be gracious to them. And it will come about in that day, that the LORD will start His threshing from the flowing stream of the Euphrates to the brook of Egypt; and you will be gathered up one by one, O sons of Israel."*[8]

So now, the stage has been set; the United States has been drawn into a land war in both the Middle East (Iraq) and Asia (Afghanistan). From the Scripture we know that from Iraq and the banks of the Euphrates River, the judgment of the earth shall come. The war which is now waging in Iraq will not end with a US victory but, rather, will become the spark which shall ignite the next world war and the great battle of Ezekiel 38.

THE COLUMBIA IS LOST

The Lord has continued to give His warnings to the people of America time and again over the years. The disaster of the space shuttle Columbia is one such example. The Columbia is named after the capital of the United States—The District of Columbia. The crash of the shuttle contains a prophetic message to the people of America. The prophecies of the Book of Obadiah speak of this event.

> *"The pride of thine heart hath deceived thee, thou that dwellest in the clefts of the rock, whose habitation is high; that saith in his heart, Who shall bring me down to the ground? Though thou exalt thyself as the eagle, and though thou set thy nest among the stars, thence will I bring thee down, saith the LORD."*[9]

America has exalted itself more than any other nation; and with the advent of the International Space Station, which is a US project, she has literally built a nest among the stars. The Lord continues in Obadiah to explain why He is bringing His judgment upon America.

"For thy violence against thy brother Jacob shame shall cover thee, and thou shalt be cut off for ever. In the day that thou stoodest on the other side, in the day that the strangers carried away captive his forces, and foreigners entered into his gates, and cast lots upon Jerusalem, even thou wast as one of them."[10]

America has chosen to stand now on the other side of the Arab-Israeli conflict, standing shoulder-to-shoulder with the enemies of God, demanding a division of the Holy Land and the creation of a Palestinian state. In the day the foreign nations cast lots for the division of the land of Israel and the Holy City of Jerusalem, America stood among them.

The shuttle Columbia was destroyed attempting to reenter the atmosphere over the state of Texas and over the county of Palestine. Could anything be clearer? The Columbia disaster is the foreshadow of God casting down the capital of America, for when you lose your capital, you lose your country. The headlines read, *"the Columbia is lost."* The message: America is lost and your judgment has begun.

The reason America is now being turned over to judgment is that she has sided with the enemies of Israel and cast her lot for the division of the Holy Land and the creation of a Palestinian state. Lest anyone think these prophecies are not relevant to these last days, and that this text is not directly referring to the shuttle disaster, look at the balance of the text in Obadiah 1:17-21. The events prophesied therein when Israel possesses the land of Edom have not yet occurred, for the text describes the events at the end of the age.

HAVING LAID STUMBLING BLOCKS
ONE BEFORE ANOTHER

In February of 2003, I was attending a solemn assembly prayer meeting where a group of believers had gathered for a weekend of prayer and fasting. Late Saturday evening, I returned to my room when the Lord spoke to me, *"Turn on your television."* I thought, how odd, normally the Lord would want us to turn off the television. I walked over and turned on the tube. CNN came on and I began to watch the tragedy in Rhode Island where a fire had engulfed a nightclub, killing over 100. The picture on the screen was of a human pile of people collapsed one upon the other in the doorway to the club, struggling with their faces in the outside cold air while their bodies remained trapped within the burning building.

As I watched in amazement, the Lord spoke again saying: "This is a picture of my people, who have laid stumbling blocks, one before another, such that they have all fallen to the ground." I stared in amazement at the pictures on TV not realizing the people in that picture all died that night, having never been freed from the pile of humanity; they had all exploded in flames. This is a picture of my people. We have all laid stumbling blocks, one before another. And the time is nigh for us to remove the stumbling blocks and to seek reconciliation one with another. I encourage you, dear reader, to do so prayerfully while there is still time, lest we too, find ourselves trapped by the stumbling blocks which we have laid one before another.

THE PASSION OF JESUS CHRIST

The latest warning to our nation is the release of the film, "*The Passion of the Christ*," produced by Mel Gibson in early 2004. The uproar and attacks from the media, the left, and the so-called religious leaders has been relentless.

Opinions surrounding the film are numerous; one point is unmistakable; the film provides a vivid and powerful picture of the suffering endured by our Lord in paying the price of the sins of His people. In another sense, it is also a warning, to a world about to be overrun suddenly by the forces of the Great Tribulation, that the King Who is coming has Himself seen pain and anguish that exceeds the experiences we will witness in the coming hour of judgment.

I am struck by how many have commented that they view this movie as a last warning to America, a final wakeup call to the demands of the Gospel of Jesus Christ. The Lord forgave the Roman soldiers who crucified him, for they did not know what they were doing. In this hour, the Lord in has promised judgment upon a people who know His will, but refuse to obey Him.

> *"Thou didst march through the land in indignation, thou didst thresh the heathen in anger"* (Habakkuk 3:12).

"I will utterly consume all things from off the land, saith the LORD. I will consume man and beast; I will consume the fowls of the heaven, and the fishes of the sea, and the stumbling-blocks with the wicked; and I will cut off man from off the land, saith the LORD" (Zephaniah 1:2-3).

AMERICA'S WORST RECESSION

In looking back over the last few years, the warnings of impending judgment appear to have been misplaced. To judge the state of the nation today, many are tempted to assume we have weathered the storm and bright, sunny days lie immediately ahead.

The picture the spin masters have painted has indeed deceived the many, while the voices of truth and reason are drowned out by the constant propaganda found in the mass media. One particular show, which I call, *Bubblevision*, is a favorite of stock market investors. Daily, the faithful are treated to a steady diet of distortions, deceptions and disinformation, all designed to hide the truth of what is really going in America.

At this writing, in the month of March 2004, the economy has recently witnessed a resounding recovery we are told. And the US stock market is rallying with newfound bullish fever. Lest you be tempted to join in the revelry of the sodomites, and be swept away by the newfound faith in the temple of man, the Federal Reserve— let us examine some of the facts of the present economic environment.

The last twelve months have witnessed the greatest debt growth in the history of our nation. Collectively, we have added $1.2 trillion in debt. As one of the nation's successful investors said, *"Give me a trillion dollars, and I will show you a good time."* And what have we gained from the trillion in debt borrowed against the inflating asset base?

Consumer spending added $260 billion to GDP, while $500 billion leaked out of the country through the trade deficit. Another $400 billion was used to pay the debt service on all of the money we borrowed previously. America cannot build a perpetual wealth on a foundation of debt.

We are told that America is the wealthiest nation in the world, and that we are experiencing a productivity miracle. The great paradox of this miracle is the average American has no savings. If we are so wealthy as a nation, and in the midst of such a great productivity miracle, why has the national savings rate collapsed? The supposed wealth of America is built upon an ever-growing pyramid of debt.

The trade deficit, the federal deficit, consumer debt, corporate debt, state budget deficits, the social security deficit... they all point out the obvious fact. We are a nation of credit card junkies, and as a country, we have mortgaged our future as if there is no tomorrow.

Compounding the problems is the fact that the spin masters on Wall Street have used deception and distortion to hide the true condition of the economy. Unemployment can remain low forever, as long as you stop counting people who have been hopelessly unemployed and have now given up looking for a job, and the so-called productivity miracle.

That, too, is a statistical distortion, a cleverly disguised lie. In the mid 1990's, the nation's economic statistics began to be adjusted for what was called "hedonic deflation," a fancy term for quality improvements. These quality adjustments have grossly overstated the national income data and the GDP data. This is the statistical basis for the so-called productivity miracle, which in reality is a mirage, built upon debt.

When the waves of judgment begin to roll over the nation in the coming years, this house of credit cards will collapse, bringing ruin to millions who never understood, unless you own your assets, you are merely renting them from the bank. Following the day of reckoning, the bankers will come and repossess virtually everything, which was owned on credit.

THE CLOUDS OF WAR

Many cannot imagine a nation as strong and powerful as the United States attacked and actually defeated by its enemies. Yet this is surely what the prophetic writings declare is in fact coming to this nation. This is the message of many of the men of wisdom in this hour. However, you may ask, *"How could such things be?"*

Let me share with you some commentary from a recent seminar by Jeffrey Nyquist, author of *The Origins of the 4ᵗʰ World War*.

THE LOGIC OF NUCLEAR WAR

"Peter Vincent Pry's central insight is that nuclear weapons might be used creatively, to win a future world war. Those who initiate such a war need not target cities at the outset. In fact, targeting cities makes little sense when the objective is to gain nuclear missile supremacy. What ought to be targeted is the other side's bombers, submarines and ICBM bases.

"The idea is to reduce the enemy to a conventional power, or a weak nuclear power, then apply blackmail by threatening unprotected cities. According to this analysis, the number of nuclear weapons at the start of a war, and the number of nuclear targets on the other side, is critical to understanding the war's dynamic and the logic of victory.

"Now that the United States is reducing its nuclear arsenal far below the number of missiles proposed by the START II Treaty, Pry's analysis is useful in attempting to understand what the Russians and Chinese want to achieve in the first decade of the twenty-first century (i.e., a war-winning numerical advantage).

"In Chapter 9 of Pry's book, under a section titled 'Future Arsenals,' we read the following statement: 'The START arsenal [by 2000] will have a marginal capability to mount counterattacks against Soviet ICBM silos (even assuming that Soviet silo-based forces are greatly reduced in the future)....'

"As Pry points out in Chapter 8, the equivalent yield needed to destroy 25 percent of the Soviet population and 75 percent of its industries has been estimated between 400 megatons to several thousands of megatons. Now that the U.S. is headed for an arsenal under 2000 warheads, there is no chance of blasting Russia back into the Stone Age if we are attacked. Table 8.2 on page 238 shows how to calculate the strategic nuclear balance in a general way.

"According to this table, America had a 1 to 1.2 ratio of nuclear forces in 1990. (DIA analyst Bill Lee maintained that Russia probably has hidden reserves of nuclear weapons, unaccounted

for since the fall of the Soviet Union, not factored into such equations.) Given Russian cheating, America's current ratio is probably 1 to 2.4. By 2012 it will be 1 to 8. There is also the issue of China's growing nuclear arsenal.

"It must be pointed out that Pry's analysis assumes absolute rationality on the Russian side in terms of executing a nuclear war. The rationality of the Russian side, however, is not a safe bet. According to Col. Stanislav Lunev, who was an integral part of Moscow's nuclear war plan (extending to the post-Soviet period), Western analysts should disdain easy assumptions about the rationality of Russia's leaders. 'These are not human beings,' he told me, 'these are crazy persons.'

"It is important to understand the extent to which feelings of national inferiority, ideological psychosis, envy, bitterness and hatred animate Russian and Chinese leaders. Human beings are not strictly rational animals. They are also emotional animals. It is worth noting that after 9/11 Chinese President Jiang Zemin spent countless hours watching video clips of the attack on the Twin Towers. He could not get enough of it. Consider the emotions that animate such persons.

"The real key to understanding a future nuclear war is not in the military rationality of such a war, but in the ideology fantasy that prompted the communists to arm themselves in the first place. The United States is not a threat to Russia any more than it is a threat to Canada or Mexico. The only reason for Russia or China to build nuclear armed forces is to destroy the United States of America; and in terms of real human values, this project must be judged as objectively insane. That is to say, no realistic thinker would expect any good result from such a project.

"Now consider the words of GRU officer Vladimir Rezun (Viktor Suvorov):

"Widespread terrorist and sabotage operations in advance of World War III are known officially in the GRU as the 'preparatory period,' and unofficially as the 'overture.' The overture is a series of large and small operations the purpose of which is, before actual military operations begin, to weaken the enemy's morale, create an atmosphere of suspicion, fear and uncertainty,

and divert the attention of the enemy's armies and police forces to a huge number of different targets, each of which may be the object of the next attack.

"The overture is carried out by agents of the secret services of the Soviet satellite countries and by mercenaries recruited by intermediaries. The principal method employed at this stage is 'gray terror,' that is, a kind of terror, which is not conducted in the name of the Soviet Union. The Soviet secret services do not at this stage leave their visiting cards, or leave other people's cards. The terror is carried out in the name of already existing extremist groups not connected in any way with the Soviet Union, or in the name of fictitious organizations.

"I already knew that war was normal to history. I knew that nuclear weapons would probably be used. But my understanding in this regard was bloodless, based on abstractions, theories, historical understanding, so it was not altogether real to me. I was anti-communist, pro-free market and favored individual rights.

"My thinking was in the liberal and conservative tradition. At the time I was reading Thomas Hobbes and Adam Smith, Macaulay and Carlyle, Boethius and Aristotle, Cicero and Tacitus. Great literature is a world unto itself, beautiful and wise. But I also read about contemporary political issues (not so beautiful).

"I read books by communist bloc defectors. Then there came this unexpected jolt, sitting there, at my reading table, 17 years ago with Golitsyn's text before me. I was prompted to reread New Lies for Old after reading Jan Sejna's claim about a secret plan to fake the collapse of the Warsaw Pact. The situation was suddenly obvious to me. I saw enemies and destroyers advancing against my country. The communists were going to give up their rotten empire to get something better. The first words out of my mouth were, 'They are actually going to do it.'

" The educated, the geniuses, the best and brightest would accept the collapse of the Soviet Union as spontaneous and authentic. They would embrace Russia's new democracy and counsel disarmament. They would be hypnotized. Nothing would penetrate their understanding, neither criticism nor warnings from

abroad. *Nothing would break the fever of their victory sickness. They would be fully and completely anesthetized.*

"The greatest genius, the most passionate argument, the most unanswerable logic would not sway them from their delusions, which would prove too deep-rooted, too thick and gratifying. What was going to happen could not be prevented. The hedonistic shopping mall regime never wanted enmity with Russia or anyone else.

"The existence of a real enemy would threaten the regime's values. Anyone who wrote of enmity was out of bounds. The very concept 'enemy' threatened the basis of the regime, negating its hedonistic assumptions. This must have been obvious to Kremlin strategists and sociologists who had studied American cultural changes during the 1960s and 70s. In fact, Nikolay Popov's 1989 essay was founded on this point.

"To summarize Popov's analysis: Russia's new task was to consciously and intentionally eliminate Stalinism so that America would feel free to set aside her nuclear weapons. This suggests that the Kremlin long ago understood America's national psychology. They knew that America would not ruthlessly exploit her advantage after 1989 and 1991.

"The West preferred shopping and having fun. Politics and war had become the mean little ministers of 'a good time.' This attempted reversal of history's pattern might well prove fatal. According to my own analysis, the only thing holding the West's defensive strata together was anti-communism (i.e., anti-Stalinism).

"Therefore, as Popov explained, 'our main task today, in addition to an honest analysis of our past and an elimination of the remnants of Stalinism... is to divorce Stalinism from communism in the eyes of the world.'

"The new Iron Curtain would be a curtain of denial constructed by the West. The 'peace dividend' meant more welfare pork in the pork barrel and less defense spending, so the left was satisfied. It also translated into economic exuberance and a climbing stock market. The right was triumphant and self-congratulatory. The deception was perfect. Everyone was bought off, emotionally and materially. The truth did not have one chance in a million."[11]

THE WORD OF THE LORD

"In the coming weeks and months, beginning on Passover, I the Lord am coming to my people as I did in the days of Moses to call them out of Egypt. These will be the days the prophet Joel spoke of: Multitudes, multitudes in the valley of decision and no one can imagine what this will be like.

"I am coming to my people who call themselves the Church for those who call themselves the Church are not in the promised land, they are in Egypt, but I have heard the cries of the oppressed, those oppressed by religion and false doctrines. I have seen the affliction imposed upon my people by the false prophets and the false shepherds who do not speak my word in truth.

"I am coming to deliver them, all who will listen and follow me, but just as it was in Egypt, and just as it was in Babylon, so will it be again. Many will not head the call, they will chose to stay in Egypt and there they will perish.

"Understand this for this is that hour which I have spoken. Many will say to Me on that day, 'Lord, Lord, did we not prophesy in Your name, and in Your name cast out demons, and in Your name perform many miracles?' Then I will declare to them, 'I never knew you; depart from Me, you who practice lawlessness.'

"Yes, it will be many, and you will grieve to see the many reject what I am about to do, but you must stand firm and strong to the end.

"You must take Isaiah 58 to my people, declare to them their transgression, and boldly call them to repent and return to my truth. I have seen the ways of my people but I will heal them if they will come to me. I will lead them and restore comfort to those who mourn, but there will be no peace, says my Father, for the wicked.

"Who is hearing this message from my Spirit? Where are the shepherds who still hear my voice? Among the multitudes in the valley of decision are those with a humble and contrite spirit.

They alone will be the ones who hear my voice. They alone will be the ones whom I will comfort, revive and bring out of Egypt and for them my light will break forth speedily and my glory will be their delight but the pride, the pride in those who think, who claim to be my people, how the mighty will fall.

"*Does it not say in the word of God humble yourselves lest you be humbled? This has already begun for I myself have torn the protective covering of man from the Roman church, but this is only the beginning, for the very foundations of what my people call Christianity will be shaken to their deepest roots. Humbling, humbling, great humbling is coming to the proud and the arrogant among my people. I will devastate their pet theories and their so-called doctrines that men have created out of vain imaginations. I will devastate their opinions with the searing light of my truth and those who refuse to repent will perish.*

"*This nation in which you were born totters on the brink of destruction, for America as I have already told you, it is three minutes to midnight for it is only my Father's mercy that has kept destruction at bay to this hour. How often I have spoke of my Father's great mercy, and so few have begun to comprehend even a little of that mercy.*

"*It is just as Isaiah said of this people; being unfaithful to my Father, and turning away from Him, those who lead my people speak oppression and apostasy. They conceive doctrines of falsehood from the arrogance of their heart so that righteousness is far off and truth is lacking among my people.*

"*At this Passover, by divine decree, everything in the realm of the spirit is changing. The world and most of my people will not sense it because their ears are dull. Soon they will see it and still they will not understand. I tell you what happened in natural on September 11 2001 will happen again in the spirit in this coming year.*

"*Now is the time for it to begin. The first tower to be hit was the roman church. The second plane, and the third and the fourth are already in the air en route to their spiritual targets and not one of them will crash short of their destinations for they have been de-*

creed by my Father to destroy the kingdoms of man that masquerade as the Church of God.

"Moses was in the wilderness for forty years but you will be astounded of what will take place in 40 days, and 40 weeks and 40 months. (Forty days from this word, George Bush made his first public statement of dividing the land of Israel and creating a Palestinian state). *Watch, listen and obey. Tell my people to watch, listen and obey; it will be their only salvation in the hour that is now coming upon the earth. Truly my kingdom approaches, even now it is at the door. The earth writhes in the pain of its birthing and when I come will I find faith on the earth? I tell you the truth, I will find faith but only in a remnant. Watch, listen and obey. As it was in the days of Noah, so it shall be in the days of the coming of the son of man."*[12]

The true gospel given to the apostles is radically different than the teachings of the church in the 21st century. Let me counsel you, warn you, and admonish you. Do not make the mistake of holding onto any tradition with an iron grip. Do not make the mistake of holding onto any church doctrine because the facts of history are that we have an abundance of church doctrines that were formulated by the minds and traditions of men hundreds of years after the Messiah was here.

The only people who are afraid to examine their belief system, their pet doctrines, and their traditions are those who have more faith in the traditions of men than they do in God Himself.

WHAT SHALL WE DO THEN

"For thus saith the Lord GOD, the Holy One of Israel; In returning and rest shall ye be saved; in quietness and in confidence shall be your strength: and ye would not. But ye said, No; for we will flee upon horses; therefore shall ye flee: and, We will ride upon the swift; therefore shall they that pursue you be swift. One thousand shall flee at the rebuke of one; at the rebuke of five shall ye flee: till ye be left as a beacon upon the top of a mountain, and as an ensign on an hill. And therefore will the LORD wait, that he may be gracious unto you, and therefore will he be exalted, that he may have mercy upon you: for the LORD is a God of judgment: blessed are all they that wait for him. For the people shall dwell in Zion at Jerusa-

lem: thou shalt weep no more: he will be very gracious unto thee at the voice of thy cry; when he shall hear it, he will answer thee. And though the Lord give you the bread of adversity, and the water of affliction, yet shall not thy teachers be removed into a corner any more, but thine eyes shall see thy teachers" (Isaiah 30:15-20).

Many people have asked me, in light of what is coming, what shall we do? I will attempt to provide some counsel in this regard in these final pages. First, let me comment on spiritual matters. What shall we do? Return to God. Begin to learn to walk in the Spirit. Begin to learn to rest in the Lord. Begin to learn to walk by faith, no longer trusting our money or our ability to meet our needs, but truly trusting the Lord.

In order to walk with the Lord in this hour, God is demanding that we walk with Him in true holiness with a pure heart. This must be so in order for the completeness of Christ to be found in us, and in order that we will have no doubt within us when the hour of testing begins.

We must walk with the Lord in a total commitment so that we will also be able to avoid the snares of the world, which lie at our feet. Our spiritual preparation is the most important part of preparing, for if we are not right spiritually, we have no hope to survive what is coming, for only a remnant shall be counted worthy to escape and endure the days ahead to see the sign of the Son of man in the heavens on the last day.

The Scripture itself is our guide. Jesus told us in this hour to *"pray without ceasing."* That would be a good place to start—with prayer. Our prayer lives should become a critical part of everyday. We should set aside a time and a place to pray each day, and our prayer lives should include regular times of fasting, either from food entirely or with vegetable juices.

When in times of prayer, remember to use spiritual authority speaking the Scriptures and taking authority in the spirit world over the matters you are praying about. By spiritual authority, I am referring to using the authority of the Name of Jesus to command the spirit world to come into alignment with the will of God. We should also use our prayer times for introspection, repentance and renewal.

Each of us has areas in our lives which God desires to sanctify, to bring healing and deliverance. We must have the faith and the courage to deal with these areas in the spirit of love and forgiveness. In responding to the days ahead, we should first and foremost, become people of prayer.

Second, let me speak to you about financial matters. We are currently in the midst of the greatest debt expansion in the history of the world. There are only two possible outcomes to a debt bubble: An inflationary debasement of the currency, or a deflationary collapse of the economy where the excess debt ultimately drags down the asset values which have been inflated through the debt expansion.

Understanding who owns the system and how they hold their ownership will give you insight into which outcome will occur in the present credit expansion. The world's central banks and the major money center banks are all owned by a closely-held group of wealthy families.

You must remember, Satan tempted Jesus by implying that all of the kingdoms of the world were his to give to whomever he chose. That explains how and from whom the super rich acquired their wealth. If we have an inflationary outcome to the debt bubble, the result will be a transfer of wealth from the banks and the super rich families, which own them, to the middle class debtors.

Alternatively, if we have a deflationary collapse, we will witness a wealth transfer from the debtors, through asset foreclosures, to the bankers and their families. Over the last 400 years, every major economic crisis in the western world has been deflationary. The ownership of the banking system explains why.

The powers that be use the periodic crisis, which they help create, to take back the wealth from the people. The outcome this time will be no different: a deflationary collapse awaits us. But this time will also be very, very different, given the gross imbalances that have accumulated in the external debt of the United States and the risk of substantial devaluation in the dollar.

While the inflated asset markets for stocks and housing will be falling, the cost of imports such as petroleum will likely be rising.

This will create the conditions for a complete financial collapse in the US.

The dollar will be under intense pressure in foreign markets, driving the prices of imports such as oil through the roof, and likely causing gold and other precious metals to see new record highs. At the same time, the higher costs of imported energy, and the deflationary drag of the credit contraction which will follow the bursting of the debt bubble, will likely drag the economy into a global depression of unprecedented scale.

So what exactly should we do? In part, that depends on you, where you live, your financial position, and what God is calling you to do. Generally, you should avoid debt at this time like the plague. At the same time, cash will be king, at least for a while. You should therefore keep your liquidity and conserve your cash. So if you have an existing debt on your home, and you cannot pay it off without using up all of your liquid resources, then you should build cash and refinance into a fixed-rate mortgage.

Alternatively, you could sell your house and raise cash levels. As to savings, you should consider diversifying into multiple currencies and into gold, silver and platinum. In addition, you may consider setting up an offshore bank account or an offshore trust.

Of course, these investments are still subject to US income taxation, unless you acquire an offshore annuity, which allows for legal tax deferral. Nevertheless, an offshore account is an excellent way to diversify out of the US dollar, which will face continued devaluation pressures until its ultimate collapse.

Finally, let me discuss some practical matters. Once again, you must hear from the Lord for your direct instructions, so my comments should be viewed as general counsel only. When we look at the things that are coming, the first obvious conclusion is that the cities are the most dangerous place to be for what is coming.

The cities of the US are a future disaster in the making. Lacking the necessary food production and other resources to support their populations, the cities are totally dependent upon the maintenance of the current infrastructure for the transmission of food, water, and power and for the preservation of law and order. In the days ahead of us, each of these will likely breakdown, making the cities of the US the most dangerous places to be.

For those who can accept it, the Scripture talks about leaving the country. This is a hard message to hear for many. The Lord sent a similar warning to the Jews living in Germany in the 1930's. Several Rabbi's received direct revelation from the Lord that a terrible holocaust was coming in Europe and were told the Jews should leave.

When confronted with this warning, most Jews in Europe found it unbelievable and simply ignored the warnings. For many, their end came in the ovens of the Nazi concentration camps. So it is today, the warning to leave America is too hard for many to hear. Believers have told me that the Lord would never move all of the people from one country to another. I responded by saying *"Really? Haven't you ever read the book of Exodus?"*

In summary, let me say simply, we should do what we can to get out of debt, to get out of cities, and ultimately to get out of the country. But first and foremost, we should get into prayer and hear from the Lord directly as to what we are to do personally.

May the Lord bless you and keep you from the hour, which is now at hand.

Benjamin Baruch

Passover, 2004

EPILOUGE

We have to hear the voice of the Lord Jesus Christ for the present hour—if we are moving with God, in heart felt repentance, we will need no man to teach us. The Church has stopped at the message of salvation, and the gifts of the Spirit, and has been unwilling to follow the Lord into purification.

The way is becoming increasingly narrow. Only a few will follow the Lord all the way to true purity of mind and soul. The remnant of the Lord Jesus Christ are very few and small indeed. We cannot afford to get ahead of the Lord in this last hour. We must wait for the anointing of the Lord.

The prophets in the Church are not speaking the word of the Lord, but are speaking according to the deception in their own hearts. Deceiving and being deceived, they will wax worse and worse. We have a few short months left to repent, and then the door will close and the judgment will begin. Many people have turned from the Lord, and have chosen other men as their covering.

The holy remnant has come out of the false churches and is now being set apart unto the Lord alone. The Lord is even now beginning to gather His remnant together from the four winds. This last hour is so crucial. We must bring every area of our lives into perfect obedience to the will of the Lord.

The door to grace will be open for just a little bit longer, and then it shall be shut. Those who have entered in with perfect obedience, surrendering all to the Lord, shall be protected. Those who are without shall be judged. We must be moving with the Spirit of God in this last hour if we don't wish to miss the hour of our visitation.

The remnant is of a kindred spirit, fitly joined together by God. The Lord has gone to prepare a place for His little remnant flock. Jesus Christ, our Lord and Savior, will plainly show us the Father and reveal to us His perfect will, and it is Christ Who will set us free to do the Father's will.

He will equip His saints to stand in the hour that is ahead. We must do our part, and keep our hearts with all diligence. Humility is the most precious grace we may develop within our souls. The bride of the Lord Jesus Christ is adorned with grace and humility. The higher the calling, and the greater the spiritual attainment and gifts, the greater the temptation to become high-minded. Humility is an ornament which can never be fashioned by self-effort. It only comes from a genuine work of the Holy Spirit. As the bride advances more and more into the heavenly revelation, there is an increasing danger of becoming exalted. The beautiful grace of perfect humility is not only an ornament reflecting the glory of the Lord, but also a shield against the adversary of our souls. Let us seek humility daily, in prayers and fasting. Only the humble will see the day the Son of Man is revealed within His saints. The way of the Lord Jesus Christ is the cross, and death to all that is of self. We are standing at the threshold, and will soon enter the hour of testing. Only those found fully consecrated in the Lord Jesus Christ will be able to stand. We have no idea how strong-willed and rebellious we are. Our safety lies in humility before the Lord. We must watch every thought, and bring them into captivity before the knowledge of the Lord. If we judge ourselves, we will not be judged. If we continue in self-will and rebellion, we will be destroyed. The Lord Jesus Christ is coming soon to be glorified in His saints. It is our choice whether we will found in Him when He comes.

May God bless you all! I wish to share a few final words with my special friends at the office, who were there to witness the early birth pains of the kingdom of God in my life. The Lord Jesus Christ has blessed me mightily, through His word and His Spirit, and through my family and my many friends. I wish to express my love and thanks to each of you, for all you have done. Of all the parables our Lord Jesus Christ taught, the parable of the Field-stone will always remind me of the days when I walked and labored beside you. Permit me to share it in my own words. The kingdom of heaven is like a treasure, a precious jewel of infinite value, which was hidden as a Field Stone. Throughout the years, many great men had passed over that field, yet none of them recognized the word of God, which had been hidden therein. One day a little servant, while working in that field, found the treasure. He immediately ran, and sold everything that he had, and purchased that field. Having bought the great treasure, which is the true word of God, he went out rejoicing and proclaiming the truth to the whole world. All the people of the earth would soon hear the word, which had been hidden as a Field Stone.

> *"Let us hear the conclusion of the whole matter: Fear God, and keep his commandments: for this is the whole duty of man. For God shall bring every work into judgment, with every secret thing, whether it be good, or whether it be evil" (Ecclesiastes 12:13-14). "The Son of man shall send forth his angels, and they shall gather out of his kingdom all things that offend, and them which do iniquity; And shall cast them into a furnace of fire: there shall be wailing and gnashing of teeth. Then shall the righteous shine forth as the sun in the kingdom of their Father. Who hath ears to hear, let him hear"* (Matthew 13:41-43)

Let me share a final prophesy which I share with my Father, whom I have always loved.

> *"Behold, I will send you Elijah the prophet, before the coming of the great and dreadful day of the LORD: And he shall turn the heart of the fathers to the children, and the heart of the children to their fathers, lest I come and smite the earth with a curse"* (Malachi 4:5-7).

Most of all, I wish to thank My Beloved Lord and dearest Friend, Jesus Christ. You have heard my cry, Lord, and You rescued me. In this final hour, You have remembered Your covenant with me. Though I was unfaithful to you Lord, in Your great mercy, You have remained faithful to me. I am truly the least of your saints, and in myself, I am unworthy to even speak Your Name. But you have clothed me with Your robe of righteousness, and put Your word of truth in my mouth. Forever I will sing Your praises on Mount Zion. Amen and Amen!! Baruch haba be' shem Adonai! Hallelujah! Hallelujah! Blessed is he who comes in the name of the LORD. Praise the Lord! Praise the Lord!

Brother Benjamin

CHAPTER ENDNOTES

<u>CHAPTER 1 ENDNOTES</u>

1   Matthew 24:5.
2   *Strong's* Number 4105.
3   2 Timothy 3:13.
4   *Strong's* Number 1114.
5   1 John 3:7-8.
6   Ezekiel 9:4-6 NAS.
7   2 Timothy 4:3-4.
8   2 Peter 3:3.
9   *Strong's* Number 1703.
10   John 15:18-21 NAS.
11   *Strong's* Number 5278.
12   Daniel 12:11.
13   Daniel 11:31.
14   Daniel 11:21.
15   Daniel 11:21.
16   Daniel 11:23.
17   Daniel 11:24.
18   Daniel 11:36.
19   *Strong's* Number 2195.
20   Daniel 11:27.
21   Jeremiah 30:7.
22   Daniel 12:3-4.
23   Daniel 9:25-26.
24   Isaiah 53:5.
25   Isaiah 1:9.
26   John 3:16.
27   Micah 5:1.
28   Isaiah 9:6-7.
29   Genesis 22:7-8.
30   Psalm 22:1.
31   Psalm 22:12-15.
32   Psalm 22:7-8.
33   Psalm 22:15-16.
34   Luke 12:49-51.
35   Jeremiah 30:7.
36   Nehemiah 6:15.

37   Isaac Newton, Observations upon the prophecies of Daniel and the Apocalypse of St. John. (London 1733) 135.
38   Newton 133-134.
39   Newton 137.
40   Revelation 1:10.
41   Isaiah 63:4.
42   Isaiah 61:2.
43   Newton 133-134.
44   Daniel 9:26.
45   Daniel 9:27.
46   Jeremiah 30:7.
47   Numbers 23:24.
48   Daniel 9:24.
49   *Strong's* Number 3722.
50   *Strong's* Number 2856.
51   *Strong's* Number 2377.
52   *Strong's* Number 5030.
53   *Strong's* Number 4886.
54   *Strong's* Number 6944.
55   Leviticus 27:28 NAS.
56   Exodus 26:34.
57   Isaiah 62:12.
58   Isaiah 6:11-13.
59   Leviticus 2:10.
60   Numbers 18:9 NAS.
61   Zechariah 13:8-9.
62   Song of Songs 8:5.
63   Deuteronomy 33:12.
64   Luke 21:36.
65   Daniel 9:27.
66   Hebrews 10:8-10.
67   Daniel 9:27.
68   Daniel 9:26.
69   John 5:43.
70   Isaiah 28:15.
71   2 Thessalonians 2:3.
72   Televised news announcement of the signing of the Peace and Security Agreement.
73   Exodus 32:28.

74 Acts 2:41.
75 Isaiah 28:14-15.
76 Leviticus 25:23.
77 Rabbi Zalman Baruch Melamed Arutz, Sheva Israel National Radio.
78 Deuteronomy 12:2-18 NAS.
79 Shimon Peres, *The New Middle East.*
80 Daniel 5:28.
81 Isaiah 28:20 NAS.
82 Monte Judah, *Yavoh He is Coming*, January 1997.
83 Isaiah 28:18-22.
84 *Strong's* Number 3617.
85 Isaiah 10:22-23.
86 Ezekiel 37:11-14.
87 *Intelligence Digest*, "Russia Brings the Mideast War Closer," 19 September 1997.
88 *Intelligence Digest*, "Cyprus Missile Crisis looms closer," 17 April 1998.
89 *Terrorism and Security Monitor*, April 1998.
90 Amos 8:2.
91 Mark 13:28.
92 Daniel 2:35.
93 Isaiah 28:21.
94 Isaiah 28:21.
95 Zechariah 12:3.
96 Zechariah 12:10.
97 Zechariah 13:1-6.

CHAPTER 2 ENDNOTES
1 Daniel 12:8-9.
2 Isaiah 29:11-14.
3 1 Samuel 3:1.
4 Psalm 74:9 NAS.
5 Isaiah 49:2-4.
6 Isaiah 4:4.
7 Matthew 11:7-14.
8 Daniel 2:20-22.
9 Isaiah 8:20.
10 Revelation 13:1-18.
11 Revelation 17:3-9.
12 Genesis 41:32.

13 James Lloyd, *Apocalypse Chronicles, Role Reversals and Prophetic Parallels.*
14 *Apocalypse.*
15 *Apocalypse.*
16 *Apocalypse.*
17 Daniel 2:43.
18 *Los Angeles Times* 27 March 1998: A10.
19 *The Economist* December 1992.
20 Alexander G. Higgins *The Scranton Times*, 29 January 1997, AP article.
21 Daniel 7:4.
22 Daniel 8:23.
23 Daniel 8:24.
24 Revelations 13:6.
25 Daniel 8:25.
26 Daniel 8:24.
27 Daniel 8:24.
28 Daniel 7:25.
29 Daniel 7:25.

CHAPTER 3 ENDNOTES
1 Amos 3:7-8.
2 Amos 7:14.
3 Jeremiah 9:14.
4 Ephesians 4:11.
5 Revelation 11:1-7.
6 Genesis 18:17-19.
7 John 15:15.
8 John 10:27.
9 Amos 3:8.
10 Jeremiah 4:7.
11 Proverbs 28:1.
12 2 Chronicles 36:15-16 NAS.
13 Rosha Judah, Prophets Still Speak, The Sound of a Trumpet, 1991.
14 Numbers 12:6-8 NAS.
15 Luke 6:22-24
16 1 King 17:1.
17 Luke 1:80.
18 Marvin Byers, Yasser Arafat—*An Apocalyptic Character*, (Hebron Press, 1997) 21-22.

19 Marvin Byers, *The Final Victory: The Year 2000* (Treasure House, 1994) 25.
20 Byers, *Yasser Arafat* 29.
21 *Strong's* Number 3478.
22 John 10:14-16.
23 *Strong's* Number 1577.
24 *Vine's Expository Dictionary of Biblical Words*, (Nashville: Thomas Nelson Publishers, 1985).
25 Matthew 15:24.
26 Matthew 27:42.
27 John 1:49.
28 Romans 9:6-7.
29 Romans 9:27-28.
30 Luke 12:32.
31 Romans 11:1-5.
32 Romans 11:25-29.
33 Ephesians 2:11-13.
34 Hebrews 8:8.
35 Genesis 32:28.
36 Galatians 6:16.
37 Matthew 5:17-18.
38 Romans 11:5.
39 Jeremiah 3:23.
40 1 Peter 4:12.
41 Revelation 3:10-11.
42 Proverbs 29:18.
43 1 Samuel 3:1.
44 Amos 8:12.
45 Isaiah 9:16.
46 Jeremiah 23:19.
47 *Strong's* Number 5591.
48 1 Thessalonians 5:2-4.
49 Joel 2:32.
50 Proverbs 14:34.
51 John 14:15.
52 Matthew 7:21.
53 Jeremiah 8:20.
54 Matthew 7:23.
55 *Strong's* Number 6117.

[56]   Matthew 24:9-10.
[57]   Jeremiah 9:4-7.
[58]   Daniel 12:10.
[59]   Richard M. Rives, *Too Long in the Sun*, (Partaker Publications, 1996) 128.
[60]   Rives 128.
[61]   2 Timothy 4:3-4.
[62]   Jeremiah 15:19-21.
[63]   Psalm 4:3-5.
[64]   Revelation 2:14.

CHAPTER 4 ENDNOTES

[1]   Genesis 15:1.
[2]   Mark 9:7.
[3]   Isaiah 33:10.
[4]   Isaiah 28:22 *paraphrased*.
[5]   Joel 1:15.
[6]   Joel 2:1-2.
[7]   Luke 12:49-51 NAS.
[8]   Amos 5:18-19.
[9]   Obadiah 1:15.

CHAPTER 5 ENDNOTES

[1]   Revelation 14:8.
[2]   Revelation 17:1-2.
[3]   Matthew Henry, *Complete Commentary on the Whole Bible,* Revelation 17.
[4]   David Wilkerson, *Set the Trumpet to thy Mouth* (New Kensington, PA: Whitaker House, 1985).
[5]   Dumitru Duduman, *Through the Fire without Burning*, (Hand of Help Ministries).
[6]   Dr. Jeff Bakker, speaker Dallas Prophecy Conference, Dallas, March 1997.
[7]   Mike McQuiddy, *The Promise*, (Cornerstone Publishing, 1997).
[8]   Henry Gruver, Joyful Sound Ministries, 601 Walker, Woodbine, IA 51579.
[9]   Jeremiah 50:41-42.
[10]   Jeremiah 50:9.
[11]   Jeremiah 50:41.
[12]   Jeremiah 51:6.

13 Jeremiah 51:13.
14 Revelation 18:7-8.
15 Jeremiah 51:27.
16 Ezekiel 38:11.
17 Ezekiel 39:6.
18 *Strong's* Number 339.
19 Jeremiah 51:62.
20 Jeremiah 50:22-24.
21 Jeremiah 50:31.
22 Jeremiah 50:32.
23 Jeremiah 50:38.
24 Jeremiah 50:40.
25 Jeremiah 50:46.
26 Jeremiah 51:5-6.
27 Jeremiah 51:14.
28 Jeremiah 51:58.
29 Jeremiah 51:61-64.
30 Jeremiah 50:8.
31 Joel 1:14-15.
32 Jeremiah 50:28.
33 Jeremiah 51:8.
34 Jeremiah 51:13.
35 Jeremiah 51:30.
36 Jeremiah 51:33.
37 Jeremiah 51:41.
38 Jeremiah 51:45-46.
39 Jeremiah 51:49-50.
40 Revelation 18:11.
41 Revelation 18:16-18.
42 Jeremiah 50:4-5.
43 Jeremiah 50:20.

CHAPTER 6 ENDNOTES
1 Isaiah 3:12.
2 Isaiah 1:9.
3 Isaiah 8:11-22.
4 Isaiah 37:32.
5 Isaiah 10:21-22.
6 Isaiah 11:12.
7 Isaiah 13:14.

8   Isaiah 13:19.
9   Isaiah 14:1-2.
10   Isaiah 26:20-21.
11   John 15:1-6.
12   *Strong's* Number 4679.
13   *Strong's* Number 5553.
14   Isaiah 45:20.
15   Isaiah 48:20.
16   Isaiah 48:21-22.
17   Isaiah 65:8-9.
18   Daniel 11:41.
19   Habakkuk 1:5.
20   Habakkuk 2:1-3.
21   Amos 9:12-15.
22   Micah 2:12-13.
23   Zephaniah 2:7-9.
24   Zechariah 8:7-23.
25   Numbers 24:16-18.
26   Psalm 60:8-9.
27   Amos 9:11-12.
28   Obadiah 1:8-17.
29   Psalm 108:9-10.
30   Micah 2:10.
31   Micah 2:12.

CHAPTER 7 ENDNOTES
1   Revelation 17:4-5.
2   Revelation 17:8-12.
3   John 16:11.
4   John 12:31.
5   Luke 10:18-19.
6   2 Thessalonians 2:7-8.
7   2 Thessalonians 2:9-12.
8   Micah 5:1-2.
9   Micah 5:6.
10   Revelation 17:13-14.
11   Revelation 17:15-17.
12   Revelation 17:18.
13   Revelation 13:1-18.
14   Revelation 13:2.

15 Monte Judah, speaker, Beth Yeshua, Orange County, CA, Nov. 1996.
16 Monte Judah, Beth Yeshua.
17 Tim Cohen, *The Antichrist and a Cup of Tea*, (Prophecy House, 1998).
18 Monte Judah, "Yahov He is Coming," Jan. 1997.

CHAPTER 8 ENDNOTES

1   Psalm 11:3.
2   Ephesians 2:18-20.
3   Revelation 19:10.
4   2 Peter 1:19-21.
5   Daniel 12:10.
6   John 16:33.
7   Job 36:33.
8   Psalm 77:18.
9   Job 40:9.
10 Deuteronomy 32:2.
11 Hosea 9:7.
12 1 John 2:3-6.
13 Mark 8:35.
14 Proverbs 1:7.
15 Proverbs 9:10.
16 Proverbs 14:26-28.
17 Isaiah 11:1-4.
18 Hebrews 12:14.
19 Isaiah 35:8.
20 Obadiah 1:17-18.
21 2 Corinthians 7:1.
22 1 Peter 1:16.
23 Rosha Judah, "The Signet Seal, Holiness to the LORD," *The Sound of the Trumpet*, 1991.
24 Matthew 7:14.
25 *Strong's* Number 2346.
26 *Strong's* Number 2476.
27 *Strong's* Number 1715.
28 *Strong's* Number 2729.
29 *Strong's* Number 1628
30 Revelation 2:7-3:22.1-3
31 Ephesians 1:3-4.
32 Ephesians 1:5-8.

33   Ephesians 1:9-10.

34   Ephesians 1:11-14.

35   Joel 3:13-16.

36   Genesis 18:14.

37   *Strong's* Number 1285.

38   Genesis 6:18; 9:12-14; 9:9.

39   Henry, Genesis 9:8-11.

40   Genesis 15:1.

41   Genesis 15:5-6.

42   Genesis 17:7.

43   2 Samuel 23:5.

44   Psalm 89:3-4

45   Galatians 3:14.

46   Galatians 3:16.

47   Galatians 3:17-18.

48   Genesis 15:7-9.

49   Genesis 15:9-10.

50   Genesis 15:17-18.

51   Henry, Genesis 15:17-21.

52   Isaiah 62:1.

53   Genesis 18:17-19.

54   Daniel 9:4.

55   *Strong's* Number 157 .

56   Proverbs 18:24.

57   Isaiah 41:8.

58   Proverbs 27:6.

59   *Strong's* Number 7453.

60   Revelation 12:1-6.

61   *Strong's* Number 4592.

62   Henry *Commentary.*

63   Byers *Final Victory* 36.

64   Matthew 12:50.

65   John 16:19-23.

66   Zechariah 14:21.

67   Luke 17:30-33.

68   2 Peter 2:1-3.

69   Jeremiah 51:20-24.

70   Micah 5:1-5.

71   Jeremiah 30:6-7.

72 Luke 17:30-33.
73 Revelation 12:5.
74 *Strong's* Number 6629.
75 Isaiah 13:2-5.
76 Jeremiah 50:25.
77 *Webster's American Heritage Dictionary* (Boston: Houghton Mifflin, 1981) 888.
78 Isaiah 41:15.
79 Jeremiah 51:20.
80 Ezekiel 1:4.
81 Isaiah 29:6.
82 Psalm 104:4.
83 Zechariah 12:6.
84 Isaiah 9:19.
85 Rosha Judah, "A More Sure Word of Prophecy," *The Sound of a Trumpet*, Jan. 1997.
86 Psalm 25.
87 Psalm 103:17-18.
88 Isaiah 35:4.
89 Isaiah 40:10.
90 Isaiah 66:15-16.
91 Isaiah 13:3.
92 Proverbs 19:10.
93 Deuteronomy 1:30.
94 Revelation 19:11.
95 2 Samuel 22:35.
96 Zechariah 10:5.
97 Psalm 144:1.
98 Joel 3:9-15.
99 2 Samuel 22:5-22 *paraphrased*.
100 Malachi 3:1-5.
101 Isaiah 66:14-16.
102 *Strong's* Number 784.
103 *Strong's* Number 5492.
104 *Strong's* Number 2534.
105 *Strong's* Number 3851.
106 Isaiah 10:16-21.
107 Luke 12:4-7.
108 Deuteronomy 20:3-4.

109 Deuteronomy 31:6.
110 Deuteronomy 31:8.
111 Joshua 10:25.
112 Judges 6:10.
113 Judges 6:23.
114 1 Samuel 12:20-25.
115 2 Kings 6:16-17.
116 Isaiah 35:4.
117 Isaiah 41:13.
118 Joel 2:21.
119 Isaiah 43:1-7.
120 Exodus 29:37.
121 Ecclesiastes 12:3-5.
122 Isaiah 2:11-12.
123 Rasha Judah, "His Vanguard and Torchbearer for Truth" *The Sound of a Trumpet* 31 Dec. 1995.
124 Luke 12:32-37.
125 Revelation 1:17.
126 Jeremiah 46:27.
127 Lamentations 3:57-61.
128 Psalm 37:3-40.

CHAPTER 9 ENDNOTES
1 Isaiah 2:11-12.
2 Proverbs 8:13.
3 Proverbs 16:18.
4 Ezekiel 7:1-10.
5 Obadiah 1:3-4 NAS.
6 Zephaniah 1:12-13 NAS.
7 Zephaniah 1:14-18 NAS.
8 Isaiah 16:6.
9 Isaiah 16:7-8.
10 Isaiah 16:9-10.
11 Isaiah 16:11-12.
12 Isaiah 16:13-14.
13 Isaiah 17:1.
14 Jeremiah 48:6-12.
15 Jeremiah 48:15-17.
16 Jeremiah 48:28-30.
17 Jeremiah 48:32.

CHAPTER 10 ENDNOTES

1   Isaiah 13:3.
2   Mike McQuiddy, speaker Kingdom Builders International, Los Angeles, Feb. 1997.
3   Mike McQuiddy, Kingdom Builders.
4   1 Samuel 15:22.
5   Isaiah 1:19.
6   Luke 22:36-38.
7   Mike McQuiddy, Kingdom Builders.
8   Luke 13:34-35.
9   Revelation 18:1-4.
10   Revelation 3:10.
11   Jeremiah 51:46.
12   Jeremiah 51:43.
13   Daniel 7:21.
14   Daniel 7:23-25.
15   Stuart Best, "Report From Iron Mountain," video, Stuart Best, Best Video Productions.
16   United States, Department of State Publication 7277, *Freedom from War*, (Washington: GPO).
17   United States *Freedom from War*.
18   United Nations, Commission on Global Governance.
19   Norman Cousins, Chairman, Planetary Citizens of the World We Chose, 1985.
20   President George Bush, State of the Union Address, Washington, DC 29 Jan. 1991.
21   Malachi Martin "Pope John Paul II" *Keys of Blood*.
22   *Intelligence Digest*, "Mass Destruction Terrorism: Fact or Fiction," Sept. 1997.
23   David Armstrong, Chicago Corp. 20 April 1996.
24   Michael A. Pacer, *San Gabriel Valley Tribune* 4 August 1996.
25   *USA Today*, 5 March 1997.
26   Janet Reno, interview, *Larry King Live* CNN.
27   Senate Investigating Committee on Education, State of California, 1953.
28   David Rockefeller, 14 Sept. 1994.
29   Maurice Strong, closing speech, Earth Summit, Rio de Janeiro, 15 Jun. 1992.
30   "Preamble" *Biological Diversity Treaty*.

[31]   Maurice Strong, lecture, Swedish Royal Academy, Stockholm, 27 Apr. 1994.

[32]   Maurice Strong Swedish Royal Academy.

[33]   Texe Marrs, *Summary of the Biological Diversity Treaty* Living Truth Ministries.

[34]   *Strategic Investment*, "Free Agents in an Unfree World," 17 Dec. 1997.

[35]   Steven Jones, Esq., 14th Annual Criminal Law Seminar, Aspen, CO, Jan. 1996.

[36]   President Clinton, Inaugural Address, Washington, DC 20 Jan. 1997.

[37]   "Executive Order # 12852" The White House, Office of Press Secretary.

[38]   "Memo to Friends," Lucis Trust, New York City, Aug. 1995.

[39]   *Mark Skousen Newsletter* "Review of Tragedy and Hope," 979 - 980.

[40]   *Southern California Christian Times*, Mar. 1996.

[41]   Robert Schuller, *Time Magazine*, 18 Mar. 1985.

[42]   Thomas Jefferson.

CHAPTER 11 ENDNOTES

[1]   2 Timothy 3:1-5.

[2]   1 Timothy 4:1-2.

[3]   Isaiah 28:15.

[4]   Isaiah 28:17.

[5]   Isaiah 5:13-16.

[6]   Micah 6:9-12.

[7]   Romans 6:16.

[8]   Matthew 7:22-23.

[9]   *Strong's* Number 93.

[10]   Henry, Luke 13.

[11]   *Strong's* Number 646.

[12]   2 Thessalonians 2:3-4.

[13]   Henry, 2 Thessalonians, 2.

[14]   Luke 17:26-37.

[15]   Hebrews 11:7.

[16]   John 17:15.

[17]   *The Rapture Truth.*

[18]   2 Timothy 4:3-4.

[19]   Dave Mac Pherson, *The Incredible Cover Up—Exposing the Origins of Rapture Theories*, (Medford OR: Omega Publications, July 1991).

[20]   Mark 13:27.

21   1 Corinthians 15:51-52.
22   Revelation 11:15.
23   Revelation 3:19-22.
24   Daniel 7:21-22.
25   McQuiddy, *The Promise*.
26   *The Maranatha Baptist Watchman*, Aug. 1997: 4.
27   *The Last Trumpet Newsletter*, Oct. 1997.
28   Isaiah 29:9-10.
29   Amos 9:10.
30   *Voice in the Wilderness*, Apr. 1998.
31   Ezekiel 22:18-21.
32   *Strong's* Number 5509.
33   *Strong's* Number 5472.

CHAPTER 12 ENDNOTES
1   Revelations 3:3.
2   Luke 21:36.
3   Matthew 16:1-3.
4   Jeremiah 8:7 *paraphrased*.
5   Jeremiah 9:5 *paraphrased*.
6   Genesis 6:3,11-13.
7   Amos 9:6.
8   Deuteronomy 34:7.
9   1 Corinthians 5:7-8.
10   John 4:23-24.
11   Psalm 72:16.
12   Adapted from the Poem by Alice Tompson, Born Oct. 13, 1897, Died May 9, 1993.
13   Leviticus 23:10.
14   Revelation 14:4-5.
15   Rasha Judah, "His First Fruits Barley Harvest," *The Sound of a Trumpet*, Mar. Apr 1996.
16   Malachi 3:16-18.
17   Psalm 71:1-4.
18   Psalm 71:5-7.
19   *Strong's* Number 4159.
20   Proverbs 2:21-22.
21   *Strong's* Number 3498.
22   *Strong's* Number 8549.
23   *Strong's* Number 3498.

24   Luke 21:36.
25   Rasha Judah, "His Vanguard" *The Sound of a Trumpet*, Apr. 1998.
26   Numbers 17:8.
27   Numbers 16:5.
28   *Strong's* Number 1250.
29   2 Chronicles 31:5.
30   Ecclesiastes 1:9.
31   Zechariah 10:1.
32   *Strong's* Number 2385.
33   Ecclesiastes 12:5.
34   Jeremiah 1:10-11.
35   1 Samuel 2:10.
36   *Strong's* Number 7481.
37   Psalm 77:18.
38   *Strong's* Number 1534.
39   *Strong's* Number 215.
40   *Strong's* Number 1300.
41   *Strong's* Number 7264.
42   Job 38:25.
43   *Strong's* Number 6963.
44   Exodus 19:10-11.
45   Hosea 6:2.
46   1 Samuel 12:16-18.
48   Isaiah 33:12-14.
49   2 Corinthians 5:11.
50   Rasha Judah, "His First Fruits Barley Harvest."
51   Deuteronomy 16:9-10.
52   Revelation 7:1-3.
53   Psalm 49:1-5.
54   Psalm 90:12-13.
55   Psalm 90:10.
56   Haggai 2:18-19.
57   Ezekiel 36:8.
58   Leviticus 25:8-10.
59   Nelson's Illustrated Bible Dictionary, (Nashville, TN: Nelson Bible Publishers, 1986).
60   Nelson's Illustrated Bible Dictionary.
61   Isaiah 61:1-2.
62   Daniel 9:25.

63   Greg Killman, *Celestial Events*, 21 Nissan 5776 .
64   "Just how hot is it going to get?" *US News and World Report*, 4 May 1998.
65   Rasha Judah, "Jesus is LORD," *The Sound of a Trumpet* 1997.
66   Hosea 4:6-13.
67   Hosea 1:11.
68   2 Thessalonians 1:7-10.
69   Zechariah 10:1.
70   Deuteronomy 32:2.
71   Romans 8:18-19.
72   Deuteronomy 32:22-43.
73   Micah 4:5-8.
74   *Strong's* Number 6760.
75   *Strong's* Number 5080.
76   *Strong's* Number 7489.
77   *Strong's* Number 7611.
78   *Strong's* Number 4475.
79   Obadiah 1:17-21.
80   Micah 5:2.
81   Micah 1:3-4 NAS.
82   Revelation 6:1-2.
83   Zechariah 9:13.
84   Rasha Judah, "The Hour of His Judgment is Come," *The Sound of a Trumpet* 1998.

Final Words Endnotes

1   2 Samuel 23:3-5.
2   2 Peter 1:19.
3   John 9:4.
4   Daniel 9:25-26.
5   Luke 17:30-31.
6   Matthew 24:15-21.
7   Colossians 1:27.
8   Isaiah 27:11-12 NAS.
9   Obadiah 1:3-4.
10   Obadiah 1:10-11.

[11] Jeffrey Nyquist, *Winning the Next World War: Penetration, Surprise & Combination*; Peter Vincent Pry, *The Strategic Nuclear Balance*, vol. II, Nuclear Wars: Exchanges and Outcomes (New York: Taylor & Francis, 1990) Chapter 8, "War Outcome." Nikolay Popov, *Literaturnaya Gazeta* (Mar. 1987) "We Are All in the Same Boat" [an open confession].

[12] A prophecy from a woman of God.

ABOUT THE AUTHOR

Benjamin Baruch works with Get Ready Ministries Association, a group of like-minded ministries helping the body of Christ prepare for the coming difficult times leading to Christ's appearance.

At Christian Get Ready Network you can subscribe to the Millennial Trumpet for periodic articles, ministry and speaking announcements and news: www.christiangetready.net

Also, you can listen to Benjamin and Pastor Pretlow on -
The Millennial Voice program—Christian Get Ready Network

COMPLEMENTING BOOK

A book to help complete your study on this very important topic is Pastor Charles Pretlow's book:

"REVELATION SIX Get Ready - *for the great and terrible day of the Lord is drawing near.*"

This volume offers practical how to knowledge in helping the sincere Christian become ready. In-depth and insight, Revelation Six addresses the daily *working out* one's salvation, God's way and exposes the damning and destructive teachings that are so widespread within the body of Christ.

www.getreadyresources.com

Your prayers and support are most welcome. Time is running short and Christian Get Ready Network, its members and Get Ready Publishing and its authors' mission is to get the truth out in time to the body of Christ.

This is not an easy task. We appreciate your participation in helping us accomplish our mission.

The following pages are an overview of the **Get Ready Now!** mission with ministry engagements presented by Benjamin Baruch and Pastor Charles Pretlow.

MINISTRY ENGAGEMENT INFORMATION

Get Ready Now!

Learn how to
Stand and Endure
to the End!

"Therefore you also must be ready; for the Son of man is coming at an hour you do not expect." (Matthew 24:44)

Many Christians are not ready for the coming of the Lord. The unveiling of the kingdom of heaven will be preceded by persecution, political turmoil, economic depression, trouble and intense spiritual oppression.

Get Ready Ministries Association's mission is to help discerning Christians prepare for these coming days by presenting a series of messages in conjunction with the books —

The Day of the LORD is at Hand
by Benjamin Baruch
-and-
REVELATION SIX *Get Ready*
by Pastor Charles Pretlow

The following information covers ministry topics to assist you and those in your ministry, congregation and Christians in your community to Get Ready Now, God's way.

The Lord is starting to purge and cleanse all sincere Christians and in the coming days our trials of faith will become more fiery. Many of us are not ready to endure the hard times that lie ahead. Christians are in denial, believing they are ready and able to stand during the end of the age but like Peter, Satan will sift them.

There is no time left to soften this warning. America and the Christians of this great nation can expect the beginning of severe judgment at anytime. Pray that we will have enough time to get ready and that we not squander what precious time we do have left.

To help become prepared, this series of messages is now available to help likeminded Pastors, elders, and the sincere and discerning Christian learn to become ready, God's way. To learn how to cooperate with the Lord in His discipline and advance training for the tough times that are already upon us.

Those of us in leadership are to be the messengers that help each other and God's people become ready to greet the Lord without being ashamed, nor miss the last trumpet call.

Our Lord warned, *"But take heed to yourselves lest your hearts be weighted down with dissipation and drunkenness and cares of this life, and that day come upon you suddenly like a snare; for it will come upon all who dwell upon the face of the whole earth. But watch at all times, praying that you may have strength to escape all these things that will take place, and to stand before the Son of Man"* (Luke 21:34-36).

We recommend reading both books to help you understand the intensity and the urgency of these messages. Quantity discounts are available for ministry and church orders.

The following are topics that you can have presented to your congregation or in your community by Pastor Charles Pretlow or Benjamin Baruch. You can request a joint ministry engagement. You can go online to submit a ministry engagement request. Typically, a ministry engagement will last about 2 hours. If you desire, you can request a whole day presentation, which will cover all of these topics.

Get Ready Now!
Ministry Engagement Topics

[1]   Why judgment and trouble before rapture?
Pastor Pretlow and Benjamin Baruch

[2]   America in Bible prophecy.
Benjamin Baruch

[3]   Refiner's Fire and Fullers' Soap.
Pastor Pretlow

[4]   Having the Mind of Wisdom.
Benjamin Baruch

[5]   Spiritual Warfare and Standing in the Gap.
Pastor Pretlow

[6]   The call for the true Church—*winning the war!*
Pastor Pretlow and Benjamin Baruch

[7]   Other topics as led by the Holy Spirit.

These messages that Pastor Pretlow and Benjamin Baruch share have taken years of study, research and a disciplined life under fiery trials ordained by the Lord. Solid doctrine is presented that will help the sincere disciple of Christ get ready and do God's will during the coming terror filled days. A road map filled with Biblical principles that, when embraced will bring true sanctification, cleansing and healing as the kingdom of God approaches.

Those in your congregation and Christians in your community will be blessed when exposed to the dynamic, intense and practical speaking style of these two men of God. Once you hear these harder teachings of Christ and true end time instructions—you will never be the same!

ABOUT THE SPEAKERS

Benjamin Baruch Professional Investment Advisor, a Chartered Financial Analyst and a Certified Public Accountant is the author of the groundbreaking work, The Day of the LORD is at Hand. The book provides insight into the last days prophecies of the Bible including information surrounding the future of America and what the people in America can do to protect themselves and their families in the years immediately ahead.

The Day of the LORD is at Hand is causing a firestorm in the religious arena, challenging traditional beliefs held by many that the United States is strangely absent from Bible prophecy. Benjamin Baruch states emphatically that the United States is described directly in Bible prophecy and that the we are now living in the last days of America.

Benjamin's message is unique as Benjamin has been able to hear the audible voice of God throughout his life. In 1996, Benjamin was managing money on Wall Street and spent over a year in prayer seeking guidance from God on when to exit the stock market. Shortly after Benjamin's fortieth birthday, God answered. In a series of visions and audible revelations from God, Benjamin was shown the future of America.

Many of Benjamin's prophetic revelations have be documented by eye witnesses including his warning in the summer of 2001 that the United States was about to be attacked with planes from United and American airlines, an attack which would mark the beginning of what will become World War III. Benjamin's has toured on the Prophecy Club meeting network, churches and ministries, presenting a clear understanding into the sealed prophecies of the Bible including a detailed analysis of the future events which will shake our nation including a stock market collapse, growing domestic terrorism and ultimately nuclear war.

Pastor Charles Pretlow has nearly two decades experience in ministry and pastoral counseling. He completed his basic Bible classes at Seattle Pacific College and finished his undergraduate work at Central Washington University.

It was in 1973, while in the Marines, that he came to know Christ. In the ensuing years, he has seen much trouble, abuse and confusion within the body of Christ. He has years of experience and study in practical theology, working in a ministerial capacity with evangelical, Pentecostal and charismatic congregations, as well as independent fellowships. In 1988 he founded a home fellowship and non-denominational ministry, emphasizing pastoral counseling, that incorporated sound biblical principles to help Christians cooperate with God in the sanctification and healing process that God gives through Jesus Christ.

Over these years of ministry, he has dealt with a wide spectrum of Christians who complained of a troubled walk with Christ. He dealt with many severe cases and developed a scriptural understanding concerning the source of their difficulties.

Since his conversion in 1973, he has overcome his own obstacles and challenges that, like so many others, prevent Christians from coming to the full grace of God and a stable life in Christ. His ministry is practical—helping others work out their salvation, leaning on the Lord, and sharing from his own healing process and experiences.

In his book *Revelation Six: Get Ready*, he shares from the heart insights concerning the weak and confused condition that the body of Christ is in today. Having researched and worked in the "trenches" for over fifteen years in counseling, he has acquired deep knowledge with wisdom and understanding concerning the problems facing so many Christians today.

Pastor Pretlow resides in Colorado with his family. He loves the great outdoors, camping and traveling. He has a deep love for children of all ages and has had the privilege of coaching high school football and other youth sports programs.

He is the founder and director of Word of the Cross Ministries International (WCMI) Get Ready Publishing and Christian Get Ready Network. He is preparing to publish his next two books; *Called to Lead by Example* and *Can Christ Heal the Divided?*

For conference and ministry engagements, you may contact

Christian Get Ready Network

PO Box 58 ~ Westcliffe, CO 81252

719.783.2335

contact@christiangetready.net

www.christiangetready.net

Schedules for both Pastor Pretlow and Benjamin Baruch are subject change. Please call for itinerary confirmation.

Printed in the United States
50051LVS00004B/127-144

9 780976 457497